The PRIME MINISTERS

REFLECTIONS ON LEADERSHIP FROM WILSON TO JOHNSON

STEVE RICHARDS

Atlantic Books
London

First published in hardback in Great Britain in 2019 by Atlantic Books, an imprint of Atlantic Books Ltd.

This paperback edition published in 2020

10 9 8 7 6

A CIP catalogue record for this book is available from the British Library.

Paperback ISBN: 978 1 78649 588 4
E-book ISBN: 978 1 78649 589 1

Printed in Great Britain

Atlantic Books
An imprint of Atlantic Books Ltd
Ormond House
26–27 Boswell Street
London
WC1N 3JZ

www.atlantic-books.co.uk

The PRIME MINISTERS

REFLECTIONS ON LEADERSHIP
FROM WILSON TO JOHNSON

'A thoughtful and compelling book… the chapters on
Tony Blair and Gordon Brown are the jewels in the
crown, but the entire set glitter.'

Observer

'Brilliant.'

Independent

'You could not ask for a better qualified guide… than
political journalist Steve Richards… the whole book
brims with counter-intuitive insights.'

Prospect

'Extraordinary.'

Kirsty Wark

'Smart and incisive, from a fine scribe and a wise watcher.
Steve Richards is a joy.'

James Naughtie

'Entertaining, informative and timely.'

Evan Davies

'A pure pleasure to read.'

Polly Toynbee

About the Author

Steve Richards is a political columnist, journalist, and presenter. He regularly presents *The Week in Westminster* on BBC Radio 4 and has presented BBC radio series on Tony Blair, Gordon Brown, David Cameron and Theresa May. He also presented the BBC TV programmes *Leadership Reflections: The Modern Prime Ministers*, *Turning Points* and *Reflections: The Prime Ministers We Never Had*. He has written for several national newspapers including the *Guardian*, the *Independent* and the *Financial Times*. He also presents a popular political one man show each year at the Edinburgh Festival and across the UK.

To Lachlan, who was born as one prime minister fell and as another hopeful figure prepared to acquire the thorny crown.

CONTENTS

PREFACE TO THE PAPERBACK EDITION

I finished writing the first edition of *The Prime Ministers* on 24 July 2019, the day Theresa May stepped down as prime minister. Her premiership had been short and tumultuous, a wildly oscillating ride, from an early honeymoon during which her colleagues and a fickle chorus of political commentators assumed she would be in post for many years, to a speedy descent as she struggled to survive as leader. In the final months of her leadership no one knew what would happen next, as May's bid to deliver Brexit suffered one historic parliamentary defeat after another. Yet such were the volcanic explosions following her tearful departure from Number Ten that her leadership has been almost forgotten, obscured by subsequent upheavals that make her traumatic era seem almost tranquil.

Every prime minister of the modern era has endured phases of nerve-shredding stress, but Boris Johnson's first year in Number Ten tops the lot for mind-boggling, energy-draining drama. In April 2020 he almost died in intensive care, after catching coronavirus, which had already transformed the way he governed and the way the rest of us lived. Before the pandemic wreaked havoc, Johnson had taken the UK out of the European Union and won a general election – two epic events that were soon dwarfed by another. His leadership or, to be more precise, what happened to him as a leader was of supreme significance well before he had served a full year as prime minister.

Yet the lessons of leadership arising from other modern prime ministers apply equally to Johnson's frenetically fraught early months in power. His predecessors also faced unprecedented challenges, even if none of them ended up in intensive care, and were justified in feeling daunted. The devaluation of sterling, the three-day week, the 'winter of discontent', the Falklands War, the miners' strike, the ERM crisis, the outbreak of foot-and-mouth disease, the war in Iraq, the financial crash and Brexit all seemed impossibly stressful at the time, with unclear causes, solutions and consequences. And so it was with coronavirus. The difference was in scale: the pandemic caused the biggest emergency since 1945, but the same range of prime ministerial skills was required to deal with it as with the other major crises of modern times.

As this book argues, successful prime ministers are political teachers capable of guiding the country through frightening and destabilizing times, making sense of what is happening and why. They need a clear message, and that means he or she must have a command of detail and coherent policies. An early, astute reading of unexpected crises before they have fully taken shape is also an essential requirement of leadership. Throughout the sequence from the early stages of a national emergency, the prime minister must seek to take a party, Parliament, the media and the country with them. Each modern prime minister ached to reach the very top, and then discovered that power often made them miserably neurotic and insecure rather than euphoric. The additional chapter on Boris Johnson in this edition marks a leap in the speedy pace of events, yet it also signifies continuity in terms of what is required of a leader.

In the late 1990s, when he was becoming famous as a journalist, before his career in politics, Johnson once told me that he thought politics was the new rock 'n' roll. He was a star pundit then, and the early New Labour era under Tony Blair had a glittering and glamorous dimension. Johnson was a critic of that government, but he was a beneficiary of the broadcasters' tendency in those years to conflate politics with showbiz. Significantly, he was the first modern prime minister to have started his career as a journalist. He was fascinated by the performance of politics.

At the end of 2019 Johnson had cause to feel a sense of prime ministerial euphoria over the way he had performed. He had pulled off many political feats, from his perspective, as he led his party to election victory and took the UK out of the EU. In early 2020 he and his advisers were planning to radically reform the UK in the post-Brexit era. But soon Johnson found – just as his predecessors had – that being prime minister is a gruelling role, far removed from rock 'n' roll. He started to look drawn and tired, as many of those who ruled before him had also done. Inevitably, the stress of responding to the pandemic took its toll and he was then hospitalized after he caught the virus. As the numbers dying in the UK began to rise, Johnson's job became as far removed from showbiz as it was possible to be.

Other prime ministers had been through similar emotional journeys: joyfully reaching the peak, flourishing in the new terrain, before finding the burdens at the top to be almost too heavy to bear. Johnson was unusual in moving from one extreme prime ministerial sensation to its opposite in the space of a few months, and after less than a year in Number Ten. His leadership style was unique, breaking informal rules that his predecessors chose to follow, but he could not transcend the most unyielding law of British politics. Leadership is arduous and demands a range of qualities that few possess.

—

INTRODUCTION

There are memoirs by prime ministers. There are biographies of prime ministers. This is the first book to reflect at some length on all the modern prime ministers, from Harold Wilson, who ruled first in 1964, to Boris Johnson, who entered Number Ten following the seismic general election in 2019.

Some modern prime ministers are viewed more vividly than others. Margaret Thatcher and Tony Blair are still recalled with a multicoloured intensity. The explosive consequences of Boris Johnson's, Theresa May's and David Cameron's leaderships will still be taking shape for another decade at least. Other prime ministers are ghostly, distant figures, even though there are many lessons from their leaderships that are urgently relevant.

This book is an attempt to make sense of their leaderships, to take a step back and look at the political stage as it seemed to them. The reflections aim to bring to life the complex three-dimensional human beings who made it to the very top – a triumphant ascent that became, for some, a nightmare when the peak was reached. Shakespeare is cited as much as other, more recent political observers. The lessons learned will also hopefully appeal to those in any field who are interested in the qualities required of leaders.

My definition of 'modern' prime ministers is based on two factors. The leaders from Harold Wilson to Boris Johnson were part of the television era, when a more direct and potentially hazardous form of communication with the electorate took hold. The later ones were also navigating the social-media revolution, one in which politics speeded up. Wilson became neurotically angry about newspapers and the BBC, as did all his successors at various points. Even so, if he was worried about a poor performance at Prime Minister's Question Time he would have nearly twenty-four hours to await the verdict of the next day's newspapers. Today, advisers to prime ministers alert them to the verdict on Twitter immediately after the event, while twenty-four-hour rolling television news is a constant, never-ending commentary. Wilson's immediate predecessors, Alec Douglas-Home and Harold Macmillan, faced no such pressures. Macmillan read Jane Austen in the afternoons quite often. Now even he, a lover of literature, would be distracted by Sky News and Twitter.

The other defining factor is that these are the prime ministers I knew directly or observed closely. What was written about them at the time, and to some extent since, did not seem to me anywhere near the full story. I never met Wilson, but I observed him at first hand. The other prime ministers I knew, with varying degrees of access. The purpose of the book is not to attack them from the left or the right. That has been done a thousand times before. I do not accept the political fashion that the divide between left and right has become irrelevant. On the role of the state, raging questions about how to deliver decent public services and how governments can mediate in a global economy, the left-versus-right divide is as relevant as ever. But to write relentlessly about recent prime ministers from one perspective would not be especially illuminating. Instead, based on a career in political journalism that has so far included many conversations and interviews with prime ministers, aspirant prime ministers and their numerous critics, this book aims to challenge prime ministerial caricatures. In doing so, I seek to reflect on the qualifications of leadership and on how perhaps no one is, or can be, fully equipped for the mighty tasks involved. Looking at each of the prime ministers again, I am constantly surprised by what I see – by their unexpected strengths and weaknesses.

I turn to them now, at a time of epic national crisis, partly because the Brexit drama in the UK was brought about, and then deepened, by failures in leadership. Conversely, the dangerous anti-politics mood – both a cause and a consequence of Brexit – is deepened by misreadings of leaders and politicians more generally. Some voters felt 'left behind' with good cause and ached to 'seize back control' as work patterns became fractured and public services were fragmented in the name of 'empowerment', only to disempower. But the leaders who were culpable for hopelessly misjudged policies did not act out of wilful malevolence or for reasons of corrupt venality. Their motives were more interesting than that. There is no evidence to suggest that modern prime ministers were criminal, corrupt or lacked integrity, as is widely assumed. Their flaws were epic, but had little to do with their perceived sleaziness. Yet most prime ministers left office tormented by perceptions of their rotten lack of integrity.

This book is by no means a defence of modern prime ministers. How could it be, when contemplating such a diverse group? The modern prime ministers faced many crises, and caused some of them. The deepest is the Brexit saga, one that was partly the consequence of panic-stricken and weak leadership. Indeed, the current leadership crisis in the UK is a result of the lack of impressive leaders of depth, fuelled by the vast numbers of self-proclaimed potential leaders who are deluded enough to assume that a nation's destiny lies in their inexperienced hands. Leadership is now an urgent theme in the UK and across much of the Western world.

———

In the autumn of 2016 I recorded six unscripted television talks for the BBC on modern prime ministers. Each talk lasted thirty minutes and was recorded in a single take. The historian A. J. P. Taylor was a model of sorts. In the 1960s and 1970s he spoke, without an autocue or any notes, on topics ranging from how wars start to how they end, and from Bismarck to Lloyd George. Taylor was mesmerizing and mischievous on many different subjects. I focused on the easier task of looking at modern prime ministers, the backdrop to a political journalist's life. I was keen to do so because politics on television can be cluttered and speedy. I am a big fan of letting topics breathe in order to give context to current events. Nothing makes sense without context. The series was called *Reflections on Leadership* and the prime ministers featured were Harold Wilson, Margaret Thatcher, John Major, Tony Blair, Gordon Brown and David Cameron. The talks have been repeated several times and are often available on BBC iPlayer. There were subsequent series on other themes, including one on *The Prime Ministers We Never Had*.

This book is based on those television talks, but differs from them in several ways. The chapters are longer than the original transcripts, and four additional prime ministers are considered: Edward Heath, James Callaghan, Theresa May and Boris Johnson.

In the television talks there was no space to compare the conduct of the different prime ministers, but in these chapters all of them recur, like characters in a crowded Iris Murdoch novel. They recur for a purpose: the conduct of one shines light on the others.

I find the demands of leadership, and the characters of leaders, so endlessly fascinating. Prime ministers tend to be viewed at the time they are in power, and subsequently, as cartoon stereotypes. The newspapers in the UK are on the whole biased to the right and they still influence nervy BBC editors. But the much bigger bias is one that favours political fashion at any given time. This leads too often to what the former BBC director-general, John Birt, once brilliantly described as a 'bias against understanding'. I am biased in favour of understanding, partly because the characters of our prime ministers – as well as the demands placed upon them – thereby become more compelling, and not less.

One of the lessons of leadership is that fashionable assumptions are nearly always wrong. A prime minister can walk on water. Later the same prime minister can be mad and a criminal. A prime minister can be a 'modernizer', whatever that overused term means. Later the same prime minister can be hopelessly out of step with the times. A prime minister can be admirably dutiful, a committed public servant. The same prime minister can be a self-interested liar, no longer to be trusted. The extreme perceptions held in relation to the same individual do not add up. What if both are wrong? Whatever my views about her policies and their consequences, I am fascinated by Thatcher's skills as a leader. Although widely lauded by some journalists and writers to the point of deification, her precise qualities as a leader have in some respects been underestimated. The same applies to prime ministers who have been largely forgotten. Wilson, in particular, merits considerable rehabilitation. Conversely, the flaws associated with modern prime ministers are based on misunderstandings about the pressures on leaders, and a tendency in the anti-politics age to assume the worst.

Sometimes we choose to see what we want to see, or are told to see, rather than what is happening in front of our eyes. This is a lesson of leadership that I learned at a youthful age, and one that I have applied ever since. Do not assume that what you are told to see is what you are seeing. For me, this lesson took the form of a political rally that I attended in the 1970s, only just a teenager and yet drawn towards the theatre of politics.

During the October 1974 election I went to see the then prime minister, Harold Wilson, speak at a rally in north London. This was the distant era when security was less tight and anyone could get in to big campaigning events with ease. Wilson had been prime minister since February of that year, having won a handful more seats than the Conservatives. The mid-1970s were a sensational time to become interested in politics. There were two elections in 1974 and a referendum on Europe in 1975. Big politicians seemed to be on the campaign trail in nerve-shredding contests all the time. When there were no elections or referendums, the Labour government struggled to win key votes in the Commons. Parliament also became the location for epic dramas. It was no coincidence that James Graham's glorious play *This House* was set in late-1970s Westminster and became a hit in the twenty-first century. In the 1970s there were charismatic politicians lighting up the political stage at Westminster and out on the campaign trail. Politics was as exciting and unpredictable as football and almost as glamorous as rock music, two more familiar teenage passions.

Wilson intrigued me. I had read in the newspapers that he was exhausted, paranoid and useless. Some television interviewers appeared to be disdainful, as if they shared the assumptions of the influential newspapers they read. Yet Wilson was prime minister having performed better in the February election than most pundits had assumed. He was leading a country in turmoil and was planning a referendum on Europe. Coming to politics fresh and for the first time, I felt a bit like Hercule Poirot, who would often turn to his sidekick, Hastings, and make an observation along these lines: '*Mon ami*, something is not quite right. We jump to conclusions, but they are not necessarily the right conclusions.' From my uninformed perspective, something did not add up. How could a prime minister facing a range of nightmarish challenges be exhausted, paranoid and useless?

I wanted to make sense of Wilson by seeing him live during that dark autumnal campaign in 1974. As a teenager I went to live gigs as well as buying records. For me, David Bowie and the Sex Pistols only started to make much sense when seeing them perform. I assumed that a prime minister might acquire greater definition at a live event as well.

At the rally I attended during the October 1974 election, Wilson was the star turn at a large and packed town hall. The prime minister walked onto the stage to the sound of comically incongruous pop music. At first he looked old, grey and stooped by the burdens of leadership. He was dull, looked well beyond his fifty-eight years and repeated tediously familiar phrases like a machine: '...the social contract... price freezes... help with rents...' I was both excited to be seeing a prime minister live and wondering whether the media caricature was right. Perhaps Wilson had peaked long ago and this was a ghostly shadow, a prematurely aged and lifeless leader.

Then there was a dramatic twist. After around ten boring minutes of the speech, a protester threw an egg at Wilson. The contents trickled inelegantly down the prime minister's face and onto his crumpled suit. I looked on in horror, wondering what the tired, old and useless prime minister would do. Wilson looked up after the egg had landed and declared: 'You know, I'll tell you something very interesting. During the June 1970 election, after six years of a Labour government, somebody threw an egg at me like the man has just done, the one who's being escorted from this hall. In February 1974, during the election campaign a few months ago, nobody threw an egg at me at all. I think that the contest was an egg-free campaign. And now somebody has thrown an egg at me again.' Wilson paused. He brushed the yolk away from his ruined shirt and looked up again and said with great mischievous passion: 'Which goes to show you can only afford to throw eggs under a Labour government.'

There were spontaneous cheers in the hall, people were laughing and suddenly Wilson looked ten years younger. He had changed the political mood beyond recognition. For the rest of his speech he sprang into life, as if liberated by the egg challenge. The audience left raving about what a class act he still was. In the space of a couple of hours I had seen the Wilson of caricature and the Wilson who could think speedily and transform the political mood. So it was during his final phase in power between 1974 and 1976. He was exhausted, drank too much whisky, lacked much visionary purpose, viewed colleagues and others with suspicion and loathed most of the media. But he won two elections and a referendum on Europe and, uniquely, left Number Ten on his own terms. He continued to master complex policy detail while plotting several steps ahead of his internal and external opponents. His old friend Barbara Castle was convinced that if Wilson had stayed on, he would have beaten Margaret Thatcher at the next general election. I am not sure about that, but I am certain that the fuller picture of Wilson is more interesting than the caricature. Instead, we chose to see what we wanted to see. In Wilson's case, we still do.

Much later, in the mid-1980s, the then Labour MP and former adviser to Wilson, Gerald Kaufman, told me that 'Wilson had learned to have a sense of humour'. The observation added to Wilson's ghostly enigma. He had been very funny that evening in 1974 and could use wit like a weapon. Apparently this was not a natural attribute, but one that he had deliberately acquired. He had the timing of a stand-up comic, without having a natural sense of humour. Unlike some of his successors, Wilson recognized that humour was a powerful force in politics.

Each modern prime minister has the equivalent of the Wilsonian rally – a sequence that does not make full sense of how they are perceived. In subsequent decades, Margaret Thatcher was sometimes portrayed as mad in her evangelical convictions. Edward Heath, Jim Callaghan and John Major were portrayed as useless. Tony Blair became a deranged war criminal. Gordon Brown was seen by some as bonkers. David Cameron was apparently a lazy dilettante. Theresa May was a dangerously self-absorbed leader who stubbornly led her party to the right after the 'modernizers' had taken it triumphantly to the 'centre ground'.

Again, we were choosing to see what we wanted to see. I feel like Hercule Poirot once more: none of this makes much sense. What if Thatcher's projection of shrill certainty was partly an act, at least until her final phase when her lofty and elevated status had blunted some or her sharper political instincts? Sometimes she was brutally unyielding in her simplistic convictions, but not by any means all of the time that she led. She could be smartly pragmatic, too.

If Heath, Callaghan and Major were useless, how did they survive at, or close to, the top for so long in often dark circumstances? If Blair was a thoughtlessly crusading warmonger, how to explain his sleepless mission to bring peace to Northern Ireland? Perhaps Blair possessed other flaws that propelled him towards Iraq. If Brown was so unreliably temperamental, how to make sense of his record-breaking tenure at the Treasury (the longest-serving Labour chancellor) and his focused response to the financial crash in 2008? If Cameron was lazy – the so-called 'essay crisis' prime minister, as he became known to some – how to explain his leadership of a coalition that introduced more radical reforms from the right at a speedier pace than any government in recent times, including Thatcher's? The 'essay crisis' epithet implied that he acted only at the last minute when a deadline loomed, opting to 'chill' the rest of the time. But no modern prime minister has time to chill for very long, not even the self-assured and occasionally over-confident Cameron. His reforms might have been misjudged, but that is a different matter. How was May's leadership, deeply flawed in so many ways, a leap to the right when she was the first Conservative leader since Heath to argue that the state could play a benevolent role in some circumstances and that markets did not always work? In some respects, under the influence of her close adviser Nick Timothy, May was to the left of her predecessor, but was seen as being to the right partly because, as the most tribal of Tories, she felt the need to appease the Brexit hard-liners in Parliament and in the party membership.

Step back a little and nothing quite adds up. Thatcher's claims to be giving power to the people were widely hailed, when all but the affluent were being disempowered. Blair and Cameron were portrayed as 'modernizers' without much scrutiny as to what the term meant. In some respects, both were fearful of moving on from the era in which Thatcher had cast her spell. Both paid homage to the recent past as much as they leapt away from it. May was praised for being dutiful and honest, when she was sometimes being self-interested and making assertions at odds with reality. How was Brown perceived as a stealthy chancellor when he became so well known for being stealthy? How was Wilson devious when he was so famous for being devious?

The characters of leaders are more interesting than they seem to be, but their conduct is also explained by the many actual or imagined external constraints. The modern prime ministers possess Shakespearean qualities and suffer dark fates brought about partly by character and partly by other factors beyond their control.

My favourite essay title when studying Shakespeare's plays was 'Character is Destiny. Discuss'. The instruction to discuss was a wonderful way of understanding politics as much as the great Shakespearean tragedies. Although Shakespeare's characters were creations of genius, three-dimensional and complex, their tragic destinies were determined by much more than who they were. Their fates were rooted in the wider context of the plays, the other characters, the situations they were in, the need to sustain a plot for a night out at the theatre. As my English teacher used to joke, Hamlet delayed murdering Claudius partly because the play would have ended very quickly if he had acted immediately. There were also many external factors that explained the delay.

In *Hamlet and His Problems* (1921), T. S. Eliot argued that the external factors in *Hamlet* did not fully justify the character's behaviour: 'Hamlet (the man) is dominated by an emotion which is inexpressible, because it is in *excess* of the facts as they appear.' I would argue that being told by your father's ghost that he was murdered by his brother, who is now king and married to your mother, was enough to justify all that Hamlet expressed. Either way, there was something rotten in the state of Denmark, and the rotten element needs analysing to make sense of Hamlet's actions. Hamlet's character alone did not make his destiny inevitable. Similarly, Othello was furious in his jealousy partly because he had good cause to be jealous. He assumed his wife had been unfaithful. Othello had the misfortune to face Iago. He might have acted differently if he had a less villainously deceptive ally, but then the play would have been different. Again, character alone did not determine destiny. I could write a whole book on Macbeth and the degree to which his character determined his destiny. I would argue it did so only to a limited extent.

The essay theme taught me how to view politics. A leader acts partly because of the appalling constraints he or she might face at any given time. The characters of the prime ministers matter hugely, but Wilson, Callaghan and Heath would have led differently if they had not faced economic turmoil, and Blair and Brown would have been unrecognizable as leaders if Labour had won elections in the 1980s rather than being slaughtered. Major might have been a genuine 'modernizer' if he had not faced the nightmare of a party divided over Europe. Heath might have been a more imposing leader if he had not been beaten by Wilson in the 1966 election, his first as leader and a calamitous debut.

To make sense of a leader's rule, an understanding of the context matters as much as the personalities of those who acquire the crown. Heath, Wilson in 1974, Callaghan, Major, Brown, Cameron and May faced daunting contexts. Thatcher, Blair and Wilson, in his first term in the 1960s, made their preliminary moves against political backgrounds that were benevolent. In spite of the benevolence, Blair and to some extent Wilson saw daunting constraints wherever they looked, some real and some imaginary. Labour prime ministers tend to regard themselves as imposters, disturbing the natural order, where England – not the rest of the UK – ensures that Conservative governments are elected. The sense that they have much to prove partly explains why Wilson was wary of tackling the vulnerable pound before devaluation was forced on him in 1967, why Blair went to war in Iraq in 2003 and why Brown wooed senior bankers. The Shakespearean irony is that in seeking desperately to prove they were part of the natural order, Labour prime ministers moved towards their doom.

Leaders become more interesting when situations are viewed from their nervy perspectives. They are obliged to appear in command, when most of the time they are not. If a prime minister confessed to an interviewer that he or she had no idea about the state of the UK economy at some future date, they would seem 'weak'. Yet the state of the global economy, over which they have little or no control, will play a major role in determining the fate of the UK's fortunes. Quite a lot of the time prime ministers have to act with their fingers crossed, needing to keep voters on board, a party together, an economy on track, public services at a high standard (although some prime ministers have not seen this as a priority) and to respond around the clock to a noisy media. From the outside, they can seem lofty and arrogant. From their point of view, the challenges of leadership can seem almost impossible to meet. Commentators and interviewers may attack leaders for acting weakly, evasively or bizarrely if they convey any hint of their sense of political incarceration. Yet even prime ministers with big majorities can feel trapped.

In spite of the presidential culture in UK politics and the obsessive focus on leaders and potential leaders, the qualities required for the titanic demands of leadership are under-explored. Partly for good reasons, a leadership contest tends to divide along ideological lines and did so even when UK politics appeared, deceptively, to be moving in a less ideological direction in the late 1990s and early twenty-first century. After the 1997 election, Conservative contests were based largely around candidates' positions on Europe. Polls suggested that Ken Clarke, a towering figure in the Conservative Party who had held numerous ministerial roles, was the most popular candidate with the wider electorate in the many contests in which he stood, and yet he never had a chance of winning because of his pro-European views. In Labour's 2010 contest, Ed Miliband won as the candidate to the left of New Labour, but not as far to the left as Diane Abbott, another candidate in that muted battle, which now seems like ancient history. In 2015 Jeremy Corbyn won because he was the change-making radical. He brought the leadership contest to life because he had convictions and was not too timid to express them. A candidate's views and convictions, where they stand on Europe and on the wider political spectrum, are pivotal in leadership contests, and so they should be.

Their qualifications for leadership are also pivotal, but are much less scrutinized. If it had not been for the Conservative Party's obsession with Europe, Clarke would have been a more popular and better-qualified leader than William Hague, Iain Duncan Smith and David Cameron. Clarke described his hobby as standing in leadership contests and losing. He stood against all those victorious candidates in various eccentric leadership contests. In some respects

Yvette Cooper was more suited to leadership than Jeremy Corbyn, who won Labour's 2015 contest. She did not stand a chance in spite of her greater experience, her capacity to master policy detail and her authoritative voice in the Commons. The rise of Corbyn highlighted an ache for a leap away from orthodoxies that had taken hold in the UK since 1979. Inevitably Corbyn lacked the leadership skills to make a success of his ascendancy. He became close to invisible for large periods of time after he won the contest, as the storms raged. Corbyn had been a backbencher since 1983, with no need to agonize over the demands of leadership. His sudden rise was the equivalent of a tennis player in a local park being asked to play on the Centre Court at Wimbledon. The demands are different.

The 2015 Labour leadership contest was important for marking a rare break with the past. The BBC and *The Times* newspaper were both demanding that candidates should apologize for the Labour government's 'profligate spending' – seen widely, and wrongly, as the cause of the financial crash. Candidates agonized over how to deal with this narrow, outdated interrogation. Up popped Corbyn and declared the Labour government should have spent more. He was ahead of the media zeitgeist. Soon the Conservative government abandoned its plans to wipe out the deficit largely by spending cuts. But Corbyn's exuberant ideological confidence, an important qualification of leadership, should not have obscured the obvious fact that he lacked other pivotal qualifications.

This makes politics an unusual vocation. When vacancies are advertised for senior posts in other fields, previous experience of running an organization is often specified as an essential qualification. Similarly, if a passer-by popped into the National Theatre and declared a wish to play Hamlet, he or she would be told that some previous experience of acting in demanding roles would be necessary. Playing the equivalent of Hamlet at the top of politics requires no previous experience, however. The opposite is the case. Perversely, not having any previous experience can be an overwhelming advantage. Donald Trump became the most powerful elected leader in the world by proclaiming his lack of experience in politics. In the UK, Tony Blair and David Cameron became prime ministers with no previous ministerial experience. In 2010 Nick Clegg became deputy prime minister in a coalition facing daunting economic turmoil. He had been an MP for only five years.

Yet it should be a statement of the obvious that having served as a Cabinet minister, observing and working closely with a prime minister, must be a significant advantage for a candidate seeking to be a leader and to rule from Number Ten. Other demands of leadership also transcend a candidate's convictions. Leaders must have the capacity to communicate and persuade, internally and with the wider electorate; they must manage unruly parties, giving the impression of unity when intense division is unavoidable; they must translate their convictions to policy detail and then ensure successful implementation of the policies. In the UK, responding to the media is another essential requirement. Even in its fragmented state, the media still mediates politics. Few people watch leaders perform unmediated; they watch or read from a media outlet of some form or another. In reflecting on modern prime ministers, here are a few of the lessons of leadership that I have learned.

The longest-serving modern prime ministers are Harold Wilson, Margaret Thatcher and Tony Blair. These election winners were different from each other in many ways, but shared a common quality. At their peak, they were all political teachers. They sought to make sense of what they were doing or of what was happening around them. This was especially the case with Thatcher and Blair. Thatcher was an instinctive teacher, making complex ideas and contentious policies become reassuringly accessible. Her ability to teach was helped by the fact that she did not delve deeply into the complexities herself. She seized on terms like 'freedom', 'the people' and 'choice' in ways that voters and activists in her party could relate to. Blair could frame an argument more effectively than any modern leader and would advance the arguments across all media outlets most days of the year. He introduced monthly press conferences in Downing Street, a highly effective innovation – at least for him. During the late phase of Blair's leadership, the media would be full of stories about his bleak vulnerability. Up he would pop for two hours at a press conference, putting the case that his expediency was a form of 'boldness' (one of his favourite terms) and answering all questions from fickle journalists who had become fleeting admirers once again. In his early phase Wilson, too, was a teacher, witty and evidently able, making his form of social democracy seem safe and yet exciting in its overdue modernity.

Wilson won four elections. Thatcher and Blair both won three. There were many factors that explain their durability, but the common one was their skill as teachers. This is a form of artistry that is different from 'spin', an overused term that became derogatory. There is nothing sinister in prime ministers seeking to present what is happening in the best possible light. But the teacher prime ministers do more than that. They sense instinctively that voters will not listen to lists of aspirations or policies without having a sense of the values that underpin them. So few leaders, and aspirant leaders, recognize the need to explain, opting instead only to assert. They never explain *why* they are acting in the way they are. They only proclaim that their actions are the right ones. Thatcher was fascinated by the 'why' question and liked to answer it. One of May's failings, as she navigated the impossible waters of Brexit, was an indifference to explanation and persuasion. She possessed no language to make sense of what she was doing, or the skill to frame an argument. Even if she needed to be opaque to keep her party together, there were ways of making evasiveness seem purposeful. She opted for near-silence punctuated by speeches every six months or so, which sought to paper over the cracks, but never did so.

There is, though, an important twist that highlights the degree to which leadership is multi-dimensional. This trio of teachers does not represent the deepest thinkers in the list of modern prime ministers, although Wilson had a grasp of policy detail and a strategic wiliness that were a form of depth. When it came to policy detail, Blair and Thatcher often skated on thin ice. Curiously, the two prime ministers who thought most deeply and had the widest range of insights were not long-serving. Both also suffered traumatic leaderships. They were Edward Heath and Gordon Brown, both of whom became unfashionable even before they had left office, and even more so subsequently.

Heath arrived in Number Ten in 1970 with a highly developed sense of how he saw the UK's place in the world, unique for a modern British prime minister. Most prime ministers begin their time in Number Ten with no clear international outlook. Thatcher had campaigned in the 1975 referendum for the UK to stay in the Common Market and had even argued in the late 1970s that the UK should join the European Monetary System, the embryonic move towards a single currency. Only in government did she adopt a foreign policy that was tonally hostile to the European Union, while never advocating withdrawal, and that was intensely Atlanticist.

Blair was a supporter of the euro and yet he 'loved the pound' as he made his way to power in 1997, hoping conveniently to be a 'bridgehead' between the US and the EU – convenient in that the metaphor conveys diplomatic muscularity rather than incoherence. Wilson and Callaghan were opponents of the UK's membership of the European Community and yet were the two figures who secured the voters' consent for membership, when they were back in government. Cameron was an opponent of the UK leaving the EU and yet held a referendum that brought about its departure. In opposition he hinted at doubts about the war in Iraq, but as prime minister he authorized air strikes in Libya that led to a similar chaos that arose in post-war Iraq. May arrived pledging to unite the UK over Brexit and led the most spectacularly divided government, party and country in modern times. Heath was different. He was convinced that the UK's destiny lay in Europe and he negotiated its membership with an unqualified focus and enthusiasm. He also arrived in Number Ten with a deep knowledge of how government and the parliamentary party worked, as a former Cabinet minister and chief whip. Yet his three and a half years as prime minister were stormy as well as brief.

The other prime minister who could range widely, and who thought deeply about policy and politics, was Gordon Brown. He arrived in Number Ten as Labour's longest-serving chancellor, buttressed by a profound sense of political history in general and of the Labour Party more specifically. He could delve below the surface in analysing policies and the ideas behind them, the only senior figure from the New Labour era who dared to reflect on the relationship between markets and the state, the limits of 'choice' as a driving force in the delivery of public services, and who sought to claim Adam Smith as an economist of the centre left. He had regular conversations with the then Archbishop of Canterbury, Rowan Williams, as well as with authors, poets and historians. But Brown was equally at ease with the populist soundbite. He devised the phrase 'tough on crime, tough on the causes of crime', as well as 'prudence for a purpose'. He was obsessed with the media and with securing the support of Rupert Murdoch and his newspapers. Brown had range, a capacity for mastering detail and a hunger to project.

Yet his period as prime minister was around the same length as Heath's and in some ways more turbulent. Heath was never challenged while prime minister. There were several attempted internal coups against Brown, who also faced the nerve-shredding nightmare of the 2008 financial crash. He left office in 2010, having finally achieved his aching ambition to be prime minister in the summer of 2007. He dreaded being a 'tail-end Charlie' prime minister, and yet that is what he became.

Heath and Brown were very different in many ways, but had similar failings that overwhelmed their capacity for range, depth, curiosity and intelligence. Neither was good at handling colleagues, even if they commanded intense loyalty from those who worked closely with them. Both assumed that voters followed politics as closely as they did and would understand the nuance of what they were trying to do. Heath introduced a pay policy – a way of controlling inflation by restricting increases in wages, and prices – that had a certain logic to it, one that came in three different phases. Most voters found each phase an act of provocation, rather than a reasoned way of managing soaring incomes. Brown sought endlessly to make sense of the global economy, of the opportunities and the need for governments to do more to counter the downsides. Most voters paid no attention. Both men lacked empathy and were wooden as performers. Brown became wooden when he acquired responsibility for the economic brief after Labour's defeat in 1992. Prior to that, he was a lively and witty speaker. He faced the mighty Nigel Lawson when he was acting shadow chancellor in the late 1980s, and often got the better of him. Heath was never a great performer, but was at his worst by far as prime minister. Before he became leader, he conveyed a certain dynamic authority rooted in a partly unjustified self-confidence.

Both men faced complex political backgrounds when they became prime minister. Heath had been slaughtered in his first election as leader in 1966 and never fully recovered his authority. Many in his party thought he would lose again in 1970. Heath was conscious of having much to prove. He never looked a 'winner' – a perception that is hugely authority-enhancing – except for the briefest of honeymoons after the 1970 election victory. Brown waited a long time for Blair to leave Number Ten and, when he got in, faced the delicate task of indicating distance from Blair, but not too much, as he wanted the support of newspapers that had only been sympathetic to Labour because of Blair. Both Heath and Brown were partly destroyed by mistimed elections. Heath went early and lost. Brown very publicly contemplated an early election and then did not call one, fatally undermining his strategic and policy ideas as well as his public voice. In some respects, they were the two biggest figures in modern times and yet they struggled to stay afloat at the top.

In both cases, the Cabinets over which they ruled were relatively passive and united. Another essential requirement of leadership is the skill to manage the frontbench, the parliamentary party and the wider party. In the UK there is a presidential culture and yet the system is inescapably party-based. If a party is divided, a leader has a duty to bind it together. This is relentlessly tough. The much-derided Wilson had no choice but to be a party manager, given the scale of the divisions in the Labour Party during his leadership. He led a Cabinet that included Tony Benn and David Owen, Michael Foot and Roy Jenkins, all political giants who disagreed on the big issues. The largely forgotten James Callaghan was the most effective manager of all the modern prime ministers. He led the divided Cabinet that he inherited in 1976 from Wilson through stormy economic times. There was not a single resignation over policy throughout his three or so years at the helm. The contrast with May is revealing. She lost more ministers through resignations over policy than any modern prime minister. She had the excuse that she was dealing with Brexit, an even thornier challenge than the ones facing Callaghan. Nonetheless, his Cabinet had many bigger and more charismatic figures in it than May's and he kept them all on board, a deft act of leadership. Yet it did him no good in electoral terms. Callaghan lost the only election he fought as leader, in 1979.

Keeping a Cabinet and a party together is not enough to win an election. Winning elections is an essential quality of leadership, and Callaghan lost. Those who become prime minister without winning an election lead with far less confidence. Brown ached for his own mandate, but blew the election timing and had to carry on awkwardly until the 2008 financial crash gave him fresh purpose. He had a strategy to move on stealthily from Blairite New Labour for around a year and then call an election. Such was his early popularity, which he had not anticipated, that he got caught up in a frenzy over a much earlier election that he did not in the end call. May felt obliged to woo the hard-line Brexiteers in her party, having become prime minister without winning an election. When she sought her own mandate, she lost her party's majority and became weaker still, or at least she acted in a politically fragile context, even if she was largely unyielding in her approach to leadership.

Winning and governing successfully requires a UK leader to espouse and implement policies that bind members while appealing to a wider electorate. This is not easy. One of Thatcher's great strengths was to act with radical conviction while convincing enough of the wider electorate that she was on their side. In doing so, she changed her party rather than appeased it – epic leadership. Blair challenged his party's convictions and rarely appeased them, but while Thatcher moved to the radical right, Blair was more cautious and technocratic, arguing for 'what works'. No one supports what does not work. Wilson managed to excite his members and the wider electorate in the run-up to the 1964 election with his plan to harness the 'white hot heat of this technological revolution'. Only leaders at their peak can be change-makers in policy terms, keeping their party with them and winning the backing of most voters. Yet remove one of those three components from the sequence and leadership becomes impossible, or pointless.

Leaders must also know how much space they have in which to act, on what is always a crowded political stage. This is an overlooked qualification for leadership, but an essential one. Commentators will be urging prime ministers to do X or Y, without acknowledging that if they did X or Y, their party would fall apart. To be successful, he or she must be an astute reader of the rhythms of politics. What are the underlying trends? How long will a damaging story run? How far do they dare to go in terms of policy? For various reasons, Wilson, Major, Brown, Cameron and May led with virtually no room to move at all. After 1997, Blair had more room than he dared to realize. Until the end, Thatcher was astute in recognizing just how much room she had – cautious at first, bold after the schism in the Labour Party that led to the formation of the Social Democratic Party (SDP). Wilson was a brilliant operator, given the ridiculously cluttered political stage that he faced for much of his leadership. Cameron created space by forming a coalition, which he managed with considerable skill. May had more space than she realized when she first became prime minister, and then none at all after she called an early election in May 2017 and lost her party's majority. To his surprise, Brown had space during his early honeymoon as prime minister – space he made the most of until he became distracted by the temptation to hold an election. After that he was doomed, but his long tenure at the Treasury meant he was supremely well qualified to respond to the 2008 financial crash. An economic emergency cleared the stage for him and he could act.

———

Of the ten prime ministers in the following chapters, I got to know most of them one way or another and observed them all in the flesh. As well as seeing Wilson speak live, I went to the spectators' gallery in the Commons to see him perform at the despatch box in the mid-1970s. He was wily and in command, yet he looked knackered, as he did at the rally in the October election. I interviewed Heath several times, including on the night Thatcher fell from power, when he was on an unqualified and transparent high. I also interviewed him at his home in Salisbury a few times for GMTV's *Sunday Programme* and Heath usually invited us to stay for tea afterwards. He made the biggest impression on me when I was at university in the early 1980s. He came to give a talk on foreign policy and spoke brilliantly, without notes, for an hour and then answered questions. His command and range were scintillating, although he was no orator.

I met Thatcher for the first time when she was guest at our primary-school summer fete. The school was in her constituency. She was Education Secretary at the time and I had been assigned the task of showing her around the stalls at the fete. Thatcher had a go on the coconut shy and, at her first attempt, succeeded in throwing a ball with such determined ruthlessness that the coconut fell to the floor within a nanosecond. Here was a sign of things to come. She was competitive and knew her targets. Her visit was on an unusually hot day and, in her speech, she made a joke about how the headmaster's bald head was exposed to the sun and perhaps he should borrow her hat. The headmaster, Mr Sharpe, struggled to hide that he was a little taken aback by the reference to his baldness. Thatcher did not notice his fleeting discomfort – again a sign of things to come. I traded on this early meeting. She never forgot encounters, however trivial.

'Do you remember that time you were triumphant at the coconut shy at Queenswell School?' I asked her once.

'Of course I do,' Thatcher replied. She reminisced with a smile that suggested to me that, contrary to her reputation, she did possess a slight sense of humour, an awareness of how things could be a little ridiculous. I should add that of those people I have met who knew her far better, no one agrees with me on this.

I interviewed Callaghan several times, including for what I assume was one of his last long interviews, which I quote in the chapter on his leadership. He had a capacity for reflectiveness after his leadership that he did not always possess when he was in power. I observed Major at close quarters as a BBC political correspondent, although did not know him. As political editor of the *New Statesman* in the early New Labour era, I saw a lot of Blair and Brown and managed to remain engaged with both throughout their increasingly tense relationship. This was unusual. Most commentators were either 'Blairite' or 'Brownite' and were barred from contact with one circle or the other. I was seen as more of a Brownite because I recognized qualities in Brown, and his close allies, that most 'Blairite' commentators refused to see or disapproved of. But any journalist would have been able to recognize qualities in Blair, too. Both had failings. Quite a lot of their differences were ideological and strategic, although these were largely hidden at the time, and since. Roy Jenkins, a senior Cabinet minister, former SDP leader and author of weighty biographies, once said to me at the height of the New Labour era that it must be difficult being a commentator when there were only two interesting figures in politics, Blair and Brown. He compared it to the time of his political peak, when there were charismatic, enigmatic titans in both the main parties. In retrospect, there were other big figures around in the New Labour era, but they wielded little power, such was the control of the duo at the top.

As David Cameron sought to adopt some of New Labour's techniques from the other side of the political spectrum, he wooed non-Conservative commentators including me, at least when he was leader of the Opposition. I seemed to be the chosen columnist when he took trips to East Anglia. I travelled with him three times on day-trips to Norwich. One of them coincided with the height of the expenses scandal, and Cameron had to break off from the itinerary to sack someone or other from the frontbench. He acted with an elegant ruthlessness and then got on with the demands of his visit with a cool energy. He passed a test of leadership: to act with speedy brutality when necessary and then to compartmentalize. He returned to the task in hand as if nothing had happened. Blair was the best for compartmentalizing – almost eerily so, by the end. He could have a cup of tea and discuss market economics while a vain police inspector waited to interview him about 'cash for honours', an outrageous police inquiry that carried the possibility of jail for Blair and his senior advisers.

After trips or meetings with Blair and Brown, I returned with lots of notes and ideas. Cameron was something of a blank canvas. He asked me a lot about Blair and Brown. Perhaps that was the sole purpose of my trips with him to Norwich: to provide him with information. His small entourage was efficient, friendly and relaxed, perhaps too relaxed. I was surprised how high the stakes were for Blair and his advisers when he went on excursions, even towards the end of his leadership. I recall one visit with him to Manchester during which we visited the set of *Coronation Street*. I was in the car of his press secretary, David Hill, on the way back. Blair was in a different car and he phoned Hill several times to seek assurances that the trip had gone well – and this was after he had won three elections. Prime ministers are human. Blair had been battered by onslaughts after Iraq, but had been received enthusiastically by the cast of *Coronation Street* and by onlookers. He could not quite believe it, and needed Hill to make sense of what had happened. No wonder he was so dependent on Alastair Campbell to guide him through the torrents of media and public scrutiny. Brown was just as dependent on individuals, especially Ed Balls. Brown might have terrified some Cabinet colleagues and external opponents, but he listened to the relatively youthful Balls on policy and strategic decisions, often phoning him several times a day even when he was prime minister and Balls was running his own department as a relatively new Cabinet minister. In terms of policy-making, Balls was the third most influential figure of the New Labour era, after Blair and Brown.

I got to know May a little while presenting GMTV's *Sunday Programme*. The show was broadcast live at the ridiculously early hour of 7 a.m. In opposition, May was one of the few frontbenchers willing to come on live, getting a taxi from Maidenhead. I assumed she was merely being conscientious, but came to realize that wilful ambition played a part, too. She was impeccably polite and solicitous. The other regular live guest was Jeremy Corbyn. He lived relatively near the studio and was also willing to come on whenever we asked him, sometimes at short notice. The two occasionally appeared on the same programme and would stay for a quick cup of tea at the end. This was at the height of the New Labour era. If anyone had told me that one would be prime minister and the other leader of the Opposition, I would have assumed it to be a drug-induced fantasy, at least in the case of Corbyn, who showed no signs of being burdened by personal ambition. May gave no indication then of being the 'bloody difficult woman' that Ken Clarke identified during the short, eccentric Conservative leadership contest in 2016. Her obstinacy and insularity developed when she was a long-serving Home Secretary. She learned then the wrong lessons about how to lead, assuming that an unyielding insularity would work in Number Ten, as it had done at the Home Office.

My first column was published in *The Spectator* when I was still a political correspondent for the BBC. I shared the cover of that magazine in September 1995 with Boris Johnson; we had both written on New Labour as it emerged under Tony Blair. Johnson was the magazine's main political columnist and would later become its editor. I got to know him a little when I became political editor of the *New Statesman* and we were used as pundits on a range of programmes during the early New Labour era. We also occasionally formed a panel of two on Radio 4's *The Week in Westminster*. Every now and then I also appeared with him on *Head 2 Head*, a much missed programme on the BBC News channel in which two commentators debated a topical issue for half an hour.

I admired him for wanting to be a politician and detected an underlying seriousness as well as boundless personal ambition and a capacity to play the charming fool, a beguiling combination for some. Nonetheless, I did not see him as a future prime minister. Some of the factors that stopped the likes of Michael Heseltine, Denis Healey, Michael Portillo and others taking the top job applied to Johnson on a more spectacular scale. They included perceptions of disloyalty, transparent ambition and a reluctance, almost a shyness, to cultivate large numbers of political allies. After the Conservatives were slaughtered in the 2019 European Parliament election, none of these factors mattered. The party members wanted an exuberant performer and Brexit supporter to challenge Nigel Farage, the victorious leader of the Brexit Party. Johnson proved many commentators wrong in seizing the crown.

In the following chapters I attempt to root their leaderships in context, seeking to understand how it seemed to them at the time, and the dilemmas and opportunities of power. Any further references to my conversations with the modern prime ministers and other senior politicians are in the Notes. These characters were all deeply flawed and, unsurprisingly, given that they made it to the top, they had great qualities, too. All are more complex than the caricatures that defined them. None had all the qualifications of leadership. Perhaps such candidates for power do not exist. But if the job were advertised in the way other senior positions are, here is what the advertisement would specify.

The Country is Looking to Elect a Prime Minister

He or she must have the following qualifications:

- He or she must be a political teacher with a skill for explanation and making sense of complex issues. This is an essential qualification.

- He or she must be able to manage a party that is bound to be divided, and must also lead that party with a sense of purpose and ideological verve.

- He or she must respond astutely to the demands of the media at any time of any day.

- He or she must link values to policies in ways that bind a party and appeal to the wider electorate.

- He or she must show a deep understanding of the wider currents of domestic and foreign policy and a developed sense of political history.

- He or she must read the political rhythms in order to assess correctly the space available to act as prime minister.

- Highly desirable: experience of government before seeking to lead one.

- Voters are expected to take into account the constraints on a prime minister when making an appointment, but probably will not do so.

———

Harold Wilson was the first of the modern prime ministers to apply.

1

HAROLD WILSON

Harold Wilson is the most misunderstood of post-war prime ministers. He enjoyed a political honeymoon of intoxicating popularity, with high personal poll ratings and a generous media, from his election as Labour leader in 1963 until soon after his landslide election victory in 1966. Soon after Wilson's big election win, the way he was perceived changed wildly. Neither his ambitious senior colleagues nor much of an increasingly disdainful media sought to recognize the impossible context in which he made his many energy-draining, stressful and often successful moves. After he ceased to be Labour leader there was little desire to understand Wilson, either. Instead something odd happened. The leader who had dominated British politics during the heady 1960s and for a pivotal part of the dark 1970s became a ghostly figure very quickly. From being the most talked-about figure in British politics for more than a decade, Wilson was rarely referred to. By the time Labour returned to power in 1997 he had become part of 'Old' Labour. The Labour Party's complex past, and its longest-serving leader, were dismissed as being no more than part of a distant chronology that had become irrelevant at best.

Yet the present constantly redefines the past. After 2010, the era of large or landslide election wins had passed. Deeply divided parties struggled to govern and to oppose. Once again a referendum on Europe was contested amidst economic turbulence. Suddenly we were closer to the fragile parts of the Wilson era than we were to the landslide parliaments of 1997 and 2001, or to the 1980s when Margaret Thatcher won huge majorities. For the few who bothered to look, Wilson acquired a new relevance. There were lessons to learn. From being a ghost, he had now become a potential guide.

After the 1964 election Wilson became prime minister with a tiny majority of just four seats. Ten years later he became prime minister in a hung parliament, and then in one with another puny majority. In order to make sense of more recent events, there is an urgent need to understand Wilson, to return him from the shadows. For most of his leadership he led a deeply divided party. The policies that divided Labour included the UK's relationship with the EU – or the Common Market, as it was known in the Wilson era. Other divisive policy areas included state ownership and nuclear disarmament. After 2010 there were many echoes from the Wilson era.

Most specifically, the echoes relate to Wilson's final phase in power, which is much overlooked and yet highly significant and instructive. Those final years in power, from 1974 to 1976, reveal partly how leaders are perceived. We choose what we want to see, or what we are told to see, rather than what is in front of our eyes. What we chose to see was an exhausted, paranoid, devious prime minister who had lost all sense of purpose and moral mission. What was happening in front of our eyes was rather different.

The caricature was not a complete distortion. Stereotypes of leaders are always based on an essence of truth, and there was something to the narrowly defined image. Wilson was tired beyond his years. He was only in his late fifties and looked much older. He lacked any great visionary zeal. But he still had spark and the skill to transform a political mood. He could think quickly and strategically. He was artful. He could master complex policy detail.

The lesson about misleading stereotypes applies precisely to the last period of Wilson's leadership, which began in March 1974 and ended with his resignation in March 1976. These stormy, nightmarishly challenging years highlight vividly the need to go beyond stereotype. This is the period of his leadership that is largely ignored, to the point that it is rarely referred to. Even Wilson's best biographer, Ben Pimlott, rushes over the final phase of power.[1] In order to learn the Wilsonian lessons, we must start at the end rather than the beginning.

The tired Wilson achieved a range of extraordinary feats in those final two years. Winning in February 1974 was one of them. He only just won. Edward Heath and the Conservative government in power at the time secured more votes, but Wilson's Labour Party won a handful more seats.[2] Even so, that narrow win was a significant triumph for Wilson, for several reasons.

The February 1974 election was the most bizarre of modern times, taking place against the backdrop of a miners' strike, a three-day week under Heath's government and power cuts. Sometimes Britain was literally in the dark, although wisely Heath lifted some of the tougher restrictions during the campaign itself. Still, it was highly unusual for an election to be contested in the depths of winter, even if most of the lights were fleetingly back on.

Wilson's narrow win in February 1974 was remarkable, however puny the margin of victory. Above all, no one had expected him to return to power – including Wilson himself. The diaries of his frontbench colleagues from that era are darkly comic. Tony

Benn writes towards the end of the February campaign: 'I saw Harold probably for the last time as Labour leader. He was tired and exhausted.' Barbara Castle and Roy Jenkins make similar observations. They sensed that Wilson's career was about to end. Benn, who was often an astute reader of political rhythms, could hardly believe it when he was back in power as a Cabinet minister and wrote in his diary: 'A week ago, I thought I might be out of parliament altogether and now I'm in the cabinet as Secretary of State for Industry.'[3]

In his own memoir – an important source for understanding the multi-layered complexities in relation to Wilson – Roy Jenkins wrote: 'My last encounter with Wilson before polling day was on the final Sunday afternoon when we spoke at a big Birmingham Town Hall meeting and talked for some time afterwards. He seemed tired, depressed and expecting defeat, keeping going with some difficulty and gallantry until by Thursday night he would have completed his final throw in politics. We are both wrong.'[4] Jenkins returned to government as Home Secretary. He had been a historic reformer as Home Secretary in Wilson's previous government. After the February 1974 election Jenkins moved back to the Home Office, with much less enthusiasm for the task ahead. Soon he was to leave British politics for Brussels, before returning sensationally to form a new political party.

Wilson was at least as surprised as Jenkins to be in government once again. His senior adviser at the time, Bernard Donoughue, revealed subsequently that Wilson had expected to lose and did not want to give journalists the pleasure of seeing him defeated. Bizarrely, Wilson had planned to hide from the journalists in the aftermath of defeat, arranging for a discreet flight back to London from his Huyton constituency in the north-west of England, without appearing in front of the media at any stage. The deranged plan was for the pilot to land in an obscure part of Bedfordshire, and Wilson would then be driven away to a hidden venue. The idea was wild enough to suggest that, at this late stage in his career, Wilson had lost all reason in relation to his dealings with the media; but then again, parts of the media had given him cause to become irrational. In his early years as leader most newspapers, even the Conservative-supporting ones, had hailed Wilson as a 'modernizer'. By 1974 all the newspapers, including the non-Conservative ones, had become highly critical of him, to his despair. The BBC had also turned against him. In 1971 it broadcast a programme on Wilson and his shadow Cabinet with the provocative title *Yesterday's Men*. Both the title and the programme were not only biased, but wrong. Yesterday's men were back in power before very long. Wilson was justifiably furious with the BBC. He would have struggled with the later era of rolling TV news and Twitter, when no party leader could even contemplate disappearing from public view in the immediate aftermath of an election. As it turned out for Wilson, there was no need to attempt an elaborate escape. Instead he became prime minister again: quite a spectacular alternative route to determined anonymity.[5]

The assumption that he would lose – often an assumption that feeds on itself – was not the only reason why Wilson's return from the seemingly political dead was an unusual triumph.

By February 1974 the Labour Party was divided in ways that made it almost impossible to lead. The divisions were unusually intense partly because there were titanic figures on either side of all the epic issues from that era. Leading is easier when mediocrities fall out with each other from within a party. It becomes a nightmare when political giants articulate conflicting visions. From the very top down, Labour was split over Europe, over whether more industries should be nationalized and over the degree to which public spending was the way out of the economic crisis or a contribution to it. These were divisions of unique range. From the late-Thatcher era onwards, the Conservatives were split over Europe, but broadly agreed with each other on economic policy and public-service reforms. Labour's leading figures did not agree with each other on very much at all.

All the titans around Wilson's frontbench also enjoyed deep support within the Labour Party. They were impossible to lead, and yet Wilson led them back into government. Those he appointed to his new Cabinet included Denis Healey, James Callaghan, Roy Jenkins, Tony Crosland, Shirley Williams, Tony Benn and Michael Foot. This group concurred on very little. In addition, most of them wanted to be leader and regarded Wilson with disdain. But it was Wilson who had taken them back to government. The Labour Cabinet formed in 1974 was the weightiest, most experienced and most charismatic of all the governments elected since 1945. The weight and charisma lit up the political stage and, at the same time, added to the burdens of a prime minister needing to manage big political egos.

There is a third reason why Wilson's return to power in February 1974 was extraordinary. After he was unexpectedly defeated in June 1970, when someone threw an egg at him for the first time in an election campaign (see Introduction), he almost disappeared from public view. He was deeply disappointed and shaken by defeat. Election outcomes are surprising in their capacity to surprise. Wilson had not expected to win in February 1974. He had not expected to lose in 1970. Almost as a way of coping with the trauma after the 1970 defeat, he kept a low public profile and spent a lot of time writing his memoirs. He was not seen that often in public. Parliament was not televised, so voters did not see or hear his speeches in the Commons. There were no TV news channels following leaders around at every hour of the day. It was much easier to disappear. And Wilson largely disappeared.

In the twenty-first century a leader who unexpectedly loses an election is almost always doomed. Indeed, leaders who lose when they are expected to do so also tend to resign in the immediate aftermath. Wilson discovered what Tony Blair would call a 'third way' – a political magician's third way. He disappeared from public view, but did not resign. He stayed on as leader of the Opposition and won another two elections.

The final two election victories were part of the underestimated phase of his career. He began in February 1974 as prime minister of a minority government. Wisely, he chose not to try to form a coalition; probably that option was not available to him. The outgoing prime minister, Edward Heath, had already sought a coalition with the Liberals and failed.[6]

Wilson liked and admired the leader of the Liberals, Jeremy Thorpe, but kept astutely clear of any negotiation about a partnership in government. Instead when Heath moved out, Wilson moved in, the leader of a single-party minority government. He had become a smart reader of the rhythms of politics, a pivotal qualification for leadership. He knew when to make a move and how to do so. While Heath negotiated with Thorpe over the frenzied weekend after the election, Wilson was filmed walking with his Labrador, seemingly relaxed but ready for action. The only action he contemplated was to be prime minister of a minority Labour government.

If David Cameron had followed Wilson's precedent after the 2010 election, he might have found the space on the political stage to rule more assertively as a new prime minister and to carry his party with him more authoritatively. Wilson governed for a few months with a minority administration, held a second election – the one where another egg was thrown at him in October – and won a small overall majority. Almost certainly Cameron would have secured a majority in a second election if he had chosen this course, and probably a more substantial majority than Wilson secured. Being younger and far less experienced, Cameron was not as sharp a reader of the complex political rhythms.

Wilson won a tiny overall majority of four seats in October 1974. He thought the margin would be bigger and was disappointed, the third successive election in which he was surprised by the result. But to win an overall majority of any sort in the context in which that election was contested – raging inflation, industrial unrest again, after a brief pause when Labour came to power six months earlier – was another electoral achievement. Above all, establishing Labour as a majority government was near-miraculous, because the party's divisions over Europe were intensifying.[7]

In a way that Cameron failed to do, Wilson held a referendum on Britain's membership of the Common Market – and won. He won decisively. In navigating the victory, he made several moves that Cameron did not make when he held, and lost, the referendum on Europe in 2016. Cameron was a world expert on Tony Blair and New Labour, so much so that his leadership was partly an act of imitation. But he would have been well advised to spend more time studying the unfashionable Wilson, leading a party divided over Europe into a referendum.

Wilson's first smart move was to ensure that the political consequences of merely offering the referendum worked decisively for him. There is no point in a prime minister pledging a referendum, with all the risks involved, unless the offer in itself works for the leader.

He was a reluctant convert to the idea of a referendum on Europe. Like Cameron, he pledged to hold one not because he had discovered a passion for direct democracy, but to prevent his party from splitting fatally over the issue. Wilson made the offer well in advance of the elections in 1974 and his party calmed down a little. There was an acceptance that the referendum would settle the issue, that Cabinet ministers would publicly disagree with each other during the campaign and that the voters would decide.

The sequence before the formal referendum campaign was rather messier under Cameron. There was a fundamental difference. The Conservative prime minister had hoped to persuade all of his Cabinet to support the case for staying in the EU. Cameron felt an intense sense of betrayal when some of his Cabinet, particularly Michael Gove, came out against remaining in the EU. The stakes were high as he embarked on his renegotiation, precisely because he had hopes of convincing most, or all, of his Cabinet to back him.[8]

Wilson had no such hopes for his Cabinet. He knew, from the beginning of his renegotiation, that his ministers would be split on the issue. Ironically, the overt scale of the division in the Labour government simplified matters. Wilson had given up hoping for unity long ago. The knowledge of the split helped him, crucially, in limiting the significance of his 'renegotiation' of the UK's membership of the Common Market. But while the prospect of a referendum had cooled the political temperature in Wilson's party in some respects, Cameron's offer raised the temperature in his. Cameron was under almost unbearable pressure to deliver a 'renegotiation' that reassured the likes of Gove and Boris Johnson, who was the Mayor of London when Cameron first proposed a referendum. Wilson was under no such equivalent pressure because he knew that he could never persuade Tony Benn, Barbara Castle, Peter Shore and Michael Foot, four of the big Cabinet heavyweights who had resolved to campaign for the UK to leave Europe. The purpose of Wilson's renegotiation was therefore much more limited. It was a fig leaf to justify his support for EU membership, when he had opposed joining in the first place.

Before the February 1974 election, Wilson secured a significant electoral benefit from the referendum pledge. He successfully nudged the Conservative MP, Enoch Powell, to declare his support for Labour on the basis of the offer. Powell resigned as a Conservative MP at the start of the February campaign, an ominous opening to the election for Heath. The fleeting support for Labour of the Conservatives' intellectual populist in a closely fought election was a significant bonus for Wilson. For him and his party, the referendum was paying off even before he had held it.

Powell despised Heath, but as a politician, Wilson was as far removed from Powell as it was possible to be. Wilson was the pragmatic leader who had been on the frontbench for most of his political career. Powell was the right-wing troublemaker who was sacked from Heath's frontbench after his explosive 'Rivers of blood' speech in 1968 and would never serve in a senior capacity again. The impact of Powell's intervention is not easy to measure precisely. But his resignation as an MP, and his support for Labour, conveyed a vivid sense of a deeply troubled Conservative Party at a time of national crisis. Such an impression could only have helped Labour, a party that almost managed to hide its own deep troubles during the two elections in 1974.

Wilson went on to win the 1975 In/Out referendum on the UK's membership of the Common Market by a big margin – around

67 per cent voted to remain – a more historic victory than his two election wins the previous year. In terms of timing, he waited until he was virtually certain he would win. He found excuses to wait until one opinion poll after another pointed to a decisive victory for staying in the Common Market. For several years public opinion had been as febrile as it was in the build-up to the 2016 referendum on whether the UK should stay or leave the EU. Polls in the early 1970s suggested strong opposition to the UK's membership. It was far from clear in early 1974 that a referendum would deliver the result Wilson sought – one that backed continued membership. The anti-marketeer Tony Benn had been a passionate advocate of a referendum, partly because polls suggested that his side could win. Wilson waited until he was wholly confident of victory. When he called the referendum for June 1975, every poll pointed to a substantial win for the UK staying in the Common Market. This was not the case in the 2016 referendum, when polls suggested a much closer contest.

During the campaign Wilson was smarter still. He was more than self-aware enough to know how unpopular he was by 1975. In some ways he was too self-aware, one cause of his neurotic introspection. Still, in some respects Wilson was correct in his self-awareness. Voters were fed up with him, as they tend to be with any leader who has been on the political stage for a long time. More than two decades later an outgoing Labour prime minister, Gordon Brown, reflected that in the modern media age, public figures had around seven years on the political stage before voters tired of them. By June 1975 Wilson had been a leader of his party for around twelve wearying years. As a result, he took careful steps not to make the referendum about himself. He delegated his Foreign Secretary, James Callaghan, to renegotiate Britain's terms of membership cosmetically, announced the referendum at a point when the polls showed decisive margins in favour of staying in, and then he all but disappeared during the campaign. Wilson made two or three weighty interventions, but gave no one the chance to frame the campaign as a test of his own leadership and, therefore, an opportunity to kick him. His low profile made it difficult for the 'Out' campaign to suggest that voters could bash Wilson. Equally, Wilson's political opponents felt at ease campaigning for 'In', knowing that the prime minister would not acquire huge personal capital if the referendum backed continued membership of the Common Market. The campaign was not about him. In terms of personalities, the referendum was dominated by sparkling or weighty figures. Roy Jenkins, Shirley Williams, Jeremy Thorpe, Edward Heath and, to some extent, even Margaret Thatcher put the case for the UK's continuing membership. Tony Benn, Michael Foot, Barbara Castle and Enoch Powell were the main advocates for withdrawal. Wilson was almost nowhere to be seen.

In 2016 one of the reasons why some Labour voters struggled to back 'Remain' was their sense that they would be giving an enormous boost to Cameron and his chancellor, George Osborne, the two dominant figures in the campaign. Perhaps the duo were not self-aware enough at the start of that fateful referendum. Again, they should have studied the late-Wilson era, where there were lessons to learn.

Cameron did not seek to learn them. He fought a high-profile campaign, which was admirably energetic in some respects. But the referendum became partly about him and his political future. No one who wanted to bring down Wilson would have used the referendum to achieve their objective. He won without making the entire sequence partly about his own fate. He chose to be irrelevant.

—

In relation to economic policy, Wilson was also agile in this final overlooked phase of his leadership. He left much of the hard grind to his chancellor, Denis Healey, a formidably robust figure, and yet one who became ill with exhaustion by the end of his five and a half years at the Treasury. To some extent Wilson also gave a lot of space to his new Employment Secretary, Michael Foot, whom he hailed publicly as the great success of the new government. For a leader who was not especially interested in character, Wilson was unusually clear-minded at making Cabinet appointments. Like Powell, Foot was as far removed from Wilson as it was possible to be: a left-wing rebel, a bibliophile and writer. Wilson had been an expedient and ambitious frontbencher for most of his political career, was no lover of books and was an inelegant writer. Yet Wilson recognized that Foot was moving towards a more pragmatic approach without reneging on his deeply held convictions. So he put Foot in a key post. As Employment Secretary, Foot was trusted by key union leaders, especially the mighty Jack Jones, General Secretary of the Transport and General Workers' Union.

At first, Wilson based the government's relationship with the unions around a vaguely defined social contract. The vagueness was deliberate. As Wilson recognized, precision would have been far too dangerous. Agreement between government and union leaders would have been impossible if the details were explored too fully. The idea behind the contract was that, on a voluntary basis, the government would deliver a social programme and some price controls that the unions welcomed, while the unions would act with restraint in relation to pay. Wilson had opposed Heath's formal incomes policy, in which limited pay rises were imposed by the government over three successive phases, so he had no choice but to hail a voluntary alternative. Heath had become prime minister in 1970 as an opponent of incomes policy, but like other prime ministers in the 1970s he became so panic-stricken that he turned towards one – in his case, a highly convoluted one.

The only problem with Wilson's social contract was that some union leaders, or their members, were reluctant to deliver their side of the deal. Immediately after returning to power, the government had ended the miners' strike by awarding a substantial pay rise, more or less what the National Union of Mineworkers (NUM) had been seeking. The settlement triggered a debate about whether the miners were a 'special case'. Unsurprisingly, other unions concluded that the miners were not, and also sought pay deals on a similar scale. Inflation soared further, although the trigger for the high inflation of the 1970s had nothing to do with the British government. The tripling of oil prices in 1973 was the context against which unions, most obviously the NUM, became more muscular. The market gave more power to the miners, as Enoch Powell recognized from the right.

In one of his final acts, Wilson performed with Wilsonian guile. Trapped by publicly declared opposition to an incomes policy in any form, Wilson set tough guidelines on pay. He insisted that they were voluntary, but that his government would use emergency powers to enforce them if the unions failed to adhere to them voluntarily. Wilson was an early pioneer of Tony Blair's 'third way'. He announced a voluntary pay policy that could become compulsory, just as Blair banned fox-hunting in a way that allowed fox-hunting to continue.

These were grim contortions. From the perspective of the Treasury, Denis Healey despaired of what he regarded as Wilson's weak manoeuvring. Indeed, most Cabinet ministers were scathing of Wilson at this late stage, although many were to change their minds retrospectively.[9]

Yet Wilson's contortions managed to keep the show on the road, more or less. Like Heath before him and Jim Callaghan afterwards, Wilson was gripped by the need to avoid the high unemployment levels of the 1930s, the likes of which he had seen at first hand during his political upbringing. He wanted to avoid strikes that could wreck an already fragile economy. Incomes policies had failed spectacularly under Heath. Wilson navigated his third way, but shared with Heath a determination to avoid high unemployment. In the 1970s there were Heath's incomes policy, Wilsonian guile that disguised an incomes policy, and James Callaghan's later incomes policy. An alternative approach arrived in 1979.

As well as winning elections and a referendum on Europe, keeping a divided Cabinet together and establishing an incomes policy that did not appear to be one, Wilson has one more claim to distinctiveness in that short period of his final premiership. He chose the moment of his departure, resigning in March 1976. He is the only prime minister in modern times to leave Number Ten according to a carefully planned timetable of his own choosing. How ironic that after years of feverish speculation that Wilson would be forced out by an internal coup, he chose voluntarily both the timing and the manner of his going. The contrast with Margaret Thatcher is powerful. For much of her time as prime minister – at least after the Falklands War in 1982 – there was not much speculation about her being forced out. Yet in November 1990 she was removed against her wishes in the most dramatic of circumstances. She never recovered from an intense, raging sense of betrayal. Wilson, who had spent much of his leadership looking over his shoulder and neurotically fearing a coup, left with rare dignity.

Few expected Wilson's departure. He had told a handful of close friends that he would go when he was sixty, and he did. He chose the timing, he chose the context and to some extent he chose his successor, in that he made it relatively easy for the senior colleague he wanted to succeed him, Jim Callaghan, to be the victor in the contest that followed. Consider the tortuous, agonized context of most prime ministers' departures. Wilson took a bow calmly, which was remarkable given all the speculation about possible leadership coups since around 1968. In the end, no one forced him out.

All his successors left in traumatic circumstances. Callaghan lost the election in 1979. Thatcher was forced out by Cabinet colleagues and by some in her parliamentary party. Major was slaughtered in the 1997 election. Blair was forced out by Gordon Brown and his parliamentary allies. Brown lost an election. Cameron lost a referendum. May left reluctantly and tearfully as her Cabinet and party turned against her. If a leader is defined partly by the manner and context of his or her departure, then Wilson is uniquely placed.

And yet it was this final period that diminished his already declining reputation. By 1974 Wilson had become, in the eyes of most voters and ministerial colleagues, an untrustworthy trickster, a leader who viewed politics purely in managerial terms, with no vision, and indeed no principle. Like all caricatures of leaders, there is some truth in this one; but like all leaders, Wilson was a complex, multi-dimensional human being. His overt expediency did not present the whole picture, nor was his wilful pragmatism a wholly fatal flaw.

His leadership in relation to Europe is one example of this. Towards the end of his leadership Wilson had a conversation with his friend and colleague Barbara Castle. She revealed the discussion many years later:

> He was a man of principle. Harold always wanted to go into Europe, but he didn't want to get too ahead of the party. In the early 1970s, I remember he was having a terrible time. He was making pathetic evasive speeches and some of his friends became very worried about him. I said to him, 'Harold, you've got to come out on Europe, one way or another.' He replied, 'Barbara, I regard it as my sacred duty to keep the party together. I know where I want to go on Europe, but I'm not going to do it if it wrecks the party.' And then he said to me, 'I've been doing this for eight years over Europe and it's been hell.'[10]

Wilson's side of the conversation is the pragmatists' charter.

He opposed Britain's membership when he was Opposition leader in the decisive Commons vote in advance of the UK joining in 1973. He did so not because he was a convinced opponent. He had no choice, as this was the position of most in his party. Wilson knew that if he had joined the forceful minority in favour of entry, his party would have fallen apart.

Originally Wilson was opposed to a referendum, but he changed his mind when he saw that it was the only way he could keep his frontbench and wider party together. In February 1974 he claimed that his support for membership would be dependent on a successful renegotiation, and he took the same line in October 1974. In reality, he had been a pragmatic supporter of staying in the Common Market once the UK had signed up. However, he had no choice but to twist and turn to keep his party together. Wilson is not alone in this. For UK leaders of both main parties, Europe has demanded wiliness attached, in some cases, to a principled strategic endgame. Wiliness is draining. Managing an unruly party is the least glamorous dimension to leadership, but is an essential demand. By the early 1970s Labour had become impossibly difficult to manage. But we tend to notice the leader's behaviour without always acknowledging the context. Plucked out of context, Wilson appeared pathetically expedient, a mere manager without vision or principle.

The caricature was partly true, as all caricatures of leaders tend to be. Behind the scenes, Wilson's management in his last period as prime minister was dysfunctional. His two senior advisers, Joe Haines and Bernard Donoughue, loathed Marcia Williams, Wilson's long-standing aide and friend. In their memoirs, both describe scenes of breathtaking hysteria. Haines reveals a wild plot that could easily take the form of a fictional thriller, suggesting that Wilson's personal doctor, Joe Stone, proposed killing Williams with a lethal injection.[11] The level of internal despair must have bordered on the deranged, for murder to be contemplated. At the height of the intense loathing between the courts of Blair and Brown, murder was never considered.

But both Haines and Donoughue acknowledge that while Williams' behaviour drove them – and sometimes Wilson – to the edge of despair, as she allegedly stormed out of meetings or failed to turn up at others, she had great strategic insights. To some extent Wilson obeyed her, a supposedly mighty prime minister following the whims of an erratic friend. But Wilson followed her advice partly because he admired her and rated her judgement on the basis of a long relationship.[12]

Marcia Williams was one of the many enigmatic figures from the Wilson era. She rarely gave interviews after she emerged from behind the scenes to take a seat in the Lords. She never spoke in the Lords. Yet throughout Wilson's long career she was a constant factor and a significant influence. While Haines and Donoughue came to view her with disdain, others liked and admired her. Even after Wilson turned against Tony Benn, she showed an affection for Benn's unfailing charm; and Benn, who by the early 1970s despised Wilson, approved of Williams' mischievous political energy. While she could be intolerant, she could also be kind. Williams was at Mary Wilson's side before and after Wilson's funeral on the Isles of Scilly in July 1995, the two of them walking arm-in-arm on the high street of St Mary's, where the Wilsons had purchased a modest bungalow. Wilson's funeral was both cinematic and restrained. On a hot day that made the Scillies seem like Greek islands, the small town of St Mary's was invaded by the stars of glossy New Labour and by those who had been unglamorously and unfairly defined as 'old Labour'. Tony Blair and Gordon Brown were there, alongside James Callaghan and Michael Foot. Mary Wilson and Marcia Williams were always side-by-side, in the public spaces of a town that briefly hosted a coming together of Labour's generations. In his death, Wilson fleetingly unified his party.

Between March 1974 and Wilson's departure in March 1976 there was little scope for arm-in-arm friendship of any sort. Like their leader, Wilson's advisers were exhausted and surprised to be there. They struggled to work together from hour to hour. There was hardly any room for vision or long-term strategic planning.[13]

Yet, at his best, Wilson did have some ideological verve as well as a deep pragmatism that could sometimes lapse into desperate managerial lunges. His leadership qualities and flaws were formed early in his political career. This is very common in leadership. The seeds of leaders' success and downfalls are often the same and are sown very early on. Most vividly in the cases of Margaret Thatcher and Tony Blair, their dark fates were sealed as they rose to the top.

So it was with Wilson. The factors behind his rise also explain his fall. As an Oxford student Wilson was hard-working, achieving a distinguished first in PPE, but unlike many of his Cabinet colleagues he was not gripped by party politics or the glamour of the Oxford Union. A key influence was his socialist-history tutor, G. D. H. Cole. In his memoirs, Wilson wrote a typically formal and distant tribute to Cole; he was incapable of flowery emotion: 'I had long held G. D. H. Cole in high regard and found this closer contact with him most congenial.' His endorsement was wooden, but it was with the encouragement of Cole that Wilson eventually joined the Labour Party. He continued: 'It was G. D. H. Cole as much as any man who finally pointed me in the direction of the Labour Party. His social and economic theories made it intellectually respectable.'[14]

These are the deadly dull words of a student most emphatically not roused by an ideological crusade. Even so, like many of his political contemporaries in both the main parties, high unemployment in the 1930s shaped Wilson's views and gave him a degree of conviction. Wilson twisted and turned on many issues, but not on what he regarded as the social and economic scourge of unemployment. Again he writes with the limited passion of an accountant explaining a tax return, but his conclusion on unemployment is climactic:

> My attitudes had been clarifying for some time and the catalyst was the unemployment situation. I had seen it years before in the Colne Valley, with members of my class jobless when they left school. My own father was still enduring his second painful period out of work. My religious upbringing and practical studies of economics and unemployment in which I had been engaged at Oxford combined in one single thought: unemployment was not only a severe fault of government, but it was in some way evil, and an affront to the country it afflicted.

For leaders, early impressions are defining. Being younger than Wilson and Heath, Margaret Thatcher dared to risk high unemployment in her early years as prime minister. For her, the 1930s were a more distant decade. Her approach to social and economic policy was determined more by what she saw as the weak vacillations of the Heath government in which she served as a loyal, dutiful and energetic minister. John Major was obsessed with the threat of soaring inflation, even though the risk was not especially high during his leadership. He had been brought up politically on high inflation in the 1970s, being acutely aware that it was those on lower incomes who felt most destabilized by rising prices. Tony Blair was defined by his party's four election defeats in the 1980s and early 1990s. For Wilson and his opponent, Edward Heath, and his Labour successor, Jim Callaghan, it was the unemployment of the 1930s that they were determined to avoid.

In the 1970s each of the three prime ministers could see that their corporatist policies were failing and yet they could not change them, for fear of returning to 1930s-style unemployment. Leaders are trapped by their pasts. None fully escape from them, even if the external circumstances of the present are unrecognizably different. We may choose to see what we want to see in our leaders. Leaders choose to see what happened in the past, rather than what is happening in front of their eyes in the present.

Wilson's own politics deepened when he worked with the economist William Beveridge on the early stages of what became the Beveridge Report on social security and unemployment, published in 1942, which led to the creation of the NHS and the founding of the welfare state. He began working with Beveridge in 1937, before joining the Civil Service. Beveridge was demanding, and Wilson often began his working day at seven in the morning. They worked long, earnest hours without any great personal rapport. Yet Wilson's views were beginning to form quite strongly at that point, combining a sense of fairness as a defining theme in politics with a forensic awareness of poverty and inequality, the statistics that highlighted the plight of the poor and some of the possible ways of addressing it. Sometimes Wilson described himself as a statistician, a term he regarded as high praise. He became a Labour Cabinet minister at the early age of thirty-one. Attlee made him President of the Board of Trade in 1947. At that point Wilson was more a grey technocrat than a future leader. He was assiduous, hard-working and conscientious, but not charismatic at all.

More than any other modern prime minister, Wilson changed as a public personality. The transition evolved long before he got to Number Ten, but it was quite a metamorphosis nonetheless. After the 1950 election a sequence took place that was to shape the rest of his career. The sequence had all the key ingredients to turn a technocrat into a leader, one who became an alert reader of strange political rhythms. To be an astute reader of political rhythms is a necessary qualification for leadership. Edward Heath and Theresa May were poor readers of the political rhythms. Most of the other modern prime ministers were readers by instinct. Wilson acquired the skill as a result of what happened in the early 1950s.

The prime minister, Clem Attlee, had become a considerable admirer of the future leader, Hugh Gaitskell. He made Gaitskell chancellor in his re-elected government after the 1950 election. On the whole Attlee was a thoughtful team manager, but at times he could be coldly insensitive in his handling of ministers. Although younger than Gaitskell, Wilson thought he was better qualified for the senior post. Unsurprisingly, having presided over the creation of the NHS, Aneurin Bevan also believed that he should have been promoted to the Treasury or given another top job. Attlee had given little consideration to managing their respective ambitions, fully formed in the case of Bevan and growing in the case of Wilson.

The two of them, Wilson and Bevan, displayed defiance when Gaitskell as chancellor proposed prescription charges in order to pay for growing demands on defence spending. This was in 1951, a pivotal year for Wilson and his party. Bevan and Wilson resigned from the Cabinet over the issue – an explosive move for a relatively fragile government with a tiny majority. Bevan's departure was much more noteworthy at the time, the glittering star of the Cabinet walking out over policies relating to the purity of the NHS, public spending and the importance that should be attached to defence spending. But in the longer term it was the departure of Bevan's more junior colleague that had more significant consequences.

For Wilson, the drama was one of great profundity. This was not only because he had resigned from the Cabinet, a big moment for anyone in a political career. His resignation taught him that managing the Labour Party was about a series of interrelated highly charged factors: how a leader manages colleagues, the ambitions and egos of those colleagues, the ideological divisions between right and left, and the danger to a Labour government when all of these factors coalesce over a single policy area.

The prescription-charge issue remains totemic and exposes a divide that continued in the Labour Party throughout the 1950s into the 1960s, and arguably well into the twenty-first century. The questions erupting in the aftermath of the resignations became familiar ones. What form should, or could, universal healthcare take? How should the demand for health provision be paid for? What priority should a Labour government give to defence spending? What are the overall spending levels required to provide decent public services? These are timeless and thorny questions.

Wilson concluded, more or less from 1951 onwards, that if he became leader in the future, one of his objectives would be to prevent ideological or policy divisions revolving around strong personalities turning into fatal opposition, which appeared to be Labour's fate in the 1950s. His own experience as a Cabinet minister who was provoked into resignation for reasons of ambition, positioning and conviction defined his later approach to leadership.

Arguably he made his first wily moves during those years of seemingly eternal opposition. There was an assumption in the party, and in the media, that Wilson was a Bevanite, largely because he resigned from the Cabinet with Bevan. Yet in the heated internal battles between followers of Bevan on the left and those on the right of the party, Wilson stood largely above the fray. This lofty positioning enabled him to appeal to both sides when a vacancy unexpectedly arose. This is about the only parallel between Wilson and Theresa May. As Home Secretary, May declared her support for 'Remain' in the 2016 Brexit referendum, but deliberately kept a low profile during the campaign. She was the only senior minister not clearly defined by the referendum – a key part of her armoury as she moved speedily into Number Ten in the summer of 2016. Wilson had been regarded as a 'Bevanite' and yet was never quite a 'Bevanite'. He got his chance to lead in 1963, when Gaitskell, then leader of the Labour Party, died suddenly. Here is another rather dark lesson about leadership, certainly in relation to the Labour Party.

The two most electorally successful Labour leaders both inherited the crown in unexpected contexts, when the previous leader died suddenly. Wilson became leader in 1963, very close to the next general election that was held the following year. Tony Blair became leader after John Smith's unexpected death in 1994, relatively close to the next general election, which many anticipated would be called earlier than it was. Neither Wilson nor Blair was tormented and undermined by endless speculation about their leadership-scheming ambition, because there was no obvious vacancy. Endless predictions about a particular individual becoming leader can kill off any chance of that individual rising to the top. In the case of both Wilson and Blair there had been no energy-sapping speculation, a framing that can make aspiring leaders seem unattractively self-serving. The assumption was that Gaitskell would be leader for many years to come. The same assumptions were in place when Smith died suddenly in 1994. In a party as full of tensions as the Labour Party, an unexpected vacancy seems to be the best context for a Labour leader to win a contest and move towards a general-election victory.

In striking contrast, those who become Labour leaders after an election defeat at the beginning of a parliament have gone on to lose. That was the fate of Ed Miliband, who became leader after the 2010 election and lost after five wearying years. Neil Kinnock took over after Labour's slaughter in 1983 and, for him, the long haul became a problem in itself. Kinnock was seen to be too often immersed in thorny party matters rather than acting as a determined prime minister-in-waiting. Theresa May gave Jeremy Corbyn a boost by calling an early election when he was still a fresh leader, albeit a battered one, having fought two leadership contests in the space of twelve months. But Corbyn did not win the 2017 election, even though the removal of May's majority was an electoral triumph for him. For Labour, the election winners acquired the crown halfway through the parliament when no one was preparing for a contest or even anticipating one. Almost immediately on becoming leaders, Wilson and Blair were seen as prime ministers-in-waiting, a flattering perception that feeds on itself. Kinnock and Miliband were never seen widely as prime ministers-in-waiting – also a self-feeding perception.

———

The unexpected death of Gaitskell gave Wilson his chance, and he performed with energetic, mischievous guile as leader of the Opposition. In a short period of time he managed to convey a dazzling modernity, even though he looked older than he was. Later the gap between his actual age and the way he looked was to widen considerably, but voters and the media chose to see what they wanted to. At the beginning of Wilson's leadership quite a lot of voters and much of the media saw youthful modernity, and at the end they saw an old man, when Wilson was more politically agile than he looked.

As a new leader, Wilson recognized the potency of wit, an underused weapon in leadership. Of the modern prime ministers, only Tony Blair deployed wit with the same deadly force. David Cameron was witty at times, but often in the style of Blair. Imitation is common in leadership. Wilson partly copied Harold Macmillan, his opponent for many years and a political figure who greatly influenced him. Often, in the case of leaders, their main opponent or the opponent they grew up with politically exerts a disproportionate influence over them. Blair was greatly influenced by Thatcher, and Cameron by Blair. With Wilson it was the often charmingly amusing Harold Macmillan whom he partly sought to copy.

Macmillan was witty. Wilson became wittier. In 1962, when a weakened Macmillan sacked several prominent Cabinet ministers in what became known as the 'Night of the Long Knives', Wilson popped up and said, 'I see Harold Macmillan has sacked half his Cabinet – the wrong half.' That was all he had to say. It was a perfect soundbite in the era before the term had even been invented. Political journalists and voters laughed with Wilson and they got the message behind the joke: that Macmillan had become fatally incompetent.

Like Blair, Wilson chose as his theme 'modernization', that overused, safe and evasive apolitical term. But Wilson framed an argument in a way that excited the left as well as other parts of the electorate that he sought to win over. He famously delivered a speech at his party's 1963 conference, the one before he was elected as prime minister, in which the central theme was about harnessing the 'white hot heat of this technological revolution'. The focus on technology made him sound entrepreneurial and modern in a way that appealed to businesses and the media, while the 'harnessing' theme gave the speech a statist social-democratic perspective. Both wings of his party, and many Conservative newspapers, were excited by the Wilsonian vision, a phrase that was soon to become a contradiction in terms.

In his early years as leader, Wilson enjoyed almost as positive media coverage as Tony Blair in his long honeymoon phase after becoming leader in 1994. But Wilson never fully recovered when the media turned on him. Being human, leaders never do. Also being human, Blair did not recover when the media, or parts of it, turned on him.

When Wilson won by a tiny overall majority in 1964, he showed he was genuinely serious about harnessing the technological revolution. He ambitiously set up a Department of Economic Affairs to act as a counter to the Treasury, the intimidating department of economic orthodoxy that dominates Whitehall. Other prime ministers had contemplated such a move, but had pulled back. Wilson acted. He put his old rival, George Brown, into the top post and told him to adopt a robust industrial strategy. Brown was a formidable character when sober, but too often he was drunk. The department never found its footing in the Whitehall orbit and imploded quite quickly. Nonetheless, the attempt at establishing an alternative economic department was an example of Wilson's radical ambition. In the early days he sought to be more than a party manager. Equally important, he had the space to be more than a manager, leading a party that was in awe of his skills and excited to have regained power. A useful way of making sense of a leader is to look at the space he or she has on the political stage. At the beginning Wilson had a fair amount of space. By the end he had virtually none at all.

Wilson won again in 1966, this time by a landslide. Many of his critics argued that the landslide parliament was his lost opportunity, a terrible failure of leadership. He had a near three-figure majority and failed to make radical changes. The criticism is valid. Wilson was already, at this point in his leadership, becoming obsessed with keeping the show on the road and managing what was becoming once more an unmanageable party. He failed to make the most of a landslide parliament, when a prime minister is much freer to act. But Wilson also suffered the near-fatal blow of a devaluation crisis in 1967, early in this theoretically malleable parliament. He was never the same again, irrespective of what legislation he could or could not have got through the House of Commons.

Here is another lesson in leadership. In the UK a formal

devaluation kills off political careers. Prime ministers do not fully recover from them. John Major's already limited authority and self-confidence never revived after the UK fell out of the Exchange Rate Mechanism (ERM) in September 1992. The Conservatives did not lead in the polls again until after their slaughter in the 1997 election – and for a long time after it. Major's life became a form of political hell from the day the pound left the ERM.[15] Wilson made matters worse by attempting to play down the significance of the 1967 devaluation. In a TV broadcast on 18 November he asserted, in relation to the lower pound: 'That doesn't mean, of course, that the pound here in Britain, in your pocket or purse or in your bank, has been devalued.' Like many prime ministers in a crisis, Wilson went too far in his attempt to reassure voters. His reputation for being untrustworthy, evasive and devious took rigid shape with the sterling crisis and his handling of it. He never shook it off.

Up until the devaluation crisis in 1967 Wilson had enjoyed an unusually good media, for a Labour leader. After devaluation, most of the newspapers and parts of the BBC went for him. Wilson, who was thin-skinned, could not bear the onslaughts. The attacks changed him. The sunny modernizer moved speedily towards becoming the wary old man.[16]

As he became warier, Wilson also had to deal with a range of internal feuding and scheming from big figures who were growing under his leadership. By 1969 there was so much speculation about his leadership that Wilson had to use a speech to declare wittily: 'You may have been wondering what has been going on in recent days. I'll tell you what's going on. I'm going on.'[17] Here is another lesson from his leadership that few follow. When in trouble, make a joke of it.

Much of the speculation focused on Wilson's most successful Cabinet minister, Roy Jenkins, a reforming Home Secretary of historic significance and then a steady, stabilizing chancellor. But Jenkins was not the only possible alternative. James Callaghan also had ambitions to lead. So did Denis Healey, who was then Defence Secretary. Tony Crosland, president of the Board of Trade in the late 1960s, had his devoted followers. In the end the ambitious rivals preferred Wilson to any of their competitors. In some respects it is safer for a leader to have lots of rivals rather than one, as Blair reflected privately towards the end of his period in power.[18]

From the left, Tony Benn's relationship with Wilson became dire. Yet at its lowest ebb, Benn could see no other option as leader. After being demoted from the Department of Industry to Energy Secretary after the 1975 referendum, Benn was furious, but noted in his diary on Tuesday 10 June:

> If Harold goes, I should think Denis Healey would take over
> as the strong man in a crisis, or perhaps Jim [Callaghan]. Roy
> [Jenkins] would not get it and I certainly would not because the PLP
> [Parliamentary Labour Party] would be too nervous I would lose
> them the election. I suppose I have a vague interest in Wilson going
> on...[19]

For all the media speculation about the fate of prime ministers, Benn's reflections are a glorious illustration as to why leaders remain in place. Even for those humiliated by a leader or in deep disagreement over policy direction, the alternatives are often worse.

Benn was reflecting in 1975. Several years earlier, following the devaluation in 1967, Wilson's authority was hugely diminished. The decline in his authority as leader was one of the reasons why he failed to implement Barbara Castle's White Paper proposals known as *In Place of Strife*, a framework within which trade unions could function with some constraints and some formalized freedoms. The proposals were published in 1969 when Wilson was still reeling from the destabilizing devaluation, speculation about whether he might, or should, be toppled, and a sense – widely shared in his Cabinet – that his leadership lacked purpose. Wilson could not persuade his Cabinet, let alone the rest of his party, to back the proposals. Several Cabinet ministers, most notably Wilson's successor, Jim Callaghan, had strong connections with the unions and were resistant to reform. Their resistance was short-sighted. The reforms that were finally implemented were Margaret Thatcher's, after the chaos of the 1970s.

Many commentators have argued since that if Wilson and Castle had prevailed with *In Place of Strife*, the 1970s would have been entirely different. There is something in the assertion. But Wilson acted weakly in relation to Castle's proposals, because he was in a weak position. A leader cannot become strong simply by declaring an unswerving determination to prevail. If Wilson had been in the honeymoon phase of his leadership, ambitious Cabinet colleagues might have been less stroppy. But his honeymoon had passed. If a leader cannot convince his most senior colleagues – in this case, Callaghan and several other major figures were ferociously against *In Place of Strife* – he or she is not going to get a policy through.

A leader cannot impose a policy and face a revolt that would destroy his or her leadership. Knowing that his space on the political stage was narrowing, Wilson did not seek a futile confrontation. *In Place of Strife* was a sensible, modest, forward-looking document. Its ministerial author, Barbara Castle, was on the left of her party. The paper never stood a chance of being implemented when most of the Cabinet was opposed. Prime ministers can only be strong when they are in a politically strong position.

Even so, the landslide government had one policy that Wilson personally instigated which highlights his instincts as a social reformer – the instincts that had taken shape in the late 1930s. The Open University (OU) was Wilson's big idea. He drove the policy through with the support of Jennie Lee, Bevan's wife. Lee was Minister for the Arts and reported directly to Wilson on the progress of the project. The institution became a creation in some ways as remarkable as the NHS, although on a much smaller scale. The OU opened up the possibility of adults becoming students, liberating some of them from unfulfilled lives. Later, Wilson described the OU as his proudest policy achievement. He did so with justification.

Perhaps Wilson would not have survived for so long as prime minister in the era of rolling news and Twitter, when fleeting rumours can become a full-blown political crisis for a leader in the space of hours. But he stayed doggedly in place for several more years after speculation about his possible demise began in 1968. He fought three more general elections and a referendum before resigning voluntarily.

His durability became a feat of leadership in itself. In the end, for all the frenzied speculation in the UK's media about the possible fall of a prime minister, they tend to be hard to budge. The reasons for Wilson's staying power apply more widely. Internal dissenters can rarely unite around a single alternative leader. Potential leaders worry that another rival might be victorious if they make a move for the crown. There is no single cause to justify making such a move.[20]

Despite the confidence-sapping devaluation of the pound, as the next election moved into view the economy had stabilized under the calm but determined Roy Jenkins, who replaced Callaghan as chancellor. With considerable optimism, Wilson called a general election in June 1970. But the unexpected happened, as is often the case in general elections. The polls got the outcome wrong and Wilson lost. Most polls had predicted a comfortable Labour majority. Wilson was more popular than the publicly awkward Ted Heath. The economy was performing relatively well. One of the great myths of UK politics is that a party wins when its leader is more popular than his or her opponent and the economy is doing well. Margaret Thatcher was less popular than Jim Callaghan in 1979. The economy was growing faster than had been anticipated in 1997 when John Major was defeated. Major won in 1992 when the economy was in the doldrums. Cameron won in 2015, even though austerity economics was scheduled to last at least another five years. For Wilson, the June 1970 defeat competed with the devaluation in 1967 as the event that most shook his confidence in a way that was transformative. For a leader, the sense of rejection that accompanies an unexpected defeat is almost unbearable. It is bad enough when leaders are ready for the humiliation because they had expected such a bleak outcome. The blow is much worse when they are unprepared. As with economic crises, they never fully recover.

When Wilson won again in February 1974 he did so cleverly, by focusing on the issues that he knew, almost by instinct, voters cared about: prices, the standard of living, getting the miners back to work. His personal campaign avoided the great ideological debates in the country, and certainly in his party, at the time. He simply ignored them. He was not overtly ideological, to the fury and disdain of both left and right. When Wilson did resign in March 1976, to the stunned amazement of most of his Cabinet, he gave one long interview to the BBC. When asked what his greatest achievement was, he replied in part that it was keeping the Labour

Party together in a challenging era. At the time, and for some years to come, that observation seemed pathetic and anticlimactic. Here was a long-serving prime minister. When he became leader, Wilson was far more experienced than Blair, Cameron or even Thatcher. As a leader he had experienced many intense political dramas. He led his party, one way or another, to four election victories in dark economic circumstances.

At the end of it all, he concluded that a great achievement was keeping his party together. The claim condemned him because, from that moment onwards, commentators and writers wrote of Wilson as the devious managerialist who was not up to the task of meeting the crises erupting around him. Indeed, as a leader, Wilson appeared to have ended in the worst of all worlds: being famous for being devious, therefore making it impossible for him to be successfully devious. Successful devious leaders are those that no one regards as being devious.

But in retrospect, Wilson's leadership of a deeply divided party seems like an immense achievement. Labour's election-losing divisions in the 1980s, and after Labour left power in 2010, show that a party that Wilson led for so long has an almost unique capacity for fracturing and losing elections. In the heat of all the battles during Wilson's leadership, Cabinet ministers loathed him. The political diaries are full of their anger. Tony Benn, who rarely expressed personal abuse towards anyone, noted at one point, 'Harold looked at me with his piggy eyes.'[21] Benn was often furious with Wilson. Roy Jenkins was equally distant. Michael Foot disapproved of him. So did Denis Healey.

But after Wilson died, Benn, Jenkins and others began to change their minds. Away from the intensity of all their internal battles, Benn made this observation during his tribute to Wilson in the

House of Commons: 'Harold Wilson recognised that for a bird to fly it needed two wings, a left wing and a right wing.'[22] Jenkins, in his memoir, was more generous in some ways about Wilson than he was about his close old friend and ally, Hugh Gaitskell. He recognized retrospectively that Wilson had given him the space to introduce the social reforms of the late 1960s, which were another historic landmark of that government.[23] Wilson was not especially concerned with the life-changing progressive reforms, but he let Jenkins get on with implementing them. The unlikely figure of Wilson created the space for Jenkins to legalize abortion, end theatre censorship and introduce other substantial socially liberal reforms.

So what seemed a puny conclusion from Wilson at the time – 'I kept my party together' – now seems like a titanic achievement. By maintaining a form of unity, he gave colleagues the room to be more creative than himself and led an unleadable party to election victories. His journey was tough and, apart from the early honeymoon phase, unglamorous. There were rarely moments of great crusading joy. By the end there was no ideological verve. But in some very fundamental ways Wilson's leadership was far more effective than historians have recognized so far. In the light of what happened to his party subsequently – and what happened to another prime minister who also held a referendum on Europe – they will come to realize the scale of his achievement in the future.

Wilson's successor as prime minister in 1970, Edward Heath, assumed that he was an unrecognizably different type of leader, more serious and less playful, with a greater sense of moral mission. Yet Heath was to suffer a similar fate to Wilson. He was also tormented by economic and industrial turmoil. Unlike Wilson, however, he was not to last very long at the top, partly because he was not playful enough.

2

EDWARD HEATH

Few leaders were better prepared for the tasks of leadership than Edward Heath by the time he became prime minister in 1970. Heath had flourished in the intense student politics of Oxford University in the 1930s. As a student he had travelled widely in Europe. While rising to the top in politics, his ministerial responsibilities included a demanding negotiation to join the Common Market under the leadership of Harold Macmillan, a test of any potential leader's stamina and durability. In addition, Heath had been an energetic and reforming Cabinet minister at a point when a tired Conservative government lacked momentum. Earlier, he had been chief whip at a highly sensitive and traumatic period, giving him a developed sense of how the parliamentary party behaved and how to make it behave. He was also the first leader of the Conservative Party to be elected by MPs, an authority-enhancing act of democratic engagement.

This was quite a CV for leadership, compared with most other modern prime ministers. Yet, as prime minister, Heath endured a traumatic, dark and brief tenure at Number Ten. His political career ended in terrible failure and a long sulk, as he observed his successor transform the Conservative Party and win landslide elections. How to explain the mismatch between Heath's considerable qualities and mighty qualifications for leadership with the hell that erupted around him soon after he became prime minister?

Such was the enduring sense of failure associated with Heath, his fall and his subsequent transparent grumpiness that these qualities are easily overlooked. They might even seem to relate to an entirely different figure than the one who ruled in troubled times, called an early election and lost. But before being elected leader in 1965, Heath had been an unusually self-confident Cabinet minister. Even more unusual, he left his Cabinet posts with greater self-confidence than he had when he arrived. He made a practical impact, implementing some radical changes with a wilful resolution and buttressed by a clear 'one nation' philosophy. Indeed, Heath was the last 'one nation' Conservative to lead his party. David Cameron claimed to come from the same tradition, and probably genuinely thought he was, but he was much closer to the Thatcherite model. Heath's politics lay well to the left of Cameron's. Although Heath was never as popular as Harold Macmillan, or acquired the same variety of ministerial roles as Rab Butler, who never made it to the top, his career before he became leader comes closest to offering a precise definition of what it was to be a 'one nation' Tory – another of British politics' overused and imprecise terms.

As a bonus for his party, seeking wider electoral appeal in the mid-1960s, Heath was the son of a carpenter, brought up in Broadstairs and therefore far removed from the Etonian grandeur that had become a problem for the Conservatives. Wilson had ruthlessly mocked the privileged affluence of Tory leaders. He could not do so with Heath. All these factors were in the minds of MPs who backed Heath in the first formal election of a Conservative leader.

Heath had another essential quality at the time of the leadership election. He wanted the job with a greater single-minded intensity than his rivals. His main opponent in the contest was Reginald Maudling, a former chancellor and therefore more senior than Heath. Although ambitious, Maudling was a more laid-back politician who fought a languid campaign. Heath was focused on winning. One lesson of leadership is that an aspiring leader must be willing to work around the clock to win. Heath went for it with tireless determination. As a former chief whip, he understood the parliamentary party, which had the vote for the first time. He worked the tiny electorate sleeplessly. Maudling had more charm and political agility, but as the contest intensified he could still relax and enjoy a drink or two. He relaxed too much.

Heath deserved to win. He was fully formed when he became leader of his party, having been engaged with politics in various forms for decades. He knew more or less what he stood for, by the mid-1960s. As far as Heath was concerned, government was not always the problem but could also sometimes be part of the solution, whether in framing new welfare policies or intervening in markets. No Conservative leader had a similarly benevolent view of the state until the election of Theresa May in 2016, when she occasionally put the case for government as a force for good – at least she did when Nick Timothy was her special adviser. At the same time Heath was driven by a desire to make government more efficient. Unusually, as a Cabinet minister, he became interested in how his departments were run and how to make them more effective. When he became prime minister he similarly resolved to make Whitehall and local government more efficient. Partly he was a technocrat, but not wholly. He had some sense of ideological purpose, too.

Heath was part of the glittering generation of politicians who went to Oxford in the 1930s. All of them were shaped in different ways by the decade that ended in a second world war. In Heath's case, he travelled intensively around Europe during university vacations. He was in Spain during the civil war, in Nuremberg for the Nazi rallies, in Salzburg for the annual festival of music and the arts, an event that attracted legendary conductors from that era. Heath also hitchhiked his way across France. Only Denis Healey, amongst the embryonic politicians from 1930s Oxford, travelled as widely and with the same level of intense fascination. Heath's journeys played a part in his youthful opposition to appeasement, an issue that threw up so many themes and opportunities for students with an insatiable appetite for politics.

Unlike Harold Wilson, and later Tony Blair and David Cameron, Heath adored student politics at Oxford. The raging themes combined domestic and international affairs in a way that meant even student politics could not be too insular or parochial. The future of the UK and much of the world was at stake. Heath's first major speech at the Oxford Union in 1936 outlined his opposition to appeasement. In June 1937 he was elected president of the Oxford University Conservative Association as a pro-Spanish Republic candidate. In his final year at Oxford, Heath was president of Balliol College Junior Common Room, an office held in subsequent years by his near-contemporaries Denis Healey and Roy Jenkins, and as such was invited to support the Master of Balliol, Alexander Lindsay, who stood as an anti-appeasement 'Independent Progressive' candidate against the official Conservative candidate, Quintin Hogg, in the epic 1938 Oxford by-election.

Heath described Lindsay, a socialist, as his biggest influence at university, although he stressed that the consequence of political discussions was to strengthen his 'innate Conservatism'.[1] Heath became a forbidding and self-absorbed figure, deepening his beliefs as a result of contact with someone well to the left of him. He became president of the Oxford Union in 1939, his final year at Oxford. Part of his university experience was a potent brew of intense foreign-policy debates, engagement with socialist ideas via Lindsay, electioneering, campaigns, manoeuvring for posts in student politics and travelling. By his early twenties Heath had been the most politically active of modern prime ministers, taking formative stances that were unavoidably contentious at the time, campaigning against the foreign policies of the Conservative prime minister, Neville Chamberlain, while being a committed Conservative.

Yet, curiously, the modern prime ministers who immersed themselves in politics at university were not electorally successful. Heath went on to lose three elections. Gordon Brown was as comparably addicted, a brilliant and in some respects glamorous student at Edinburgh University, who dated a Romanian princess and became a youthful rector of the university. He lost the only election he fought as party leader and prime minister in 2010 or, more precisely, he did not win it. The election led to a hung parliament. Already politically ambitious, Theresa May was active in the Oxford Conservative Association and, according to the journalist and her contemporary, Michael Crick, was quite a good speaker at the Oxford Union. She lost her party's small majority in the 2017 election. Student politics help to form embryonic politicians, but are not adequate preparation for the hurdles of leadership or a sign as to who will flourish as leader subsequently.

And there is another curiosity. Some of Heath's contemporaries or near-contemporaries glittered more at Oxford and later in the

House of Commons. Denis Healey, Roy Jenkins, Tony Crosland, Michael Foot – all from the left – were more exuberant and charismatic than Heath. At some stage in their careers all sought to be prime minister. But it was Heath who became one. He wanted it more than they did.

The route to leadership was tough, but one that Heath travelled with deceptive ease. He deceived himself, as well as his party, that he would be similarly at ease with leadership. Heath was a subtle chief whip under Anthony Eden during the epic drama of the Suez Crisis in 1956, a traumatic episode for a restive parliamentary party. When Egypt's President Nasser nationalized the Suez Canal, Eden felt the need to prove his own and the UK's imperial swagger by launching a military response, one opposed by the US and a significant number of his MPs. It was the first post-war example of a prime minister misreading the national mood and his own party in relation to a military venture. Tony Blair was another who was to misread it, although Blair assumed that voters and the media would expect him to back the US in a military venture. In both cases, Suez and Iraq, there was a pattern. There was exuberant media support followed by disillusionment. Heath's task during the Suez Crisis was to maintain the loyalty of increasingly bewildered MPs and then be a key mediator, after Anthony Eden's resignation.

After Eden resigned in January 1957, Heath's duties included informing Rab Butler that he would not be Eden's successor, at precisely the point when the normally modest Butler assumed he would be. In conveying the message, Heath passed a key test of leadership. He could act ruthlessly. In addition to being the deadly messenger, he had told senior party figures involved in managing the succession that Conservative MPs would prefer Macmillan, with his textured flair, to the less publicly flamboyant Butler.

When Heath delivered the news in a one-to-one meeting, Butler was devastated. Uncharacteristically, Butler had gone so far as to prepare a prime ministerial address to the nation, on the assumption that he would be Eden's successor. Butler was rarely over-excited or unrealistic in his assumptions about how high he would rise, but on this occasion he had good cause to assume that he would be prime minister. By 1957 his career had been as wide-ranging as that of any incoming prime minister. Butler had guided MPs towards supporting Indian independence when he was a youthful minister in the 1930s; had been a reforming Education Secretary, a modernizing party chairman, a solid chancellor and Eden's deputy. This was not bad preparation for leadership, but Heath told Butler that he was not the chosen one. 'I had a sad mission to carry out, but there was nothing I could do to soften the blow. "I am sorry, Rab," I said, "it's Harold". He looked utterly dumbfounded.'[2] Such exchanges, demanding unavoidable ruthlessness, are formative for aspirant leaders. They become stronger.

Heath also held two substantial departmental Cabinet posts before becoming leader. In each he was far more dynamic than most of his ministerial colleagues. As Labour Minister under Harold Macmillan, he was the model of engaged pragmatism. He maintained a largely constructive dialogue with the unions, regarding Sweden as a model of sorts. On a visit to Sweden Heath wrote that 'I was struck by how much employers and unions socialized together. The atmosphere of co-operation coupled with the high level of their social services, confirmed my belief that good industrial relations were both the product of, and essential to, a prosperous and fair society.'[3]

Here was Heath's version of 'one nation conservatism' taking shape. As Labour Minister, Heath was a believer in selective forms of state intervention, introducing a Local Employment Act that provided incentives for industry to locate to areas of high unemployment. He rejected right-wing calls for a royal commission on trade unions – demands that aimed to curtail the rights of unions. Expediently but contentiously, he agreed a pay deal with the railways that avoided a strike. This pragmatism gave him the dangerously misplaced confidence that a balanced approach to industrial relations would serve him well as prime minister. As ever, the seeds of a leader's rise were a cause of his fall. Heath looked back to his ministerial past and complacently assumed that a similar approach would work as successfully in the storms of the early 1970s.

His next ministerial post also set the scene for his short period in Number Ten. Macmillan appointed Heath to be Lord Privy Seal at the Foreign Office. In effect he was Foreign Secretary in the Commons, with Alec Douglas-Home, the official Foreign Secretary, still in the Lords. Macmillan was the first prime minister to decide that the UK should join the Common Market, then consisting of six countries. Heath was the second, after his election victory in 1970. After Heath, no prime minister, with the partial exception of Tony Blair, conveyed any great public enthusiasm for the European project. Under Macmillan, Heath's task was to negotiate the terms of membership. The challenge was nowhere near as great as Theresa May's task of negotiating the UK's departure from the EU, but it was still mountainous. During the talks Heath made twenty-seven visits to Brussels, eleven to Paris and twenty-seven to other countries.

Macmillan and Heath faced an impossible barrier. Perhaps wisely, President de Gaulle saw only the deep ambiguities of the UK. The French president feared that the UK misunderstood the European project and might undermine the cause by a semi-detached approach, reinforced by its apparent close relationship with the US. De Gaulle's veto in 1963 meant that Macmillan's detailed planning for membership could not take effect.[4] The rejection did not deter Heath. If anything, the blocking of his early efforts made him more determined to join later.

Heath did not like losing and he was difficult to push to one side. At the earliest opportunity he returned to the cause. His commitment to Europe was deep and unyielding. He was not interested in Europe as a political device to play dangerous games in the UK political arena, as other leaders were. He was committed to Europe as a cause. This made him unique amongst modern prime ministers.

In his final Cabinet post under Alex Douglas-Home in 1963, Heath was given the job that helped to define him as a significant reformer. In the dying days of the long-serving Conservative government, Heath was made president of the Board of Trade, the job that had also provided Harold Wilson with a platform in Attlee's government. Heath made more of it than Wilson. In a drab political context, a governing party running out of steam, Heath was energized. His abolition of Resale Price Maintenance, known as the RPM, had near-revolutionary consequences in terms of its impact on voters' lives.

The RPM had allowed manufacturers and suppliers in the UK to set the retail price of their goods. The effect was to prevent large retailers with greater buying power from undercutting the prices charged by smaller shops. Heath sided with the supermarkets, while taking on some powerful manufacturers and Tory-supporting small businesses. As he did so, the Conservatives' chief whip warned him that the policy would split the party – quite a warning as an election approached. Heath went ahead.[5] The act marked a turning point in the growth of the major supermarket chains in the UK. As food shopping formed a prominent part of voters' lives, Heath had been a radical change-maker.

It took dogged determination and wilful political courage to implement the meaty reform during the election year of 1964. Risks over policy are rarely taken when elections loom, but Heath took a large risk. Again, the experience gave him a false sense of what could be achieved by focused determination in government, and in his own abilities as a dynamic policy-maker.

His successful ministerial career was partly shaped by his determined drive. Heath was ambitious and ferociously competitive, a qualification for leadership. He loathed losing and never contemplated giving up, in the event of defeat. The same competitive spirit propelled him to win the Sydney-to-Hobart boat race in 1969, when he was a long-serving leader of the Opposition and a relatively inexperienced sailor. There was a stubborn quality. He was hard to cast aside.

At the same time, he had deeper interests outside politics than any of the other modern prime ministers. Above all, music was a great passion. Even when facing draining challenges, he had time for music and to conduct concerts with a hint of exuberance never seen in his role as a leader and prime minister. The sailing helped to humanize him. Heath's boat, *Morning Cloud*, became as well known as any of his policies. Theresa May, the other shy prime minister, became fleetingly popular for the awkward dance that she performed with more gracious gyrators during a visit to Kenya in 2017. The media mocked her, but focus groups suggested that May's clumsy dance was one event in a stormy leadership that voters noticed and liked. Heath seemed more human when he sailed and conducted at concerts, more animated than when he was a political leader.

His drive was the constant factor in all these diverse pursuits. He wanted always to prevail, winning a music scholarship to Oxford University and becoming a decent musician; and not only taking part in sailing competitions, but winning them. Heath was as wilful as any prime minister in his determination to get to the top, and had fewer distractions in his burning ambition.[6] This unyielding hunger marks out some of those who become prime minister, compared with those who do not.

Given the range and depth of Heath's political repertoire, why did his leadership include three election defeats and a traumatic, short-lived premiership? What went wrong, when so much had gone so smoothly up until the point when he became leader? Do intense political experience, inside and outside government, a deeply held sense of purpose and forbidding ambition not matter very much when it comes to leadership? Of course they do. Heath's leadership was bleak in spite of his qualifications for the top job. There are other reasons why it all went spectacularly wrong.

———

Heath's immediate route to Number Ten was a haphazard one. Most leaders of the Opposition who become prime ministers have, or affect, a sense of sustained momentum. Thatcher and Blair dazzled with energy and apparent purpose from the day they were elected leaders of their parties to the day they won a general election. Cameron also did so, if more erratically. Heath stumbled more awkwardly towards Number Ten.

The context was strategically challenging when he became leader in 1965. The Conservatives had been in power for thirteen years, losing to Labour narrowly in 1964. For a long-serving governing party, electoral defeat is unavoidably devastating. Leading figures tend to be exhausted after being senior ministers. They are also unused to the intense but different demands of Opposition. In this case, the Conservatives were facing a dazzling and wily Harold Wilson at his peak. Why did they lose in 1964? Was there comfort in the narrowness of their defeat, or was that a complacent interpretation of the way their party was perceived? Heath was keenly interested in the questions, as any leader would be, but he lacked the magician's art of making his answers seem big and compelling. Being leader of the Opposition is partly an art form. He or she has only words to make an impact and cannot be tested by policy implementation. Heath was not especially interested in words or projection. Although more passionate about the arts than any other modern prime minister, he was not a political artist.

In his first party conference speech as leader in October 1965, Heath did what David Cameron was to do later, in a more expansive manner. He portrayed Labour as backward-looking compared with the Conservatives:

> It is no paradox, strange though it may seem, that in a period of rapid change like this, what the nation needs is leadership from a progressive and modern Conservative Party, for it is only we Conservatives who will get moving and seize the opportunities which exist for us as a country. It is only we Conservatives who will act, and it is only we Conservatives who will remember and care, as change goes on, for the individuals – and there are always many who find it difficult and uncomfortable. Above all, it is only the Conservatives

who will have the foresight and the sense of history to keep and protect those elements which are fundamental and valuable in our society, to keep the things which make this country the place where we want to live.

Influenced by New Labour, Cameron made 'change' his defining motif when he became party leader. Heath was a more substantial figure than Cameron and yet he was not interested in framing big themes to match his assertions. To claim his party was the 'progressive' option was an act of counter-intuitive provocation that might have led him towards fertile terrain. But Heath chose not to develop the narrative. During his leadership there were not many further references in the years to come to a modern and progressive Conservative Party.

Instead, the narrative was confused and blurred. Heath was much more gripped by policy, the details of policy and determined implementation, an interest that was to his credit and a necessary qualification for muscular leadership. Yet in opposition after so long in government, any party needs a leader who can bring people together in an exercise of political renewal. The Conservatives elected a political loner, who preferred to work with a small number of trusted and largely devoted advisers. Heath was not one who could easily inspire.

When voters got a chance to give their initial verdict on the party's first elected leader, Heath was slaughtered. In 1966, the year after he won the leadership, Labour won a landslide, a nearly 100-seat majority. This was ominous for the Conservatives. Heath was the fresh leader on the scene, and yet Wilson shone more brightly. In an era when television was beginning to dominate election coverage, Heath was wooden and humourless. During an election campaign or outside one, he had no great interest in how messages were conveyed in the medium that was watched by millions of voters. During his leadership, even when prime minister, a year could pass without Heath giving a TV interview. Many modern leaders are fascinated by television and how they come across on the screen. Heath could be self-obsessed but, again like Theresa May, he gave little thought as to how he was seen or, indeed, whether he was seen.[7] Such reticence defined the way Heath and May were perceived, unhelpfully from their points of view.

The 1966 election defeat was hugely significant for Heath's leadership. On one level, he carried on as if not much had happened. Landslide defeats would wreck the confidence of most leaders and fatally undermine a party's backing of a leader. This was not the case with Heath in 1966. He concluded, without hesitation, that he had only been elected leader a short time before the general election; he could not be held responsible for a calamitous defeat, as there had been no time for him to revive his party's fortunes. Characteristically, he did not for one nanosecond contemplate resignation. Less characteristically, his party did not consider removing him, either. Both leader and party decided that another leadership contest was out of the question. Heath was given more time to make his mark.

Yet on another level, the defeat framed Heath's leadership. He had lost, outwitted in every way by Wilson. Although he and his party carried on without contemplating a change of tack, he had less space than other Opposition leaders to impose his will. So early on he was a loser. Only perceived winners have the space on the political stage to do as they want. This unflattering context – an early calamitous election defeat – explains partly why a leader with a clear and coherent sense of ideas did not convey momentum and direction. A loser is rarely allowed the luxury of perceived clarity and dynamism.

His party had its doubts about Heath, and part of his mission was to reassure rather than inspire. After the 1966 election he became incoherent as a leader. The late 1960s represented an odd phase in political leadership. After the trauma of devaluation, industrial disputes and a failure to win Cabinet support for trade-union reform, as proposed in the White Paper *In Place of Strife*, Harold Wilson had lost his way, or was widely perceived to have done so. Yet Heath had not found his. He had been more suited to government than to the performance art of opposition.

There were few moments that attracted great game-changing attention as Heath made his publicly awkward moves towards the 1970 election. He courageously sacked Enoch Powell from his frontbench after Powell delivered his deliberately provocative and immediately notorious 'Rivers of blood' speech in 1968. Powell had a following in the Conservative Party and could hold a conference hall with mannered but intoxicating oratory. Heath's act was a commanding and, to some extent, defining act of his leadership.

Yet at the Selsdon Park Hotel gathering of the shadow Cabinet in 1970, shortly before the general election of that year, Heath appeared to move towards Powell in terms of economic policy. More precisely, he allowed Harold Wilson to frame the way he was perceived, as a result of an uneventful and shapeless meeting of his frontbench team. The meeting, soon to be mythologized, was to discuss strategy and ideas, with an election moving close into view. In reality, the event was meandering and inconclusive. The sole radical idea floated at the meeting was that the NHS should meet only 80 per cent of treatment costs, with individuals taking out insurance to meet the other 20 per cent – a form of electoral suicide that was rejected speedily by Heath's shadow chancellor, Iain Macleod. Nothing much else of any significance was agreed.

Selsdon was a talking shop for frontbenchers. Like most leaders, Heath was wary of deciding a programme with an entire shadow Cabinet. But political journalists had turned up at Selsdon Park expecting some exciting developments. Macleod, a former editor of *The Spectator*, alert to the rhythms of news, recognized the need to generate some headlines.

As a result, Macleod persuaded those present that even though they hadn't decided anything, they should at least give the impression of being decisive, so he drafted a statement that expressed general support for law and order, trade-union reform, tougher immigration controls and the free market. Since it proved to be a slack week for news, the Selsdon Park conference was widely reported and interpreted as evidence that the Conservative Party had swung to the right.

This was a view that Harold Wilson was only too willing to endorse and he coined the term 'Selsdon Man' in response, even though Heath did not regard the meeting at Selsdon as signifying the adoption of any kind of new political philosophy. On the other hand, he did little to contradict the impression, since it served his purposes at the time to be seen as offering something new to the British electorate. Distinctiveness was not what Wilson had in mind when he invented the term. Wilson meant that Heath had leapt to the right – what he assumed would be the vote-losing right.

Heath sent out conflicting messages, misunderstanding one of the fundamental requirements of his role: an Opposition leader must at least convey a sense of determined coherence even if, in reality, much is incoherent. His close allies were convinced of his moderate 'one nation' philosophy and yet Heath did little to challenge the mythology around Selsdon in the build-up to the 1970 election.

Unsurprisingly, his government became confused, following the election held in the same year. Was it going to be tough on unions, as implied by 'Selsdon Man', or closer to Heath's approach as a conciliatory Labour Minister? Was it to be a small-state, free-market government, as 'Selsdon' appeared to suggest, or take a more balanced approach, as Heath's closest allies assumed? There were gaping gaps in the programmes of Wilson, Blair and Thatcher when they were in opposition, but in their very different ways the three leaders knew where they wanted to go in government and spoke accordingly. Heath was less clear. In opposition, what is said and done has a huge influence on a leader in government. Blair's equivocation about a single currency, when in opposition, made it much harder for him to put the case to join, as prime minister. Thatcher's relative caution in the build-up to the 1979 election meant that she had no choice but to be cautious in the immediate aftermath of victory. Indifferent to framing a narrative in opposition, Heath became a prime minister who was too easily blown off-course, because he had not established his chosen course with clarity and in public.

In spite of his failings as an Opposition leader, Heath won the election in 1970 – to everyone's surprise except his own. His confidence had been mildly undermined by defeat in 1966, but he had plenty in reserve to sustain him. He did not rate, respect or like Wilson, and assumed voters would take a similar view, even though opinion polls suggested that Labour was on-course for victory. In this assessment Heath was correct. By 1970 the Labour government had been thrown off-course following the trauma of devaluation, industrial unrest and internal tensions as senior figures contemplated their chances of becoming Labour prime minister. Wilson in particular had lost authority and his own self-confidence.

Heath was the only alternative and he won. The victory was a triumph of endurance: five years as an Opposition leader, which included a big election defeat. With one exception, the night of the victory was the best in Heath's career. The exception was the celebratory mood on 1 January 1973 when the UK joined the Common Market.

Heath had been a relatively weak leader of the Opposition, never fully recovering from being defeated in 1966. The weakness led him to convey unclear messages as to what his governing philosophy would be. But that did not mean Heath arrived in Number Ten without a clear sense of his own ideological purpose. William Waldegrave, a close ally, elegantly defined what that was. Waldegrave understood Heath better than most and was also a stylish writer. Like Wilson, Heath was a wooden writer of prose. His writing did not save him from the unflattering stereotypes that formed during and after his prime ministerial trauma. Waldegrave came to the rescue in explaining Heath's governing ideas much more powerfully than Heath himself ever did.

The economy rationally managed; Europe as the modernising catalyst (the Treaty of Rome embodying as it did commitment to free enterprise); British industry revitalised by European competition and Europe (with Britain) returned to the centre of the world stage as equal partners with the US; a rational reform of trades union law; huge capital investment in new projects like the Channel Tunnel; a fair solution to the problems of Northern Ireland; class barriers and prejudice swept away. All this and more was to be done, and quickly (as well as dealing with the usual menu of unforeseen crises). The model was how Heath had swept away Resale Price Maintenance in the dying days of Douglas-Home's government, confounding reactionaries and lobby groups. [8]

This was a vision as dynamic as any of those espoused by other prime ministers as they walked into Number Ten after an election victory; indeed, more galvanizing than some who lasted a lot longer in power. Heath lasted for slightly more than three and a half years. Very quickly his government struggled amidst industrial and economic chaos. The ambiguity of Heath's approach in opposition was only a small part of the explanation for his inability to communicate his ideas effectively. There were several other factors.

———

Partly, Heath was an unlucky prime minister. Only Gordon Brown could compete in terms of misfortune, soon after he moved into Number Ten. There is a cliché that leaders create their own luck. That is true to a limited extent, but leaders need luck that extends well beyond their own orbit of control. Heath had none.

His first misfortune was also a tragedy, and happened almost immediately after the 1970 election. Heath's chancellor, Iain Macleod, died of a heart attack in July. Prime ministers' choice of chancellor is nearly always central to their fate. Even though Geoffrey Howe came to annoy Margaret Thatcher intensely, he was an indispensable architect of Thatcherism, arguably more so in terms of policy detail than the lady herself. If Howe had disappeared in the summer of 1979, with his early budgets already written and his dogged capacity to turn her instinct for slogans into substantial economic policy, she would have wobbled even more than she did in her early years. Without Gordon Brown, Tony Blair would have had no economic policy; there was no one sitting around his Cabinet table qualified to replace Brown in 1997. David Cameron would have been lost without George Osborne, who arguably had even more space than Brown to shape policy and strategy.

Macleod had the potential to be as significant for Heath as those chancellors were for Thatcher, Blair and Cameron. He was a stylish counterpart to the awkward new prime minister, with an interest in communication and language that Heath lacked. Macleod had been editor of *The Spectator* and could sparkle when making speeches. He was loyal to Heath and shared a similar 'one nation' outlook, in a party already starting to show embryonic signs of the divide that Thatcher was to describe at the end of the 1970s as 'wets' v. 'dries'. From Thatcher's perspective, the 'wets' were the villains, opposing her monetarist policies and her opposition to intervening very much as unemployment soared. The 'dries' were her supporters. Heath and Macleod were embryonic 'wets'. Macleod had an economic programme of sorts, even if the perceptive and constantly curious Roy Jenkins sensed that Heath and Macleod were too alike, both unable for virtuous reasons to contemplate higher unemployment, while being confused in their attitudes towards the role of the state as an intervening force.

But for a prime minister to have a sophisticated, loyal chancellor with similar views and a greater capacity to communicate than him, there were only upsides. These were never realized. After Macleod's death, Heath replaced him with a middle-ranking mediocrity. Anthony Barber was propelled into the Treasury suddenly, without a thought-through set of economic ideas and policies. From the beginning he lacked weight, authority and a clear sense of purpose – unsurprising as Barber had no idea he was going to be chancellor in a new government, a role that demands years of preparation, until he became one. In effect Heath became his own chancellor, determining the oscillating economic policies. For leaders, such autonomy never works. When Thatcher sought to give her adviser Alan Walters too much influence over economic policy, she began to sow further seeds of her demise. Her second chancellor, Nigel Lawson, resigned over the attempted dominance. By instinct a control freak, Heath had even greater control freakery thrust upon him with the death of his key Cabinet colleague. It was a personal tragedy beyond Heath's control that began the dark sequence of events.

Other forms of misfortune partly determined Heath's fate. There was little he could do to stop war erupting between Israel and a number of states in the Middle East in October 1973. In response to the conflict, the Arab members of the Organization of the Petroleum Exporting Countries (OPEC) implemented an oil embargo for some countries and a quadrupling of oil prices for others. For Heath, the timing was a nightmare. The National Union of Mineworkers imposed an overtime ban in November 1973, with the aim of securing pay increases well above the limits of Heath's incomes policy. Heath might have been able to cope with the miners' strike, but faced also with reduced oil imports and higher energy prices, he had no choice but to introduce a state of emergency in December.

He was also unlucky in his main internal opponent. Leadership is partly about managing dissenters, but Enoch Powell was impossible to manage. Heath was a hopeless manager of people, but even a tactile charmer would have struggled with Powell.

Enoch Powell was not especially ambitious in career terms, or tribal in his attachment to the Conservative Party. He was at least as content on the backbenches as he was on the frontbench. Powell was largely untroubled when he left the Conservative Party in 1974. His lack of ambition and tribalism made him a much bigger threat than any internal dissenters, who would not consider leaving their parties and hoped to be a leader of that party. Powell was immune to the patronage that empowers most leaders, and would happily sacrifice party loyalty to maintain his principles. At the same time, Powell had doting admirers in the Conservative Party and could cast a spell over them whenever he spoke. He was an academic with a highly developed populist streak, happily appealing to those voters who feared or loathed immigrants, while espousing a nationalism that became a form of defiant patriotism. He was a powerful orator, the best speaker in the Conservative Party, and flourished in front of a big audience, while being a shy bibliophile away from the political stage.

Powell left the Conservative Party and became a Unionist MP in October 1974. He was a unionist, a passionate anti-European and was opposed to Heath's many attempts to support troubled industries. Powell was most emphatically in the 'dry' camp on economic issues, although that led him to some surprising and counter-intuitive conclusions at times. He supported the miners' pay demands in the autumn of 1973 because the quadrupling of oil prices had increased their worth in the marketplace. He challenged Heath on most policy issues, from the 1970 general election until he announced that he was not standing as a Conservative candidate in the February 1974 election. Major, Cameron and May were tormented by dissenters. None of their tormentors were in the same league as Powell.

But bad luck and his erratic performance as leader of the Opposition cannot, and does not, solve the mystery of the contrast between Heath's relatively smooth path to the leadership and the wild oscillations when he became prime minister. Heath was thrown further off-course almost immediately, facing industrial unrest that was far more determinedly intense and widespread than when he was Minister for Labour in Macmillan's government. The scale threw him. Heath looked back to his ministerial past for guidance, but there were no equivalents of scale when he had engaged successfully with union leaders in a distant context.

Strikes by the dockers and the power workers forced him to introduce two states of emergency within the first six months of winning power. The need to ration heating and lighting in December 1970 led to a rush on candles. Rooms lit by candles became one of several primitive symbols that marked Heath's rule. He was supposed to be a modern leader, fascinated by how government could be organized more effectively and updated to meet the demands of the modern era. Yet voters needed candles to light up their homes within a few months of his premiership.

For Heath, what became a familiar sequence unfolded early in his rule. Lord Wilberforce, who was appointed to arbitrate on the destabilizing early disputes, awarded the power workers a pay increase of 15 per cent, a rise that implied the striking workers had a stronger case than ministers had acknowledged. At the same time, the ruling triggered higher pay demands from other unions. Heath often seemed to be on the wrong side of pay disputes. A union would make a claim and he would resist, but then an independent body appointed by his government would more or less back the union.

In spite of the early strikes, or perhaps because of them, Heath pressed on with his own plans to place the unions in a new legislative framework. His Industrial Relations Bill in 1971 was tougher than Harold Wilson and Barbara Castle's *In Place of Strife* proposals, but less severe than some of the later reforms implemented by Margaret Thatcher. Heath's plans were less subtle than either Wilson's or Thatcher's, and badly timed. Thatcher was much cleverer when it came to the important matter of timing. She introduced incremental reforms rather than a single Industrial Relations Act. Accumulatively her changes were far more stifling than Heath's, but she chose her moments to act. Wilson dropped his *In Place of Strife* proposals at the early whiff of trouble from his own Cabinet and subsequently adopted the vague social contract and other wheezes. At the worst possible time, as industrial relations soured and the unions became more muscular, Heath proposed legislation that sought to define 'unfair industrial practices', the introduction of secret ballots and a 'cooling-off' period before strike action could take place. The Act eventually came into force in March 1972, but never took practical form. The unions resisted.

This is another element of the mystery in relation to Heath's rule. He sought constructive relations with the unions and yet proved to be less politically sophisticated than Thatcher, who challenged the unions only when she was confident of winning, deploying blunter instruments than Heath would have contemplated. Under Heath, many unions adopted the simple but effective tactic of failing to register with his new Industrial Relations Court, established to regulate labour laws. Within six months the government had effectively abandoned its own Act.

Unlike his career as a Cabinet minister, but with echoes of his leadership in opposition, Heath was all over the place. He wanted to tame the unions, but was not aggressively anti-union as Thatcher was. He met with them just as regularly as Labour prime ministers did, whereas Thatcher had nothing to do with them. Heath occasionally spoke the language of embryonic Thatcherism, but when there was a steady rise in unemployment in 1971 – and despite his vaguely declared policy not to help 'lame ducks' – he authorized the rescue of Rolls-Royce in January, and

Upper Clyde Shipbuilders in June of the same year, interventions more in tune with his wider philosophy.

At the beginning of 1972, when unemployment went over the one-million mark and miners began a strike, Heath opted to intervene further, not out of weakness, but out of a long-held belief in intervention. An Industry Bill empowered his government to assist individual companies, resulting in increased state investment in British Steel and in the coal industry.

The plan was in line with Heath's moderately interventionist instincts. He had pursued similar policies when he was Labour Minister under Macmillan. Now his moves appeared to be a panic-stricken response to fast-moving events, partly because they were. He managed to make what he believed in, as a matter of conviction, be perceived as weak-kneed 'U-turns'. This was the opposite of Thatcher's leadership. Even when she was being weak, she gave the impression of being strong and consistent. Heath became trapped because he had spoken loftily of a new approach to economic policy in his final years as Opposition leader, without fleshing out fully what he really meant.

Heath's character is also part of the solution to the mystery: why was he such a troubled leader, even though he arrived in Number Ten with such weighty qualifications? As with Shakespeare's tragic heroes, character alone cannot explain destiny, but in Heath's case it played a significant role. He could be transparently self-absorbed, grumpy and rude. He did not have a devious bone in his body, but the lack of deviousness meant that he could not hide how he felt. The eldest child of a relatively poor family in Kent, Heath went on to be the only unmarried prime minister of modern times. He was publicly shy and awkward, while being unable (or disinclined) to disguise these qualities. If he disapproved of someone, he showed it, too. After he was succeeded by Margaret Thatcher, Heath was open about his disdain for her and the transparency of his contempt sealed his reputation as a grump. In a column for the *Daily Telegraph* in 2008 the author, Craig Brown, wrote about Heath's rudeness. It triggered so many responses from victims of Heath's insensitivities that he wrote a follow-up with examples. Here are two of them:

> My favourite Heath story is when he was on the campaign bus with a bunch of apparatchiks and journos. The bus was involved in a minor crash. No one was hurt, but one middle-aged lady was thrown to the floor and was obviously shocked. Heath immediately called for brandy, impressing the rest of the bus with his decisiveness and compassion. When the brandy arrived, he drank it himself.

The second relates to an exchange with a single journalist, as recalled by Brown:

> In his wonderful memoir, *Cold Cream*, Ferdinand Mount describes Heath as the holder of the UK Allcomers' Record for Incivility. Heath concluded an interview with the young, tipsy Mount by saying, 'I didn't realise this was going to be such a superficial interview', while fixing him with a glare of 'loathing and contempt'.[9]

Here is a key lesson: self-absorption and rudeness are disqualifications for leadership. And they are central to the failures of Heath. When he needed colleagues and others to work with him, and to want him to flourish, quite a lot struggled to find much goodwill towards him.

Like Theresa May, Heath was a poor communicator. He was almost casual in his ambiguity in opposition, and that left him in some ways unprepared for the epic demands of prime ministerial power, in particular for explaining what he was trying to do. He was even worse in government, not trying very hard, or in ways that were accessible, to make sense of what he was seeking to do.

Heath had assumed, like Gordon Brown, that leading a government was a small leap from being a successful Cabinet minister. The gulf between the two is gaping. His lofty manner – partly, in itself, a failure to focus on communication – alienated some unions, even though union leaders who negotiated with Heath in fraught circumstances came to respect him. They recognized his integrity and grounded decency in relation to issues and policy, even if he had no capacity for interpersonal relations.

When a prime minister appears to lose grip, the chaos feeds on itself. The hunger for agreement with the unions, and his desperate desire for order as his government lost control, propelled Heath to dump his previous opposition to an incomes policy. The same dark sequence happened to Wilson and Callaghan. The three prime ministers from the 1970s could all see the dangers of rigid incomes policies, and yet all three were drawn towards them as they appeared to offer some shape amidst the fearful shapelessness. At least they were a way of controlling wage inflation when inflation was starting to soar, or appeared to be a means of doing so.

Modern British prime ministers from Wilson to May all discovered that they were not as strong as they thought they were, or as weak as they had feared. In the 1970s, incomes policies and referendums were dark attractions, as an apparent response to prime ministerial powerlessness. The prime ministers thought they were an escape from political hell, but in most cases they propelled them towards their bleak fates.

Heath's incomes policy was characteristically complex. Like Brown, Heath could delve deep as he reflected on policy. Unlike

Brown at his peak, Heath misread the political rhythms that often determined the fate of policies. His incomes policy was to be introduced in three phases, a theoretically sensible attempt to impose restraint incrementally. But the policy inevitably triggered rebellions at each stage. After striving in vain throughout the autumn of 1972 to reach a voluntary agreement with the unions, Heath felt compelled to introduce a ninety-day statutory freeze on salaries. This was followed in April 1973 by Stage Two, under which pay rises were limited to £1 a week plus 4 per cent. Stage Three, unveiled in October 1973, limited pay rises to £2.25 or 7 per cent per week, up to a maximum of £350 per year.

The logic was one of phased generosity. Heath had thought through the substance of each phase with characteristic care, but failed to see the fatal dangers. Each phase was a cause for further strikes. More fundamentally, the phases were not generous enough. The miners' strike followed the introduction of Stage Three. Heath responded to the growing crisis with drastic measures, announcing a three-day week and a wider range of power constraints. TV stations closed at 10 p.m. in the evenings. Football matches started earlier in the day to avoid the use of floodlights. Like May, Heath was not a theatrical prime minister. Like May, he presided over epic, nerve-shredding political theatre.

During a cold winter, the UK was in a crisis of primitive and yet epic proportions, a darkness that Heath made no attempt to hide. In a TV broadcast at the end of 1973 he acknowledged that this would be a 'harder Christmas than we have known since the war'. This was the background to his decision to call an election in February 1974, posing the question 'Who governs Britain?' The voters replied, in effect, 'not you' and delivered a hung parliament and a few more seats for Labour than for Heath's Conservatives.

The framing of the election was typical of Heath. His question had a superficial appeal to a prime minister calling an election. Heath assumed most voters would give backing to the democratically elected government rather than to non-elected trade-union leaders. But leaders who are political artists would recognize the dangers of framing an election in this way. They would note in their multi-layered calculations that the need to ask the question would reflect badly on a government struggling to govern. Heath was not a political artist. He assumed, with his rigid stubbornness and lack of empathic artistry, that his question would produce one answer: we want *you* to govern.

———

There are in this sequence several lessons of leadership. Again, like Gordon Brown, Heath could become almost indiscriminately immersed in policy detail, assuming that if the multifaceted complexities made sense to him, they would make sense to his party and the wider electorate. Unlike Heath, Brown was gripped obsessively by the need for a strategic course, even if he lost his skills as a navigator when he became prime minister, and in his final years as chancellor. Heath never had the skills, or sought them. He acted as if what he said and did were explanation enough and that his chosen course was the one that would prevail. Heath thought his own conversion to legalized wages and price constraints made sense. At a time of rising inflation and industrial unrest, a staged incomes policy of increasing generosity and yet firm rigidity was the only available course. But he never effectively explained this, and he lacked the guile and charm to stick to the course, or to persuade others to do so.

Some trade-union leaders respected his integrity. The president of the NUM, Joe Gormley, preferred negotiating with Heath than with Wilson, whom Gormley did not trust. But Gormley still led the miners' strike that forced Heath to announce the three-day week. Thatcher had more expedient guile. She chose to take on the miners ruthlessly only when stocks of coal were high. Heath challenged them when oil prices had soared and he desperately needed the coal. He was being defiant when he had no levers to support him, and when those he was confronting had acquired incomparably greater strength in the marketplace.

Heath's misreading of the rhythms of politics brought about his downfall. He fought a mistimed election on the wrong issue. Prime ministers often get the timing of elections badly wrong, or struggle to deal with the issue of timing. In some senses the Fixed-term Parliaments Act of 2011, rushed through for shallow and immediately self-interested reasons by the coalition government after the 2010 election, liberated prime ministers from making the choice. The liberation was limited, though. Theresa May showed how easy it was to subvert the Act when she called an early election in 2017. In the light of the 2017 result, May should have studied – before she went to the country earlier than she needed to – what happened to Heath when he called one early in February 1974.

In theory, Heath could have stayed on as prime minister for nearly eighteen months longer before holding an election. He went early for the substantial reason that he could find no way through in his dealings with the NUM and other unions. He had negotiated sleeplessly with the NUM, taking over responsibility for industrial policy, just as he had done with most aspects of detailed economic policy.

In UK politics, certainly before the Fixed-term Parliaments Act and to some extent afterwards, speculation about the need for an election was often feverish. Would, or should, John Major call an election after the first Gulf War in 1991? Would, or should, Gordon Brown call an early election in 2007? Would the Brexit crisis from 2016 trigger an election? The speculation in itself can be deeply destabilizing for a prime minister. Heath was resistant to an early election over Christmas and New Year, in spite of some senior colleagues urging him to call one. He succumbed only when he could see no alternative way through.

There were other reasons he called an early election. Like May in 2017, Heath went early because he assumed he would win. No prime minister volunteers an early election on the assumption they will lose. The Conservatives were ahead in the polls, Labour was deeply divided on several policy areas, Harold Wilson was seen as tired, politically lonely and paranoid.

But Heath's framing of the campaign (the government versus the striking miners) was too crude and the timing turned out to be ill-judged. Having warned voters a few weeks earlier that they were about to endure their hardest Christmas since the war, Heath sought to win an election. There was some sympathy with the miners, not least when, during the campaign, an independent report suggested they deserved a more substantial pay rise than Heath was proposing. It was on 21 February, in the middle of the campaign, that the Pay Board released a report on miners' pay, which unexpectedly revealed that they were paid less in comparison with other manufacturing workers, contrary to the claims of the National Coal Board. Four days later there was further bad news for Heath, with the latest trade figures showing that the current-account deficit for the previous month had been £383 million, the worst in recorded history. Heath claimed that the figures confirmed 'the gravity of the situation' and the need for a new mandate, prompting Labour's Roy Jenkins to respond, 'He presumably thinks a still worse result would have given him a still stronger claim.'

Although Jenkins thought Heath was heading for victory, he highlighted the flaw of the outgoing prime minister's pitch. In effect, Heath's contorted argument to the voters could be summarized as 'Things are going so badly that I deserve to win.'

He did not do so, and Heath's attempt to cling on to power was as doomed as Brown's attempt in 2010. But the context was worse for Heath. Before the 2010 election, political commentators had thought the Conservatives under David Cameron would win the election with a substantial majority, assuming that their own hopes and partisan judgements were shared by the wider electorate. When voters elected a hung parliament, it was Cameron who was disappointed and Brown who was buoyed by a result that was better than expected.

With Heath, the opposite applied. The media and most politicians had assumed he would win with relative ease, and therefore his attempts to cling on in a hung parliament seemed more stubbornly unrealistic. He explored the possibility of a coalition with Jeremy Thorpe's Liberals, but the talks were fleeting and Heath had left office, never to return to government, by the Monday after the election. He had called an election to resolve an industrial crisis. Instead the crisis was to deepen.

Heath's meeting with Thorpe over the weekend after the February election has a novelistic quality. The two leaders – soon to be consigned to different forms of powerless hell – fleetingly wondered whether both could be part of a mighty new governing partnership. The duo could not have been more different: the shy and introverted Heath meeting up with the exuberant Thorpe.

Jeremy Thorpe's tragic fall was part of the whacky turbulence that swept the UK in the 1970s. He had been the vivacious star of the February election campaign, more energetic and mischievously charismatic than either Heath or Wilson. Largely as a result of Thorpe's leadership, the Liberals won more than six million votes, but only fourteen seats. In spite of the relatively small number of seats, Thorpe was still in a strong position to negotiate terms for a coalition, or at least he was in theory.

A hung parliament is the dream for the UK's third national political party, giving them considerable bargaining power in the formation of a government. Oddly, the first two post-war hung parliaments have turned into a nightmare for the Liberals. In 2010 they formed a coalition with the Conservatives, a partnership that nearly destroyed them at the 2015 election. Soon after February 1974, Thorpe became a huge problem for his party rather than an asset. He was forced to resign the leadership in 1976, and in May 1979 Thorpe lost his seat in North Devon as he waited to face trial for alleged conspiracy to murder. Minutes after losing his seat he was asked by the BBC's Robin Day, live on TV: 'Do you think that the fact that you are facing a trial for conspiracy to murder contributed to your defeat?' With characteristic quick-witted charm, Thorpe replied: 'Put it this way, Robin, I don't think it helped.'

Thorpe was a gracious showman who was also curious enough to be a good political listener; he was fascinated by debate and the arguments advanced by political opponents. He was also gay and a promiscuous risk-taker, in an era when it was not possible for a leader to be open about homosexuality in politics. Heath had tentatively offered Thorpe the post of Home Secretary in a coalition government. Given the scandal soon to erupt around him, Thorpe would have been a former Home Secretary before very long.

While it lasted, a Heath/Thorpe coalition would have been well to the left of the Con/Lib coalition that was eventually formed many decades later, after Margaret Thatcher had transformed British politics, propelling the prevailing consensus well to the right. When Heath negotiated fleetingly with Thorpe, the Thatcher era had not happened and was not even taking embryonic shape.

The arrangement was not attempted. No agreement was reached between Heath and Thorpe over the Liberals' support for a change in the voting system. Thorpe must have had personal doubts and did not try hard to persuade his sceptical party about the merits of a partnership with the Conservatives. Having lost his party's majority, Heath might not have had the authority to lead a partnership with the Liberals. He was finished as a prime minister, with no time to pursue developing ideas about new structures for Northern Ireland, public-service reforms, the role of the state and, above all, the UK's new role as a member of what was then known as the Common Market.

Heath left office in the bleakest possible circumstances and yet, after fewer than four years as prime minister, he was guaranteed to become a historic leader. With typical dogged focus, he was the prime minister who took the UK into Europe. In doing so, he showed the energy, resourcefulness and mastery of detail that he had deployed as Macmillan's Minister for Europe. It remains doubtful whether anyone else could have negotiated the deal, if only because no alternative leader from that era cared as much.

Given the UK's stormy relationship with the rest of Europe, Heath was attacked unfairly at the time, and subsequently, for taking an elitist approach to his mission and for not being truthful about the loss of sovereignty. A significant section of his parliamentary party was opposed to membership, with Enoch Powell being the most articulate internal adversary once more. Heath won the vote in the Commons only by offering a free vote on the issue, enabling Labour rebels led by Roy Jenkins to back him. Heath agreed to a free vote only at the last moment. The device saved him, and his dream of joining the Common Market. His reluctance to deploy the device was another illustration of how poor a reader he was of the rhythms of politics. Like Theresa May later, Heath's instinct was to opt for the attempted imposition of unyielding parliamentary discipline. As a former chief whip, he loathed the idea of free votes. Yet it was a free vote that saved his dream, enabling him to secure parliamentary backing for membership of the Common Market.

The accusations of lofty elitism and deceit about the loss of sovereignty have no basis in reality. Heath was not a natural teacher on any front, including Europe. This was a fatal flaw in relation to many policy areas. He failed to explain accessibly and coherently what he was trying to do in relation to economic and industrial policy. The same applied to Europe. He negotiated with other European leaders and put the case to the UK Parliament, where a majority of MPs was supportive even if the Labour leadership was opposed, or at least affected opposition while being privately more ambiguous.

As a result of Heath's indifference to communication, and Labour's equivocations, the UK made a historic leap without great public engagement at first. Heath was a leader who did what he believed to be for the best, but he did not have the language or the inclination to be a campaigning persuader. The likes of Thatcher and Blair never stopped campaigning. Heath never really began, when he was prime minister.

Yet he did so afterwards, and with compelling authority. When Wilson put the UK's continued membership of the Common

Market to a referendum in 1975, Heath rose to the challenge and was one of the leading campaigners, being far more high-profile than Thatcher, who was by then leader of the Opposition. Questions about sovereignty were explored and debated in much greater depth in 1975 than they were during the 2016 referendum. Heath explained well his understanding of what it meant to be a sovereign country in a wider world.

In the 1970s the BBC and ITV broadcast political programmes at peak times, and with a greater willingness to allow discussions to breathe. To take one example of many, ITV broadcast a debate between Heath and the then Employment Secretary and anti-marketeer, Michael Foot. The title was *A Question of Sovereignty*. The two of them debated for an hour. Foot put the case that the likes of Boris Johnson and Michael Gove occasionally argued in the 2016 referendum, but at greater length.

Foot insisted that the Common Market was not democratic and that it represented a transfer of power to non-democratic institutions. With an echo of Jeremy Corbyn's concerns about the European Union, Foot expressed worries that a radical Labour government would be blocked from implementing some policies, especially in relation to state ownership.

Heath responded at length. The exchanges became bad-tempered at times. Foot preferred to debate with witty adversaries. Heath never used wit, a big flaw in his political personality. But he made clear that he regarded sovereignty as the 'power of a nation to look after its citizens... sovereignty is to be used and not hoarded'. He pointed out that the Council of Ministers was accountable to the parliaments and electorates, and that the European Commission could not act without the permission of the Council of Ministers. He argued that, as with NATO, the UK 'contributed its sovereignty' for a wider purpose.[10] There was no mendacity or deliberate distortion. Heath and other prominent supporters of membership took a different view of how sovereignty worked in an increasingly interdependent world, and expressed it openly. They did not downplay the issue.

Heath and Roy Jenkins, who was back as Home Secretary, led the 'In' campaign. They would both have been dismissed as part of an 'out-of-touch elite' in 2016, but they were commanding then. Heath had lost an election less than eighteen months earlier, but he was back as a key campaigner and was respected, too, as the prime minister who took the UK into Europe, putting the case powerfully in a campaign. Heath had a much higher profile than the prime minister, Harold Wilson. Heath's authoritative prominence in the 1975 referendum was in itself a sign that the UK had not then been infected deeply by the anti-politics bug. A year before, Heath had lost two elections. In the 2016 referendums, former prime ministers were hidden away by the 'Remain' campaign, out of fear that in advocating 'Remain' they would trigger support for Brexit. In 2016 Heath would have been nowhere to be seen. In 1975 he was allowed to be ubiquitous.

Heath's role in the referendum was a triumph, but his post-prime ministerial career was not smooth. He loathed Margaret Thatcher, partly because he would have disliked whoever had removed him from the leadership against his wishes. He was a bad loser. One of the many reasons he fumed against Harold Wilson was that the Labour leader beat him in three elections and outwitted him several times in between. Heath's determination to prevail could be both a strength and a terrible weakness. But his torment over Thatcher was also to do with her policies, many of which he genuinely opposed. If Heath had been more effective at explaining what he was for, and why her policies outraged him, he would have seemed less self-serving. Instead he appeared to be succumbing gracelessly to the biggest sulk in British politics. The intensity of his transparent disdain for Thatcher was only purged when she fell from power in November 1990.

On the day Thatcher resigned as prime minister, Heath was a panellist on BBC1's *Question Time*. Before the programme was broadcast, a BBC political correspondent interviewed him in the programme's green room to get his reaction to her fall. Heath was too shy to look directly at the interviewer or anyone else in the green room, but he was openly jubilant: 'I hear you want to get my reaction to her removal from power… I think that will be possible.' He paused and laughed joyfully, the famous shoulders heaving up and down with unqualified pleasure. In the interview Heath argued that the fall of Thatcher was good news for the country and for the Conservative Party. He did not utter a single word to soften his message or even express sympathy for her, on what would have been a deeply traumatic day.

He had been waiting a long time for this moment – since February 1975, to be precise – when she had replaced him as Conservative leader. Heath had never been an actor. He could not hide his fuming frustration during the many years that followed his enforced resignation. Now he could not disguise his joy. He was like a spoilt child who had finally got the gift he yearned for.[11]

Heath had always possessed the intellectual gifts to forensically demolish a lot of Thatcher's simplistic populism, but managed to suggest most of the time that he was motivated solely by personal jealousy. On the night of her fall, he reinforced the sense that his feud with her was beyond reason. That was partly because it was. He loathed her with a burning intensity. As Thatcher cast her spell in the 1980s, some Conservative MPs expressed bewilderment as to how their party had elected Heath as their leader and then stuck with him for nearly ten years. They saw him as a failed leader and then a disloyal former prime minister, a combination so unattractive that Heath's rise to the top was a mystery to star-struck Thatcherites.

Some leaders empathize as a matter of instinct, knowing what needs to be done in order to appear gracious and dignified. Heath did not give grace and dignity much thought. He was the victim of his own thoughtlessness. Yet, like perceptions of Wilson being old and paranoid, the image of a joyful Heath on the night that Thatcher fell is only one part of a much bigger story. Heath was the awkward, lonely leader who still commanded intense loyalty from those who worked for him, much like Gordon Brown, who could be even more explosively temperamental at times. But above all, Heath was so much bigger than his inability to act with endearing elegance on the public stage. The depths of this most complex of political figures gradually became hidden, but they were on view in the early phase of his career.

What has happened since Heath died would have troubled him far more than the torment he endured as the despised Thatcher won her landslide election victories. A police investigation into allegations that Heath had been guilty of sexual abuse was carried out, with the highest media profile, including one police press conference outside Heath's home in Salisbury. The subsequent investigation came to the convoluted conclusion that Heath would have been questioned over sex-abuse claims if he was alive, but that 'no inference of guilt' should be made from the fact that he would have faced questioning.

Some of those who worked closely with him observed that they saw no evidence that Heath was gay, and even if he had sought to abuse teenage boys, there would have been no chance.[12] There were protection officers with him at all times. Heath reflected on this constraint in one of his final TV interviews with Nanette Newman, before the allegations against him were made: 'I've had protection officers since 1965 when I became leader of the Opposition. You get used to them being around.'[13]

Heath might have coped with the trauma of a clumsy, defensively naive police investigation, but he would have been horrified by the referendum on Brexit in 2016, a shallow act of direct democracy that threatened to undo his historic act as prime minister, the moment the referendum was called. Heath endured many of his political assumptions being challenged by Thatcher, but even she never contemplated leaving the EU when she was prime minister. The publicly displayed agonies of Heath's old pro-European colleagues who lived through the 2016 referendum – Michael Heseltine and Ken Clarke – are ones that Heath would have felt with even greater intensity. He would have found Brexit unbearable.

Instead, while he was alive, he witnessed the Labour Party moving from being an anti-European party to one that was for a time strongly pro-European. The role of Wilson and Callaghan, who both voted against entry in 1973, was to cement the UK's position as a member. For Callaghan, who became prime minister in 1976, his relations with European leaders were an upside to his leadership. There were few other upsides for him. Callaghan's leadership was just as nightmarish as Heath's, and for precisely the same reasons.

3

JAMES CALLAGHAN

Take a look at any footage of Jim Callaghan and he comes across as a calm and steady political figure. In some respects, this impression is accurate. Callaghan was a relatively stable, rooted politician and was not especially flamboyant or temperamental. There seemed to be no mystery about him. He was never accused of being an enigma. Although sometimes irascible, he always looked solid, the hair neatly greased back, slightly receding but not at an unmanageable pace, with the large glasses that framed a mischievously cheerful face. He usually wore a smart suit, a crisp white shirt and, quite often, a neat red tie. Unlike Wilson, Callaghan did not age noticeably as a public figure. When Callaghan left Number Ten in 1979 he did not look greatly different from when he became a relatively youthful chancellor in 1964. Over the years he was always prominent, ebullient, assertive, irritable, decent and, at times, bewildered by events.

Yet there is a strange twist to the career of sustained prominence. Callaghan's career was wildly oscillating and the patterns were not reliable. He was the committed trade unionist who was tormented by the trade unions when he was prime minister. He was an old-fashioned Eurosceptic who cemented the UK's membership of the European Union. He was the brilliant manager of a divided Cabinet, but left behind a Labour Party suffering more internal strife than at any point in its history. His leadership was a triumph of Cabinet government and also signalled its demise.

Callaghan was a short-serving prime minister, in office for just over three years. Many lessons of leadership arise from his brief tenure; few were learned. In the introduction to this book, the skills of Hercule Poirot were cited as ones that might help to make sense of the modern prime ministers. This applies in particular to Callaghan. In the first half of our investigation of Callaghan the mysteries are laid out: the apparent contradictions, the fractured patterns that shaped the career of a seemingly solid, old-fashioned politician. In the second half the mysteries are solved, or at least the attempt at a solution is made. As Poirot might have noted, 'In the case of Monsieur Callaghan, nothing was quite as it seemed.'

Like John Major later, Callaghan was a prime minister who had not been to university; and again like Major, he was deeply insecure about his limited education. Both prime ministers were surrounded by Cabinet ministers from Oxbridge. Both were too aware of the difference between their backgrounds and those of the ministers over whom they presided. Callaghan came from too poor a background to be able to afford the costs of university, an enduring regret. Yet his career was extraordinary. He was the only modern prime minister to have held the three senior Cabinet posts: before moving to Number Ten, Callaghan had been chancellor, Home Secretary and Foreign Secretary in that order, a chronology that in itself was curious. The move to the Home Office in 1967 was a demotion from the Treasury, a sign that his career was heading downwards. Unusually for a demoted Cabinet minister, he moved upwards again several years later, triumphantly defying the normal laws of political gravity to become Foreign Secretary in 1974. Having been around for a long time, he made the final leap to Number Ten in 1976.

As Labour's first prime minister for thirteen years in 1964, Harold Wilson in effect made Callaghan the second most powerful figure in his administration. The two were not especially close and already Wilson was wary of rivals. But Wilson gave Callaghan the central task of running the economy, even if he created a rival Department of Economic Affairs under the erratically charismatic George Brown. Callaghan and Brown had been rivals for several years. Both had stood in the 1963 leadership contest, losing to Wilson. Brown was more exuberant and, when he was sober, was one of the more formidable Labour politicians of the 1960s. Quite often he was drunk or had drunk too much and could not hide his consumption in public. Callaghan was much the steadier of the two, but from the beginning he struggled at the Treasury. He inherited a negligently managed economy from a tired, long-serving Conservative government. Indeed, the outgoing chancellor, Reginald Maudling, left Callaghan a note in which he declared, only half-jokingly: 'Good luck, old cock… Sorry to leave it in such a mess.' Outgoing Treasury ministers should never leave notes for their successors, even for a laugh. The Labour Treasury minister, Liam Byrne, wrote a note as he left in 2010, stating, 'There's no money left.' Incoming ministers quoted the words for years to come.

In Callaghan's case, the inherited mess as described by Maudling included a balance-of-payments deficit of £800 million. Labour chancellors face tougher hurdles than Conservative ones. The markets are warier and the media is less supportive. They feel a greater need to reassure. Callaghan had not expected the deficit to be so steep and felt compelled to introduce an emergency budget, which included public-spending cuts and a hike in interest rates to stem a panic selling of sterling. Even after he had acted, the markets looked on at the conduct of a Labour chancellor with hawkish disdain.

The greater the disdain, the more reluctant Wilson and Callaghan were to act against an overvalued currency. The desire to challenge perceptions fuelled by a hostile media is the curse of Labour governments. In seeking to appear strong in areas where they are perceived to be weak, Labour governments become weaker still. Tony Blair's various military interventions were partly explained by his fear of being seen as 'soft on defence', and Labour's reputation in the 1980s as being 'anti-American'. In seeking to prove that he could be tough in relation to 'defence', Blair moved towards the nightmare of Iraq. Although winning a landslide in 1966, Wilson and Callaghan were determined not to feed the perception that Labour could not be 'trusted' with the economy. In their reluctance to act of their own volition in relation to sterling, they were forced to devalue in 1967, a traumatic humiliation for the chancellor in particular, even though the devaluation started to revive the economy.

Chancellors who suffer an economic trauma under their watch rarely recover. Callaghan offered to resign and Wilson moved him to the Home Office, swapping him with Roy Jenkins, who quickly acquired a reputation for economic competence at the Treasury, one that Callaghan never secured.

Fast forward to 5 April 1976 when the once humiliated chancellor became prime minister. Not only had Callaghan managed to recover from his bleak phase as chancellor, but he had become much more authoritative. He inherited an economic nightmare that was far worse than that in 1964 when Maudling left his 'good luck' note behind. Neither Heath nor Wilson had managed to find a way to deal with the increasingly muscular unions. Inflation was raging. The government was running out of money and lacked any obvious means of raising more. Callaghan had the tiniest of majorities in the Commons at the beginning and, with a relatively elderly parliamentary party, was soon to be leading a minority government. Yet the former chancellor was not impeded by his past. Instead he proved to be a guide through the economic storms – not always a reliable one, but steady enough to retain high personal ratings in raw polls. Even Callaghan's opponents struggled to portray him as a leader out of his depth in terms of the tottering economy, even if at times he was.

The final dramatic event under Harold Wilson's leadership had set the scene for Callaghan. Days before Wilson left Number Ten, the government had lost a vote in the Commons on its public-spending White Paper. The proposals for spending cuts in the defeated White Paper were relatively modest compared with those that his chancellor, Denis Healey, was to advocate soon after Callaghan became prime minister, but enough Labour MPs rebelled to block the plans.

That was the immediate context when Callaghan moved into Number Ten. Very quickly the nightmare got much worse. Once again the markets moved in for the kill, as they had done when Callaghan was chancellor. Sterling came under intense pressure during the long, hot summer of 1976. As Healey noted in his memoir:

> By this time the Conservative press was screaming for public spending cuts; its frenzy was not discouraged by the Treasury's own misleading statement that public spending was taking 60 per cent

of GDP and by the official Treasury forecasts which overestimated that year's PSBR [public-sector borrowing requirement] by over £2 billion… it was all I had to go on and it was worrying the markets…[1]

Frenzied and irrational debate shaped government policies in the UK long before the era of so-called 'Fake news'. In some respects, the fakery was more dangerous in the 1970s, as the reporting of economic policy came from seemingly respectable sources – national newspapers and broadcasters.

Attempting to appease the combination of the UK media and the markets, Healey proposed £1 billion of spending cuts in July 1976. This was largely an act of appeasement, and not rational policy-making. As ever, such forces are never appeased when they sense blood. Sterling was under pressure again in September. Healey described the next four months as 'the worst of my life'. He famously turned back, on his way to catch a flight to Hong Kong where he was due to attend a meeting of Commonwealth finance ministers. Instead Healey stayed in London to intensify his negotiation for a loan with the International Monetary Fund (IMF). In return for the loan, the IMF demanded further severe spending cuts. Almost on the spur of the moment, Healey decided courageously to head for Labour's conference in Blackpool and spoke from the floor, with a supportive Callaghan looking down from the platform above.[2]

Healey talked for a few minutes, provoking loud boos and cheers as he spoke of coming from the 'battlefront' to explain to the conference why the austere course was necessary and unavoidable. The images remain extraordinary: a chancellor speaking from the conference floor, with a red light indicating that his time was up, as those attending showed their passions live on TV. The watching prime minister – the most observed of the observers – knew what the sequence portended: the political nightmare of getting agreement for more drastic spending cuts without a majority in the Commons, and with an assertive party in revolt.

On the whole, Callaghan and Healey got their way. They negotiated a loan with the IMF in the autumn of 1976 and introduced spending cuts, after many Cabinet meetings, sessions of the party's National Executive and parliamentary battles. There were numerous storms to come. The IMF loan and the spending cuts marked a historic outbreak of turbulence in themselves. Yet here is the first example of the fractured pattern: Callaghan, the failed chancellor, having the authority to be the prime minister to prevail, in a much deeper crisis nine years later.

Europe is the second example. Here again, there was no pattern. Callaghan started out as something of an old-fashioned British nationalist, more strongly opposed to the UK's membership of the Common Market than Wilson. In speeches he made bad jokes about the French. Opposed to the UK's membership in 1971, he declared in a speech of tabloid crudity, 'If we have to prove our Europeanism by accepting that French is the dominant language in the Community, then my answer is quite clear, and I will say it in French in order to prevent any misunderstanding: *Non, merci beaucoup.*' This was silly on many levels, but reflected Callaghan's fairly simplistic wariness of the Common Market.

Yet as Foreign Secretary from 1974, Callaghan conducted the renegotiation of the UK's EU membership in order to win a referendum on continued membership. Wilson delegated much of the responsibility to the more energetic Callaghan. Like Wilson, Callaghan had voted against the UK joining the Common Market in the parliamentary vote under Heath. Like Wilson, he played a key role in ensuring that the UK would remain a member of the Common

Market or European Union, well beyond their own political careers. As prime minister, Callaghan formed a close relationship with the German chancellor, Helmut Schmidt, and at no point expressed any doubt about the UK's membership. In joint interviews the two of them pulled off a neat informality. 'I agree with Helmut...' / 'Jim and I always agree...' Callaghan was nowhere near as committed as Heath, but he became more or less at ease with Europe.

As prime minister, Callaghan had more harmonious relationships with European leaders than he did with trade-union leaders in the UK. Yet he was the most committed trade unionist to have become prime minister. After the economy and Europe, Callaghan's relationship with the unions was the third example of the oscillating rhythms and disruptive patterns of his career.

Indeed, Callaghan's relations with the trade unions generated the most Shakespearean twists. He chose to be shaped by his genuine rapport with the unions, and most union leaders respected him, at least until he became prime minister. More than any other modern Labour prime minister, Callaghan was steeped in trade unionism. At the age of seventeen, he worked as a clerk for the Inland Revenue at Maidstone in Kent. While working as a tax inspector, Callaghan joined the Maidstone branch of the Labour Party and the Association of the Officers of Taxes (AOT), a trade union for those in his profession. Within a year of joining he became the office secretary of the union. In 1932 he passed a Civil Service exam that enabled him to become a senior tax inspector. The same year he became the Kent branch secretary of the AOT. The following year he was elected to the AOT's national executive council. In 1934 he was transferred to Inland Revenue offices in London.

Following a merger of unions in 1936, Callaghan was appointed a full-time union official and to the post of Assistant Secretary of the Inland Revenue Staff Federation (IRSF). He resigned from his Civil Service duties in order to become a senior figure in a trade union. His union position at the IRSF brought Callaghan into contact with Harold Laski, the chairman of the Labour Party's National Executive Committee and an academic at the London School of Economics. Laski encouraged Callaghan to stand for Parliament. His commitment to the vocation of a trade unionist led to a political career. Wilson learned to be close to the unions, while Tony Blair and Gordon Brown felt the need to convey distance from the unions. After being elected an MP, Callaghan retained close links with the unions, out of instinct, conviction and ambition. The links endured through all the political dramas until the tragic final scenes, when some of those to whom Callaghan had felt close contributed to his fall.

On the eve of Callaghan's victory in the 1976 leadership contest, the *Guardian*'s columnist Peter Jenkins noted that 'By a process of elimination the mantle has fallen upon the Keeper of the Cloth Cap',[3] a patronizing evocation of the old-fashioned trade unionist rising to the top, but also a reflection on Callaghan's enduring association with the unions. At times the unions formed the buttress of his support in the Labour Party. He reciprocated by representing their points of view often in Cabinet and beyond – most famously in 1968 when the Cabinet minister Barbara Castle presented her proposals for a modest legislative framework for trade unions, *In Place of Strife*, and Callaghan opposed them without qualification. If he had supported them, they might have stood a chance of being implemented. The unions were opposed and, without delving too deeply, Callaghan opposed them, too. Yet when he became prime minister, he found himself battling it out with some union leaders in conflicts of historic significance.

Images of the so-called 'winter of discontent' in the early months of 1979 were centre-stage in Conservative broadcasts up until the 1992 election, such was their potency. There were plenty of disturbing images for the Tories to deploy: the consequences of lorry and train drivers, ambulance drivers, gravediggers and refuse collectors taking industrial action. The Callaghan years, as much as the Heath era, were seen as ones in which the government lost control over the unions. At times Callaghan did not know what to do with them. Like Heath and Wilson, he changed tack several times, opposing and then adopting an incomes policy. Nothing seemed to work for him, in terms of resolving the tensions. The strikes were a result of Callaghan's attempt to control inflation by a forced departure from the government's supposedly voluntary social contract with the unions, by imposing rules on the public sector that kept pay rises below 5 per cent. The imposition was meant to be an example to the private sector. However, some unions conducted their negotiations with employers within mutually agreed limits above this limit. While the strikes were largely over by February 1979, the government's inability to contain the strikes earlier helped to propel Callaghan towards his doom. He no longer knew what his relationship with the unions was – a bewildering position that challenged his political identity and purpose.

Callaghan faced his changing relationship with the unions as prime minister of a deeply divided Cabinet in a hung parliament. As with Wilson, there were mighty ministers in Callaghan's Cabinet with competing views on economic policy, the economy being the key test of a government at any time. On the whole, Callaghan got his way in policy terms without provoking a single Cabinet resignation during his time as prime minister. Given the composition of the Cabinet, this was almost an act of genius.

Sometimes Callaghan's judgements in terms of policy were wrong, but in relation to managing his Cabinet he was always subtle and sophisticated. His astute handling of deep division is the fourth example of a wild pattern. Callaghan was a master at achieving unity, and yet he left behind a party that was impossibly divided.

During his first nerve-shredding summer as prime minister, Denis Healey noted that at first only Roy Jenkins[4] and Edmund Dell[5] were prepared to accept any spending cuts at all. Tony Benn was developing his alternative economic strategy, a programme that included import controls and extensive state ownership. The newly elevated Foreign Secretary, Tony Crosland, argued – correctly, as it turned out – that the situation was already under control and there was no need for further spending cuts. At the time, the IMF demanded the cuts and the UK Treasury had calculated that they were necessary. Healey wrote later:

> The consummate skill with which Callaghan handled the cabinet was an object lesson for all prime ministers. His technique was to allow his colleagues to talk themselves to a standstill in a long series of meetings... as they did so they came to recognise that their proposals would involve as many cuts as the IMF route.[6]

Roy Hattersley, an ally of Crosland's in these seemingly eternal Cabinet meetings, agreed: 'We met day after day. There was the Chancellor's view. Tony Benn's view. Tony Crosland's view. Each was fundamentally different... and yet we came to an agreed position.'[7]

From his very different ideological perspective, Benn concurred: 'Jim used to say when we disagreed subsequently, "But your point was put at length in the cabinet" and that legitimised the policy... I was very fond of Jim.' Benn added that when he clashed with

Callaghan, as he often did, they would have a conversation along these lines: 'Jim would say to me, "I'm not as nice as I look" and I said to him, "Neither am I…" On that basis we got on very well.'[8]

This was partly retrospective papering over wide cracks. Benn's diaries are crammed with a fuming sense that the Callaghan government was betraying the Labour movement, while Callaghan could hardly hide his despair at what he regarded as Benn's reckless disloyalty.

Yet there was an essence of truth in Benn's recollection of Callaghan's leadership. By the late 1970s, Benn was the most talked-about politician in the UK, feared and loathed by some, yet idolized by a significant section of the Labour Party. He was a mesmerizing speaker of unbounded energy and determination. Even so, he never resigned from Callaghan's Cabinet and accepted that he had lost arguments over economic policy, having been given the space to make his case. As Hattersley observed, Callaghan held as many Cabinet meetings as was necessary until a consensus emerged that the prime minister had sought from the beginning. Nearly always Callaghan backed Healey. The beleaguered chancellor, who was not quite as robust as he appeared to be, was hugely grateful to Callaghan for his reliable supportiveness.[9] Callaghan held together a Cabinet that included Benn, Michael Foot and three of those who went on to form the SDP: David Owen, William Rodgers and Shirley Williams. Compare Callaghan's record as a manager of Cabinet with Theresa May, leading in a similarly nightmarish context: she lost two Brexit Secretaries and a Foreign Secretary in the space of a few months in 2018, along with a record-breaking number of other Cabinet ministers and junior ministers.

The management of his Cabinet was Callaghan's greatest triumph as prime minister, a triumph of leadership. He had the confidence to let dissenting ministers put their case forward, before asserting his own position and nearly always prevailing – the dream model, as far as prime ministers are concerned. In another curious irony, his subtle management of the most divided government in modern times triggered the end of Cabinet government.[10] Callaghan's collegiate approach was a vindication of Cabinet government and yet his mastery of a warring Cabinet became the death-knell for collective rule. The concept of senior ministers debating policy candidly in some detail, before a prime minister was in a position to implement his or her programme, went out of fashion, simplistically dismissed as 'weak' leadership.[11] The main figure claiming weakness was the leader of the Opposition, Margaret Thatcher. She made the claim with good cause. She appeared 'strong' in comparison. But even then, in her early years, Thatcher had a genius for turning a self-interested assertion into a widely held point of view, the new consensus. Cabinet government became a sign of 'weak leadership', so much so that Tony Blair later followed the Thatcher style partly in order to be 'strong'. Callaghan's astute management of his Cabinet went out of fashion even before he left office, as Thatcher made her moves.

———

As ever with Callaghan, there was another twist. Civil war within the Labour Party followed his astute enforcement of Cabinet collective responsibility up until 1979. After election defeat, Callaghan stayed on as leader. Benn decided not to serve in the shadow Cabinet and instead toured the country rousing party activists with his brilliant oratory, accusing the Labour government of betraying party members and demanding new forms of accountability within the party, as well as for the economy more widely. With verve and wit, Benn was reflecting and articulating the anger of many activists. At the 1979 party conference, delegates turned on Callaghan, accusing him of betraying members in opting for a cautiously expedient manifesto rather than choosing a more radical programme. The angry election post-mortems at the conference were broadcast live on BBC2 as part of the BBC's conference coverage. As TV theatre, the debates were electrifying. But for Labour, the open warfare was calamitous. Callaghan was both the leader who brilliantly maintained Cabinet unity and the leader who was pathetically impotent as civil war erupted.

There was yet another seemingly conflicting sequence during Callaghan's leadership. He was a tribal Labour leader who would never have contemplated leaving his party. When Tony Blair and Gordon Brown proclaimed a divide between new and old Labour in 1994, Callaghan suggested in a rare intervention that he was 'original Labour'.[12] This was authentically mischievous without being overtly disloyal to Blair, at a point when he was on the eve of becoming prime minister. Callaghan was indeed original Labour, a trade unionist who climbed the ranks of the parliamentary party, despairing at times of what Labour had become during his period at or close to the top, but never being anything other than Labour.

In spite of his tribalism, it was Callaghan who agreed the Lib/Lab pact in 1977 when he was prime minister and went on to form a close relationship with the Liberal leader, David Steel. The Lib/Lab pact was far less rigid than a formal coalition, but is the only example of two parties working together in the Westminster Parliament before David Cameron and Nick Clegg joined hands in 2010. By the late 1970s, Callaghan was a wily operator. As a leader who had kept his Cabinet together during the IMF crisis, he knew how to manipulate Steel, a new leader of a much smaller party. But Steel was astute, too. Both derived quite a lot from the strange arrangement. Callaghan secured what was, for him, the equivalent of gold dust: a degree of parliamentary stability. He did so without having to agree a formal coalition with the Liberals, a move that would have torn his Cabinet and his party apart. Instead he agreed vaguely to a consultative committee with leading Liberals, and the space for Liberal spokespeople to 'shadow' their equivalent Cabinet ministers. When the chancellor, Denis Healey, was asked what influence his Liberal shadow, John Pardoe, would have on policy, he replied, 'None whatsoever.'[13]

But Steel, a greatly underestimated leader and a figure of some historic importance, also got something out of the arrangement. After the trauma of Jeremy Thorpe's resignation as Liberal leader, amidst allegations that he was involved in a conspiracy to murder a former male lover, Steel's party needed a renewed sense of purpose and seriousness. Being close to government, or appearing to be so, gave the third party some momentum.

Steel ended the loose arrangement with the Labour government after fifteen months, but he remained close to Callaghan. Indeed, Callaghan would sometimes treat Steel as a confidant. Although there was no formal pact, the two of them continued to discuss policy and strategy. As an example, Callaghan had a conversation with Steel over whether he should call an election in the autumn of 1978. Steel urged him to do so, predicting another hung parliament. He pledged to form a post-election coalition with Labour, one that would have been very different from the Thatcher government that was formed in 1979.

Callaghan did not take Steel's advice. But although Callaghan was tribally Labour, circumstances forced him to discover that he could form a rapport of sorts with a leader of another party. It helped that Steel was a figure firmly rooted on the centre left, and in some respects to the left of Callaghan.

Callaghan had other ways of demonstrating a flexibility in his politics that was at odds with his seemingly rigid and unchanging personality. He came from the party's right, and yet he had a rapport of sorts with his deputy, Michael Foot, who was of the left and a political romantic far removed from Callaghan. Indeed, it was Callaghan who chose to make Foot his formal deputy. He did so for pragmatic reasons, but the relationship deepened once he had taken the decision to formalize Foot's role. Callaghan had been an expedient senior frontbencher for decades. Foot had only become a minister after the February 1974 election, preferring before then to be a writer and journalist of elegant and committed prose, a brilliant left-wing orator whose political hero was Nye Bevan. In spite of their striking differences, Callaghan managed Foot deftly, and Foot took his role seriously. He was the mediator in the divided Cabinet, holding endless meetings with Tony Benn, Peter Shore and others who were closer to his political outlook. Callaghan also made Foot Leader of the House, the ideal post for a parliamentarian with a feel for the Commons at a time of theatrical fragility.

By the mid-1970s Foot was close to Neil Kinnock, a newish Labour MP on the left who had voted several times against the government in Wilson's final phase. As a former rebel, Foot knew well those Labour MPs, including Kinnock, who were inclined to vote against the government. He worked assiduously to minimize the destabilizing revolts. Parts of the left were wary of Foot's loyalty to Callaghan, but Foot, who would one day be leader, was convinced that a struggling Labour government was incomparably better than a Conservative one. Late in his career, Foot became expedient, without losing his socialist convictions. Callaghan gave him the space to develop his expediency. It is telling that Foot was far less enthusiastic about Wilson, even though Wilson brought him into the Cabinet.[14] From Benn to Foot and on to Steel, the leader of another party, Callaghan was a skilful manager of colleagues. He needed them all on board for the rocky ride. The ride would not have been possible if some of them had stormed out. There he was, the self-proclaimed 'original Labour' leader, working with the leader of another party and wooing the stars of other wings of his party. He was the non-tribal tribalist.

More widely in the Callaghan era, there was a strange disjunction between the conservatively cautious personality and the times in which he ruled, as there was with Theresa May after she became prime minister in 2016. Callaghan was a seemingly uncomplicated prime minister who led at a time of dark political drama and parliamentary theatre. As Home Secretary in the 1960s, he would never have contemplated the social reforms implemented with historic verve by his predecessor at the Home Office, Roy Jenkins. Indeed, Jenkins and Callaghan were worlds apart. Jenkins was the daring reformer, the author of dazzling political books, the lover of good wine, illustrious social gatherings and a Lothario. Callaghan was the modest family man who relaxed on his farm. In political outlook, Jenkins was a liberal progressive. Callaghan was a solid labourist, with a sense that his fellow trade unionists valued law and order, family life and reliably rising living standards. Blair turned to Jenkins for inspiration, but when the Labour leader from 1994 sought to woo Conservative newspapers such as the *Daily Mail* and its Middle England readers, he had a streak of Callaghan's politics.

Yet in spite of the conservatism and relative caution during Callaghan's leadership, there were knife-edge votes in the Commons so nerve-shredding and bizarre that the scenes of mayhem became the plot of a brilliant play in the twenty-first century. *This House* by James Graham evocatively portrayed the parliamentary mayhem of the late 1970s. The largely unshowy Callaghan led a government that provided the backdrop for a West End hit. Those great political actors Margaret Thatcher, Tony Blair and David Cameron got no West End drama in which their government was the dramatic context, even though each of them has been the source for various films and novels. It was Callaghan and his precarious government that formed the backdrop to a timeless production about high-stakes parliamentary theatre.

Although Callaghan was not an actor in the league of Wilson, Thatcher, Blair and Cameron, he did like the performance of politics. He was the only prime minister to sing songs with a joyful exuberance when delivering a speech at a conference or at a political gathering such as the Durham Miners' Gala. He did not have the wit or cunning of Wilson, but he was playful. Unlike the shy and self-conscious May – the first prime minister to dance onto the stage, at the start of her speech to a Conservative conference – Callaghan could be an authentic performer. His background was far removed from the Oxbridge political games that excited Edward Heath as well as many of his Labour rivals. Yet he could play the games of politics and could occasionally enjoy the fun.

The contrasts, fractured patterns, contradictions and dramatic ironies were already striking when Callaghan finally secured the crown at the age of sixty-four. He was older than the departing Harold Wilson, who made great play of his long-planned intention to retire at sixty. After Wilson announced his resignation in March 1976, Callaghan won the leadership against the most formidable set of candidates who had stood in a contest for any party since

1945. While his rivals had been students and stars at Oxford before lighting up the political stage, Callaghan had not been to university and had a less-glittering public personality, in spite of the tendency towards mischievous playfulness. He won the contest with ease against his ambitious colleagues and was in one key respect by far the best qualified of the candidates, having served at the top of the Cabinet longer than any of the other leadership contenders.

Callaghan's slow rise to the very top is an example of his almost unprecedented wilful staying power. Only Gordon Brown displayed the same resolute determination to move from 'leader-in-waiting' to leader. Most perceived leaders-in-waiting never become leaders, partly because of the pressures that arise from the perception.

The candidates who stood in the 1976 leadership contest after Wilson's resignation were all 'leaders-in-waiting' at one time or another, in contrast to the barren New Labour era, when Brown was the only one. One of the other candidates in the 1976 contest, Michael Foot, was to become a leader. The others who stood were Tony Benn, Anthony Crosland, Denis Healey and Roy Jenkins. Although a good speaker and a lively interviewee on TV and radio, Callaghan was the least sparky of a competitive field. All the candidates had depth and political vivacity. The others were scintillating writers, orators of varying brilliance, gripped by ideas and history. In contrast, Callaghan chose not to shine at times, at least in his victorious leadership contest. Sensing that his greatest strength was to be seen as being above the fray, Callaghan played little part in the 1976 Labour battle. This was an era when it paid to be laid-back. Wilson had kept a low profile in the 1975 referendum and won. Callaghan was rarely heard or seen during the 1976 leadership contest and he won, too. Labour MPs alone selected the leader, and in this case the new prime minister. On the basis of his longevity and his combative authority, a large majority of MPs chose Callaghan. Michael Foot came second. In a sign of what was to follow, Foot topped the poll in the first ballot, but Callaghan came through to win by a big margin in the second.[15] As the former Labour MP, Giles Radice, pointed out in an illuminating book, it might have been possible for one of Healey, Jenkins and Crosland to be leader. Labour's glittering social democrats chose to be rivals rather than to coalesce around one of the three, a move that would have involved the other two casting aside their leadership ambition. Few in politics are ready to make such a sacrifice.[16]

Although there appeared to be no mysteries in relation to the enigma-free Callaghan as he rose erratically to the top, there were plenty of riddles and conundrums. How did he flourish later in his career, having been a failure as a chancellor, not least becoming the sensible 'sunny Jim' leading a country in dark economic times? How did he become a pro-European, having been at times a crude anti-marketeer? Why was an ardent trade unionist incapable of forming a constructive relationship with the trade unions as he moved towards his fall? How to explain his role as an astute unifier when prime minister, and yet the leader who left behind a party tearing itself towards seemingly eternal Opposition? How was a prime minister who made Cabinet government work effectively also the figure who brought about the demise of Cabinet government? Why did high-stakes parliamentary theatre form the backdrop to the leadership of a figure who was less actorly than several prime ministers? This is where Hercule Poirot's skills as an investigator must be applied. Here are the answers to the riddles and conundrums, and with them come several lessons of leadership.

Callaghan's staying power was both a personal triumph and the consequence of a less hysterical age. Politics became even more unforgiving after Callaghan had left the fray. We should not exaggerate the scale of the difference. With good cause, Callaghan – and Wilson even more so – felt besieged in the build-up to devaluation in 1967 and beyond. The media could torment and destroy politicians then, too. Even so, there was more space in the mid- to late 1960s for political recovery. The media's coverage of politics, although ragingly intense and partisan enough to make leaders paranoid and insecure, was less screeching than it subsequently became. In the 1960s there were no political programmes on a Sunday, no rolling TV news; newspapers gave more space to parliamentary debates and less to the soap opera of politics; and, of course, there was no social media. Callaghan could move to the Home Office from the Treasury and get on with the job, his authority within the Labour Party not greatly undermined by the around-the-clock scrutiny that was to follow a few decades later.

But even then, in the 1960s, TV had become a dominant medium. Callaghan's career was boosted considerably because he was a brilliant television interviewee, another key to his durability. Being an effective interviewee is an important part of a leader's or aspiring leader's ammunition. Of modern prime ministers, only Tony Blair beats Callaghan as an intoxicating interviewee. Callaghan was engaged, calm, witty and authoritative. He managed to perform well even when he was struggling at the Treasury. These are important attributes when political authority is being challenged. He was a prime minister, and aspiring prime minister, in an era when TV interviews were broadcast regularly at peak time and at length, often with a panel of distinguished and weighty columnists. There were far fewer political interviews, but their rarity meant they had much more impact. Callaghan had the knack of appearing and, to some extent, being candid, while also managing to be discreet. Again, only the very different personality of Blair had a similar skill as an interviewee.

There were only a handful of political writers for newspapers in Callaghan's era, and their output created far greater waves than political writers do today in the age of social media. Callaghan took on the commentators with verve when he faced them in a TV studio. He enjoyed the format. There are several full-length interviews on YouTube from the time when Callaghan was prime minister navigating his way through the economic fog. No viewer could discern how dark it all appeared to be, from Callaghan's demeanour in a studio. He was relaxed and engaged, unless an interviewer irritated him, in which case he made his irritability part of his engaging repertoire. He would often retort along these lines: 'I know what you'll do with my answer. You will put the answer to another of my colleagues, hoping that he or she will disagree. So I'm not going to answer... Come on, Robin [Day], you've had several attempts but you're not going to get anywhere.' The viewer could not help but empathize with the evasive politician. Callaghan became unfashionable as a leader very quickly, but any aspiring leader could do worse than take note of his skills as an interviewee. They assisted him greatly when he was down, as he was quite often in his oscillating career. His capacity as a performer explains partly how Callaghan kept going when others would have fallen.

His position within the Labour Party was also a pivotal buttress after his short-lived tenure at the Treasury. In the UK there is a presidential culture, but a party-based system. The relationship between aspirant leader and party is therefore crucial. By the time he became chancellor, Callaghan was already a formidable figure within his party and beyond. He had become an MP after Labour's

1945 landslide and had held several portfolios in the parliamentary party by the time he became chancellor nearly twenty years later. He was close to being fully formed by the time economic storms overwhelmed him in the 1960s, and had a developed sense of who he was as a public figure by the time he became prime minister. Compared with the fourteen years they spent in Parliament, before Blair became prime minister and Brown took over as chancellor, Callaghan had been around for a long time and was harder to remove from the political stage as a result, even if he made mistakes.

The Labour Party, or enough of its influential components, was supportive of him for other reasons. Football supporters like to cheer players who are local, chanting that they are 'one of our own'. Callaghan was one of Labour's own. This was another reason for his durability. His father, who had been a chief petty officer in the Royal Navy, died suddenly when Callaghan was nine, leaving his mother to struggle on without the aid of a pension. His education was patchy, a part of his past that he would often highlight. He made the right to a decent education one of his great political passions. As prime minister, his first significant speech was on the importance of a decent education for all. He had neither the time nor the political space to develop his ideas in this area, but the intent was genuine and intensely felt.

The appearance of authority when he became prime minister was partly a facade. For effective leaders, the facade is not an act of duplicity. Quite often leaders need to appear calm when they are not, funny when they are fuming, determined and focused when they are lost.

In public, Callaghan became calmer and more self-confident than he was. There were times as prime minister when he despaired.

Unlike Theresa May, he could hide his nervy anxiety when the cameras rolled. Behind the scenes, he would occasionally display red-faced indignation and doubt about policy direction, which is unsurprising given the external circumstances. At one never-ending meeting of Labour's ruling National Executive Committee in the late 1970s, Callaghan looked up at one point and declaimed: 'Why don't we throw away the keys and stay here for the rest of our lives?'[17] He was prime minister at the time. In spontaneously exploding at his incarceration at Labour's HQ, he exposed as ridiculous the pompous declaration of some in the media that it is their duty to 'hold the powerful to account'. A lot of the time even prime ministers are powerless and are accountable, in a thousand different ways, every minute of the day. Non-elected figures are often far more powerful, wealthier and largely unscrutinized.

But under scrutiny, Callaghan conveyed calm in public, even when he was privately alarmed. At times, and in private, the impossible scale of the task came close to overwhelming him, but the avuncular, authoritative public face was nearly always in place. MPs and party members make their judgements based partly on the public personalities of senior politicians in their party.

Callaghan kept going when flimsier politicians would have fallen. His senior adviser in Number Ten, Bernard Donoughue, noted that 'Although apparently an agnostic, his Baptist upbringing showed through when, especially during a crisis, he would suddenly burst out singing hymns. Before he left his Commons room for the big debate on our pay sanctions policy he sang to us one of his favourites, "We'll meet again with the Lord".'[18] There were many crises from 1976 till his fall in 1979. Callaghan must have sung a lot of tunes. But his personality, his position within the Labour Party and the quieter volume at which politics was reported at the time all contributed to making Callaghan a symbol of solidity when he was prime minister, even when the economy was tottering chaotically.

There was another reason why Callaghan as prime minister seemed to epitomize calm in the midst of a bleak tempest. He was so evidently keeping the creaking show on the road in a way that nobody else in his party could. Most obviously, he had won a leadership contest and, unlike Theresa May, did not undermine the authority-enhancing benefits of winning by calling an early general election. May never recovered from losing her party's majority in the 2017 election. In spite of all the crises that erupted around Callaghan and the intense divisions, there was no serious speculation about a leadership challenge while he was prime minister. Partly because of his reasonably secure position internally, he was able to manage an unruly Cabinet. As a prime minister he appeared to be strong in part because he was. No one threatened to challenge him.

The next riddle is connected with calculated, cunning politics. The explanation as to why a successful period of Cabinet government led to the demise of this form of rule comes in the form of the then leader of the Opposition, Margaret Thatcher. Given the wider turmoil, she saw by instinct an opportunity to present herself as the model of 'strong leadership' compared with the 'weak' Callaghan, who was forever chairing crisis Cabinet meetings. She derided such teamwork, insisting that she would lead from the front and would have little time for internal discussion. This, too, was partly an act, but a highly effective one nonetheless.[19]

Subsequently Cabinet ministers, including those who were highly critical of her leadership, insisted that to some extent Thatcher did allow and encourage Cabinet discussion as prime minister, even if she became irritable when probed intelligently for too long. But Thatcher had framed an argument around 'strong leadership' in order to make Callaghan's collegiate style seem weak. The bigger leap came with the leadership of Tony Blair, who dismissed his party's past as 'old Labour' and took as his guiding philosophy the idea that 'new Labour' must be entirely different from all that was associated with the 1970s – including Cabinet ministers speaking their minds.

As fashions change, Blair, who was widely praised initially for showing 'strong' leadership, was then heavily criticized for turning away from Cabinet government, most specifically in relation to the war in Iraq. This was unfair on Blair's leadership. There was nothing to stop Blair's Cabinet acting as Callaghan's ministers had done. On the whole, Blair's Cabinets chose to be pathetically subservient and unquestioning, with the exception of Blair's chancellor, Gordon Brown, who managed to pressurize Blair with almost the same intensity of all of Callaghan's ministers put together. Callaghan had to manage his Cabinet because his ministers chose to be assertive. Blair's ministers were grateful to be in power and saw Blair as the leader who had taken them there.

Callaghan also proved to be a wider team player as prime minister. He had no choice but to be. That is the key. The tribal leader had to look beyond his tribe and found the experience a congenial one. For much of his time as prime minister, Callaghan had no Commons majority and a substantial number of Labour MPs inclined to vote against their frail government. Prime ministers in hung parliaments have to work with what they have got. Callaghan had David Steel. He was lucky to have a thoughtful leader of the Liberals. He knew how to get the best out of potentially awkward people partly, again, because he had to. Without forming an internal alliance with Michael Foot, his government might well have collapsed.

Callaghan was a pragmatist, working with whoever he needed to and often changing with the flow of the tides. He was against the Common Market until the UK joined, after which he recognized that departure would be counter-productive. He was against incomes policies until he feared that no other option was available to him, at which point he favoured incomes policies. He was an ardent trade unionist out of conviction and self-interested calculation. When self-interest and conviction demanded a different response, he became less ardent. Callaghan was a poor reader of long-term political and economic trends, but he was flexibly astute at responding to the more immediate rhythms. He could be stubborn until he sensed a need to change, and then he could swiftly pull a reverse gear.

Given these agile attributes, at odds with his apparent rigid old-fashioned politics, here is another riddle: why did Callaghan quickly become an unfashionable prime minister, referred to dismissively (if at all) in the decades that followed? This is a leader whom Denis Healey, a figure who was not easily impressed, placed second only to Attlee in the pantheon of Labour leaders.[20] Shelves creak with books on Attlee. There are few on Callaghan.

Part of the answer is obvious. Prime ministers who serve briefly at the end of an era, and without winning an election with their own distinctive agenda, are easily dismissed. Roy Jenkins, who had more curiosity about leaders and leadership than any of his colleagues, dismissed Callaghan as a 'tail-end Charlie', a quote that tormented Gordon Brown as he agonized over how to win an election in his own right after Blair's long reign. Callaghan ruled only from April 1976 until the election that was forced on him in May 1979. This election campaign triggered the Thatcher revolution that made Callaghan seem like ancient history very speedily.

The end of Callaghan's reign was also traumatic and bleak, arguably bleaker than the fall of any other prime minister in the modern era, including even that of Theresa May. The darkness took many forms. Like Brown, Callaghan clumsily mishandled the timing of the election. He had dropped a few hints that he might call an election in the autumn of 1978, when some polls suggested that Labour had a chance of winning, or at least being the largest party in a hung parliament. David Steel was by no means alone in advising Callaghan to call the election. His deputy, Michael Foot, urged him to go to the country earlier. Healey, too, was of the same opinion. So were senior trade-union leaders. In July 1978 Callaghan was interviewed on peak-time TV by a panel of journalists. He was asked about the possibility of an early election and replied truthfully that he would have a summer holiday and decide after that. His words merely fuelled speculation, as he had not ruled out the idea. Like Gordon Brown, he was too transparently keeping all options open.[21]

Over the summer holiday he concluded that he would lose an autumn election. Subsequently, in a dramatic television broadcast in September 1978, Callaghan announced that he would not be calling one: 'The government must and will continue to carry out policies that are consistent, determined, that don't chop or change and that brought about the present recovery in our fortunes.'[22]

Prime ministers always hope that something might turn up, if they stay on. Hope is a huge driving force for leaders. To outsiders it might appear that a prime ministerial cause is without hope, but prime ministers rarely reach the same conclusion. Even in the depths of despair, they wonder if there is a way through. In addition, Callaghan was not in despair. For all the intense pressures on him, he was enjoying the job that he had waited so long to get. He did not want to give it up.

Sometimes he even appeared to be enjoying himself too much, a bizarre problem for a prime minister who is deeply aware of the political and economic turmoil. Only a fool would not be aware.

Famously, in the depths of his final winter as prime minister, Callaghan had been photographed at a sunny international conference in Guadeloupe. The gathering took place just a few months after his decision not to call an election. He returned with a suntan to a freezing UK that was enduring the chaotic consequences of various industrial disputes, declaring at the airport: 'I don't think other people in the world would share the view [that] there is mounting chaos in this country.' The headline in the *Sun* newspaper the following day was: 'Crisis? What Crisis?'[23] Here is another vivid reminder that so-called 'Fake news' existed long before the eruption of social media. The headline was an exaggerated summary of Callaghan's comments, but it cemented an impression of a prime minister who was 'out of touch' – a cliché that makes little sense when applied to any politician dependent on winning elections. His actual words were complacently phrased, but Callaghan was far from out of touch. Governing had become close to impossible, and no prime minister becomes detached in such circumstances. Yet Callaghan's strength as a communicator became his weakness. His calm authority misleadingly conveyed an indifference to the chaos.

The 'Crisis? What Crisis?' saga was just one of many that erupted around Callaghan, as if he was being punished for dragging out an unruly parliament beyond its natural life. Prime ministers such as May and Heath were torn apart for calling early elections. The political gods turned on Callaghan for seeking to avoid an election until the last possible moment.

The so-called 'winter of discontent' was at its worst as he returned from sunny Guadeloupe in January 1979. This doomed Callaghan to defeat. The strikes and the failure of the government to impose its own pay policy without triggering industrial unrest combined to make Labour's electoral task far more mountainous after he had lost the election.

The election defeat in 1979 was preceded by the government losing a vote of no confidence in the Commons. Callaghan was only the third prime minister in the twentieth century to lose a vote of no confidence.[24] Such a parliamentary defeat is a humiliating way to open an election campaign. Until the Fixed-term Parliaments Act, rushed through for superficial reasons by the 2010 Con/Liberal Democrat coalition, a prime minister had a degree of freedom about when to call an election, a freedom that often tormented the individual who had to make the decision. Callaghan had been forced into an election, placing him on the defensive and making the Opposition leader, Margaret Thatcher, seem already a powerful player before she had acquired power. She had won the decisive vote that triggered an election. The dynamic was flattering for Thatcher and made Callaghan appear even weaker.

The build-up to the no-confidence vote was theatrical in its stressful unpredictability. This was another twist of the Callaghan era. Curiously, interest in the Callaghan era has faded, yet the real-life drama was epic and edgy. Ian Aitken was the *Guardian*'s political editor in the late 1970s, reporting on every twist and turn. On Aitken's death, another journalist, David McKie, evoked vividly what it was like being a reporter at Westminster during Callaghan's premiership:

> For much of the day he [Aitken] would operate not in the members'
> lobby of the House of Commons, to which senior political
> correspondents enjoyed privileged access, but much more in the
> corridors and the bars. Of these, the greatest, at any rate in the
> 1970s and 80s, was Annie's Bar, a particularly important information
> exchange when the life of James Callaghan's government was
> imperilled almost nightly, as it was from 1976 to 1979... At some
> time between 7 p.m. and 8 p.m., Ian would move to the telephone,
> assemble his notes, some of which had been made on torn-up
> cigarette packets, and dictate a story that was a model of its kind.[25]

It is the phrase 'imperilled almost nightly' that conjures up the challenges of leadership in a hung parliament with a restive, rebellious governing parliamentary party. The government was finally killed off in the no-confidence vote, after a day of frantic negotiations with minority parties, whips on both sides summoning a few dangerously ill MPs on stretchers, and some epic speeches in the Commons as the deadline for the 10 p.m. vote drew closer. The final full speech of the parliament was made, appropriately enough, by the great parliamentarian Michael Foot, as Leader of the House. He was funny, gracious and passionate in his defence of the tottering government. After the wit and passion of Foot's words, MPs headed for the lobbies. Callaghan lost the vote of no confidence by a single vote, 311–310. Afterwards, amidst much frenzy, he stood up at the despatch box and declared that he would now 'Take our case to the country' – the final affirmation of a Labour prime minister in the Commons for eighteen years. The defeat added to the sense of chaos that marked Callaghan's leadership. Yet in some respects this particular compelling and nerve-shredding parliamentary drama was irrelevant. Callaghan would have had to call an election later that year, even if he had won the no-confidence vote. There is no reason to assume the election outcome would have been different in the autumn. There were deep currents driving the tides.

During the 1979 campaign Callaghan turned to his senior adviser, Bernard Donoughue, and observed: 'You know there are times, perhaps once every thirty years, when there is a sea change in politics. It then does not matter what you say or what you do. There is a shift in what the public wants and what it approves of. I suspect there is now such a sea change and it is for Mrs Thatcher.'[26]

Callaghan's observation appears prophetic, in the light of what followed. Yet for a smart reader of the political rhythms, he was late to recognize the tidal wave that propelled Margaret Thatcher towards power. His insight also provided him with a convenient get-out clause, implying there was nothing he could do to reverse that tidal wave.

Elections elsewhere suggest this was not the case. France elected a socialist president in 1981 at about the point at which Thatcher's popularity was so low that *The Times* ran an opinion poll under the headline 'The Most Unpopular Prime Minister This Century'. The tidal change was a limited one. The waves did not engulf West Germany, an economically more vibrant country, which often elected social-democratic chancellors as part of a coalition. Northern European countries, all with economies performing better than the UK's, were often governed by social-democratic parties.

Callaghan explained what he meant by his tidal metaphor in a candid interview many years later. In December 1996, months before the New Labour landslide, he reflected on the historical forces that shaped the assumptions of his leadership and, by implication, those of the other prime ministers who ruled in the 1970s before Thatcher:

A new generation was growing up in the 1970s and had reached the stage where their ideas were becoming popular – and we failed to adjust to that. To understand the reason one has to go right back to the war and before. In the thirties, what we now call the market economy failed. There was the 'Great Depression' with millions unemployed. As soon as the war came that disappeared. We had a centralised economy which provided work for everyone. So when my generation came into the public eye we said there was no going back to the twenties and thirties and we said 'Look what happened during the war – a centralised economy has shown that we can plan for success...'

But by the 1970s a new generation had grown up that did not have our wartime experiences and didn't think it was relevant. So I think we failed to recognise the new expectations of the younger generation. The think tanks of the right – we failed to pay any attention to them.[27]

Callaghan was intelligently insightful, admirably reflective and yet too defensive. He was speaking when Tony Blair was walking on water, heading towards a big victory in the 1997 election, while Callaghan had lost his. Leaders who only fight and lose an election are tormented by their failure and usually agonize for the rest of their lives about what they did wrong. Gordon Brown adopted a self-deprecating approach in the years that followed his defeat in 2010. 'Don't take my advice. I lost an election,' he would say in his rare public appearances, normally at book festivals.

Although, in the same interview, Callaghan was subtly critical of Blair at times, he was also coming to terms with New Labour's overwhelming popularity as it turned its back on the centralized state and hailed markets and the private sector as agents of delivery. If Callaghan had been interviewed after the 2008 financial crash, he might have taken a different line. But he was also onto something. For noble reasons, those leaders shaped by the 1930s – Heath, Wilson and Callaghan – feared, with good cause, the social and economic consequences of unemployment. As erratic defenders of the corporatist state, Wilson, Heath and Callaghan had several objectives, but above all they intervened to protect jobs. For them, there could be no return to the 1930s. But as they agonized over what to do about pay, prices and jobs, they almost failed to notice the rise of an alternative set of beliefs and assumptions, personified partly by the leadership of Thatcher. They were defined by orthodoxies that no longer applied, in the same way that later disciples of Thatcher could not see that the ideas behind Thatcherism were partly the cause of the 2008 financial crash, and not the solution to the dark consequences.

Having a vision, some ideological momentum and policies that make tangible sense of that vision is essential for a leader to endure and develop. This is not easy, and the combination is rare. Some leaders have visionary ideas or phrases, but lack the policies. Others have policies in which they believe, but do not have the ideological verve to bring them together into a coherent whole. Callaghan was not a visionary, and would probably have taken it as an insult if he had been described as such. But he was opposed by Margaret Thatcher, an ideological populist with a simple but clear sense of what had gone wrong and of what was required to put it right. Callaghan had none of the skills required to counter with a populism from the left. His appeal depended on a projection of solid competence. That only works if an economy, and much else, is running smoothly. No one could claim this was the case in the late 1970s.

Wilson had, in part, acquired an unfairly negative reputation for wiliness and a lack of vision long before he retired from the leadership. Callaghan was regarded by colleagues, and even by the anti-Labour newspapers, as more solid. Yet he lacked clarity of purpose, too. For partly understandable reasons, he changed tack almost as often as Wilson.

Nowhere was the clarity less clear than in Callaghan's relationship with the trade unions. He ensured that the *In Place of Strife* proposals never had a chance of implementation and then, with a Shakespearean twist, became arguably the biggest political victim of the weak legislative framework that he had helped to bring about. Some of the unions turned on him, or his attempts to impose pay restraints, and Callaghan was at a loss to know what to do about it. A large part of him still regarded himself as a trade unionist, and yet some trade unions were making his life hellish. Bernard Donoughue reports a despairing Callaghan asking in January 1979, 'How do you announce the government's pay policy has collapsed?'[28]

That is quite a question for a prime minister to ask, even in private. Yet pay policy had indeed collapsed spectacularly. In the autumn of 1978 Callaghan had attempted to impose a 5 per cent ceiling on pay rises. Within weeks of his announcement, workers at some companies (including Ford, then a big employer in the UK) were demanding 15 per cent. Public-sector unions sought higher increases. In December legislation required to enforce the pay policy was defeated in the Commons. In February 1979 the 5 per cent ceiling was raised to 10 per cent. The pressures on Callaghan over this period – partly self-induced – were as intense as those on Theresa May as she sought to navigate Brexit in a hung parliament.

They were self-induced in the sense that Callaghan, like Heath and Wilson, failed to understand what was happening and what needed to happen. Thatcherism did not have to be the answer to the chaos of the 1970s, but it became the only answer for a time, or at least the only answer that commanded enough support for a government to govern.

For all his ebullient authority, Callaghan was all over the place in terms of policy coherence when he was prime minister. His first speech to his party conference as prime minister, delivered in September 1976, is widely cited as the first move towards Thatcherite monetarism. Thatcher saw monetarism – governments controlling the supply of money circulating in the economy – as the solution to high inflation and the generator of sustained economic growth. In a script written partly by the economist and Callaghan's son-in-law, Peter Jay, the newish prime minister told his party:

> We used to think that you could spend your way out of a recession, and increase employment by cutting taxes and boosting Government spending. I tell you in all candour that that option no longer exists, and that in so far as it ever did exist, it only worked on each occasion since the war by injecting a bigger dose of inflation into the economy, followed by a higher level of unemployment as the next step. Higher inflation followed by higher unemployment. We have just escaped from the highest rate of inflation this country has known; we have not yet escaped from the consequences: high unemployment.

But this was not an endorsement of monetarism in the way that Thatcher was to espouse it in the early phase of her premiership. In the same speech, which was confused and contradictory, there was also a strong defence of public spending in many areas of government. Callaghan was also addressing an immediate crisis: the demand from the IMF for further sweeping spending cuts. Yet as Healey was later to reflect: 'The whole affair was unnecessary. The Treasury had grossly overestimated the PSBR.'[29]

Callaghan was not to know this at the time, and after his traumas as chancellor he had become fixated with the need to reassure the markets. He needed to put the case to his party, and be seen doing so. In some ways he was being politically courageous. Yet his attempts to sway his party and reassure the IMF and the markets left him lacking an argument, or the space to frame one against Thatcher. In the end, he could only argue that Labour would not cut public spending as brutally as she would. In doing so, he had handed her victory in the ideological battle, almost before it had begun. Those like Crosland and Benn, from very different perspectives, who had opposed the spending cuts were not the reckless extremists they were portrayed as being.[30] In some respects, their analysis was more closely related to the economic realities and, unlike Callaghan, they came equipped with ideological armoury, a narrative to challenge Thatcher's instinctive and, in some respects, simplistic anti-state populism.

The oscillating relationship with the trade unions was mirrored in Callaghan's erratic approach to incomes policies. Like Heath and Wilson, Callaghan often opposed incomes policies, only to turn to them. For these three prime ministers, incomes policies were like a 'femme fatale' in film-noir thrillers. Legal constraints on pay attracted them, even though they knew deep down that in adopting them, they were walking towards their doom. Incomes policy brought about the fall of Heath. Wilson got into a contorted nightmare seeking to impose a pay policy without calling it a pay policy. Callaghan noted the agonies of his predecessors and opposed pay policy, before fatally adopting one.

In spite of strong international relationships, Callaghan was not a visionary in foreign affairs, either. He failed to articulate powerfully what he was up to. This was in contrast to most of his colleagues, a number of whom wrote entire books articulating their visionary politics. Crosland was Labour's great philosopher in the 1950s. Benn's books included *Arguments for Socialism* and *Arguments for Democracy*. Healey and Jenkins had written many articles and books that gave a clear guide to their ideological journeys. There are none from Callaghan. He was a social conservative, committed to family, law and order, the value of a good education and improving the lives of the poor. His opening broadcast as a new prime minister focused almost entirely on his old-fashioned values, as well as the need for tough decisions on easing government debt. Later, Callaghan was to look back and recognize his lightly-worn ideological baggage as a flaw rather than a strength:

> 'You see I never had a really developed theory of Socialism. People like John Strachey or Denis Healey or Barbara Castle or all those lucky people that went to university.'
>
> 'Do you feel that you missed something by not going?'
>
> 'I feel I missed a great deal. I gained things that they never had through having a practical life but I missed the discipline of thought and the opportunity to exchange ideas with other people who were thinking in the same way. I think that I would have enjoyed going if I'd had the opportunity.'[31]

Callaghan had been surrounded by Oxbridge titans. As he hinted, his strength was a practical focus on the matters in hand, but the most formidable leaders need a weighty sense of thought-through purpose. When Callaghan observed the 'sea change' during the 1979 election, he was partly seeking to make sense of the rise of a radical Conservative leader with an ideological mission. In contrast to Thatcher, he was openly uncertain about how to deal with the mountainous challenges and had no guiding ideology to lead him. These are problems for a leader, even one who was sometimes celebrated for his hard-headed, well-intentioned pragmatism.

There is another reason why Callaghan's reputation sank rapidly or was viewed with indifference. He mishandled his approach to leadership after the election defeat in 1979. Some prime ministers are casually negligent about their post-prime ministerial careers, in a way that changes how their entire leaderships are perceived. Thatcher and Blair were viewed differently, and more critically, by some partly because of their conduct after they left Downing Street. Major's reputation grew on the basis of his behaviour post-Downing Street. Callaghan's reputation fell for very different reasons than Thatcher's or Blair's, but is also partly explained by what happened after he lost power in 1979.

Callaghan decided to stay on as Labour leader. He thought he could calm down a deeply divided party after the trauma of power, creating a path for Denis Healey to succeed him. He calculated that Healey was such a contentious figure, after more than five years as Labour's chancellor, that a period of solid leadership from a leader with no further ambition was required before Healey could win.

Instead, the divisions deepened and there was no stability whatsoever. Callaghan had little authority to impose his will, as both sides of the divide knew that he would be going fairly soon. Under Callaghan's fading leadership, internal rule changes were made that began to give new powers to party members.

Labour's party conferences in 1979 and 1980 – Callaghan's final annual gatherings as leader – were febrile, the fieriest in the party's history. Furious speakers talked of the betrayal of the Labour government, with Callaghan looking down once more from the platform. The 1980 conference was especially dramatic. From the podium, Tony Benn pledged that the next Labour government would nationalize the banks, abolish the House of Lords and leave the Common Market within days. At a fringe meeting, Shirley Williams, soon to leave the Labour Party, spoke of a 'fascism of the left'. Callaghan looked weak and impotent. Indeed, during the

1980 conference his sudden resignation was clumsily leaked to the media. It was a dark ending to a long career at the top of British politics. Callaghan wanted Healey to be his successor, but Michael Foot was chosen by Labour MPs instead. Ever since, Callaghan's reputation has been poor, defined by images of the 'winter of discontent', his inability to keep the left of the party in line and the dominance of Margaret Thatcher, who swept him aside.

He was more or less airbrushed from history soon after he stepped down from the leadership in the autumn of 1980. Unlike Wilson, Callaghan continued to be physically and mentally alert for decades to come and yet, after he retired as an MP in 1987, he was largely forgotten or ignored by his party.

Labour's successive leaders wanted nothing to do with him, for different reasons. Although they had worked well together in government, Michael Foot – Callaghan's immediate successor – wanted to pursue a policy programme well to the left of the former prime minister's beliefs. Most specifically, Foot was a committed believer in unilateral nuclear disarmament and Callaghan was a passionate opponent, even speaking out publicly and angrily against Labour's defence policies in the years to come. When Neil Kinnock followed Foot, after Labour's 1983 electoral slaughter, the new leader was desperate to be seen moving on from the nightmare of the late 1970s. He sought no public association with Callaghan. More woundingly for Callaghan, Tony Blair, after becoming leader in 1994, turned to Roy Jenkins for guidance, as an experienced former Labour Cabinet minister and SDP leader. He made no attempt to seek advice from the last Labour figure to have occupied Number Ten.[32]

Callaghan lacked the vision to be a great prime minister, and the circumstances would have made greatness impossible: a hung parliament, raging inflation and a divided party. But the agile manner in which he prevailed over dissenting ministers of intimidating weightiness, and navigated his way through the nightmarish terrain of the UK economy – while explaining to the country via authoritative TV interviews what he was seeking to do – were historically significant achievements. Callaghan looked at Thatcher and Blair with envy as they led with landslide majorities. But his envy was misplaced. Probably he would not have been a very different prime minister if he had faced a more malleable Commons, given that he got his way more often than not as prime minister. His way was erratically resolute and conservative, amidst an epic sea change that he recognized only when it was too late to make an ideological case for an alternative route. He left the stage clear for Margaret Thatcher.

4

MARGARET THATCHER

Margaret Thatcher is the great change-maker of modern prime ministers. The sweeping alterations to Britain during her premiership took a distinct form. By the end of her leadership, she had transformed her country beyond recognition – a remarkable feat for a leader – and the 1970s seemed like a distant land. After eleven years of her rule, parts of the UK flourished, as an entrepreneurial spirit was unleashed. She won three elections in a row. Yet as a result of her dominance, parts of her country no longer knew where to turn for accountable leadership. She was the hyperactive leader who did not believe in an active state; she was the strong leader who left the UK with weak forms of democratic leadership. This was one of the most significant consequences of her time in power. By the time she left office, local government had either been abolished or reduced to cranky irrelevance. Even a city as big as London had no body to represent it. If the Tube trains did not turn up or buses did not arrive, travellers had nowhere to turn to make their protests. In other parts of the country, jobs that had once been for life were not available for even a small part of a life. While parts of the economy boomed spectacularly, some voters lost control of their previously orderly lives, and others felt as if they had been left behind. Margaret Thatcher was a control freak who was not specially interested in how others sought some sense of control over fractured public services. Instead she was a believer in the concept of 'freedom' almost unmediated. She deployed the term 'freedom' like a weapon, refusing to acknowledge that the concept is complex or nuanced. She sought to set the people free. Which voter would opt for incarceration?

Part of Thatcher's genius, and a reason for her historic endurance, was a capacity to make sense of the vibrant or impoverishing chaos that she unleashed. Instinctively she could articulate what she genuinely believed. She made her sometimes shallow radicalism seem like sound common sense. Thatcher was freeing people from the manacles of the state and, on the whole, quite a lot of people were grateful. Some were making money and could do more with their lives than they had been able to during the shabby, nerve-shredding 1970s. Thatcher was strong, and her ghostly predecessors had been weak. In her strength, she made the state – in most of its various manifestations – weaker.

Margaret Thatcher is the most analysed of modern prime ministers. Unsurprisingly, there have been many books about her; only Winston Churchill has inspired more. As a modern prime minister, she has the field of largely flattering biographies almost to herself. The reasons for the enduring interest are obvious. She was a determined, wilful reformer, transforming not only her country, but her party, too. In terms of domestic policy and her later approach to Europe, Thatcher's influence lasted much longer than Churchill's, extending well beyond the end of her career and, indeed, her death.

Seeking to fully explain Thatcher's addictive love of politics from an early age is almost impossible, the equivalent of solving the mystery of the Beatles' masterful musicianship. Her father, Alderman Roberts, the hard-working owner of a grocer's shop in Grantham, was the key early influence, in the same way that Paul McCartney's father was a factor behind his love of music. Neither fully makes sense of what followed. Thatcher cited her father often. He believed in concepts that were to shape her outlook: 'individual responsibility' and 'sound finance'. The latter formed the basis of her future economic policies. Although her brilliant biographer, Charles Moore, reveals that she had boyfriends and set aside time in her pursuit of them, her immersion in politics was total, and unusual in an era when politics was largely a male vocation. From early in her life she became intoxicated by politics and by the Conservative Party, the ideas, the performance, the battles. After she had left Number Ten she continued to intoxicate many of those in her party.

One of the questions posed during the 2016 Brexit referendum was: 'How would Thatcher have voted?' The question continued to be asked for a long time after the result. Following the 2008 financial crash, the Conservatives' youthful leaders, David Cameron and George Osborne, turned to the 1980s for guidance on how they should respond. Their economic policies were recognizably Thatcherite. A more sensitive figure than his reputation suggested, Osborne was in tears during Thatcher's funeral. Thatcher's ideas shaped and defined him, and Cameron, probably more than they dared to realize. She had cast a spell long ago and, remarkably in the fast-moving world of British politics, her capacity to intoxicate a new generation of Tories had not diminished. In their different ways, Labour leaders also paid homage to the potency of her leadership, until the election of Jeremy Corbyn in 2015. Even Corbyn's supporters referenced Thatcher. Some suggested that he was the left's answer to her. This represents the dominance of a rare political force.

Yet for all the worship and scrutiny, Thatcher possessed two qualities as a leader that remain under-explored. The first was those instinctive skills as a political teacher. All leaders announce policies and take strategic positions. Many do so most days of the week. Surprisingly few explain *why* they are doing so. They make announcements as if the declarations need no explanation. The most effective leaders explain as well as announce. Thatcher was explaining what she was up to most of the time, in a populist language that voters could easily relate to.

The second overlooked quality was her unerring ability to read the unpredictable political rhythms and apply them to her advantage, while also acting with conviction, or at least appearing to do so. With good cause she is seen as a 'conviction politician'. But she was wily, too. The fact that most voters regarded Harold Wilson as devious exposed the limits of his wiliness. Thatcher was seen as deeply principled and courageous, showing that she was devious enough to keep her political calculations well hidden. Perhaps sometimes she hid them from herself. But until close to the end, they were there.

Most leaders fail to read properly what is happening on the crowded political stage, let alone respond in ways that enhance their position. But Thatcher possessed a rare ability to recognize the space she had on the political stage to act either radically or cautiously. She was a restless, impatient leader and yet she took the time at each phase of her career, again almost instinctively, to judge how far she could go in sating her hunger for radical change. Thatcher was both impulsive and cautious. She usually knew which of the two characteristics should prevail at any given time. Until the dramatic final phase of her leadership, she was able to control her own impulsiveness.

Before exploring both qualities and an under-examined, but deep flaw, there is a wider lesson from Thatcher's leadership, one that is a common theme with all our leaders and prime ministers. In a way that is Shakespearean in its epic theatricality, the origins of a leader's rise to the top are often the cause of their downfall. They do not see that they are moving towards their fall by acting in ways that earlier had propelled them to the top. Harold Wilson's career is an earlier example and Tony Blair's is a later one.[1] To some extent, the same dark sequence applies to the other modern prime ministers.

This was precisely the case with Margaret Thatcher. Oddly, given the vivid drama of Thatcher's leadership, her rise and fall are connected to the dry theme of local government, and how to raise finance for councils. Her remarkable ascent to the top of the Conservative Party happened, at least in its breathlessly fast-moving final phase, because of the last two portfolios she was given by the then leader of the Conservative Party, Edward Heath. The first of these portfolios made her responsible for the Conservatives' approach to local government and housing. The second pitched her into battles over economic policy. The first was at least as important as the second.

After the Conservatives' defeat in the February 1974 election, Heath appointed Thatcher, previously his diligent and loyal Education Secretary, to the seemingly humdrum post of shadow Environment Secretary. She irritated him, but no more than that, at this particular point in what had always been a cold relationship. Thatcher had acquired what appeared to be a dull remit, in the aftermath of one of the great dramatic elections of recent times. But it was this supposedly humdrum brief that gave her the opportunity to become the headline-grabbing populist Tory politician during turbulent times.

When she became shadow Environment Secretary she started working on a policy that she privately had some doubts about: the abolition of the rates system, the local property tax from which councils raised some of their revenue. Like most taxes, rates were unpopular and she began working on ways to abolish them, putting in characteristically long hours in order to come up with a striking proposal.

In August 1974, when most Conservative politicians were exhausted and on holiday after their traumatic period in power and the lost election in February, Thatcher held a press conference. Again, characteristically, she was not on holiday, preferring to focus on property taxes rather than lie on a beach. She now proposed that the next Conservative government would abolish rates. In the August news vacuum, she commanded the front pages with her plan. She attacked the likely rate increases and promised that, in the short term, a Conservative government would reduce them by spending more from the centre, while imposing 'efficiencies' on councils. With a flourish not altogether backed up by substance, Thatcher pledged to remove the property tax over time and replace it with one that reflected the ability to pay. This was a safely vague alternative, although it proved a convoluted proposition. She partly sought to address her wariness of central-government spending with a pledge to increase it, in order to keep local taxation under control. Her lengthy assertions in the summer of 1974 are worth reading in full, as they suggest that she could be a confused thinker at times:

The capacity of governments to spend has gone beyond the capacity of ratepayers to pay. The first essential therefore is to limit total public expenditure. This means looking at existing expenditure in terms of value for money and scrutinising any proposed increases. Stories of large staffs, high expenses payments to councillors and needless subsidies to those who can afford to pay for things themselves cause alarm and anger among ratepayers and taxpayers alike. In this situation some reassurance about next year's rate burden is needed... I believe that the least we can do for next year is to transfer to the exchequer the cost of teachers' salaries... Other expenditure such as that on the police or fire services could rank for increased grants in the same way as the last Conservative Government decided to put 90% of the cost of student grants on to the exchequer. It would be a condition of any such transfer that local authorities would not spend more in other directions. Otherwise the citizen as both taxpayer and ratepayer would be worse off than before the changes. In the long-term the system of local government finance must be changed so that it reflects the ability of people to pay.[2]

The contradictory messages – higher public spending while reining in public spending, insisting on the freedom of councils to make decisions while imposing new constraints – did her no harm at all. They were to do her much more harm when she returned to this theme towards the end of her career. In August 1974 she lit up the political sky, as far as bewildered Conservatives were concerned. Their internal polling suggested that most property owners welcomed help with their rates bills and paid little attention to the detail.

During August 1974, Thatcher was also the star of a party election broadcast, an important outlet when a second general election was moving into view. In the broadcast she hailed a property-owning democracy, including an expensive plan to subsidize mortgages. She also vaguely reiterated her plans to abolish the unpopular property tax. Then, during the October election, Thatcher was the star of another Conservative Party broadcast. The dry remit of shadow Environment Secretary was giving her the kind of peak-time TV exposure that her colleagues would have died for. She had not sought the glamorous slots, but even then she was a performer and discovered that she enjoyed performing.

At this early phase she was contemplating a replacement to the rates based on the ability to pay. When she revisited the policy in her 1987 manifesto, she was no longer bothered by the ability-to-pay principle, with fatal consequences. Soon after that triumphant 1987 election campaign her new plan to abolish the rates by replacing it with the poll tax would propel her towards her doom. But in the summer of 1974 Thatcher was heading for the top of her party, although she did not realize it at the time.

She was fortunate not to know. Potential leaders are placed at a considerable advantage when they do not recognize how close they are to the crown. Recognition leads to nervy, self-conscious ambition and a giddy excitement, a near-fatal combination. As we have seen, one of the persistent lessons of leadership is that most leaders-in-waiting do not become leaders. In the summer of 1974 neither Thatcher nor anyone else realized that she was in such an elevated position. She became a leader without being a leader-in-waiting, a major factor in her ascendancy.

A few weeks after Thatcher's hyperactive summer, Harold Wilson, once again prime minister, called a second election. It was to be held in October. Thatcher was the Conservative star of the contest. In another dark campaign, where politicians were battling it out over who could be least unpopular, there she was, self-confidently saying in effect, 'I can do something that a lot of you would like.' She had been a severe Education Secretary, famous for ending free school milk, but in this subdued autumnal election she had changed into an early Santa Claus, promising help with mortgages and the end of rates. Polls suggested her policies were popular. Desperate to win the election, or not lose it too heavily, Conservative strategists deployed Thatcher regularly on TV throughout the campaign. In her star appearance during the party election broadcast, she explained in safely broad terms her approach, and highlighted how she would help those facing big mortgage repayments – another set of proposals that she privately had doubts about. But she conveyed no doubts whatsoever in public. During this period of her career she learned the art of unswerving advocacy, whatever her private doubts. Suddenly the former Education Secretary of limited prominence became one of the great Tory media stars.

The timing of her rise was accidental, but a form of political perfection for a potential leader. Other factors outside her own direct control also played into her hands. After the October election and another defeat for the Conservatives, Heath unintentionally delivered for her again, by putting Thatcher in his shadow Treasury team. Growing in confidence as a public performer, she more than held her own in the House of Commons, even against the formidable Labour chancellor, Denis Healey. Conservative MPs took note. Thatcher was seen to be flourishing in the key area of economic policy-making, just as a significant number of Conservative MPs were beginning to decide they had endured Heath's leadership long enough. By then he had lost two elections in a year. In retrospect, the level of support for Heath was remarkable, given his record of election defeats, even if he was taken aback by the disloyalty of those who turned against him.

Heath, more than anyone else, gave Thatcher the chance to become leader of her party, by making her shadow Environment

Secretary first, and then giving her an economic brief. He never forgave her for succeeding him, but she was his inadvertent creation.

After the October 1974 election defeat, some Conservative MPs wondered whether the right-wing candidate in any leadership contest should be Sir Keith Joseph. Thatcher and Joseph were close ideologically, while being incomparably different political personalities. Joseph agonized almost visibly as he moved from being a hyperactive Housing Minister under Harold Macmillan, and a relatively high-spending Social Services Secretary in Heath's Cabinet, to becoming an advocate of free-market conservatism and monetarism after the party's election defeat in February 1974. Thatcher endured no equivalent ideological stress. Joseph was a deeper thinker, but a much poorer communicator and without a populist bone in his political body. Thatcher adored him and assumed that he would stand in a leadership contest, if one were held. This genuine assumption helped her enormously. While few perceived her as a leader-in-waiting, she was content to focus on Joseph as leader of the Tory right.

However, during the latter part of 1974 Joseph lost credibility as a potential leader, with a series of controversial speeches that highlighted his distinct unsuitability for leadership. In one speech he suggested that poor people should stop having so many children, an argument that at the very least conveyed a lack of sensitivity when framing a case. Joseph had poor judgement. He had a thousand ideas before breakfast, but in expressing them he alarmed significant sections of the electorate and the media. He was a deep-thinking intellectual, but a political innocent. In contrast, Thatcher was highly political and not as deep-thinking – a more convenient combination for modern leadership. Already she was learning to frame radical policies in ways that had a populist appeal. She was as ideological as Joseph, but the difference was that she was a natural communicator and most of the time knew how far she could go in her public declarations. Joseph was an awkward conveyer of ideas, and possessed no safety valve to prevent avoidable controversy. Neither Joseph nor Thatcher had a great interest in the media at this point, but Thatcher had an instinctive sense of how to use newspapers and broadcasters. There were occasions when Joseph gave interviews to broadcasters when he had no idea whether they were live or recorded, or quite what the distinction might imply.

Painfully self-aware, Joseph did not try very hard to build support for a challenge to the leadership. He knew his cause was doomed. Thatcher was the obvious alternative candidate on the right. Her prominence just when a leadership contest seemed inevitable was an early example of her luck as a potential leader. She was to become a lucky leader, too.

She was fortunate in that the leadership contest was perfectly timed for her and she didn't look self-serving. She had been carrying out her duties as a middle-ranking shadow Cabinet member rather than scheming for the top job. Thatcher had nothing to be transparent about; she was not calculating her moves towards the leadership until close to her battle with Heath in early 1975. By then a lot of Tory MPs ached for a contest. Thatcher would be the right-wing candidate, even though she hadn't displayed a great deal of ideological verve, or a sense of intense personal ambition. She had been solidly loyal to Heath as he battled with the unions and conducted various policy U-turns. She had got on with her job at Education without ranging very much further, publicly or privately. To Heath's fuming surprise, she challenged him early in 1975.

A combination of her starring role from February 1974, including her headline-grabbing policy to abolish the rates – a proposition that she never forgot – and the implosion of Joseph's leadership bid meant that she became a candidate in the contest held in February 1975. The contest was both intimidating and relatively undemanding. For her, the context was close to political bliss. Heath had lost three elections and was a curmudgeonly and awkward campaigner, unable to hide his dismay at being challenged by this annoying woman with strident right-wing views, whom he had tolerated on his frontbench.

But on another level, Thatcher was taking on the party's establishment, and with little time to prepare for the psychological challenge of a contest. Most of the Tory heavyweights backed Heath in the contest. They included those figures perceived to have wider appeal in the country, such as the popular and emollient Willie Whitelaw, who had been under pressure to stand himself, but was too loyal to Heath to contemplate such an act of insurrection.[3] Others who backed Heath were his shadow chancellor, Robert Carr; Lord Carrington, who was to become Thatcher's Foreign Secretary; and James Prior, Thatcher's first Employment Secretary. Their support for Heath showed the degree to which she was the insurrectionary candidate, and her willingness, once leader, to work with them.

'One nation' Tories, those regarded as moderate pragmatists, gathered around Heath not only out of loyalty, but because they were part of an ideological battle, even if the divisions were only vaguely defined. Thatcher was campaigning from the right, but largely with a series of clichés about rewarding hard work. She was filmed for ITV's *World in Action* washing up at home, before dashing off for a meeting – a woman of action. In other interviews she conveyed a restless energy, but was sharp enough not to be too clearly defined. After Thatcher won the contest, the *Guardian*'s columnist Peter Jenkins suggested that we knew little about the Conservatives' new leader, despite the fact that she had dominated the media. It had been 'Thatcherated', as he wrote the day after she was elected. He added that in spite of Thatcher's ubiquity, little was known about the direction in which she would lead the party.[4]

Heath knew more than Jenkins seemed to do. After he was defeated in the first ballot of the contest he looked up at his adviser, William Waldegrave, and declared, 'It has all gone wrong then.' In his memoir, Waldegrave suggests that the outgoing leader was referring to the end of 'one nation' conservatism as well as his own career. If Heath was indeed looking beyond the death of his career, he was prophetic. 'He realised that his defeat meant that a sea change was coming over the British right.'[5]

Whitelaw entered the second round of the contest, but by then Thatcher had momentum, benefiting with good cause from launching a challenge in the first place. In this contest, and for many years to come, Thatcher was smart at making the most of perceived momentum. She often appeared as if she was being thrust forward unstoppably by a gust of wind, almost as if resistance was pointless.

Even so, in the immediate aftermath of her leadership victory, she did not stride on indiscriminately. Instead she displayed one of her more overlooked qualities as a leader. In the early years of her leadership Thatcher recognized that the amount of space available to her on the political stage was extremely limited. She might have appeared strident, but in policy terms and in her use of patronage as party leader, she moved cautiously, knowing she had no choice but to do so.

Her genius was to know when she had more space to act. She was politically agile. This was her wiliness, an essential part of leadership. At the beginning she wisely appointed most of Heath's allies to senior posts. She knew this was not the time to make ideological appointments. Thatcher might have won the contest, but her relative inexperience and the range of internal doubters made her fragile, and she knew it. She was disinclined to spend time on introspective reflection, a major flaw, and yet she sensed how far she could go without needing to calculate for too long.

Thatcher made Willie Whitelaw her deputy. Whitelaw proved to be loyal, but occasionally candid. Arguably he was too loyal at times, wary of challenging her unless he had no choice but to do so. She was not to know this when she appointed him to the second most senior post in the party. With his authority and experience, Whitelaw might have made life difficult for her.

Those she later dismissed as 'wets' – Jim Prior, Peter Walker and Ian Gilmour – were also appointed to senior positions in her shadow Cabinet and first government. Norman St John-Stevas, a mischievous observer of Thatcher's rise, was also given a post, even though Thatcher had no time for mischief or humour. This was not because she had no sense of fun. Contrary to the mythology, she could sometimes fleetingly see the funny side of situations, but she had no tolerance of humour deployed against her and no understanding of topical comedy references. Indeed, her populism did not extend to an affected attachment to popular TV culture or sport, a big difference with some of her successors and predecessors.

Even if she did not pretend to follow sport or fashionable TV, beyond the glorious satire *Yes Minister*, Thatcher was one of the great political actors and relished politics as performance, in contrast to the UK's second female prime minister, Theresa May. Thatcher also gave the impression of unyielding purpose. From February 1975 to the election in May 1979, her leadership was a model of how to move a party towards a more radical position without fatally alienating its more cautious wing. Her dance with colleagues in the early years was a delicate one, compared with the more punk routine a few years later, when she knew she had the space to let her hair down.

Part of the fascination is that Thatcher kept her internal critics more or less at bay without being tonally emollient, or especially cautious, in the expression of her ideological verve. Her correspondence with colleagues in the late 1970s, chronicled illuminatingly on the Thatcher Foundation website, is full of exclamation marks and written shrieks of assertive disapproval. One such document on the website is the draft 1979 manifesto, with Thatcher's scribbled handwriting on every paragraph proposing, from her perspective, smart revisions. There are exclamation marks and question marks as paragraphs are underlined by her. She was a natural sub-editor. Her proposed revisions made the final version in 1979 far more accessible.

In interviews she made clear that she would not have time for long Cabinet discussions on policy if she won the election. She gave a long interview to the *Observer*'s Kenneth Harris a few months before the 1979 election, in which she conveyed unqualified intolerance towards internal dissent: 'As Prime Minister I couldn't waste time having any internal arguments. My Cabinet would have to be a conviction government.'[6]

Indeed, after her election as leader in 1975 she had an insatiable appetite for discussing why she had reached her unyielding convictions – a hunger that was novel in British politics. Most leaders of the Opposition, especially those with limited experience, avoid reflecting on their ideological beliefs, if they happen to have any. They prefer to deploy banal terms such as 'modernization' and the 'radical centre' in their search for wide electoral support. As part of their cautious strategy they avoid challenging interviews. In striking contrast, Thatcher sought to meet her hunger for debating ideas almost immediately after becoming leader of the Opposition.

From the time when she became leader of the Conservative Party in 1975 to her election as prime minister in 1979, Thatcher never shied away from formidable TV interrogators, both in the UK and the US. One of her favourite US programmes was *Firing Line*, an hour-long interview with the right-wing radical William Buckley. She appeared on his show on several occasions as leader of the Opposition. Buckley shared many of her convictions, but that made him in some respects a tougher interviewer. He was steeped in the work of F. A. Hayek and many other philosophers that the Republican right was turning towards. He could be scathing to interviewees on the right. But Thatcher could not get enough of his programme, even though her appearances, broadcast only in the US, were of limited value to a domestic audience in an era when they would not be seen on YouTube or highlighted by fans or critics on Twitter. She appeared on his shows because she relished the discussions. In her first appearance on *Firing Line* she framed arguments around opportunity: 'I regard opportunity as the chance to be unequal as well as the chance to be equal.'[7] Later in the same interview she declared sweepingly, 'Property is freedom.'[8]

Such assertions raise a multitude of questions. What is the role of the state in addressing inequality for those who have limited opportunities? What does Thatcher mean by 'opportunity', given that inequality of opportunity is deeply entrenched? Does she accept that she had more 'opportunities', as the wife of a millionaire? Why is property necessarily an agent of freedom? What precisely does she mean by 'freedom'?

And on we could go. But the assertions, when repeated to UK audiences on TV and other platforms, had a wide and accessible appeal. It is not easy to argue that voters should not own properties or should not be 'free'. In 1979 Labour tried to challenge some of her ideas by opposing the sale of council homes. It lost the election. Who can be against 'opportunity' and yet win the argument? The challenge for Thatcher's opponents was to frame the debate in a different way, showing how the state can be an agent of freedom and opportunity. They failed to do so confidently and effectively, although Labour's deputy leader after 1983, Roy Hattersley, made the best attempt. His book outlining Labour's ideas and values was called *Choose Freedom*, a title that purloined from Thatcher two of her favourite words. But Hattersley made little impact when his book was published in the late 1980s. He was too late. By the late 1970s Thatcher was framing arguments that moved the tides rightwards. The policies would follow, but first she made the arguments. Labour had given her the space to do so, by failing to come up with a coherent and accessible left-of-centre alternative. There was a powerful left-of-centre critique to be made that might have challenged

Thatcherism in the late 1970s and beyond, but the left split in many different ways, whereas over time much of the Conservative Party coalesced around Thatcher.

As Opposition leader, Thatcher was also fearless in facing interrogations in the UK. In July 1977 she appeared on BBC1's *Panorama*, then a more nuanced and weighty programme. For nearly an hour Thatcher was interviewed by the broadcaster David Dimbleby and three of the more formidable columnists from that era, Peter Jenkins, Anthony Shrimsley and Mary Goldring. This was in the era when there were only a handful of political columnists, each of them influential. Thatcher more than held her own, although the BBC helped by giving the programme the flattering title of *The Alternative Prime Minister*. Once again she was blunt in her ideological arguments, unswervingly self-confident, but again less specific in terms of policy. At one point she was asked, 'Are you a pragmatist?' She replied astutely and revealingly: 'I'm a pragmatist in the true sense of the word… putting your principles into practice.'

In seeking definition, another of the interviewers asked her, 'Are you right-wing?' Without hesitating, Thatcher made the term one that could have wide electoral appeal: 'Define what you mean by right-wing… you can't look after hard-working people unless you create enough wealth to do so… My views don't differ very much from Iain Macleod [Heath's short-serving chancellor, who died of a heart attack and was widely seen as having been much closer to Heath's politics than to Thatcher's] … If you want lower taxes it's called right-wing… If you support the police it's called right-wing… If you want to sell council homes it's called right-wing… If you want to uphold standards in education it's called right-wing… If you call that right-wing, I'm right-wing.'

She went on to argue that the 'whole philosophy of the Conservative Party revolves around the freedom of the individual... a belief in the sanctity of the individual'.

Any individual voter watching the interview might well like the idea of being sanctified, but in order for a country to be governed effectively there needs to be powerful and efficient mediating agencies. Thatcher was less interested in the binding forces and much more enthused about 'liberating' individuals from what she, and quite a lot of voters, regarded as the stifling state. Her focus was potent. For voters, it is more flattering to hear that the alternative prime minister valued them, above all, as individuals. The state would get off their backs and allow them to flourish. At this stage, because Thatcher framed arguments that were accompanied by relatively vague policies, Peter Jenkins asked her whether her heart was on the right, but her head was on the centre. Her response was unequivocal: 'I'm in politics to say and do what I believe... I do believe in things passionately [and] I have to compromise... but I'm not an eternal compromiser.'[9]

Many years later, some of Ed Miliband's closest advisers suggested that he 'do a Thatcher' and take part in a series of tough interviews in which he posed radical arguments. Miliband liked to think of himself as Labour's Margaret Thatcher. But he was too fearful of the intimidating TV interview, and too constrained by his New Labour upbringing, to be her equivalent from the left. Her equivalent from the left was Tony Benn in the 1970s and 1980s and, to some extent, Jeremy Corbyn when he succeeded Miliband in 2015. But unlike Thatcher, Corbyn was wary of the long interview with sceptical interviewers. He hardly ever took part in interviews. Thatcher relished them.

But in one important respect she was playing safe in her radical assertiveness. Once again, almost instinctively, she could sense what would work for her electorally. The wider political context of the late 1970s was the key to making electoral sense of her early ideological declarations and her assertive leadership style.

As prime minister, Jim Callaghan chaired seemingly never-ending Cabinet meetings before heading off to struggle through equally interminable gatherings of Labour's National Executive Committee, so Thatcher's insistence that she would not tolerate much Cabinet dissent seemed compelling, in contrast to the seemingly weak prime minister. Part of Thatcher's risky ideological relish was therefore utterly expedient; there were immediate advantages for her in claiming to be ideologically self-confident when her main opponent appeared to be bewildered by seismic events. In effect, she was implying 'I am strong. Callaghan is weak' – not a vote-losing pitch in British politics.

She was also championing the individual, when corporatism was in obvious and vivid crisis. It was not especially daring to talk about the need to set individuals free when the state was failing so vividly. She had both eyes on the wider political situation, even though she seemed to be gripped by ideological verve. Crucially, she knew this verve placed her in a flattering light compared with her troubled, traumatized political opponent, a prime minister facing economic crises and industrial unrest in a hung parliament and with a divided Cabinet. Here was an early example of Thatcher sensing how much space she had on the political stage and using it to teach a political lesson, in the coming together of her two distinct skills. She could perform with a degree of crusading zeal partly because she was a performer with convictions, but also because the troubles of Callaghan meant that it was in her interests to convey 'strong leadership'.

In the early years there was a constant interplay between her two leadership skills. She was a teacher, making accessible sense of what she was up to. Often she appeared politically daring, when she had calculated instinctively that what she was saying would win or sustain support. She knew how to win elections.

Her manifesto in 1979 reflected her distinct convictions and her capacity for expediency. Her personal introduction displayed her populism and her essential vision: that the state stifled the freedom of the 'people'. One of her favourite words was 'people':

For me, the heart of politics is not political theory, it is people and how they want to live their lives. No one who has lived in this country during the last five years can fail to be aware of how the balance of our society has been increasingly tilted in favour of the State at the expense of individual freedom... The State takes too much of the nation's income; its share must be steadily reduced. When it spends and borrows too much, taxes, interest rates, prices and unemployment rise so that in the long run there is less wealth with which to improve our standard of living and our social services.[10]

Her introduction to the 1979 manifesto showed how effectively Thatcher could frame an argument, even a highly contentious one. Most 'people' like the idea of deciding how they want to live their own lives, even if the aspiration is ridiculously simplistic. A left-of-centre politician might have replied that it is only through the state that 'people' can fulfil their potential. This was part of Roy Hattersley's case, as he sought to make an ideological narrative to counter hers, but his arguments got lost in Labour's internal battles.

The Labour leader, Neil Kinnock, also got close to challenging Thatcher's small-state populism when he spoke of the case for an 'enabling state' in his party conference speech in 1985. This was an attempt to show what the state could do, in contrast to Thatcher's caricature of 'the state versus the people'. But this was the speech during which Kinnock launched his famous onslaught against Militant Tendency, the left-wing group described widely and vaguely as 'Trotskyist', which had infiltrated parts of the Labour Party. Kinnock singled out the Militant Tendency leadership of Liverpool council, accusing them of hiring taxis to hand out redundancy notices. The highly theatrical confrontation of Militant Tendency was a pivotal moment in Kinnock's leadership and was widely regarded as one of the great speeches in British politics from the second half of the twentieth century. But as a result of his challenge to Militant Tendency, few noticed his well-argued case for the state as an enabler – an alternative route to Thatcherism. From the late 1970s until the end of her leadership, Thatcher had the space for her ideological populism. She used it ceaselessly. Her ideas and her skill to communicate them were her main political weapons.

Her words in the 1979 manifesto formed the essence of early Thatcherism: let the people be free from the burdens of the state. She pledged to 'restore the balance of power in favour of the people'. Which 'people' would be opposed to giving them 'power' – a conveniently ill-defined term from the great political teacher? In contrast to her desire to liberate the 'people', Labour would 'enlarge the role of the state and diminish the role of the individual'. Again, which individual seeks to be diminished? But Thatcher chose not to recognize that the state could enhance the lives of individuals. Such recognition would challenge her entire crusade.

In terms of policy, the 1979 manifesto was more cautious. The teacher carefully selected policies to illustrate her anti-state lessons. There would be a switch – 'to some extent' – from taxes on earnings to taxes on spending. Despite her exhalations about the virtues of low taxation, there was little detail on this. There needed to be 'responsible pay bargaining' – evasive words partly applied to bind together her shadow Cabinet, which had split over the need for incomes policies. The promise to allow tenants to buy their council homes was the most radical policy, but in setting some tenants 'free', there was no reflection as to what impact it would have on affordable housing in the UK.

Privately Thatcher was opposed to incomes policies, but she equivocated over her attitude in public and at the election. She was a firm opponent of devolution, but her 1979 manifesto promised to review the options. When she won in 1979, she clearly wanted to take her country to the right and she hoped to take on the miners at some point, partly in order to purge memories of the nightmares of the Heath government. She wanted to clamp down on public-sector pay as part of a wider attempt to cut public spending, or to cut the rate of growth in public spending.

But after 1979, with many senior colleagues viewing her warily in spite of her authority-enhancing election victory, she recognized that she had limited space to follow some of her radical instincts. She was not strong enough in the Conservative Party, and, arguably, was not strong enough in the country, to push the boundaries too far. Once again, she knew instinctively how far she could go.

When the miners flexed their muscles early in her first term in power, when she was already deeply unpopular in the polls, Thatcher gave in. She did not believe she was strong enough to win. Similarly, she was cautious on public-sector pay. She tended to give the pay awards that were due without any challenge, even though she wanted to constrain public spending.

But when she sensed space on the political stage was finally opening up for her, she moved at the speed of light. There is a much-repeated myth that after the victory in the Falklands in 1982, Thatcher became almost invincible. Contrary to this widely held view, the Falklands War was not what gave her political space on the stage. Her military victory undoubtedly changed her as a public performer: she became more regal, self-confident and assertively strident. She started to refer more often to Churchill as 'Winston', implying that the two of them were the great war leaders of our times. She saw herself, as much of the media did, as a formidable, courageous leader in the light of the war. But the war was not what propelled her to a landslide victory at the following election.

The key development that guaranteed her future election victories had already taken place by the time of the Falklands. In relation to that easily mythologized conflict, there is a misleading tendency to view her actions through the distorting prism of 'courage' or its opposite lens, 'weakness'.

In reality, Thatcher had no choice but to go to war. Her decision to do so was not 'strong' or 'weak'. The only alternative to a military response would have been her resignation as prime minister. In the immediate aftermath of the invasion by forces of the Argentinian junta in April 1982, the House of Commons met, unusually, the following Saturday. During that extraordinary historic gathering, even the Labour leader, Michael Foot – a unilateralist who sought the removal of nuclear weapons in the UK – demanded a robust military response. Foot's speech was widely praised by Conservative MPs. One of the MPs Thatcher admired most, Enoch Powell, who was by then representing the Unionist Party, implied that she would have to resign if there was no military response. He ended his speech with a challenge in relation to the pride she took in being known as the 'Iron Lady':

The Prime Minister, shortly after she came into office, received a soubriquet as the 'Iron Lady'. It arose in the context of remarks which she made about defence against the Soviet Union and its allies; but there was no reason to suppose that the right hon. Lady did not welcome and, indeed, take pride in that description. In the next week or two this House, the nation and the right hon. Lady herself will learn of what metal she is made.[11]

Whether right or wrong from Thatcher's perspective, the politically brave decision would have been to let Argentina keep the Falklands. Margaret Thatcher's decision to take on the junta and go to war was not an act of bravery. No leader is ever fully prepared for taking a country into war, and to do so demands steeliness, but for Thatcher going to war was the politically safe option. As an Iron Lady, she had to show her mettle if she wished to survive.

There were many consequences arising from her victory. The subsequent inquiry into the war, the Franks Report of 1983, was highly critical of government policy towards the Falklands in the months preceding the Argentinian invasion. But few voters noticed. Thatcher had won. That was all that mattered, as far as they were concerned. Shortly after the Falklands War, a young Tony Blair was the Labour candidate in a by-election for the safe Conservative seat of Beaconsfield. Blair noted how commanding Thatcher had become, in the eyes of voters, as a result of the war, and that victory wiped out any questions about her culpability in advance of the war. Later, when Blair made his moves towards Iraq, his former Foreign Secretary, Robin Cook, an opponent of the Iraq War, was convinced that Blair's first electoral test in the immediate aftermath of the Falklands conflict played its part in his mindset. Thatcher's Falklands victory seemed to suggest that, in the UK, wars were popular and enhanced the authority of a prime minister. What was said and done before the war was soon forgotten, if a tyrant was toppled. One of Blair's many calculations as he moved towards Iraq was that a similar sequence might apply. There was much talk after 1982 of the 'Falklands Factor'. After the fall of Saddam Hussein, Blair's Downing Street spoke with naive optimism about a 'Baghdad Bounce' – a deliberate echo.

But the Falklands War was not what gave Thatcher wider political space to move her government and the country rightwards. This was due to the split in the Labour Party. The formal schism in the Labour Party, which began to take shape in 1980 when Michael Foot was elected leader, and was formalized in 1981 with the creation of the SDP, meant there was one near-certainty in the wildly unpredictable world of politics: only the Conservative Party could win the next election. If the left-wing alternative was split in two, the non-Conservative parties would inevitably cancel each other out. There was a brief phase during the SDP's honeymoon when it looked as if the new party might sweep the country, such was the excitement generated by charismatic former Labour figures leading a new party. But the SDP was never going to defeat Labour in parts of Scotland and the north of England. Conversely, Labour was more threatened by the SDP than the Conservatives were. The SDP had been formed against Labour, and largely defined itself against Labour as a centrist party. The historic schism, rare in British politics, meant that Margaret Thatcher had the good fortune to face a split Opposition. The formation of the SDP was another example of her luck as a leader. In terms of securing her future as prime minister, it was far more significant than the Falklands.

When the schism within Labour was formalized, Thatcher started to make her more radical moves. In September 1981 she purged her Cabinet of her despised 'wets', sacking some of them and moving Jim Prior to Northern Ireland, which was in some ways a more severe punishment. She brought in Norman Tebbit to become her new Employment Secretary, replacing Prior, and a few other like-minded allies and started to become more daring, because she knew she could win the next election when facing a divided Opposition. The key reshuffle took place six months before the Falklands War.

Similarly, in the second term, having won a landslide in 1983, she became more willing to take risks because she saw that she had even more political space. For a radical prime minister, landslides are liberating. There was no internal opposition by then. She had purged her Cabinet of severe critics. The new Labour leader, Neil Kinnock, was inexperienced and faced mountainous internal challenges, while the formidable David Owen, as leader of the SDP, was more anti-Labour than anti-Thatcher at this stage in his topsy-turvy political career.[12] Seeing that her opponents were still fatally split, Thatcher knew she could make her next moves. With detailed policies relating to privatization, income-tax cuts for high earners, light regulation for the financial sector, and the defeat of the miners, Thatcherism took shape when she sensed – rightly – that she could take the risks. In policy terms, her programme from 1983 was closer to what she meant when talking about setting the people 'free' in the mid- to late 1970s.

———

In the UK, political leaders and journalists were to become overly obsessed with the benefits of 'spin' and the need for 'spin doctors', or media advisers, to guide leaders through the wild storms. But effective leaders need no guidance. Thatcher was her own spin doctor.

She was an instinctive communicator. You could agree or disagree with what she was saying, and many of her messages were banal or economically nonsensical, but they made sense of complicated, dry economic policies. She gave a running commentary on monetarism and other policies, without an Alastair Campbell figure or a Peter Mandelson to spin it for her. She had media instructors to tell her how to speak on TV, but she did not need them. Indeed, she seemed over-rehearsed after sessions with them, sometimes absurdly so. To take one example, in the late 1970s Thatcher hired a voice-coach and, following the sessions, her voice became noticeably low. Thatcher was a good political actress, but the change was too noticeable and clunky. The clunkiness was equally evident when she read out jokes written by someone else, attempts at wit that she did not fully understand. She was most effective as a performer when following her own instincts.

Her press secretary, Bernard Ingham, was devoted to Thatcher and dealt with the media. But Ingham was a civil servant and not as overtly committed as some of his successors. Of course she benefited from a largely doting set of newspapers, another significant weapon in her political armoury. Nonetheless, she spoke about politics with a partisan accessibility. During the late 1970s, in trying to explain her growing support for monetarism, she told voters that her father, who had owned a grocer's shop in Grantham, never spent more than he earned. She argued that, like her father, a country should never spend more than it earned. She was being simplistic to the point of economic illiteracy – the state is starkly different from a grocer's shop – but the lessons from her youth were powerful ways of conveying what she was trying to do, and her opponents never discovered an alternative language. Her messages were easy to understand and they appeared to make sense of what might have been more widely perceived as draconian, radical economic policies.

While she was making sense of highly complex and contentious economic policies Thatcher was building up an important and, at that point, constructive relationship with her shadow chancellor, Geoffrey Howe. In some respects Howe was as pivotal to the economic revolution as she was, and arguably even more so. That was certainly Howe's own view, even though much of the time he was a decent, modest and tolerant political figure. Thatcher found him deeply irritating, partly because of his reticent qualities, but she could not have done without him.

Howe had written his first budget before he arrived at the Treasury in 1979 and already had a good idea what his second budget would be. As Howe's colleague and ideological critic, Ian Gilmour, was to argue brilliantly in his book *Dancing with Dogma*, written after he was sacked as a Cabinet minister, some of the government's early economic policies had catastrophic consequences and were wholly counter-productive, making worse the matters they were seeking to address. To take one example, some of the early policies fuelled inflation, when Thatcher and Howe regarded inflation as one of their overwhelming challenges. But in terms of leadership, Thatcher and Howe were a model. She was the wilful communicator and he was the dutiful policy-maker. When Gordon Brown and Ed Balls planned their move to the Treasury in 1997, their model in terms of readiness for power was Howe. Brown had almost written his first budget in advance and was ready with his plan to make the Bank of England independent.[13]

Long after Thatcher had watered down her own and Howe's monetarist policies – while insisting the lady was not for turning – she continued to be a political teacher. 'We're giving industries to the people' was her explanation for privatization.[14] She was always trying to make sense of what she was doing. Tony Benn, who was in this respect her equivalent in the Labour Party, noted regularly in his diaries that Thatcher was a teacher. Although they disagreed with each other profoundly, he saw this as one of her great strengths. Benn was one of the few senior Labour politicians who recognized from the beginning that Thatcher would be formidable. Towards the end of her career, Thatcher became in turn an admirer of Benn's, turning up in the Commons to listen to his speeches on Europe and nodding passionately. Benn was a political teacher, too.[15]

The two lessons of Thatcher's leadership place her in a formidable light. She was the teacher who made sense of contentious policies, and a reader of the rhythms of politics, knowing when, as a leader with radical ambitions, she could act and when she needed to be more restrained. Both explain her longevity.

The third overlooked lesson about Margaret Thatcher's leadership is based partly on retrospective criticisms. These come as much from her former colleagues in their memoirs as from her opponents. The critics extend well beyond Gilmour, in some respects. As she pursued radical policies, sometimes with apparent success, she was often indifferent to addressing the consequences of the changes, the hardest element of policy-making. There is the glamour of introducing a policy and being hailed as a change-maker. Then there is the hard grind of making sure there are no unintended consequences. For a workaholic, Thatcher was uninterested in the hard grind of following up policies, or perhaps she was too impatient to reflect on the follow-ups that would be required. Her lack of forensic curiosity was part of Gilmour's much wider critique, but it is also a failing that was noted by other former colleagues who were less critical.

The sale of council houses, a policy from Thatcher's 1979 manifesto, was an early example of the radical dash towards implementation followed by a restless moving on. Here was an innovation that transformed not only housing in Britain, but electoral politics in general. Suddenly some tenants became house owners and they moved into the market at a point when property was booming in parts of the UK. Tenants who took the opportunity to sell in a booming private market became quite well off as a result. Some of them sold their council houses and voted for Thatcher gratefully. The prime minister was famously photographed visiting appreciative tenants who were now owners, and having cups of tea with them. She enjoyed the cups of tea and the potent symbolism of gatherings with traditional Labour voters. After the visits she showed little further interest. She overlooked what should follow on from such a dramatic reform.

After the council houses were sold off, her governments made no attempt to rebuild affordable housing on the scale required. As a result there has been a housing crisis ever since, a chronic shortage of affordable rented accommodation in particular. The shortage had several consequences, from rising homelessness to soaring housing benefit bills, as the state paid for those who could not find rented accommodation in the public sector to stay in expensive private accommodation.

Thatcher's sale of council properties – the policy that Labour later supported and accepted it was wrong to oppose in the first place – had no follow-through. Instead, she and her favourite Cabinet ministers became obsessed with new forms of ownership. After the 1987 election her Environment Secretary and close ally, Nicholas Ridley, announced a 'housing revolution'. His proposals included new quangos known as Housing Action Trusts, taking over rundown estates; and, separately, private landlords acquiring new rights to buy and rent council homes. It was a housing revolution without any new houses. The left had been gripped by the ideology of ownership in the 1970s and early 1980s, favouring more public ownership. Thatcher and Ridley, whom she greatly admired, were equally ideological from the right, in some ways even more fascinated by questions of ownership. For them, private ownership was the solution. They were not especially interested in constructing new affordable homes, how they should be built and by whom. These were tough and demanding questions. Thatcher did not even ask them, let alone answer them. She did not think policies through beyond their immediate impact. By the late 1980s young people were struggling to rent or buy, especially in cities where property prices were soaring.

The same sequence applied to the defeat of the miners in 1985, a victory for Thatcher that marked the end of the era that had partly defined her. She had been brought up politically with muscular unions wreaking havoc under Heath, Wilson and Callaghan in the 1970s. With a landslide parliament, stockpiles of coal and the NUM leader, Arthur Scargill, lacking the guile to compromise, Thatcher secured a different answer from Heath, who had posed the question 'Who governs Britain?' in the February 1974 election. Heath lost. Thatcher governed, and defeated the miners with a brutal ruthlessness.

Scargill might have lacked guile – to the fury of the tormented Labour leader, Neil Kinnock – but the cause of the conflict was, and remains, nuanced.[16] The government argued that 'uneconomic pits' should close. Scargill refused to accept that the pits were uneconomic. He had a stronger case than he managed to make with his inflammatory, confrontational style. He was a fierce and angry orator but, unlike Thatcher, he was not an effective political teacher, even when he had a strong case. Declaiming with little tonal variation, Scargill argued that the price of imported energy was bound to fluctuate and, because of this, there were huge risks in closing pits that could still produce home-grown energy. But Thatcher, the political teacher, won wider electoral support with her portrayal of striking miners acting recklessly and unpatriotically. At one point, with a reference to the Falklands War, she provocatively described the miners who had been on strike as 'the enemy within'.

As several members of her Cabinet have written since, her government made little attempt to rebuild the communities that had been dependent on mining. Cash-strapped local authorities were in no position to do very much, either. As a result, once-vibrant communities became hollowed out. There should have been a follow-through, when all those jobs were lost and there was very little to replace them. But once again Thatcher had lost interest and moved on to other areas.

Norman Tebbit was one of her colleagues who made this point in his memoirs, going beyond his caricature, as he sometimes did, to argue that her government should have intervened more to revive suddenly desolate towns and villages.[17] Tebbit was seen widely as a political thug. Michael Foot once described him as a 'semi house-trained polecat'. But he could be more thoughtful and friendly to political opponents than Thatcher was. Thatcher's more unyielding ideology precluded an interventionist approach. Her limited attention span was a factor, too.

In his memoir, Geoffrey Howe was especially critical of Thatcher's decision to abolish the Greater London Council (GLC) and the other big metropolitan authorities in England, without replacing them. Thatcher's argument was that there were too many tiers of government in England. Instead of deciding what the appropriate tiers might be, she rushed to abolish the metropolitan authorities, all of which happened to be Labour-led. She felt especially provoked by the GLC, which was headed in its final phase by Ken Livingstone, at his peak a much subtler left-wing leader than Arthur Scargill. Polls suggested that Livingstone was popular in London, in spite of the usual indiscriminate media-bashing that he received. Unusually for Thatcher, instead of attempting to beat him in an ideological battle, she abolished him, or at least his power base. But as usual there was no follow-through. In effect, she nationalized parts of London's services previously run by the GLC. Vaguely accountable quangos became responsible for running an increasingly dysfunctional transport system. The capital had no leadership and no one accountable for what was happening. The political teacher, who talked about the stifling state and giving power to the people, gave more power to the state by scrapping metropolitan councils, and left people in the big cities utterly powerless in the face of declining public services. She never understood that democratically accountable mediating agencies can empower users of public services. She had got rid of a tier of government and then largely lost interest in the consequences. Always in a hurry, she moved on yet again.

So it was with her radical economic policies. Many of them were regarded as successful. The Big Bang in 1986 – the new, light regulatory touch in relation to the City – generated great wealth for individuals and much additional revenue for the government, as London became a global financial centre. But sweeping deregulation also created an environment in which there was little control. Governments ceased to seek greater regulation, or didn't dare make the case for it. In the 1980s the seeds were sown for the financial crash that followed in 2008.

For someone who could immerse herself in policy detail if she wanted to, Thatcher could become quickly indifferent. Strong leaders must address the consequence of their reforms or the chickens will come home to roost. Some of Thatcher's roosting chickens included an acute shortage of affordable housing; widening inequality, with some communities being more or less wiped out while those in the financial sector earned a fortune; and poorly led cities with haphazard and badly run services. These were avoidable consequences of significant reforms. They were not inevitable. If she had paid more attention as to what happened next in relation to her restless radicalism, the consequences would have been nowhere near as significant.

In 2018 Michael Heseltine neatly summarized Thatcher's contradictory nature, as the shallow thinker who was capable of deeper analysis:

> If you went to cabinet with a paper that was your responsibility before you got three sentences out she would be haranguing you and yet deep down she hated people who gave in to her. She had a respect for those that did not give in. So you would wait until she drew breath and start again. You would say 'I've heard what you said but this was the point... if I may continue...' There were two Margaret Thatchers. There was the Margaret Thatcher with lots of shallow instincts and personal experiences... She would talk about a policy or idea based on a farmer she met or what tenants she met did with their council house... and this wasn't intellectually appealing... There was another Margaret Thatcher where you would seek to change a discussion from her gut instincts to more of an intellectual dialogue... then you could persuade her.[18]

Towards the end of her leadership, Europe came to dominate, with Heseltine hovering on the backbenches as a passionate pro-

European. Thatcher was the first Conservative prime minister partly to fall over Europe, but she was by no means the last. Her three immediate successors as Conservative prime minister, John Major, David Cameron and Theresa May, also fell as a result of Europe. The third successor, Theresa May, led a government in which the issue of Europe overwhelmed all others.

Over Europe and much more, Thatcher had transformed her party into one with a much more radical cutting edge. The dance between leader and party can be tense and jagged. The one between Thatcher and her party was neat and symmetrical. The Conservative Party became much more Thatcherite. She personified the changes in her own party. As part of the change, she moved the Conservatives towards a more Eurosceptic position and became, in the end, the first prime ministerial victim of that move.

In tone she was increasingly hostile to Europe, although rarely in practice. She was, after all, a great advocate of the 1986 Single European Act and of the single market that was its consequence. It was she who signed the UK up to every single treaty during her period as prime minister. But she viewed with alarm the moves towards the integrationist Maastricht Treaty. She had left power by the time her successor, John Major, signed the Treaty with several big opt-outs for the UK, but her influence lingered: she actively encouraged backbenchers to vote against Maastricht, in spite of Major's significant efforts to extract substantial concessions in difficult negotiations.

Yet to her credit, while prime minister, Thatcher was happy enough to appoint senior Cabinet ministers who took a very different position from her in what became a highly charged and emotive policy area for the Conservative Party. Her senior ministers tended to be pro-Europeans: Ken Clarke, Douglas Hurd, Geoffrey

Howe, Michael Heseltine. Her political generosity contributed to her fall. These Cabinet ministers, or former Cabinet ministers, were growing increasingly alarmed by Thatcher's tendency to be shrill at European Union gatherings and to display hostility towards the EU in the House of Commons. Days before Sir Geoffrey Howe made his famous resignation speech in the autumn of 1990, she screamed, 'No, no, no' in relation to various integrationist propositions that had emerged from an EU summit in Rome.

The removal of Margaret Thatcher marked one of the final assertive acts from senior Conservatives in favour of the European Union. This act of regicide, however, weakened their position in a party that had become ideologically wary of Europe. But Europe alone did not bring Thatcher down. The policy that made her in the first place was the one that led to her fall. Always at the back of her mind, she remembered that election in October 1974 when she became a TV star by pledging to scrap the local property tax.

In a partial repeat of her rise to the leadership, she went into the 1987 election pledging to abolish rates. In marked and fatal contrast to the mid-1970s, she had a precise alternative, the Community Charge, which soon became known, disastrously, as the poll tax. Focusing more on the abolition of the rates than on its alternative, she assumed the proposal would be as popular as it had been in October 1974. She referred to the Community Charge as the 'flagship' reform of her third term. Crucially, Thatcher made the mistake of proposing an alternative flat-rate tax. This was the policy that ultimately brought her down. In the mid-1970s her vague alternative property tax had been based on the 'ability to pay'.

The poll tax became unpopular in Scotland to the point that the Conservatives were virtually wiped out as a political force. Thatcher introduced it there first, a year early, which was seen by many Scottish voters as an unforgivable act of provocation from the Conservative government at Westminster. Arguably the rise of the Scottish National Party (SNP) began with the poll tax. The policy certainly explains the decline of the Conservative Party in Scotland up until the election of Ruth Davidson as party leader in Scotland. But when she introduced the same policy in England it proved to be equally unpopular, not only in Labour areas, but in Conservative ones, too. In particular, Conservative leaders at local government conferences were up in arms, which was wholly out of character. By instinct they were usually loyal to the national leadership. This was an early sign of the way the Conservative Party was changing. Support for the national leadership from senior activists was no longer automatic. This became a much bigger theme from the fall of Thatcher onwards. In the late 1980s the emollient Local Government Minister, David Hunt, would say to journalists as he headed towards the podium to make a speech to councillors who were previously Tory loyalists, 'Into the lions' den once more.' The lions tore him apart at every available opportunity.[19]

Chris Patten was Environment Secretary at the time and he used to take the projected poll-tax bills to Margaret Thatcher. In some cases they showed huge increases. As Patten told journalists privately, 'I show Margaret Hilda these poll-tax projected levels and she looks up to me and says, "Chris, I don't believe you."'[20] She was so convinced that the policy would be popular, and that it was necessary as a means of holding councils to account while making them more efficient, that she would not listen.[21]

But by the end Thatcher did listen. She was still alert to danger, even though she was by then losing her unusually sharp political antennae. She had lost her great skill of recognizing the space available to her on the political stage. In a frantic last-minute bid to hold on to power, she offered a whole series of revisions to the poll tax, exempting large numbers of voters and imposing caps on the amount that local authorities could charge, in a way that undermined the principle of the proposal in the first place. She showed, as she often had in the past, that in the end she was willing to compromise to hold on to power. But it was too late.

She was making increasingly frantic moves when the parliamentary party alone determined who would be leader. In effect, Conservative MPs removed her in the most dramatic internal act of political execution in modern times. They did so because enough of them feared they would lose their seats under her leadership. Having been a sharp reader of her own political strength at any given time, Thatcher strongly underestimated her vulnerability by the autumn of 1990.

This is not wholly unsurprising. She had won a landslide election victory in 1987, three years earlier. Landslide winners are usually secure. But she misread the wider political picture, particularly the degree to which the poll tax had alienated party activists (many of whom worked in local government as councillors), the despair of some Cabinet ministers and the availability of big figures to challenge her.

Often, for modern political parties, leadership crises arise because they have no obvious leaders. Towards the end of Thatcher's leadership, the Conservative Party had plenty of potential successors, all with weighty ministerial experience after a long period of Conservative rule. Above all, Michael Heseltine was waiting to pounce from the backbenches, where he had been since January 1986 after his resignation from the Cabinet.

Geoffrey Howe's resignation speech delivered in the Commons in November 1990 was the trigger. The manner of his departure provides another lesson of leadership. Leaders should treat senior colleagues thoughtfully and with sensitivity. Their seniority in government gives them authority. Howe irritated Thatcher and she could not disguise her irritability, treating him with growing disdain. Whereas she exuded restless energy around the clock, Howe was modest, mild-mannered and yet dogged. He worked as hard as her, but less ostentatiously. He had convictions as deep as hers, but did not display them with such theatrical exuberance. Howe detonated a political bomb that brought her down. His speech was vivid, full of colourful sporting metaphors, and yet delivered in his usual subdued style. The combination was political theatre at its most compelling. The modest Howe had become an actor, too. MPs listened in disbelief. Thatcher did too, taking in what she regarded as an act of treachery without quite realizing that Howe's deadly words would seal her fate.

Much has been made of Thatcher's useless campaign manager in the subsequent leadership contest. She was not a good judge of people, and her choice of Peter Morrison – heavy-drinking, lazy, secretly and promiscuously gay – to lead her campaign was another sign that she could no longer read political situations. She had become complacent. After three election victories, success had gone to her head, made her more imperious and less aware of her fragilities. To some extent such a course is unavoidable for a leader. As a new leader, Thatcher was surrounded by colleagues more experienced than her. By the end she was the mightily experienced one, working with presidents across the globe. She had become politically careless. To some extent, the same happened to Tony Blair. Even if Thatcher had appointed a political titan to run her leadership campaign, she was doomed. No leader could survive for long with Howe's words to torment her. Her former chancellor,

Nigel Lawson, had also been scathing when he had resigned a few months earlier. Backbench MPs were getting restless and fearful of losing their seats at the next election.

After her dramatic departure, Thatcher never got over what happened, most specifically the lack of loyalty from her own Cabinet colleagues, who one by one told her in November 1990 that she had to go, even after she won by a relatively small margin in the first ballot of the leadership contest.

Her fall traumatized the Conservative Party for decades to follow – a final lesson on leadership from Margaret Thatcher's long reign. There are times when parties become trapped. They need to remove a leader to have any hope of winning an election, but in doing so they are inevitably deeply troubled for a long time to come. The key figures in the removal of Margaret Thatcher were never fully trusted again by the party membership. Heseltine stood in the subsequent leadership contest of MPs and did not win. That was partly because members were telling MPs they should not support the one who wielded the knife.

But much more than that, the Conservative Party lost some sense of what it stood for. Had they turned against Thatcher because they were no longer Thatcherite? Had they turned against her because they were Thatcherite, but thought she had lost the ability to lead? Had they turned against her because they thought that not only were they no longer Thatcherite and she had lost the ability to lead, but they wanted to move towards a new position on the so-called centre ground? Even to attempt to answer the questions would have torn the Conservatives apart. Yet failure to provide a definitive answer made the party extremely vulnerable. The ambiguity of the regicide, the unanswered questions, meant that whoever succeeded her was going to find the inheritance a nightmare.

Thatcher's legacy for the country was also highly controversial. Public services were on their knees, even if some voters were incomparably better off. Communities dependent on industries that she deemed to be unproductive, or inefficient, struggled for decades to come. In different ways, both increasingly affluent voters and poorer ones became disconnected from the state in all its various manifestations. In terms of winning the battle of ideas there was no ambiguity. She was the triumphant winner. Thatcherism continued to define UK politics for decades to come, a remarkable achievement.

Although always possessing a brittle self-confidence, she was tormented in the early years of her leadership by her predecessor, Ted Heath, who behaved gracelessly towards her. Heath never got over the fact that Thatcher replaced him, and he disagreed fundamentally with a lot of the policies that she implemented. More to the point, he made it absolutely clear how he felt. She did the same with the leader who replaced her. John Major won the leadership contest in November 1990 and was her chosen successor. Yet very soon after his accession, Thatcher began to orchestrate revolts against his leadership and to give interviews suggesting he was not up to the job. It was another sign that she had lost that early ability to know when the political stage is crowding in on you, and when you need to be very careful what you say and do. A former prime minister has virtually no space on the political stage. Indeed a former prime minister has no defined role at all.

When a leader loses the crown, the best course is to say, 'Thank you very much', write your memoirs and keep out of what follows next in your party. Thatcher could not do that, which was probably a sign that those ministers and MPs who wielded the knives were right to do so. Their long-serving leader – winner of three elections and many more ideological victories – had lost her judgement as to how far she could tug at the boundaries of acceptable behaviour. For a long time Thatcher was an astute reader of politics, aware of how far she could go and adept at explaining to the voters why she was acting in the way she was. These skills enabled her to be the biggest change-maker as prime minister since Clement Attlee in 1945. When the skills faded, she was gone.

5

JOHN MAJOR

John Major became prime minister in November 1990 in arguably the most politically traumatic circumstances of any modern prime minister, with the exception of Theresa May. Jim Callaghan, another contender for this title, had faced an economic nightmare, but his transition to leadership was smooth. Major's was far from smooth, even if it seemed so at the time.

Major became prime minister after the act of regicide by Conservative MPs, when ministers and backbenchers contrived the sensational removal of Margaret Thatcher, the three-times election winner, against her will. It was an insurrectionary move that many MPs could hardly believe they had carried out.

As part of the challenging context, Major was not well prepared. Like Theresa May, he was ambitious. He had wanted the top job, but had not expected a vacancy to appear so suddenly in the autumn of 1990, just as Theresa May had not anticipated it in the summer of 2016. No one knew that the act of regicide was going to happen until it did. A few weeks earlier the Conservative party conference had been singing 'Happy Birthday' to Thatcher, and she had responded with exuberant waves from the conference platform. Major was her chancellor at the time, having been a short-serving

Foreign Secretary. He had held the two top jobs in the Cabinet, but only very briefly.

Less experienced than the candidates he defeated in the 1990 leadership contest, Major faced some titanic challenges as a new prime minister. The Conservatives had been well behind in the opinion polls and had lost a by-election in the theoretically safe seat of Eastbourne a short time before his victory. This was one of the reasons why Tory MPs turned against Margaret Thatcher. They feared they would lose their seats. The government of which Major had been a part had introduced its flagship policy, the poll tax. Major also faced a negotiation with the rest of the European Union over the forthcoming Maastricht Treaty. Some of his MPs opposed Maastricht, as did Margaret Thatcher herself. And the economy was sluggish.

His own position as a new prime minister was also deeply ambiguous. Ambiguity can help propel an ambitious figure into leadership, but can also bring him or her down. Major was Thatcher's choice as a successor. Most of her admirers voted for him in what was the last Conservative leadership contest dominated by 'one nation' Conservatives. Major beat Michael Heseltine and Douglas Hurd to secure the thorny crown. All three were well to the left of the leaders elected after Major. To varying degrees they were all pro-Europeans, with Major being the most sceptical. No one in the Conservative Party complained at the time about the narrow choice, a sign that even after Thatcher's long reign, the party's journey rightwards still had a long way to go. It became even more Thatcherite after Thatcher had fallen.

Major was not a Thatcherite, yet there was just enough in his political repertoire to convince her that he was 'one of us'. He was more of a Eurosceptic than the other candidates, although he was a believer in the UK's membership of the EU. In terms of the economy, he was obsessed by the dangers of inflation, and that gave the impression that he was economically 'dry', a supporter of Thatcherite economic policies. He was to some extent, but with significant qualifications. During the leadership contest he kept all options open in relation to the poll tax, a policy to which Thatcher was still emotionally attached. Privately he knew the tax had to be scrapped. Heseltine was against the policy from the beginning, and at this stage it was Heseltine who was the subject of the Thatcherites' fury, because he was the one who had betrayed her. But where did that leave Major as a new prime minister? Was he there as a calmer Thatcherite, or as a leader to move his party in a different direction? He never fully answered the question, even though retrospectively he was emphatic that he was part of the 'one nation' tradition of the party, pointing out accurately that he was well to the left of David Cameron, and half-jokingly suggesting that he was to the left of Tony Blair.[1]

He came closest to answering the question during the first phase of his leadership. Obscured by subsequent traumatic events, Major's leadership between November 1990 and the election in April 1992 was a triumph. Against many odds, he won the 1992 election, the Conservatives' fourth successive victory. With more than fourteen million voters backing his party, Major secured a higher vote share than Margaret Thatcher in her three election victories, even if he won only a small overall majority of twenty-three. He did this by giving the impression that there had been a change of government when he took over, without a general election. Major's style was dramatically different from what had gone before, and to a limited extent so was his policy focus. It was almost as if the Conservative Party under Major in his early phase had moved from being a party of Thatcherite crusading zeal to one closer to the Christian Democrats in Germany.

Major managed to convey a sense of change in a number of ways. Partly it was that his own personality, almost to the point of naivety, was incomparably different from Thatcher's. He was not grand, lofty or screeching in his assertiveness. While she was a strident performer, he gave the impression of being modestly self-effacing, which to some extent he was.

He loved nothing more than stopping off at a motorway café to have coffee and a fried breakfast. Although this was inevitably contrived, as every public move by a prime minister is, there was an authenticity to it as well. For a political scene so used to Thatcher, his personality was in itself refreshing and calming.

He also acted speedily to convey that he was a different leader. During an early Prime Minister's Questions, a Conservative MP asked Major a question that was critical of the BBC, assuming the new prime minister would approve of his onslaught. Major chose quite deliberately to praise the BBC. He changed his mind about the Corporation quite often in the years to come, but he started off by distancing himself from the attacks on the broadcaster by those Conservative MPs who were convinced, wrongly, that the BBC was left-wing. He also announced in an early Prime Minister's Questions some small amount of additional money for the National Health Service. The announcement symbolized at least a recognition that public services had declined in recent years and that public spending was not always a 'waste'.

Major also made a series of important appointments that indicated significant change, a softening from the Thatcher era. The key one was the promotion of Chris Patten to become chairman of the Conservative Party. It was the combination of Major and

Patten that made it look as if there had almost been a change of government. Patten was a pro-European and from the left of the party. His politics were far removed in many respects from Margaret Thatcher's. As Major and Patten set about their course with evident rapport, Major's predecessor became increasingly alarmed. This was in itself a tribute to the way Major was adapting his party to the demands of changing times.

Fleetingly, a tortured political party seemed more at ease with itself. Major appeared relaxed and looked as if he was enjoying his new job. Most Cabinet ministers felt relieved to be working with him rather than her. At first he had the authority of winning a leadership contest convincingly. There was no talk of ministerial insurrection during Major's early phase. Most MPs were loyal to him, even those who took their lead from an increasingly restive Thatcher.

As Major moved towards the 1992 election he dealt skilfully with two seemingly impossible obstacles. The first was the poll tax. During the leadership contest he was smart enough not to be entirely clear about what he was going to do with the tax. He knew that Margaret Thatcher and others supported him and the policy, so he promised no more than a 'review'. But the moment he got into Number Ten he knew exactly what he had to do. To win an election he needed to abolish what Thatcher regarded as her flagship policy. He gave the task to Michael Heseltine, the figure who had wielded the knife against her in the early stages of the leadership contest.

This was an astute appointment. Heseltine had been against the poll tax from the beginning, opposing the policy passionately and forensically when he was on the backbenches. Now he had the challenge of coming up with an alternative, a challenge that proved to be quite stressful for him. He took a long time over it. There were feverish leaks over what he might do, and other leaks over what he might not do. It was a huge issue in British politics at the time. In the end, Heseltine came up with the Council Tax, which was pretty similar to the previous property tax, the rates. Within a single parliament, a governing party had introduced a major new tax, scrapped it and announced a replacement that was close to the local tax that had been expensively abolished. Such a governing party deserved to be punished at an election, but voters were relieved that the government had abolished the poll tax. They were almost grateful. Heseltine was responsible for selling the policy to the party, which he did rather well. He did not admit at the time that he had more or less resurrected the rates, although he did so later when it was safe to reflect from a distance on what had happened.

Major's government had removed one of the great vote-losing policies that Labour had hoped would propel them to power in an election. His next challenge was Europe, the eternal issue for Conservative prime ministers.

By the autumn of 1991, the Maastricht negotiations were looming. In the proposed treaty there were two policy areas that a lot of Conservative MPs found unacceptable: the introduction of the single currency and the Social Chapter, the section of the treaty aimed at improving working conditions and employees' rights.[2] How was Major going to square the circle of signing up to a treaty while addressing those two issues? He negotiated with considerable skill. When a prime minister is confident about the mood of his parliamentary party, he or she can perform more effectively in relation to Europe. Major had grounds to be very confident – after all, only Conservative MPs had voted in the leadership contest that gave him his victory. Having removed Thatcher, they were not going to turn on him. Major used the authority of a newly elected leader to sign the Maastricht Treaty, but he got two vital opt-outs from the single currency and the Social Chapter – significant concessions that proved the European Union was far from indifferent to British demands. One of the ironies about the Conservative Party's anguish over the UK's membership of the EU was that the UK usually got its way. In this case, Major got his opt-outs. At the end of the summit in December 1991, with the next election moving into view, he declared, comically prematurely as it turned out, 'Game, set and match to the UK.'

Major's leadership eventually became hellish because of his party's response to the Maastricht Treaty, but in the build-up to the 1992 election he had manoeuvred neatly. The opt-outs just about kept his parliamentary party happy, and yet he had signed up to the treaty. He gave a number of speeches, co-written with Chris Patten, in which he talked about wanting Britain to be 'at the heart of the European Union'. The words were punctuated with much Euroscepticism. Major was not as pro-European as Patten, but the tone was markedly different from Margaret Thatcher's. The speeches also helped to establish relatively constructive relations with key EU leaders.[3]

Major made one other significant change during the 1990– 92 period. The initiative was much mocked, but it was a clever idea, based partly on models from other EU countries that had established more user-friendly public services. Major announced a Citizen's Charter, in which those who used public services would be more empowered to demand better value. Given that citizens had become virtually powerless in the face of dire public services with bewildering layers of accountability, this was a big leap, at least in theory. Voters would be able to get some of their money back, if trains failed to arrive within a certain time. There was even a cones hotline, for motorists stuck in traffic jams for hours with little evidence of work being carried out on closed motorway lanes. For some reason this became the biggest joke of all, and yet the hotline addressed a sense of impotence, as drivers were left in never-ending queues without knowing how to protest or to whom. Margaret Thatcher had declared that she would give 'power to the people' and yet had left most people powerless in the face of poor public services. As a Tory leader from a working-class background in Brixton and a former councillor who had struggled earnestly with questions over how to improve local provision, Major recognized the urgent need to improve public services and make them more accountable.

The Citizen's Charter was much maligned partly because there was little practical impact. Public services were poor, and Major was not inclined to greatly increase public spending. On the whole, voters did not notice improvements. The failure highlights a contradiction in Major's approach: a leader who recognized the need for better public services, without being willing to find the resources required.

Instead he had a different economic objective. Major was gripped by the need to curb inflation. Here is another example of a prime minister defined by his political upbringing. Wilson, Callaghan and Heath were determined to avoid the social and economic upheavals of the 1930s, most specifically high unemployment. Thatcher was resolved not to make the mistake of those 1970s governments. Major noted that high inflation impacted most severely on the poor and was alert to any danger that it might rise again. He was too alert. There were few inflationary seeds when he was prime minister and yet he sought ways of bearing down on public spending, while sensing that public spending on some services needed to rise. This preoccupation led him to support the privatization of the railways, a policy error more calamitous than the poll tax in terms of its disruptive impact on people's lives, but less politically potent. Although on most matters Major was to the left of Thatcher, this was a privatization she wisely did not dare to implement. Soon after the privatization, polls suggested that most voters supported re-nationalization. But this policy was implemented after the 1992 election, when Major was already doomed. The privatization of the railways, his stingy approach to public spending, and some of his approaches to the EU after the 1992 election meant that he never fully answered the question about whether he saw his task as to move his party on from Thatcherism. Later he was clear. He felt he never had the chance to do so fully because he was trapped by the party's civil war over Europe and by the small majority after 1992.[4]

Before the 1992 election, Major's symbolic focus on public services through the Citizen's Charter felt like another leap away from harsh Thatcherism, even if the change was more tonal than real.

In a very short period of time between 1990 and the 1992 election, Major had abolished the poll tax; repaired, to some extent, relations with EU leaders while securing opt-outs on the euro and the Social Chapter; and conveyed a concern for public services that was partly matched by policy initiatives. Indeed, it is arguable that between November 1990 and the 1992 election, Major, Patten and Heseltine were the 'modernizers' of their party – to apply that overused, vague, evasive but ubiquitous term. They were more 'modern' than the Cameron and Osborne leadership, in that they moved their party on from crude Thatcherism. Cameron and Osborne chose to define 'modernization' as being socially liberal. Major took a more challenging and substantial path. If modernization means moving on from a party's immediate past, then Major was the modernizer of the post-Thatcher Tory Party, if only until the 1992 election.

———

Major won in 1992 even though the economy was in the doldrums, with many economists predicting that worse was to come. There was a widely held assumption that Major won because of a great cliché: the voters held on to Nurse, for fear of something worse. But there was more to his victory than this cliché. It was the combination of changes that had been brought about subtly, in the period after November 1990.

Curiously, the Conservative Party learned none of the lessons from Major's victory. He won by moving to the left of Thatcher, tonally and to some extent in terms of policy. Every subsequent leader, with the partial exception of Theresa May and Boris Johnson, moved to the right and either failed to win a majority or, in David Cameron's case in 2015, won very narrowly. The combination of Major and Patten, with Heseltine, Clarke and Hurd playing prominent supporting roles, gave the Conservatives a share of the vote that their successors could only dream of.

But Major's leadership, more than that of any other prime minister, is one of two halves. If his early period is too easily overlooked, the hell that followed is almost underestimated, too. Oddly for such an undemonstrative figure, a leader who lacked language and was no performer, Major's leadership was a compelling theatrical drama of two utterly different acts. The sequence is counter-intuitive. Normally a historic election victory enhances a prime minister's authority, rather than ushering in a form of political hell. But, as ever, the seeds of Major's tragedy were sown in the very moment of triumph.

Major misread the reasons for his victory. He concluded, with uncharacteristic immodesty, that his own personal performance in the 1992 campaign was an important factor. His personality might have made a contribution to the victory, but his performance in the campaign emphatically did not. In the course of a very odd election, contested on some unusually cold days in March and early April, Major fought an embarrassingly naff campaign. On several occasions he went out on a soapbox with a megaphone, shouting at shoppers in town centres. He assumed that this kind of folksy campaigning was highly successful, that his soapbox and megaphone made a direct connection with the voters. Take a look at the footage on YouTube. The images seemed dated at the time and are absurd now, like a *Monty Python* sketch.[5]

That is not why Major won. But he thought it was one of the reasons, and he kept on repeating the same technique during the traumatic phase of his leadership after the election. His contortions looked even more ridiculous, as he was making them without much authority and with his party in revolt. In politics, we choose to see what we want to see, and not what is necessarily in front of our eyes. During the 1992 election Major was still on his honeymoon as a newish prime minister who was less lofty than Thatcher at her most imperious. When he was on his silly soapbox he got away with it, even though he looked ridiculous. Some voters saw 'a man of the people' rather than someone being silly. After the election win, during his dark period, the media and most voters saw him as weak and incompetent. When he got his soapbox out, as he occasionally did in the years that followed the 1992 election, or was door-stepped on a visit to a muddy school playing field – as he often was – he was no longer hailed for his rooted values. Now, some voters chose to see him as silly and beleaguered.[6]

Although Major won the 1992 election, his most important ally, Chris Patten, lost his seat in Bath. The loss partly explains Major's curiously downbeat response to his triumph. Indeed, on the Friday after the election, Major told Patten prophetically, 'We've pushed what should happen in electoral politics beyond its normal boundaries, and it will be almost impossible to do so again.' By this he meant that the Conservatives had won for a fourth time in a row and would struggle to win a fifth election. At his moment of triumph, he foresaw his terrible electoral fate.

He was an insecure figure in many ways, and was dependent on people he liked and could trust. He missed Patten intensely in the tragic drama that unfolded.[7]

Major's sense of doom on the day of his victory was encapsulated by Patten's defeat. The same night, Margaret Thatcher and other like-minded Tories had been at an election party hosted by the former Treasurer, Lord McAlpine. When Patten lost his seat, some of the guests raised their glasses and cheered. They were celebrating the defeat of Major's chosen party chairman and political soulmate – a vivid symbol of a deeply troubled party. The euphoria of McAlpine's guests was a sign that Major had only papered over the cracks between November 1990 and the 1992 election. This was still a party that had only recently removed its election-winning leader, was not quite sure what the removal implied and, in some respects, regretted what it had done. A section of the party represented extensively at McAlpine's gathering was becoming increasingly hostile to the European Union. It was thrilled by the defeat of the pro-European Patten.

A troubled party becomes much less troubling for a prime minister if he or she commands a large majority in the Commons.

But the other dark twist of the 1992 election was that although Major secured a historic share of the vote, he won only a small majority of seats. He had twenty-three seats more than the other parties combined. With legislation on the Maastricht Treaty looming, this was a fragile parliamentary base. Few realized the scale of that fragility in the immediate aftermath of the election. Even if Major was not exuberant after his win, he did not anticipate how quickly and deeply the turmoil would take shape.

It is widely assumed that Major's nightmare – exceeding even his well-developed sense of foreboding – was triggered by the trauma of Britain leaving the Exchange Rate Mechanism in September 1992, just a few months after the election. But by then there had already been a significant development, one that was wholly beyond Major's control.

In May 1992 – before there was a hint of the ERM drama to come, and just a few weeks after Major's election victory – Denmark voted against the Maastricht Treaty in a referendum. David Cameron was only the second prime minister to be thrown by a referendum on Europe. Major was the first, although (unlike Cameron) he had no cause to resign, as the referendum in Denmark was nothing to do with him.

At the point when Danish voters rejected Maastricht, there had been no parliamentary legislation in the UK that was required to ratify the treaty. The parliamentary sequence was still to come. When the Danes voted against Maastricht – an act of defiance from a supposedly pro-European nation – Eurosceptic Tory MPs in the UK became much bolder. They had concrete proof from another country that voters regarded Maastricht as an integrationist leap too far. Major had secured his substantial opt-outs from the treaty, but some of his MPs were still opposed to what they regarded as the fundamental purpose of Maastricht: political and economic union.

Coincidentally, two BBC political correspondents had booked to have a lunch with John Redwood, one of Major's Eurosceptic ministers, on the day after the result of the Danish referendum.[8] The lunch was in an arty basement of a Westminster restaurant. Redwood, who was not instinctively exuberant, leapt down the stairs of the restaurant joyfully. He sat at the table, looked up and said to us: 'Here's to Denmark!' He was thrilled at the outcome of the Danish referendum, and at what it might portend. But this wasn't the UK government's position. The government supported the Maastricht Treaty, with the UK opt-outs. Redwood, however, spoke of little other than the opportunities opened up via the Denmark vote, and of the need to reconsider the UK's entire relationship with the EU. It was that referendum in Denmark that emboldened Tory MPs to seek to wreck the Maastricht Treaty when Major presented the legislation in Parliament.[9]

Inevitably, when the UK tumbled out of the Exchange Rate Mechanism in September 1992, the Eurosceptics were further strengthened. For them, the humiliating collapse of the pound and the hysterical rises in interest rates, in a failed bid to prop up the currency, were vivid confirmation of their fundamental view. EU-related constraints were against the national interest.

More significantly, Major became a much weaker and less confident figure after the ERM crisis. One of the lessons of leadership is that leaders do not recover from a traumatic devaluation of the currency. In terms of self-confidence and the way he was perceived by the media, Harold Wilson never soared again after the devaluation in 1967. Major's trauma was more dramatic than Wilson's. During 'Black Wednesday' on 16 September 1992, as the UK headed towards the ERM exit, Major put up interest rates again and again until they reached ridiculous levels of 15 per cent. Then he had to give up. His top team of ministers gathered around him as he made his increasingly desperate moves.

Yet the senior ministers who were supporting Major during that traumatic day were also part of his forthcoming political nightmare. They held conflicting views on the EU in general, and on this drama in particular. The chancellor, Norman Lamont, let it be known that he was singing in the bath, after the pound left the ERM. In contrast, Michael Heseltine and Ken Clarke, supporters of a single currency, continued to defend the decision to join the ERM in the first place. On a calamitous day for British politics and economics, Major's senior ministers could not agree whether they felt relieved or downcast at the end.

From the day of the ERM saga until the 1997 election, Major and his party were never again ahead in the opinion polls, having won a decisive election victory just a few months before. At this point the crisis fed on itself, as often happens in politics; disconnected events and developments become conflated, to give the impression of a prime minister out of control. It happened to Gordon Brown after he built up speculation about an early election, but did not call one; and it happened to Major after the ERM crisis.

Away from the energy-sapping ERM saga, Major lost another close ally just a few months after Patten had lost his seat. In the same month, September 1992, David Mellor was forced to resign from a newly created Cabinet post in the clumsily named Department of National Heritage. Major and Mellor were both supporters of Chelsea FC, their political outlook was fairly similar and Major liked and trusted Mellor. But Mellor was forced out because he was having an affair. As the revelations reached fever-pitch, the woman involved claimed that Mellor liked to have his flings wearing a

Chelsea football shirt. This was a lie, made up on the advice of the public-relations guru Max Clifford, who later died in jail – the end of another dark sequence.

Major had created the new culture-focused department specifically for Mellor, who would have flourished in the role. He would have been one of the few Culture Secretaries with a real passion for culture. Within months he was gone. Major had tried desperately to keep hold of Mellor, but in the end had to give in. This was another big blow to Major's confidence, in some ways as deep as the one arising from the ERM, although much less significant. As a prime minister who had recently won an election, he had assumed at first that he would have the authority to protect Mellor. He did not regard the affair as a resignation matter. But much of the media was in uproar. They wanted Mellor's scalp, partly because he had taken a robust approach to newspaper regulation, which was part of his new remit. He had warned that some newspapers were 'drinking in the last-chance saloon'. Sections of the media sought revenge. They won, and Major lost. When a politician becomes a prime minister there is a part of them that assumes they possess unique gifts and unusual powers, sometimes with justification. Failure brings them down to earth. They are humanized to the point of feeling extremely vulnerable, rather than special.[10] When Major lost his battle with the media over Mellor's fate, he knew that the newspapers and some broadcasters would come for him again, and they did.

September 1992 was a month that demonstrated the power of the newspapers in the UK. Major was terrified of their response to the ERM sequence. At the end of that nightmarish 'Black Wednesday', he spoke to several newspaper editors, hoping that direct contact would bring about more sympathetic treatment. But he did not even get sympathy in the phone calls. The editor of the *Sun*, Kelvin MacKenzie, told Major: 'Well, John, let me put it this way. I've got a large bucket of shit lying on my desk and tomorrow morning I'm going to pour it all over your head.'[11] He did so the next day – and for a long time to come. The *Sun* had been a vibrant supporter of the Conservatives during the Thatcher era and into the 1992 election. Equally significantly, it portrayed the Labour leader, Neil Kinnock, as a dangerous fool, the Welsh windbag who would wreck the UK. Now the paper turned on Major, a significant factor in making his leadership more nightmarish.

Shortly after the ERM fiasco another crisis flared up, when the government became embroiled in a draining battle over pit closures. It was wholly unprepared for what happened and deeply troubled by the conflict. As president of the Board of Trade, Michael Heseltine announced that the government planned to close one-third of the UK's deep coal mines, with the loss of 31,000 jobs. Heseltine had spent many hours negotiating a compensation package with a reluctant Treasury, and finally extracted £1 billion to pay the cost of redundancies and assist mining communities. He assumed that the arguments that had prevailed during the miners' strike in the mid-1980s would receive even more widespread support this time, that the pits were uneconomic and there were cheaper, more efficient options. Similarly, he assumed that the compensation package would be contrasted with Thatcher's mean-spirited approach to mining communities after the pit closures that followed the miners' strike. Major made the same assumption, as far as he paid any attention to what Heseltine was planning – the ERM crisis and its aftermath were sucking up virtually all of his attention and energy.

Their assumptions were spectacularly wrong. All hell broke loose. This was partly because miners who had defied the strike in the mid-1980s were losing their jobs under Heseltine's proposals. Job losses were also threatened in some Conservative-held seats and, with a small majority, the government faced a serious backbench revolt. Above all, the mood of the media had changed. Thatcher-supporting newspapers, such as the *Sun* and the *Daily Mail*, had already turned on Major, partly because he was not Thatcher. The ERM crisis had been the trigger for the intensification of their onslaught, but these powerful newspapers had already decided Major was weak and had started to bash him around. Such newspapers set the agenda for the BBC. Based on the newspapers' hostile tone, parts of the BBC followed suit, reflecting and sometimes heightening the new, wildly critical mood.

Sensing more blood, and having already secured the departure of Mellor, the *Sun* and the *Mail* sympathetically reported big demonstrations against the proposed closures. Around 200,000 people attended one protest. Polls suggested that even Conservative voters were on the miners' side. Major and Heseltine panicked. Heseltine found the whole process nerve-shredding and draining. Political journalists who met him in the middle of the saga were struck by how he was simultaneously absorbed with, and shaken by, the crisis. At one lunch with two political correspondents, Heseltine used the entire dining table and all the implements on it to demonstrate what he was trying to do. The salt and pepper became one pit. A wine glass became another community. He was wholly wrapped up in the crisis and could reflect on nothing else.[12] Arguably the most formidable and thoughtful Conservative politician of his generation, Heseltine – the Cabinet minister under Thatcher who dared to focus on the revival of some inner cities, who later put the case forcefully for a more active state when he worked for Cameron and Osborne, and who played a big part in the fall of Thatcher and then scrapped the poll tax while devising an alternative – was fleetingly reduced to becoming a nervous wreck over the pit closures.

Major was on edge, too. The prime minister who had conveyed an almost innocent calm at the beginning of his leadership was now becoming unrecognizable as the one facing the storms. He could not bear being tormented by the media, and he was not alone in this. No prime minister copes well with the screaming front pages of disdain. Wilson was driven to exhausted paranoia. Blair made his final speech as prime minister attacking the 'feral' media. Brown awoke early each morning and read the newspapers, which meant that he was often in fuming despair before breakfast. Thatcher is the only modern prime minister not to have been tormented by the media, and that was largely because, with a few exceptions, the newspapers doted on her. Theresa May was also relatively untroubled, but that was because she took the extreme step of not reading them.

From September 1992 the media decided, almost collectively, that Major was a weak prime minister behaving weakly. The collective decision inevitably became self-fulfilling. Reading the critical newspapers, Conservative MPs became more strident in their onslaught. When weakness is perceived, a prime minister becomes weaker still.

This was the context in which Major presented the Maastricht Treaty to the UK Parliament. He had to pull every lever to get the legislation on the statute books. His struggle was an early sign of what was to come – a major staging post on the road towards the Brexit referendum in 2016.

Most fundamentally, Major discovered that the Conservative Party had become unleadable on Europe. The party conference in 1992, held a few weeks after Britain had fallen out of the ERM, was the first indication of the new febrile mood in the party. The gathering was an event of historic significance, in retrospect a key episode early on in the Brexit saga and in the related transformation of the Conservative Party.

On the whole, Conservative party conferences had been loyal rallies. Party activists attended to pay homage to the Cabinet and the prime minister. The 1992 conference was much closer to the Labour Party gatherings of the late 1970s and 1980s. Speakers attacked Major and his government for what had happened in relation to the ERM. Dissenters included the former party chairman, Norman Tebbit, who was cheered to the rafters. Packed fringe meetings on Europe were marked by intense clashes. Tory conferences were usually dull, polite affairs. This one was angry.

Tebbit's speech in the conference hall had provocative echoes of Mark Antony's at Julius Caesar's funeral. Mark Antony's address appeared to praise Brutus, while damning him. Mischievously, Tebbit claimed to be supportive of Major while inserting a very large blade into the back of the suddenly fragile prime minister. Tebbit began by expressing the hope that the prime minister would resist calls for the dumping of Norman Lamont, the Chancellor of the Exchequer, because Mr Lamont had not taken sterling into the European ERM in 1990. It was Major who had been chancellor at the time. He added: 'The cost in lost jobs in bankrupt firms, repossessed homes, in the terrible wounds inflicted on industry, has been savage... But we have established our credentials as good Europeans.'

Tebbit went on to prompt pantomime-style responses from his audience, asking them whether they wanted a single currency, and Brussels meddling in immigration controls, foreign affairs, industrial policy, education and defence. Each question was greeted with a chorus of 'No'. 'Do you want to be citizens of a European union?' he asked, to a final roar of opposition. 'Now is the time to negotiate anew. Kohl and Mitterrand no longer speak for Europe. John Major should raise the flag of patriots of all the states of Europe... Let's launch the drive for Maastricht Two; a treaty with no mention of more power to Brussels, no mention of economic and monetary and political union. It's a task in which I stand ready to join John Major whenever he is ready to begin.' Tebbit might as well have declared – as Mark Antony did of Brutus – 'And John Major is an honourable man.'

Major was sitting on the podium as Tebbit played to the crowd, looking pale while trying to convey a mild-mannered calm. He knew he was in the midst of an unprecedented drama, with many more acts to come.

The Conservative Party has never been the same since. Most obviously, the split over Europe deepened, but the conference marked a more profound and wider change in the character of the party. For years to come, party conferences had more ideological verve than Labour's equivalent events. Under Blair, Brown and the more left-wing Ed Miliband, Labour's annual gatherings were heavily controlled by the leadership, partly as a reaction against the vote-losing 1980s, when divisions were displayed vividly and in public.

Like partners in a curious dance, the Conservative conferences became wild while Labour's became controlled and dull. The Conservatives began to stage fringe meetings where insurrectionary charismatic or eccentric figures were hero-worshipped. In the mid-1990s Michael Portillo was idolized with almost the same intensity as Tony Benn had been at Labour conferences. At one Conservative conference in Blackpool, Portillo packed an entire cinema with devotees. Later Boris Johnson and Jacob Rees-Mogg became heroes of some activists. In ways that were partly admirable, Conservatives discovered the thrill of public debate, just as Labour became terrified of exploring ideas in the open. As well as Europe, other contentious themes included the role of the financial markets, the degree to which social liberalism marked a modernizing leap, the relationship between state and users, or providers, of public services. A party that had been pragmatic as a matter of conviction now became gripped by ideas. Above all, it became obsessed by Europe.

Major could not fully control the party conferences or his MPs in Parliament, some of whom voted repeatedly against the legislation required to implement the Maastricht Treaty. During the summer of 1993 he was forced to hold a vote of confidence in order to secure parliamentary assent. If he had lost, he would have had no choice but to call a general election, at a point when the Conservatives were well behind in the polls. Such a threat meant he won the vote of confidence, but the fact that he had to call it, because of the behaviour of his own MPs, was extraordinary and, again, a sign of what was to come. Cameron and May were to feel similarly tormented by their own MPs and found leadership as problematic as Major did.

In the immediate aftermath of winning the vote of confidence, Major gave an interview to ITN. At the end, assuming the tape had stopped running, he referred to the 'bastards' in his Cabinet. The words were recorded and broadcast.

Major's bastards were Eurosceptics, even though Major was himself fairly sceptical. The bastards clashed in particular with the chancellor, Ken Clarke, who opposed the idea of a referendum on the single currency.[13] The question of whether or not to hold a referendum on the euro was raging at this time. In the end, both Major and Tony Blair entered the 1997 election proposing to hold a referendum, although one was never held. This is another lesson of leadership in British politics. Referendums can be the source of intense splits and infighting. Often referendums are not held. The only UK-wide referendums have been on Europe in 1975 and 2016 and on electoral reform in 2011. Yet the rows over what question might be asked in a potential referendum, and whether a referendum should be held, come close to breaking parties at times. Mistakenly, leaders turn to referendums, or the offer of a referendum, on the assumption this will ease their burdens. The opposite happens nearly every time. The burdens only intensify. Later, Michael Heseltine described his reluctant decision to support a referendum on the euro, in advance of the 1997 election, as the biggest mistake in his career.[14]

Major had to manage a divided party and a split Cabinet. There are often intense personal rivalries and loathings, in politics as in other vocations, but a division over policy is much more serious. Major's Cabinet was unusual in that quite a lot of its members were old friends from Cambridge University. For the most part they remained friends, but they fell out over one policy: Europe. Once again, the falling-out over policy was an early sign as to what would happen with Cameron and Europe. Cameron did not learn the lesson. Friendships do not provide a protective shield in relation to the Conservative Party and Europe. The fact that Michael Gove and his wife joined the Camerons at Chequers for some festive fun on Boxing Day was not enough to sway Gove in the Brexit referendum. Gove chose to follow conviction rather than friendship.

In Major's Cabinet, friends were fighting their corner and then meeting for a drink to reflect happily on old or new times. Over the issue of Europe they followed their convictions, irrespective of friendship. Most specifically Ken Clarke, Norman Lamont and Michael Howard had been good friends at Cambridge. Yet they spanned the divide over Europe: Lamont was a critic from outside the Cabinet after he was sacked as chancellor;[15] Howard was a polite critic from within the Cabinet; and Clarke was the passionate pro-European. A leader can manage personal tensions in a government, but only the very best can manage a split over policy.

Major's attempt at managing his government and his party took a sensational turn. In July 1995 he announced that he was resigning as Conservative leader. He was still prime minister, but he intended to trigger a contest almost against himself, in order to get MPs to back him. Here, long before Brexit, was a vivid sign that the Conservative Party was suffering an existential crisis over Europe. To Major's surprise, one of his ministers, John Redwood – the one who was so excited after the Danish referendum result – stood against him. In a whacky campaign, Redwood was defeated, but Major did not win by a hugely commanding majority.[16]

Still, his victory was enough to give him the space to carry on. He carried on in a dark gloom that had not become brighter as a result of the bizarre contest.

Europe remained the cause of his gloom, the backdrop to every crisis. Even when, prior to the 1995 leadership contest, Major tried to move away from Europe in an attempt to focus on domestic policies, there was no escape from it. He lacked the capacity to excite. His language was also wooden. Unlike Thatcher, he was not a political teacher. At his party conference in 1993 he proclaimed that his government was going 'back to basics'. The slogan was almost wilfully uninspiring, as if Europe had sucked up too much passion. What he meant by 'back to basics' was a renewed focus on education, crime and housing. But one of his spin doctors said mistakenly, in a pre-speech briefing to journalists, that Major's chosen theme was also an attack on the 'permissive society'.

In more reasoned times, a misinterpretation could easily be addressed and batted away. In what were the early stirrings of a long era of hysterical unreason, one crisis after another erupted. Conservative MPs who were not in conventional heterosexual marriages, or who were having affairs, were in danger of looking like total hypocrites as they supposedly espoused a government agenda that challenged permissiveness, even though that was not the idea behind the agenda. There was one front-page story after another revealing ministerial affairs or the bizarre private lives of Tory MPs. The stories were aimed at destabilizing Major and they succeeded in doing so. Instead of escaping from the hell of Europe, Major found that when he tried to move away, matters got darker still.[17]

Even during the 1997 election campaign, when he faced Tony Blair at his most formidable, Major was still pleading with his party. He declared at one point, during one of the daily election press conferences that parties still held, with a naive hope of good publicity: 'Please don't bind my hands before I go to Amsterdam for the next EU treaty.' This was an extraordinary message from a prime minister supposedly addressing a wider electorate. Usually even desperate leaders find election campaigns liberating, as they no longer have to deal with internal party matters. To take one example, the Labour leader, Michael Foot, enjoyed the 1983 campaign, as it was a break from managing his unmanageable party. Foot did not enjoy the result, as Labour was slaughtered, but the campaign was a form of liberation. Such were the tensions in the Conservative Party that Major had to address them in the midst of an election.[18]

By then he was doomed. This was in part because Tony Blair walked on water, in the eyes of the electorate and much of the media at this point, but also because of everything that had preceded in this five-year period. The Tory Party had become unelectable. Although Major led subtly between 1990 and 1992, he was not equipped for the intense stress that followed. Arguably no one would have been, and Major certainly was not.

Ironically his brave work in initiating the peace process in Northern Ireland was a form of political escapism for him. There are several heroes in the peace process, and Major was one of them. At least negotiating with Gerry Adams, Martin McGuinness and leading unionists was a break from seeking to appease his Eurosceptics, and a much more constructive use of time. One of the lessons of Major's leadership was that the Eurosceptics could not be appeased. Neither Cameron nor May learned this lesson, with calamitous consequences for them, their party and the UK. In contrast, following secret talks with the British and Irish governments, the IRA announced a ceasefire in the summer of 1994. Adams looked to a political solution, and Major helped to give him, and others, the space to start exploring what form that might take. But by 1997 even this striking initiative was being undermined by some Conservative MPs, ardent unionists who were worried that Major had gone too far. The peace process was in danger of imploding – another victim of internal Tory divisions.

As the divisions deepened, Major got much of the blame in the media for being 'weak', as if 'strength' could magically bind a party together. He became even more sensitive about newspaper coverage, and at least as worked up as Harold Wilson. His Foreign Secretary, Douglas Hurd, later reported that allies used to hide the newspapers from Major. Having requested the first editions the night before, he would not be able to sleep, fuming at what he regarded as unfair coverage. His advisers had to hide the *Evening Standard* when the first edition arrived in the early afternoon, because he would get too worked up. His chancellor, Ken Clarke, revealed that he used to get phone calls from John Major on Boxing Day, saying, 'Have you seen page eight of the *Daily Express*?' – a page that few voters would have read on Boxing Day, or any other day.

Like other prime ministers, much of Major's despair with the media was justified. As well as being vilified for 'back to basics', his whole government was seen through the prism of sleaze, a term that became briefly ubiquitous but, as is usually the case with repeated words or phrases in British politics, hopelessly ill-defined.[19] There is no doubt that a few ministers and MPs in Major's party were 'sleazy'. Jonathan Aitken ended up in jail, and other Tory MPs were forced to stand down from various senior positions. But Major himself – for all his substantial faults and his flaws – was not remotely corrupt. He was a decent figure, trying his best in very difficult circumstances. Yet opinion polls published at the time suggested that sleaze was one of the issues that most concerned voters about his leadership. Voters' misperceptions of the innocent Major showed the distorting impact of a feeding frenzy, and were another reminder that we choose what we want to see, rather than what lies in front of our eyes.

Here is one of the lessons of leadership. When a government totters, for whatever complex reasons, the media and voters see a prime minister in an entirely different light. At which point the supposedly mighty leader is powerless to change perceptions. Indeed, attempts to do so tend to reinforce the dark prism. In this case a prime minister who was not corrupt, or 'in it for himself', was perceived in such a light because everything else was going wrong.

With hindsight, we can see another important twist. Major claimed credit for the state of the economy when he left office in 1997, but although he was unfairly tormented over 'sleaze', he has been too generously treated for the legacy he left to the incoming Labour government.

While Major could point to falling unemployment, steady growth and stable finances, he failed lamentably to address the shoddy state of public services. Any government can balance the books by not investing very much. By 1997 the NHS was in such a wretched state that hospitals were being compared unfavourably with those in Eastern Europe. In London, theatres issued warnings to audiences, urging them to leave much more time than they might anticipate to get to the venue, because public transport had become so unreliable. Across the country newly privatized trains were even more unreliable than the Tubes and buses in the capital. The infrastructure of the UK was creaking. Business leaders were crying out for more investment in capital projects. Outside London, public transport was even more unreliable. Bus services that had been privatized under Margaret Thatcher were expensive and some routes that were not profitable ceased to run. Voters who could not afford cars were left behind. The incoming Labour government was to inherit a situation where voters were aching for improved public services, without necessarily being willing to pay higher taxes. Contrary to a simplistic mythology that suggests Labour took over a booming economy, this was a challenging inheritance for Blair and Brown.

The dire state of public services was also an underestimated factor in the demise of the Conservative government, though without doubt impossible divisions over Europe, as well as the related issues of 'sleaze', were the main causes of the slaughter. Yet one of the ironies is that during the 1997 election campaign, when his party was defeated by a bigger margin in terms of seats than Michael Foot's in 1983, some of Major's messages were astute and prophetic.

He campaigned forcefully against Labour's devolution plans and on the last day he was prime minister, during the final twenty-four hours of that election campaign, he flew to different parts of the UK, warning that devolution could lead to the break-up of the UK. At the time his tour seemed rather pathetic and outdated, part of his outmoded 1950s traditionalism. As Blair walked on water, Labour's devolution plans seemed sensible, modest and very much with the times. But in retrospect, Major had a strong case. Instead of ending the momentum towards nationalism, the devolution settlement triggered a renewal. Two decades later, the UK seemed far more fragile than in 1997. Brexit was the main cause, but Labour's devolved power in Scotland provided the wider backdrop, with the SNP looking to hold a second referendum on Scottish independence. Major had appeared desperate when he was being prescient.

But his messages were not heard in 1997. When an unpopular prime minister, or former prime minister, makes a powerful case, voters turn away. Blair discovered the same as he framed potent arguments against Brexit before and after the 2016 referendum. In the 1997 election campaign Major was heading for a bleak defeat and was aware of his fate.

When he lost, he went to the Oval to watch some cricket on the Friday after the election. He looked relieved, and has looked relieved ever since. Subsequently Major became much calmer, more relaxed and, indeed, authoritative when he gave interviews. He was often witty. Voters started to listen again. He is the only modern prime minister to have looked liberated after he was brutally forced out of Number Ten. His relief suggests that, for all his early overlooked success, he was the wrong person for that particular job at that particular time.

But was there a right person available? Once again, the wider context is a reliable guide. The issue of Europe and the Conservative Party would have challenged the most titanic of prime ministers in the 1990s. Modest and insecure about his limitations, John Major would not have claimed to be a titanic prime minister.

In contrast, Tony Blair appeared to have mesmeric qualities when he became Labour leader in 1994. While no one listened to Major, Blair could utter banalities in his early years as Labour leader and they would be hailed as statements of historic significance. As Major left to watch the cricket, much of the country held euphoric celebrations to greet the arrival of the youngest of modern prime ministers. Major resented the way he was dismissed by much of his party, the media and the electorate, in contrast with the adulation around Blair. But for Blair, the euphoria became a curse.

6

TONY BLAIR

The arc of Tony Blair's leadership is the most extraordinary and Shakespearean of all modern prime ministers. After he became leader of the Labour Party in the sunny summer of 1994, Blair resolved to be trusted, respected and widely popular, not just as a newly elected leader, but as a prime minister. He assiduously wooed the newspapers and the BBC in the hope of fair coverage. He enjoyed a soaring honeymoon with voters and the media, which lasted far longer than that of any other modern prime minister. Everything he said and did in the early years was aimed at forming a new bond of trust with the electorate. There were annual reports to show that the government had delivered what it promised. There were pledges that ministers in a Labour government would be purer than pure, and would be seen as such. If there were protests, Blair sent a minister to join the demonstration, as a symbol of empathy. Poor Michael Meacher, an old ally of Tony Benn and an unlikely Environment Minister in the first Blair government, was told to join the march of the Countryside Alliance, even though it was a protest against government policies.[1] Blair ached to be a leader who was trusted in the most fundamental sense, as a prime minister of integrity.

Yet after Blair left office in 2007, he spent large amounts of time abroad, partly to keep out of a country where he provoked intense loathing from some. He could not even attend the launch of his memoirs, because of the security risks. Everywhere he went in the UK he was accompanied by bodyguards, a fate of all prime ministers, but far more necessary for Blair than for any other. When he first became leader of the Labour Party, he could utter any banality and much of the media would hail the words as an insight of profound depth and significance. A thousand columns would analyse his words and conclude, appreciatively, that the UK had a radical leader of unusual depth. After Blair left office, quite a lot of the UK turned away, even when he was speaking deeply.

To take one example: in his early years Blair would argue that Labour stood for social justice and economic competence. No party claims that it stands for economic incompetence and social injustice. Yet Blair's analysis was widely treated as if he had uncovered a magical insight of unfathomable depth. After the Brexit referendum in 2016, Blair's interventions were of the highest quality, elegant, crisp, accessible and forensic. Few appeared to take much notice.

What happened? How to make sense of his transition from a leader who walked on water and sought to navigate a 'third way' in policy-making, to a former prime minister viewed with fuming disdain. Blair's third way was similar to Harold Macmillan's middle way, even if Blair claimed for his ideas a profound distinctiveness. His third way was neither left nor right, but a route that in theory at least would keep Middle England on board, without alienating fully either the left or the right. In theory, his approach was a route towards eternal popularity. Instead, his limited philosophy propelled him towards intense unpopularity. Margaret Thatcher's career at least had a visible pattern. She emerged surprisingly and controversially. She departed suddenly, surprisingly and with breathtaking controversy. The end and the beginning make sense. Blair's end seems so different from his beginning.

———

Tony Blair was aged forty-one when he became leader of the Labour Party in the summer of 1994, the youngest leader in the party's history. The moment he became leader – indeed, even during the leadership contest that preceded his landslide victory – Blair was widely seen as the UK's next prime minister.

The authority-enhancing perception of Blair obscured almost entirely his youthful inexperience. He had not been a Cabinet minister, or a minister of any sort. He had never seen a prime minister working at close hand, from the perspective of being in a Cabinet. Instead, during arduous years in opposition, he had become the world's expert on Labour in the 1980s, and that expertise formed the basis of his calculations throughout his period as prime minister and as leader of his party. From the start of his leadership he had the forbidding, enigmatic aura of a winner, and yet electoral defeat had framed his political outlook.

Blair became an MP in 1983, the year that Labour was slaughtered in the general election. He was elected in the safe seat of Sedgefield, in the first of the Thatcher landslides – a big three-figure victory for the Conservatives, with a second to come four years later. Blair arrived at Westminster in 1983 at the same time as Gordon Brown. Their first direct experience of being candidates in general elections was of constant defeat for their party. Although they won their safe seats, Labour lost in 1987 and again in 1992.

During the 1992 election many, though not Blair, expected Labour to form the government. Under John Major, the Conservatives won for the fourth time in a row.

Blair's boundary-breaking leadership of his party is largely explained by the defeats Labour suffered in the 1980s. But there were other factors. His background played a part. Blair was educated at Fettes, a private school in Edinburgh, the son of a committed Conservative supporter who had contemplated standing for Parliament. Such a context can stir rebellious instincts and did so with Blair, but only to a limited extent. At Oxford, Blair joined a rock band and was dismissive of snooty orthodoxy. He performed in various comedy revues and plays. As a student, lawyer and politician, he was a performer fascinated by the art of performance. He was a prime minister who could perform so compellingly that he came to believe passionately in what he was arguing for, even when the ammunition was limited. As a Christian at Oxford, Blair was greatly influenced by Peter Thomson, an Australian Anglican priest, a committed Christian socialist who, when he died, was described as the 'irreverent reverend'.[2] Blair too had an irreverent streak, a sense of the absurd. He is one the few modern leaders to deploy humour and wit potently – those important political weapons. His calm and decent demeanour, combined with humour, ensured that colleagues who worked with him in Number Ten felt an intense personal loyalty, even if many of them were politically to the left of him. Blair was fascinated by charisma and was drawn to charismatic figures, irrespective of their politics; Thomson was also often described as 'charismatic'. Blair was as content socializing with the eccentric Italian prime minister Silvio Berlusconi or watching a film in the White House with President Bush as he was having a drink with President Clinton – in some respects more of a soulmate.

But contrary to the mythology, Blair's faith played little or no part in his approach to leadership. His politics were wholly secular, shaped by his sense of how to win elections, stay in power and make power as worthwhile as possible. In a political context, he was more likely to consult the *Sun* newspaper than the Bible. His commitment to the Labour Party came after Oxford, when he met his wife, Cherie, a fellow lawyer and an active Labour supporter. She was his route to the party. Roy Hattersley, who worked with Blair when he was the party's deputy leader up until the 1992 election, noted that while the rising star showed forensic brilliance and energy, he had no interest in the party's philosopher-kings. Hattersley once cited R. H. Tawney to Blair and noted that he might as well have been speaking Latin.[3]

The personal past of a leader is significant in a political career, but not decisive. A more important factor in shaping Blair's leadership was his lack of ministerial experience. He arrived in Number Ten as a youthful prime minister, fully formed as a party leader, but with no direct sense of the challenges of government in its many forms. While much of the media focused wrongly on the supposed arrogance and 'control freakery' of the New Labour leadership, there was a far more illuminating story to be told: the daunting challenge of assuming power after eighteen years of rule from a Conservative government of the radical right. Most of the senior ministers and advisers had no experience of government from the time when Labour was last in power in 1979. John Smith, the Labour leader whom Blair replaced in 1994, had been a Cabinet minister in the Callaghan government. Had he lived, he would have entered Number Ten with the kind of confidence that arises from knowing directly what government is like. Smith was cautious in many respects too, but government was not a mystery to him. New

Labour was accused of arrogance, but it was not arrogant enough – being terrified by opinion polls, focus groups and the latest verdicts in the media. Above all, its leaders had no sense of what government was like until they won stunningly in 1997.

What if Blair had been a junior Foreign Office minister, or Foreign Secretary, before becoming prime minister? At least he would have seen, and interpreted, intelligence – an explosively contentious issue in the run-up to the war in Iraq. He would have had a stronger feel for the reliability of intelligence, or the wisdom of citing it as definitive when it is inevitably tentative and often incorrect. Perhaps he would have seen at close hand Britain's so-called 'special relationship' waver, on good grounds. What if he had been Education Secretary or Health Secretary? His public-service reforms, well-intentioned though they were, might have been subtler and more finessed, in recognition of the complexities of delivering public services free at the point of need or use. Instead he was a leader with very limited experience, and that experience was largely confined to navigating the nightmarish internal politics of the Labour Party.

By 1994 when he became leader, Blair possessed a clear, well-developed and yet narrow sense of what Labour needed to do to win, following seemingly never-ending election defeats. He, Gordon Brown, Peter Mandelson and others had spent a huge amount of time together analysing what was going wrong and what was necessary, in their view, to put it right. Curiously he was the best-prepared leader of the Opposition in Labour's history, even though he had no idea that a vacancy would arise when it did. No one knew there would be a sudden leadership contest, and yet when the unexpected moment came, Blair was more than ready for the epic demands of being leader of the Opposition. This is not to suggest that he was well prepared for government. He was not. But in knowing what he wanted to do as Opposition leader, he was ruthlessly focused from the beginning. His project to win power was as tight and thought-through as Thatcher's, although very different.

Like Harold Wilson in 1963, Blair became leader after the sudden death of the current occupant. In Blair's case, John Smith died after suffering a heart attack. Smith had been a robust leader, travelling back and forth to Scotland as well as leading a party that makes impossible demands on its leaders. At weekends, he climbed the Munro mountains in Scotland in order to keep fit.

The suddenness of Smith's death was both a tragedy and part of what appears to be a dark pattern of Labour leaders winning elections. It seems that these terrible and unexpected personal tragedies pave a primrose path to elusive power for whoever takes over. Wilson acquired the crown when Hugh Gaitskell died unexpectedly. Blair is the only other leader to have done so in a dark funereal context. Both Wilson and Blair went on to win the next election. In contrast, Labour leaders who acquire the crown at the beginning of parliaments, perhaps five years before the next election toil, struggle and then lose.[4] The journey is too long.

Leadership is never easy; it is often close to impossible. Nonetheless, the context in which Blair acquired the crown was close to a dream one. The governing Conservatives were tearing themselves apart over Europe. John Major had little authority over his parliamentary party in the still-mighty media. In contrast, when Tony Blair arrived on the scene as Labour's leader there was excitement in the media about his rise, even among the Conservative-supporting newspapers. From the beginning, Blair generated a high voltage of political energy, but he did so in propitious circumstances. He looked a winner partly because he was bound to win.

Significantly, this was not Blair's own view. As he put it, with focused discipline, he was constantly fighting a 'war on complacency'. He fought the war to the point that he underestimated the potency of his appeal as the 1997 election approached. He became too disciplined. Blair genuinely assumed that a small Labour majority or a hung parliament were likely results, even up to election day in 1997, when the polls pointed to a big Labour win. The assumption determined a lot of his moves as he headed towards power.

Blair's leadership in opposition offers many lessons. Because of all those election defeats, he had a strong sense of what a party – any party – needed to say and do in order to win an election, or at least not to lose one. His heightened sense was accompanied by ideological timidity, although he argued, and believed, that he represented the 'radical centre', another imprecise term.

The concept may have lacked precision, but Blair's focus on policy detail was forensic at this stage. He was the most high-profile Opposition leader of modern times, rarely off the TV, although every now and again he would take a few days away from the Westminster frenzy on his own to analyse every proposition that was part of Labour's programme. This was to ensure, as he put it, that the policies were 'bombproof' in the context of a general election. Based on his background as a lawyer, and as an observer of Labour leaders being ill-prepared during elections, he would ask of himself the questions that he knew the media would pose in the forthcoming campaign. If he had any problems answering them, he would change the policy.

To take one highly charged example, during one of the intensive bombproofing exercises Blair hit upon a potentially explosive inconsistency in Labour's programme. He noted that Labour was proposing a referendum on whether the UK should join the eurozone, on constitutional grounds. He and Gordon Brown had justified their sudden support for a referendum on the euro on the basis that entry would mark a profound constitutional change. As ever in relation to leaders justifying a referendum, they were being disingenuous. They offered a referendum because John Major had done so, and because they were fearful of alienating Rupert Murdoch's newspapers if they did not.

Nonetheless, their public position was an apparently noble one. Voters must be consulted on a matter of such constitutional significance. Blair then noted that Labour was not offering a referendum on Scottish devolution, a policy with profound constitutional consequences, even if he did not realize quite how seismic they would prove to be at the time. Blair returned from the 'bombproofing' session and, to the astonished fury of the Scottish Labour Party, announced a referendum on the party's long-established proposal to introduce a Scottish Parliament in Edinburgh.[5] This was a brave leap. The revision meant that the election of a Labour government would not guarantee a Scottish Parliament. A referendum would follow. But Blair was not willing to be exposed on any policy during the intense scrutiny of an election.

Every policy in Labour's 1997 manifesto was bombproofed in a similar fashion. As a result, the media – albeit a sympathetic media – never caught Blair out in the absurd rituals of a UK election campaign. There were no 'cock-ups' or 'policy disarrays' that tend to mark elections in the UK. Labour leaders in particular had been destroyed during campaigns for some apparent policy cock-up or another. Blair was prepared and avoided any traps.

It might be assumed that bombproofing election manifestos is an obvious duty of leadership – in which case, many leaders are not

Harold Wilson outside the Palace of Westminster awaiting the result of the Labour Party leadership election, 7 February 1963.

The leaders of the three main political parties side by side: Jeremy Thorpe (left), Harold Wilson (centre) and Edward Heath (right) at a ceremony in Westminster, 25 November 1970.

The new Conservative prime minister Edward Heath waving to supporters outside 10 Downing Street, 19 June 1970.

Leader of the Opposition Margaret Thatcher campaigning to keep Britain in the Common Market, alongside her predecessor Edward Heath, 17 May 1975.

Labour's James Callaghan makes a point, 1978.

Callaghan and Tony Benn, the Secretary of State for Energy, answer questions at a Labour Party press conference, 23 April 1979.

Margaret Thatcher, the first woman to be elected prime minister, waves to well-wishers outside 10 Downing Street on the day of her election victory, 4 May 1979.

Thatcher shares a moment of levity with US president Ronald Reagan at a meeting to mark the UN's 40th anniversary, October 1985.

Above left: A poster of the new prime minister, John Major, replaces a poster of Margaret Thatcher on the day of her resignation after eleven years in power, 28 November 1990.

Above right: Prime Minister John Major, 1995.

Queen Elizabeth II inside 10 Downing Street during her Golden Jubilee year with Prime Minister Tony Blair (far left) and former prime ministers Margaret Thatcher, Edward Heath, James Callaghan and John Major.

Above left: Tony Blair and his wife Cherie inside 10 Downing Street after New Labour's landslide election victory, May 1997.

Above right: Blair and Brown during the first New Labour government, 27 September 1999.

Above: Blair and Brown at the Labour Party Autumn Conference – Blair's last as prime minister and party leader – 25 September 2006.

Right: Blair addresses soldiers on duty in Basra during the Iraq War before stepping down as prime minister, 19 May 2007.

Above left: Prime Minister Gordon Brown with Margaret Thatcher outside 10 Downing Street, 13 September 2007.

Above right: David Cameron, the so-called 'heir to Blair', talks to the press after winning the Conservative Party leadership election, 6 December 2005.

Below: Leader of the Opposition David Cameron listens to US Democratic presidential candidate Barack Obama during a tour of Parliament, 26 July 2008.

Prime Minister Cameron and Home Secretary Theresa May arrive for a ceremony at Horse Guards Parade in London, 21 October 2014.

Above left: Prime Minister Theresa May with European Commission President Jean-Claude Juncker, shortly after May triggered Article 50, 26 April 2017.

Above right: Prime Minister Boris Johnson outside 10 Downing Street following the Conservative Party's landslide victory, 13 December 2019.

dutiful. As an example, Theresa May got caught out in the 2017 election campaign, having not fully thought through the electoral consequences of her elderly-care proposals. In her manifesto May proposed that elderly care for affluent pensioners should be paid for partly by extracting equity from the value of their homes, a so-called 'dementia tax'. The panic in the middle of the Conservatives' campaign, when the policy was changed, was a failure of leadership. But May's inability to anticipate what might happen during the scrutiny of an election campaign was a minor lapse, compared to what had happened to Labour's leaders in the three elections during Blair's time as an MP. In the middle of elections, Labour's policies on tax and defence appeared almost to fall apart. This happened under the relentless gaze of a hostile and biased media. Even so, rows or damaging confusion about future income-tax levels, and how Labour would defend the UK, suggested that in spite of working around the clock, Blair's recent predecessors lacked the knack of bombproofing an election manifesto, a necessary part of leadership.[6]

The second skill Blair applied as leader of the Opposition was a form of genius, even if it contributed to his ultimate doom. Political leadership is an art form, and the artistry is not an added bonus; it's a precondition to success on other fronts. At all times a successful leader must give the impression of decisive purpose and momentum. Blair did so, even if the reality was much more complex.

Blair, Brown and the few other senior figures who mattered were indecisive and, indeed, divided on several key themes in the build-up to the 1997 election. They were not clear about whether they wanted to be in or outside the single currency, which was a huge issue in British politics at the time. Blair and Brown could not even agree at first on whether to offer a referendum on the issue. They prevaricated for some time after John Major had pledged to hold one. Ironically, it was Brown who was reluctant, seeking the option of joining the euro without the barrier of a referendum. Later in government, it was Blair who was keener on moving towards the euro and Brown who was passionately opposed.

Electoral reform was another significant issue in the run-up to the 1997 election, because Blair was forming a close relationship with the Liberal Democrats' Paddy Ashdown. Blair was keen on close ties with Ashdown and his party, knew that electoral reform was the policy that made a relationship possible, and yet viewed the actual policy warily. Before and immediately after the 1997 election, Blair was far from sure whether or not he wanted to introduce electoral reform. Personally, he was not keen on it, but as a leader of the Labour Party wanting to work with the Liberal Democrats, and assuming he might have to work with them in a coalition, he conveyed guarded enthusiasm.[7]

With a similar evasiveness Blair spoke of 'modernizing' welfare policies, without any clear sense of what that might mean. At the same time he and Brown were not at all sure how their rigid pledges to stick to the Conservatives' spending plans for two years, and not raise income tax for the lifetime of the next parliament, would still give them room to greatly improve public services, as they wanted to do. Indeed, Blair had proclaimed his three priorities as being 'Education, Education, Education'. But there were also similar, and equally vague, commitments to 'save' the NHS.

Under a less agile and forensically prepared leader, such evasiveness could have been disastrous. Do you support membership of the euro? Do you support electoral reform? How will you find the money to invest in public services when you won't raise income tax? What precisely will you do to reform welfare? The true answers to these questions were: 'I don't have much of a clue.'

But because of Blair's artistry as a leader, none of this mattered, at least in the build-up to overwhelming electoral victory. He gave the impression of complete confidence, direction and momentum. He managed to mock Major for the divisions in his government over the single currency, without revealing the fact that his side was just as bewildered and divided. Indeed, the number of referendums Blair offered in the 1997 campaign was a sign of how unsure he was on several pivotal issues. There were proposed referendums on electoral reform, the euro, the introduction of mayors, a Scottish Parliament and a Welsh Assembly. Blair did not hold as many as he offered, but the pledges were significant in themselves – an indication that he did not have the confidence to make the election a vehicle for profound change in relation to highly charged issues. If he wanted those issues resolved, he would win power first and then address thorny issues in referendums.

Few noticed. Much of the media, and most voters, saw only dynamism, excitement, novelty, strong leadership and a sense of purpose. If leaders look like winners, they have the space to cast spells. Even when Blair described his proposals as being 'on the radical centre' – a phrase that was both reassuring and inspiring – few noted any contradiction. In some respects, Blair made 'change' his theme, but in an unusual way. He had changed the Labour Party by promising not to do too much to change the country after eighteen years of Conservative rule. In essence, his message was that the UK had become a rundown, almost derelict mansion. He pledged to change the ashtrays. Quite a lot of voters looked forward to a renovation of the entire mansion.

Blair's genius at making the incremental seem so exciting and radical became part of his problem as prime minister. He won a landslide of huge proportions, a bigger majority than either of Margaret Thatcher's two landslides.[8] Partly because there had been a change of governing party for the first time in eighteen years, there was a sense of huge excitement. The colossal landslide triggered a further frenzy, even if the scale of the victory obscured the incremental manifesto on which it was based. The result was historic. The excitement was almost physically tangible in the immediate aftermath. There were street parties in parts of the UK. The newspapers could not contain their excitement, even those that had previously endorsed the Conservatives. And yet Blair had been elected on one of the most cautious manifestos of recent times.

The ambiguity was there from the beginning. On the night of the election, Labour politicians held a party at the Royal Festival Hall. Blair arrived in the early hours to declare, with a metaphorical flourish, 'A new day has dawned, has it not?' On one level, a new day had dawned. Here was a youthful incoming Labour prime minister after the long rule of Margaret Thatcher and John Major. At the same time, Blair was a resolutely expedient politician, wary at all times of alienating the Middle England voters and the newspapers they read. His own views were both complex and simplistic. As a matter of genuine conviction, he accepted that on some pivotal issues the Conservative rulers had been right and Labour had been wrong. Yet the sincere conviction was also a convenient one, in that it meant Blair did not have to confront some of the right-wing orthodoxies that were deeply held by powerful figures in the media and in business.[9]

As with President Obama in the United States, disillusionment with Blair was bound to come. Once again, voters saw in a prime minister what they wanted to see. At first some of them chose to see a radical change-maker. In contrast, some Tory voters saw a Labour leader who, to their delight, would not worry them, because he would not change very much. Blair hailed the 'big tent' of support for Labour, but the bulging canvas was bound to burst at some point. Here is part of the answer to the conundrum about Blair's arc as a leader: from being the country's saviour to being forced into near-exile. Expectations were high in 1997, because he was an exciting political personality and he symbolized change after eighteen years of rule from a right-wing Conservative Party. And yet, simultaneously, part of Blair's appeal was to those who had voted Conservative. He was doomed to disappoint.

Although the two perceptions of a change-maker and a leader who would not change very much are contradictory, both were true, at least in the early phase of Blair's leadership. After the election in 1997 there was a partly paralysing caution. The new government stuck to the Conservatives' spending plans, feared holding some of the promised referendums, hailed even the obviously flawed privatizations of the Thatcher/Major era and sought to help the City of London and the banks benefit from a lighter regulatory touch. Complex decisions were often kicked into the long grass. As one minister observed to a political commentator at the time, 'We've hit the ground reviewing.'[10] The observation neatly captured the tangible sense of energy in the early New Labour era, and a partial sense that the hyperactivity was not leading to deep change.

Yet at the same time the new Labour government was a change-maker. It introduced the minimum wage, the Scottish Parliament and the Welsh Assembly. The introduction of a London mayor was as significant as any reform aimed at liberating the City during the 1980s, in terms of reviving the capital, and one with no destabilizing consequences.[11] There was also the pledge, implemented belatedly in the second term, to increase investment in the NHS to the EU average – a policy that hugely improved healthcare and saved many lives. The introduction of Sure Start children's centres integrated previously fragmented services aimed at helping poorer families. New tax credits helped to make low earners better off, even if many of the voters who benefited had no idea that the extra cash came from a government policy. Blair and Brown's fear of a Middle England revolt against 'redistribution' meant that they never used that term or made much of what they – mainly Brown – were doing in relation to tax credits. The Foreign Secretary at the time, Robin Cook, noted that his constituents in Scotland assumed the extra money in their wages arose from a technical adjustment by the Inland Revenue. He urged Blair and Brown to be less stealthy and to proclaim what they were doing.[12]

Alongside all this, the Good Friday Agreement for Northern Ireland, reached in 1998, was a titanic achievement, involving courageous and tireless work from many, including Blair's predecessor, John Major. But Blair was pivotal in his willingness to keep going through long nights until the deal was signed.[13] The agreement negotiated with some previously unyielding opponents in Northern Ireland, and with the agile cooperation of the Irish government, was almost a work of art. Blair and all the other senior figures involved had to find a way through two seemingly unbridgeable perspectives: the unionists' resolute commitment that Northern Ireland must remain part of the UK – the essence of their political being – and, in impossible contrast, the nationalists' yearning for a united Ireland. Yet somehow the Good Friday Agreement formed the bridge. There would be a more clearly defined, soft border between Northern Ireland and Ireland, making the two countries far more tangibly connected than they were previously; a Northern Ireland Assembly, as part of the wider UK devolution settlement, to give a voice and potential power to all sides; as well as continued elections to the UK Parliament. A thousand other ideas and compromises helped to secure an agreement that remained fragile, but more or less in place, at least in the aftermath. Relatively minor outbreaks of terrorism in Northern Ireland did not undermine the Good Friday Agreement. The outcome of the Brexit referendum in 2016 posed a much more substantial threat.

The whole draining and lifesaving sequence played to Blair's strengths. He took risks when there was little danger of the outcome triggering the hostility of some newspapers and their Middle England readers. If there were such risks in any policy area, he became extremely cautious. On one level, he had nothing to lose politically by immersing himself in the peace process. Failure would be tragic, and yet without significant political consequence for a UK prime minister – the *Sun* would not have condemned heroic failure. There would be no obvious benefit to the main Opposition. The Conservatives had been as committed as Blair, in that John Major had instigated the peace process. Now they were under the leadership of the young and inexperienced William Hague, who would be given no political space if Blair failed. The project itself involved no ideological premise rooted on left or right. Blair's technocratic assertion 'What works is what matters' applied to the peace process in a way it did not apply to economic policy or the delivery of public services. The nightmare of the troubles in Northern Ireland liberated him from the constraining prism through which he viewed the battle with the Conservatives and the media. Even so, Blair must have been tempted to turn away from the negotiations at times, as he dealt endlessly with leaders from Northern Ireland who were capable of twisting and turning unpredictably. He lasted the course heroically.

Elsewhere, the new government introduced many smaller innovations, from free entry to museums, to the 'right to roam', which enhanced the quality of many lives. Blair and Brown were too scared to frame their policies in terms of a more active and benevolent state. They assumed that any reference to the state being active might alienate some voters and newspapers. But the government intervened selectively, and often with beneficial consequences. There was the introduction of civil partnerships, a leap as big at the time as the jump when David Cameron legislated for gay marriage. Blair's government introduced a smoking ban in public places, an innovation as important as the spending increase on the NHS. As prime minister, Blair managed to implement significant change while winning elections with big majorities – an unusual combination for a Labour prime minister.

———

Blair also changed the style of politics. He was in a constant dialogue with the voters. Thatcher was a political teacher, but she did not engage directly with the electorate very often. She hardly ever gave interviews on the *Today* programme and few TV interviews between elections. But Blair gave long interviews, press conferences and took part in a range of public events on a regular basis. He was a brilliant communicator, tonally light and flexible, framing arguments with clarity, modesty and wit. Cameron tried to copy him, but was not in the same league, as impersonators never can be. Some Conservatives referred to Blair as 'the master'. This was a doubled-edged sword for Blair, not least because the Conservatives were sincere in their endorsement.

His skills as a communicator became, over time, part of the media's obsession with 'spin'. Admittedly he was over-dependent on his main media adviser, Alastair Campbell. Both conceded that in the early years of government they continued as if they were in opposition, when successful presentation was of overwhelming significance. An Opposition leader cannot be tested by policy implementation. In government, Blair and Campbell had a tendency to mistake a presentational success for implementing policy. But the whole issue of 'spin' became overblown. Campbell's transparent duty was to place Blair and the government in the best possible light. Given the anti-Labour bias in the newspapers, and the newspapers' influence at that time, Campbell's ability to read the rhythms of news, to project positive stories and deflect negative ones, was a key part of Labour's electoral success. Gordon Brown pleaded with Campbell to work full-time for him when he was prime minister, and Tory leaders have sought an equivalent figure. The demands of the UK media are such that any leader would become reliant on a figure who understands how to address them.

The incoming Labour government also had a worked-through economic policy, although this had little to do with Blair. Gordon Brown and his senior adviser, Ed Balls, worked sleeplessly before the 1997 election to frame an economic policy that won the trust of voters, the media, the markets and business – an almost impossible challenge. Their aim was to create space to implement policies that would improve public services and address, to some extent, widening inequality, without all hell breaking loose in the markets and the media. Brown was as well prepared as Geoffrey Howe when he became chancellor in 1979. Blair was equally well prepared in some other policy areas, but gave little thought to economic policy. This became clear later when he gave his name to 'Blairism'. This school of thought found prominent advocates in the parliamentary Labour Party and the media long after Blair had stood down, yet it was an 'ism' without an economic policy.

Indeed, unlike Thatcherism, Blairism lacked a clearly defined ideology. Blair was defined by his revealing opening statement outside Number Ten, when he moved in to become prime minister in May 1997. He uttered words that were more remarkable and bizarre than they seemed at first. Amidst euphoric cheers – Downing Street was crammed with supporters, in a meticulously choreographed manner – Blair declared: 'We ran for office as New Labour, we will govern as New Labour. This is not a mandate for dogma or for doctrine, or a return to the past.'

What was so unusual about the assertion is that the core of most opening prime ministerial statements – albeit in banal or bland ways – is about the country. Blair's statement was partly about the country, but above all his message was rooted in his view of the Labour Party. He wanted to make clear from the beginning that this was not a return to 'old Labour', a conveniently vague term that created a chronological divide rather than an explicitly ideological one. From the beginning, Blair's governing philosophy was not to be Old Labour. His priority was to reassure sceptical voters that he genuinely was 'new Labour', particularly former Tory voters in Middle England, who read newspapers that were also opposed to Old Labour. If this can be called an ideology or political philosophy, it is a very narrow one. At least Thatcher had her philosophical heroes, F. A. Hayek and Milton Friedman, as guides, even if she was an erratic follower. Blair's ideological timidity was partly defined by context. He led a party that tended to lose elections. Thatcher led one that tended to win them, even though her party had been on a pretty bad run when she became its leader in 1975.

In his first term, Blair was also defined by the policies he had already inherited. When he became leader, the Labour Party had been out of power for so long it had accumulated a mountain of policies, many of which Blair had no choice but to accept. When David Cameron sought to 'do a Blair' with the Conservative Party after he became leader in 2005, he overlooked a key difference. Neil Kinnock and John Smith had done a considerable amount of detailed heavy lifting, in terms of policy and internal reform, before Blair became leader. Yet Cameron, who was not greatly interested in policy detail, inherited an empty canvas. There had been no equivalent of Smith and Kinnock, although Michael Howard, Cameron's predecessor, is underestimated in the way he kept the show on the road towards the 2010 general election, and in the selfless way in which he cleared the path for his successor.

Blair used to describe New Labour's early policy programme dismissively, and yet revealingly, as 'low-hanging fruit'. Some of the early reforms were complex – Blair meant they tended to be changes that pleased his party. Perhaps he also meant that the reforms had not originated from him. He became more excited in the second term, when he felt a little freer and could move the policy agenda to the right, closer to his comfort zone and away from his party's. That is when he began to pursue his erratic public-service reform agenda, changes to the NHS and education reforms. These often stretched the boundaries of support within his party, so much so in certain cases that David Cameron is reported to have described himself as the 'heir to Blair'. Cameron made the assertion with sincerity, and without feeling much need for painful contortion in terms of the Conservative Party's policy programme. Yet in Blair's first term the combination of detailed work carried out by predecessors, as well as the nervily forensic revisions from Blair and Brown after 1994, led to a series of formidable reforms.

Blair probably regarded his announcement that the government would increase spending on the NHS to EU average levels as 'low-hanging fruit', but it was a pledge of great significance, even if it was made in chaotic circumstances. He transformed the spending projections for the NHS on the sofa of a BBC studio one Sunday in January 2000. Crucially, even newspapers like the *Daily Mail* were demanding more spending and higher pay for nurses at around this time. In an interview earlier that month for the *New Statesman* the TV presenter and Labour peer, Robert Winston, suggested that, on the basis of his mother's recent experience, hospitals offered better health provision in Eastern Europe:

> She spent 13 hours in a casualty department before being placed in a mixed-sex ward – an environment Labour has pledged to abolish. Drugs were not dispensed on time. She missed meals, and was found lying on the floor one morning after having fallen out of bed during the night… she caught an infection and came out of hospital with a leg ulcer. It is normal. The terrifying thing is that we accept it.[14]

The *Daily Mail* and other newspapers put the Winston interview on their front pages. The BBC followed up the front pages, as it usually did.

When reflecting on leadership, Blair hailed the virtue of strategy over tactics, but at times he moved with panic-stricken and tactical haste. He often argued in private that he was strategic while Brown was tactical, but this was an example of one leader viewing subjectively his own approach over a rival's.[15] Blair often acted as a short-term tactician, from pledging suddenly to abolish child poverty, to making un-costed spending pledges. The one for the NHS was the biggest of these and Blair was wholly right to make this long-overdue spending commitment, but the announcement had not been discussed with his chancellor, Gordon Brown, let alone any of the Cabinet. The commitment to a massive spending increase was made without any sense of how it would be met. Neurotically alert to the priorities of the *Daily Mail* and the *Sun*, Blair was responding to a media campaign while coming to recognize that far more investment was required, and knowing that if he had raised the issue with Brown in advance, he would have been stopped from speaking out on the BBC sofa. So Blair chose to speak first.

He was demonstrating speedy flexibility, an important leadership skill at times, but was also revealing a wilful capacity to convince himself that his moves were the 'right thing to do', even if his latest position in relation to 'tax and spend' contradicted an earlier one. In most respects, Blair was steady in his 'third way' approach, sometimes too steady. But on 'tax and spend' he waxed and waned. Blair moved into Number Ten convinced that the priority for Labour was to show it could be ruthlessly prudent in relation to public spending. If anything, his priority was to cut taxes. He told the *Independent* before the party's conference in 1998 that lower taxes 'were the way the world was moving'.[16] Indeed, one of the reasons Brown, as chancellor, got so furious with Blair was over his contradictory instincts. After one stormy conversation with Blair, Brown returned to his advisers, Ed Balls and Ed Miliband, and declared, 'You'll never guess what he now wants from me. He wants me to increase public spending and cut taxes… without explaining how.'[17]

There was a small part of Blair that recognized his limitations in relation to economic policy-making, though this was a subject rarely discussed with his advisers in Number Ten unless they were complaining about Brown. More widely, no other Cabinet minister reflected in any depth on economic policy during the Blair era. The lack of an internal debate on the economy was in marked contrast with the Labour government of the mid-1970s, when senior ministers debated economic policy endlessly, with at least three different approaches being espoused by various ministerial heavyweights.[18]

Blair's partial recognition of his own limitations in this most fundamental area partly explains his ambiguity towards Brown.[19] After the first few years in government, quite a big part of Blair wanted to sack Brown or at least move him to the Foreign Office,[20] but he never did so. By the beginning of the second term, Brown was demanding on a regular basis that Blair depart. Typically, their first discussion after the 2001 election, when they met back in Downing Street, included a demand from Brown that Blair plan for his own departure. Unsurprisingly, Blair was far from thrilled by this. But there was still a bit of Blair that knew Brown was the only substantial economic policy-maker in his government. Every now and again Blair would thrill his closest advisers by declaring that he would sack Brown, but he never did. There was no one else in the Cabinet remotely qualified to take command of economic policy. It is to Blair's credit as leader that, reluctantly and erratically, he realized this was the case, although he also believed that Brown would be impossibly dangerous on the backbenches. He was right about that, too.

After much agonizing, Brown raised the additional money from a tax rise directly linked to the NHS, almost a form of hypothecation or earmarked taxation. He did so having moved carefully and with considerable political skill, commissioning a seemingly independent report from a senior banker at a time when bankers' views on the best way to fund healthcare demands were still respected. The senior banker recommended a rise in National Insurance – in effect, a substantial tax rise. This was a huge moment in the history of New Labour, a political project that had defined itself partly against the 'tax and spend' caricature of the past.[21] Nervily and warily, Blair endorsed the tax rise, which was formally announced in the 2002 budget. He had no choice but to do so, given that he had made the spending pledge without knowing how it would be met. Some of his senior advisers in Number Ten were so anxious about the initiative that they feared it would lose them the next election. This was soon after Labour had won a second landslide and faced the weak Iain Duncan Smith as leader of the Opposition. New Labour was always fearful and nervy about disturbing the natural order of things in the UK, and this was understandable given voters' habit of electing Conservative governments, if given half an excuse to do so. Some feared that a tax rise would fatally disrupt the natural order.

The fear was reflected in what followed. Blair was anxious to prove that every penny of the money was being well spent and was accompanied by 'efficiencies'. His chosen method was what he presented as 'reform' of the NHS. At the beginning of the second term he had appointed Alan Milburn as Health Secretary, a figure who was big on vision and flaky on policy detail. Like some of Blair's other favourite ministers, Milburn had engaging charm and fleeting political energy, but no staying power. For a time, both he and Blair enthused about 'empowering patients', 'patient choice' and creating foundation hospitals that would be largely self-governing. More widely, they sought to attract the private sector to play a larger role, partly by offering some generous conditions to lure companies into new arrangements.

Blair insisted that anyone who opposed his ideas was 'anti-reform', as if only one version of change was possible. Neither Blair nor Milburn had given much thought to how their goals would be achieved. What would happen if a hospital was forced to close, on the grounds that it had run out of money? How could patients 'choose' their hospital, without hospitals being run with lots of empty beds and spare staff, a system that would create surplus capacity? How could a market work effectively in a service where patients paid nothing directly for the service they required? In an attempt to answer these questions, vast numbers of mediating agencies were required, but that raised further issues about blurred accountability and responsibility.

In his deceptively emollient memoir, Brown's close adviser from this period, Ed Balls, made an important observation. For a moment his buoyant tone became more candid:

> New Labour was never ever about trying to turn our state schools and hospitals into a marketplace where competition and profit should be drivers of excellence; and yet people like Alan Milburn defined it in that way… We won the definitive argument on a tax rise in the 2002 budget and won it comprehensively. But instead of taking that success and applying it to other public services in need of modernisation and proper funding we just invented a new argument on health and turned in on ourselves… That as much as Iraq was the New Labour tragedy.[22]

Choosing to see what they wanted to see, reviewers overlooked the one provocative paragraph. But the words were of historic significance, and Balls was right to compare the sequence with the calamity of the war in Iraq. Instead of focusing on how effectively to spend every penny of the additional NHS cash, and showing to voters that the money was spent well, the project got lost in a huge internal row about the structure of the NHS, the degree to which internal competition was desirable or feasible, and how much the private sector could get involved. Meanwhile, Blair hailed 'patient choice' when to some extent, even with the additional resources, choice was bound to be restricted. At the same time Brown feared that if Milburn's plans went ahead, hospitals could go bankrupt, as Labour was supposed to be proclaiming its unprecedented commitment to the NHS. A messy compromise between Blair and Brown was finally agreed, but as Balls noted, the spending increase on the NHS – an epic moment for a centre-left party in government – was partly lost in internal rows and clumsy reforms.

Even so, the increased investment and some of the reforms were substantial enough to briefly transform the quality of health provision in the UK. For a short time investment was indeed as high as the EU average, but soon after the 2008 crash it started to fall again, while the chaotic structures in the NHS remained in place and were fragmented further under David Cameron's leadership.

From 2001 onwards, some of Blair's allies briefed to the chorus of supportive commentators that Brown was 'anti-reform'. Subsequently the simplistic 'reform versus anti-reform' became an enduring and wholly misleading juxtaposition in British politics. Cameron adopted the same juxtaposition when his government generated more complex structures and mediating agencies, as he 'reformed' the NHS.

———

After winning a second landslide in 2001, Blair felt freer to pursue his own agenda. As is often the case with prime ministers, this is a dangerous liberation. In Blair's case, he chose to move towards his dark end at a point when he had maximum space on the political stage. This became apparent during the first few weeks of his second term when he had a revealing conversation with the former Cabinet minister Chris Smith, who had been Culture Secretary for the entire first term. Blair did not reappoint Smith for the second term, but, as a leader, Blair was politically intelligent about being convivial to ministers he had sacked. He invited Smith for a cup of tea in Number Ten. According to Smith, Blair told him he had three objectives for the second term. These were joining the euro, reforming public services and proving that a Labour prime minister could work closely with a Republican president, at a point when senior Conservatives were parading their Republican credentials. The third objective, pursued resolutely, led towards the war in Iraq or, more precisely, the UK backing the US.[23]

George Bush had begun his first term as president of the United States in January 2001, succeeding Blair's good friend and political soulmate, Bill Clinton. Neurotically alert to whatever the Conservative Party was up to, Blair noted soon after his cup of tea with Smith that the new Conservative leader, Iain Duncan Smith, was making overtures to the Bush administration. He sensed political danger. Blair wanted to give no space to Duncan Smith, fearing that post-Clinton it might be the new Conservative leadership that claimed a greater rapport with the new Washington administration. As he had told Smith, Blair was absolutely committed to showing that he could work as closely with the Bush administration as he had done with the Clinton administration.

This was one of the key strategic calculations as he made his moves towards Iraq. That is not to say there weren't others. No doubt Blair felt there was a robust case for removing Saddam

Hussein, but if the case for war had been made by someone on the Moon or the leader of North Korea, he would not have backed the invasion. It was the fact that a US president was making the case that propelled Blair towards supporting the war in Iraq. This was partly a strategic calculation about what he saw as the need for a Labour prime minister to be seen to be close to a US president, but also one of substance. Blair knew the Bush administration would act unilaterally in Iraq, if need be. He wanted to keep them engaged with allies like the UK.

As ever with Blair, he tried to navigate a third way in relation to Iraq. Quite a lot of commentators described his approach to Iraq as a terrible lapse of judgement, a big leap that was wholly out of character. On this reading, he metamorphosed from the cautious centrist to an unyielding evangelist. This is a misinterpretation of what happened. Every step Blair took in the build-up to war was wholly in character. He did not simply back President Bush as a crusading advocate of military intervention. Blair became evangelical, but only after seeking an expedient way through the path to war.

Here were Blair's multi-layered calculations. After Bush made his speech in January 2002 about the 'axis of evil' – a sweeping term that linked the Saddam regime to the terror attacks on the US on 11 September 2001 – Blair knew for sure that the US administration was planning to remove the dictator by force. With a convenient naivety, Blair saw the case in favour of war partly on the basis of his experience in Kosovo, where liberated families gratefully named their babies after him, an intoxicating tribute. Without exploring deeply what was happening in Iraq and beyond, he assumed that an Iraq liberated from Saddam would be similarly grateful. He also became convinced that he could influence the Bush administration by supporting it, and that after the 9/11 attacks on the US he had a duty to remain a loyal ally. Soon he was to discover, as other prime ministers had, the extreme limits of UK influence. But these related assumptions were by no means his sole or overwhelming calculation. There were many others.

Blair knew little about Iraq or the surrounding region, but he was a world expert on the Labour Party and how it lost elections before he became leader. He assumed that, as a Labour prime minister, his Middle England supporters (and the newspapers they read) would expect him to support a US president when that president was challenging a brutal dictator. Previous Labour leaders had been seen as 'weak' in relation to defence policy. Blair would never be perceived in such a light. He was also aware that Rupert Murdoch would be watching him closely, and Murdoch was a strong supporter of removing Saddam by force.[24]

Blair also planned at some point to hold a referendum and to campaign for the UK to join the euro. He was normally worried by newspaper onslaughts on him, but he was entirely relaxed when the Labour-supporting *Daily Mirror* newspaper accused him of being 'Bush's poodle'. He sensed that some voters would prefer a Labour prime minister to be working closely with a Republican president and he assumed that, after such attacks, no newspaper could criticize him for being indifferent to the US and 'soft' on Europe when he led the euro referendum campaign. But the referendum on the euro never happened, even though Blair saw such a campaign as part of his historic destiny.[25] After backing the US in Iraq, he hoped to complete his global 'third way' by putting the case for the UK joining the euro.

There was one final calculation. Every leader must seek to assess where their moves will leave them politically. There is nothing wrong with this. Margaret Thatcher knew she would have to resign if she did not fight the Falklands War, so unsurprisingly she went to war. Blair assumed that backing Bush would be, at worst, the least unpopular course to take. But he had some hope, when Saddam fell, that the war would be popular.[26] The former Foreign Secretary, Robin Cook, who resigned from the Cabinet in advance of the war, recalled that the first by-election after the Falklands War in 1982 was fought in Beaconsfield. Blair was the Labour candidate and, when Cook went to campaign for Blair, he told Cook how voters were in awe of Thatcher after the Falklands. She had acquired a new aura. Cook became convinced that Thatcher and the Falklands Factor were on Blair's mind as he moved towards Iraq. He assumed that, in the UK, war leaders became popular.

Blair was also leader of a party that was bound to be divided in relation to war. Labour had a strong Atlanticist wing that would be inclined to support Bush. At the same time, Cook's wing of the party loathed Bush and parts of his administration, and was committed to the UN as a means of resolving issues. Meanwhile, on the other side of the multi-layered equation, senior figures in the Bush administration had no faith in the UN and were impatient to invade Iraq, unilaterally if necessary. This was a daunting political and international context for a Labour prime minister.

Faced with a plethora of complex calculations, Blair navigated his latest third way. The question he had to answer was not the one that is often applied to him. It was not: 'Do I want to invade Iraq?' The question he had to answer was a more difficult one: 'Do I want to back the US president, who plans to invade Iraq in order to remove Saddam?' Blair had been the United States' close ally after 11 September 2001. President Clinton had come to his aid in the Balkans, intervening decisively in a military campaign that was originally of uncertain outcome. For Blair, the question was a genuinely thorny one. A bigger, more experienced figure would still have turned away. But even a titan would have struggled with the dilemmas, which looked far more forbidding in advance of the war than they did afterwards, when Blair was lazily dismissed as a crazed war criminal.

Prematurely and with timid naivety, Blair told Bush that the UK government would support the US mission, come what may. 'I will be with you whatever' were the words of a note from Blair to Bush written in July 2002 and highlighted in the Chilcot Inquiry into the war, whose report was published in July 2016.

But Blair made that commitment as part of a negotiation in which he persuaded Bush to seek the support of the UN in enforcing resolutions that demanded the removal of Saddam's 'weapons of mass destruction' (WMD). The UN would not sanction the removal of Saddam through force in a resolution. But as Saddam had defied various UN resolutions in relation to his alleged WMD, Blair thought he had hit upon a feasible route. The focus on WMD arose from Blair's need to navigate the UN route – one that would command much wider support in his party and the wider electorate. Blair also placed polite pressure on Bush to revive the peace process between Israel and Palestine. This was his 'third way', part of a pattern in his leadership and not an aberration: seek UN backing rather than act unilaterally, and make progress in the Middle East. In order to encourage the US president, Blair assured him that even if both these routes failed, he would back military action.

There was a contrast between Blair's approach and that of his main opponent, who also supported military action. The Conservative leader, Iain Duncan Smith, was insisting that his party would support Bush, whether or not he sought UN backing.

Blair's position was distinct, but in a limited way. Without UN backing, he would be in the same place as Duncan Smith.

Very quickly, Blair became trapped. Prime ministers are often incarcerated politically, but can never admit to being so. In Blair's case, he was not used to being quite so constrained. Normally he found a way through thorny policy areas. This time there was no escape, although he did not realize this as he made his way towards his form of political hell.

From the summer of 2002 onwards, Blair spent much of his time putting forward his case for what he was doing. This happened to be dangerously ambiguous. He argued in interviews, speeches and seemingly never-ending press conferences that Saddam must remove his weapons. He did not, and could not, suggest that he or, more precisely, the US administration wanted to remove Saddam. The UN would regard such a military intervention as being against international law, and the Labour Party would become even more restive.

In September 2002 Blair published UK intelligence in a document that aimed to show the extent of Saddam's WMD. At the time he saw the document as part of his case, like a lawyer presenting evidence that would help him win an argument. Later, the dossier on Saddam's WMD was to be plucked out of context and assessed as if it were supposed to be an entirely neutral piece of work. When it was published, the document on Saddam's WMD was evidently part of a wider set of propositions that Blair was making, with increasingly desperate urgency.

By early 2003 there was still not a single senior figure in the UN who thought Blair had a hope of speedily securing a UN resolution to sanction war in Iraq. Blair had no choice but to cling to the hope of meeting this impossible objective. When he failed to agree a resolution of any significance, he blamed President Chirac, who had given a very reasonable interview insisting that, for the time being, France would oppose military intervention. Suddenly Blair was even more trapped, having assured Bush that he would be with him, whatever happened at the UN.

Blair was constrained in many other respects, too. He was not in charge of the timetable for war. While he spoke of standing 'shoulder to shoulder' with the US, he was following the US schedule. Occasionally he was assertive, but in a limited context, persuading Bush to give him time to seek, fruitlessly, a UN resolution that would give him the cover he required. Blair also succeeded in persuading Bush to make a vague pledge to renew the Middle East peace process. Bush made a brief statement in which, without any great assertive enthusiasm, he pledged to renew the focus on some form of two-state solution to the Israel/Palestine question. Blair was fleetingly upbeat as he watched Bush deliver his largely empty words on the Middle East, failing to notice the limits of his influence, or not daring to do so.

In reality the US administration was getting impatient. Why did Blair not give the weapons' inspectors more time to search for WMD? The question is meaningless and unfair. The timing was not up to him. The US wanted to act speedily not least because the temperatures in Iraq would soar if they waited much longer. Why did Blair not pull out of the conflict after he failed to secure a meaningful UN resolution authorizing force? There was not the remotest possibility that Blair would turn away and become the Labour prime minister who was not 'strong' or 'courageous' on the eve of war. Part of the purpose of his leadership had been to show that a Labour prime minister could be 'strong'. Why did Blair not retreat when up to a million people took part in demonstrations against the war in the UK on a freezing-cold Saturday in February 2003, shortly before the conflict began? By then the course was set. Blair was surprised by the scale of the demonstrations, and by the range of those taking part. Some of the marchers were 'his' constituency – those who had turned against Labour in the 1980s, but had voted New Labour in 1997 and who recognized the recklessness of this particular war. For Blair, it was far too late to pursue a different course.

If Blair had pulled back in the face of one march, he would have been without a voice in the future. Many newspapers were praising his 'courage'. The former Conservative minister Michael Portillo wrote in *The Sunday Times* that he had not realized until now 'the degree to which Blair is a principled and brave leader'.[27] Only the *Daily Mirror* and the *Independent* unequivocally opposed the war. The Conservative leader, Iain Duncan Smith, continued to side with Blair rather than with the protesters, some of whom were Conservative supporters. The least unsafe route for Blair was to carry on and claim that he was acting because it was 'the right thing to do' – one of his many conveniently technocratic and apolitical phrases that punctuated the New Labour era.

What followed was an epic tragedy. Above all, the tragedy lay in the number of deaths that arose as a result of the invasion. The estimates of the numbers who died vary and are the subject of ongoing debate, but few deny that hundreds of thousands were killed as a direct or indirect result of the war. A rare piece of accurate intelligence warned in advance that the war would heighten the risk of terrorism. Blair ignored this unwelcome pre-war information. Subsequently, Iraq became a terrorists' playground while a civil war erupted between different factions that had been held in check by a tyrant's rule.

For Blair, the war had Shakespearean consequences. At the beginning of his leadership he sought to show that he could be trusted. In the 1980s Labour leaders were not trusted on matters of defence or much else. John Major was slaughtered in 1997 partly because of sleaze and a sense that the Tories could not be trusted. Blair would be different. Blair would be 'new'. But after Iraq, he was accused of lying in order to win support for the war, and of wilfully misleading voters over the existence of Saddam's weapons of mass destruction in order to implement his crusading vision. Some voters became convinced that Blair was a war criminal who should be tried in The Hague. A few years later, when no longer prime minister, Blair confided to Alastair Campbell that he preferred being in other countries rather than his own, because of the anger that he provoked.[28]

In some respects, the anger directed at Blair was overwrought, part of the exaggerated response he generated from the beginning. The early opinion of Blair as a great radical leader who would heroically transform Britain was at odds with the cautious, defensive 1997 manifesto composed by a leader with no experience of power. The later perception of Blair as a mendacious messianic murderer is also contradicted by the evidence.

One clue as to how easily Blair is misread relates to perceptions of how he managed the Cabinet both during the build-up to war and throughout the rest of his leadership. The Chilcot Inquiry into the war was typical in suggesting that ministers were prevented from expressing their views or from scrutinizing what was happening. Chilcot concluded that there should have been 'wider discussions by a cabinet committee or small group of ministers', and that the Cabinet should 'have been made aware of the legal uncertainties' surrounding the war.[29] Yet with the exception of Robin Cook, and to some extent Clare Short,[30] who resigned after the war, the Cabinet chose not to probe. Cabinet ministers did not live in an alternative universe. They were aware of the raging debate about Iraq, the risks and the questions about its legality. Blair had won two election landslides and he had given them Cabinet posts. They were grateful and keen to deliver what he wanted. Crucially, most of them were not fully formed politicians and did not seek to be. They sought to please Blair. The very big exception to this docility was usually Gordon Brown, but on Iraq, Brown agreed with Blair. If he had disagreed, he would have attempted to block what Blair was doing, as he often did in domestic policy areas. Brown raged against tuition fees and elements of the NHS reforms, both of which were being considered at around the same time as the war in Iraq, but he did not rage against Iraq.

Blair's perceived attempts to bypass or deceive his Cabinet were part of a wider disproportianate focus on his integrity. There were many other questions that could have been raised after a deadly, calamitous war. Why did he not reflect on the internal tensions in Iraq before going ahead? Later Blair expressed surprise at the near civil war that erupted in Iraq. He need not have been taken aback if he had probed more. There were also questions, still not fully answered, about why the intelligence – even with all the qualifications – was so wrong. Blair was shallow in his reading of the Middle East and then took on the role of the persuasive lawyer as he deployed intelligence to further his case. These are serious enough allegations, but they aren't the same as suggesting that Blair 'lied' to go to war, an assertion as simplistic as some of Blair's own judgements about what would happen in Iraq once it had been 'liberated'.

But even these judgements were not made in isolation. Blair had to decide whether or not he was going to support Bush. The US would have gone to war either way. Indeed, in recognition of the multiple pressures piling in on Blair in the UK, Bush suggested that the UK could step aside – definitive evidence that the US was content to invade Iraq more or less on its own. Blair refused to accept the offer because to have done so would have wrecked his entire multi-layered strategy. He also genuinely wanted the US to be part of the international community and not to act with unilateral recklessness. For Blair, the decision to go to war was about the US and his view of the Labour Party's past as well as what was happening in Iraq.

His use of intelligence was not an act of mendacity or criminality, but he was using the hopelessly speculative material to further his cause, and he knew little about how to actually read intelligence. This is no surprise, given that his first post in government was as prime minister. He had never dealt with intelligence in a previous role.

None of these issues were explored widely after the war – Blair's misreading of Iraq and the wider region, his inexperience as a youthful prime minister, the immense domestic calculations made by any prime minister when deciding whether to take military action. Instead, Blair became a messianic figure who illegally took the UK to war and was wilfully indifferent to the deadly consequences. The long hours he worked on the Northern Ireland peace process are a challenge to a bloody caricature that was too easily formed.

———

Blair's end was as multifaceted and complex as the origins of the UK's involvement in the Iraq War. Indeed, part of the complexity was to do with how the seemingly defining conflict played only an indirect role in his fall.

After the war it might have been logical for Blair to have less confidence in his leadership. Iraq had been largely a Blair solo project, from a UK perspective, and it had quickly proven to be a catastrophe on many different fronts. Because he is a human being, the entire sequence was a draining and traumatic experience for him, and it ended with questions about his integrity, deaths and a destabilized Middle East.[31] Yet perversely Blair became more confident and determined as he moved towards the end of his time in power.

His response to Iraq was a steely determination to show that his leadership was about much more than a war. He became obsessively focused on his narrow interpretation of what constituted public-service reform and made another attempt to explore the possibility of joining the euro. There were no substantial grounds for his renewed interest in the euro at that particular time, beyond a desire to go down in history as the prime minister who was as much a pro-European as one who stood by the US when its president went to war.[32] Blair's confidence and sense of resolution were also strengthened by another election victory in 2005, a dark campaign when questions about his integrity featured heavily, and during which he and Brown had to pretend they were working well together when they were not.[33] Yet with the help of Brown and his entourage, Blair did win the 2005 election after the war in Iraq. Bush won a second election in the US, and the Australian prime minister, John Howard – a supporter of the war – also won again. The invasion of Iraq came to torment the war leaders who took part, defining them darkly, yet they remained election winners.

Blair's increasingly fractious relationship with Brown partly determined his approach in the final phase. He rationalized that with Brown challenging key policies, he had a duty to stay on in order to ensure that 'New Labour' ideas continued to prevail, compared with Brown's more social-democratic version of their project. He was sincere in his mission, but the cause was a convenient one often adopted by prime ministers. For the sake of his country and his party, Blair concluded that he had a duty to remain in power.

In doing so, he depoliticized politics during his curious, intense and yet ragged final phase. The depoliticization had explosive consequences, as voters turned away from a technocratic insistence that 'what works is what matters' – as if any leader would argue for what does not work. But Blair had to deny the salience of left-wing arguments in order to make sense of the support he attracted from sections of the Conservative Party and Conservative-supporting commentators, especially after David Cameron became Conservative leader in 2005. Indeed, the once publicly self-effacing Blair loftily detected a global phenomenon from his own freakish political journey.

He regularly declared that there was no longer a left/right divide in politics, but only one between 'open' and 'closed': advocates of free trade and internationalism against protectionists and insular interventionists. But the 'open v. closed' divide was not remotely new. Indeed, the internal splits in the Conservative Party over the Corn Laws in the mid-nineteenth century represented a split between 'open v. closed'.

Blair had concluded that the left/right divide was over, when this particular ideological chasm was deepening over the role of the state, the virtues or drawbacks of public spending, the limits of markets and the role of governments in mediating a globalized market, among other issues. Debates were erupting in new ways, not least after the financial crash in 2008. They were all themes that triggered conflicting responses from both right and left. Blair was at odds with history when he felt that his 'what works' philosophy was moving with the tides.

Fragile and yet more assertive now than when he was politically strong, in the summer of 2006 Blair flew over to Rupert Murdoch's annual conference in the United States. In his address he hailed the era of political 'cross-dressing' in which opposing parties tried out each other's clothes. The metaphor worked for Blair, but he extrapolated far too widely. His ubiquitous juxtapositions were ideologically rootless: 'boldness v. caution', 'reform v. anti-reform', 'economic competence versus economic incompetence'. Years later, Blair despaired of Labour's embrace of Jeremy Corbyn, but Blair was the leader who moved outside party boundaries and turned his political travels into a creed. His third way had become 'the right thing to do'. Such technocratic banalities were a factor in the rise of the ideologically committed Corbyn, who became an MP in 1983, like Blair. Unlike Blair, he never served on the frontbench until he became a leader with deep but untested ideological convictions. Corbyn had no leaderly experience, but he was rooted in part of a political spectrum that had never become wholly irrelevant in the way that Blair and his followers suggested.

Blair's crazy dance with Brown over his departure date was the immediate cause of his increasing assertiveness. Brown behaved with insensitive and frustrated rudeness towards Blair and his senior advisers in Number Ten, but he had a reason to feel defensive. He dreaded a legacy in which he would be paralysed as an incoming prime minister. In his final days, Blair set a series of tests for Brown, with the support of the newspapers that Brown was desperate to have on his side, too. Would he be a 'reformer', as defined by

Blair, with the support of Cameron and Osborne? Would he be as resolute in foreign affairs? Was his view of New Labour the same as Blair's? At times, Blair told Brown that he would go, then he stayed on. Brown continued to press for him to go. As Brown did so, Blair became more resilient and more determined to stay on. The dance became more crazed until Blair was finally forced to indicate publicly that he would go by the summer of 2007, ten years after becoming prime minister.

Blair had a great gift for compartmentalizing. He could focus on one issue, even if mad storms were erupting around him. In this relatively stressful period, which included an absurd and disgraceful police investigation into whether Blair and his close advisers had broken the law in seeking 'cash for honours', the fallout from Iraq and the constant battering from Brown, there were some sunny days. Blair played a major role in securing the Olympics for London. When the sporting event came to London several years later, the capital, in its buoyant exuberant metropolitan liberalism, reflected Blair's vision and virtues as a leader. He was a social progressive. Securing the Olympics was another gloriously apolitical triumph that was indicative of Blair's ideal terrain. And there were further positive developments in Northern Ireland, which made the always-fragile peace agreement more secure.

Some of the public-service reforms were also delivering positive results. As part of his productive focus on public services, Blair established a Delivery Unit that held policies and policy-makers to account. He was uneasy about hailing the state as an instrument of delivery, but his own Delivery Unit was a model of how to get a grip and make government work more effectively as a whole, even if some of the specific reforms led to costly fragmentation rather than new forms of efficiency.

Inadvertently, Blair hit upon another highly effective model of delivery and, somewhat warily at first, introduced an elected Mayor of London. The wariness was partly to do with the successful candidacy of Ken Livingstone, a figure of the left who terrified the pioneers of New Labour. Livingstone was forced to stand as an independent in the first mayoral election and won easily. He proved to be such a successful reformer that Blair endorsed him, and the mayoral model, with genuine enthusiasm when he felt it was safe to do so. Livingstone appointed travel experts from the US to improve London's dire public transport. Under the body Transport for London, the best professionals were free to innovate, while the high-profile mayor was accountable to the electorate. With the introduction of the Congestion Charge to pay for more buses, and the Oyster card, London suddenly enjoyed improved public transport. Blair was more interested in his interpretation of 'reform' as defined by his changes to the NHS, but he created an alternative model for running public services, almost by chance. Transport for London, under an accountable high-profile mayor, was a structure that greatly improved bus and train services in the capital. This is the public-service reform that was an unequivocal success.

Unsurprisingly, given the ambiguity of his leadership, Blair was forced out without being forced out. He hit upon his final third way: leaving without leaving. By September 2006 some Labour MPs started to call for Blair to go, and this time it was clear Gordon Brown was ready to strike. Blair was made to issue a statement after a fraught, animated and angry conversation with his old friend. In the statement Blair said he would leave, but only after another year or so in power.

But in another lesson of leadership, Blair's authority had already started to drain away. Even before his 2005 election win, Blair had announced that he was only planning to serve one more full term and would not contest a fourth general election. He had pre-announced his departure even before he declared in September 2006 that he would be going in about a year's time.

From that first contorted announcement in 2003, the power oozed away. Some Cabinet ministers who had been Blairite became Brownite. When Blair announced an initiative – and he announced many during his final phase – colleagues, opponents, the media, and probably the wider electorate, recognized it as time-limited. Before long, a successor would be wielding power.

Blair had made a mistake. Cameron committed the same error – following Blair, as he often did – shortly before the 2015 election, declaring in an interview that he would serve a full term, but would not fight the election after that one. He had not intended to make such a foolish declaration, but Blair was often on his mind, just as Thatcher was on Blair's.

Blair resigned as an MP after he left Number Ten. His final appearance at Prime Minister's Questions was also his last contribution in the Commons. MPs on both sides stood and cheered him as he left, departing both as a prime minister and as an MP. This was highly unusual. Most former prime ministers stay on as an MP, quite often for at least one more parliament. Cameron took the same approach as Blair, by leaving Parliament speedily.

Blair's speedy exit was part of a pattern. A lot of Blair's closest ministerial allies left politics before him or soon afterwards. His ministerial allies – figures who were supposed to be great reforming figures, like Alan Milburn, Stephen Byers, John Reid and Patricia Hewitt – did not hang around to fight for their cause, partly because Blairite ideological verve was more about him than about a deeply embedded governing philosophy. When Blair went, Blairism went, too. In marked contrast, Thatcherism continued to cast a spell long after her departure. But Blair's legacy for the Labour Party and the leaders that have followed him is as complex and daunting as the one Margaret Thatcher left for the Conservative Party. Did he win because he was not really Labour at all? Is that the only way Labour can win? Was he right at the time, but the times have changed, making him wrong now? Was he wrong from the beginning, and by the mid-1990s voters were ready to elect a leader to the left of him? The future of the Labour Party will be defined partly by what Tony Blair did, and did not, do as its leader and as winner of three elections in a row. In this sense, he continues to follow Thatcher as she leaves the equivalent questions facing the Conservatives.

Here is a curious lesson of leadership. The great election winners tend to leave their parties bewildered when they depart, or almost depart, from the political stage. Most immediately, Blair left his successor, Gordon Brown, with a dilemma that Brown never resolved. How could he show that he was different from Blair, while retaining the support of the newspapers and voters who backed Labour solely because of Blair? Brown had agonized about that question in advance, and was to do so again when he finally became prime minister.

7

—

GORDON BROWN

There are many ways of judging the effectiveness of prime ministers. How many elections did they win? What impact did their policies have on the country? How did they manage their parties and Parliament? These are three obvious criteria: the first a matter of objective record; the second always deeply subjective; and the third a combination of the two. But there is a fourth, more illuminating method of measuring leadership.

When making judgements about leaders, we must look at the context in which they led. Some leaders are lucky. Harold Wilson took to the helm when the Conservatives were perceived as exhausted and outdated after a long period of rule. A decade later, Margaret Thatcher was in some respects more fortunate. She became leader at a time when a divided Labour government was struggling to retain its tiny majority amidst economic turmoil. Tony Blair was luckier still. By 1994 the Conservatives had been in power even longer than when Wilson led Labour towards modest victory in 1964. They were furiously divided over Europe. Some Tory MPs cared more about this issue than about winning yet another election – a gift for the leader of the Opposition. The three lucky leaders made the most of the benevolent political background by striding towards historic election victories with actual – or affected – momentum.

At the other end of the scale, Gordon Brown was deeply unlucky in terms of the background against which he made his moves. Indeed, he faced profoundly challenging dilemmas throughout his career. There was no junction where he, or an objective observer, could look up at the wider political scenery and fully enjoy the view. Instead the view tended to be dark, with immense, complex political or economic challenges, even when he inherited a partially benevolent economy as chancellor in 1997. Part of the darkness was formed by Brown's internal critics, who tended to ignore the challenging background in which he made his cautious, calculating and sometimes daring moves. His angry Labour opponents often surfaced to comment anonymously on how useless Brown was, without suggesting how they would apply their apparently masterful skills to the intimidating tasks at hand. This pattern applied when Brown was shadow chancellor, chancellor and then prime minister.

The fate of leaders is determined partly by how they rose to the top: Wilson bringing together a Labour Party deeply divided in the vote-losing 1950s; Heath's successful ministerial career giving him a misplaced confidence; Callaghan's close relationship with the trade unions; Thatcher's speedy ascent as she pledged to abolish the local property tax; Major's equivocal positioning in the Conservative Party; Blair's conviction that Labour wins only by being 'new'. Both Blair and Brown were defined by their early years as MPs in the party's vote-losing years of the 1980s and early 1990s. All leaders are also shaped by their less overtly political early years, from Thatcher's upbringing in Grantham, to Major's in Brixton. Of all the modern prime ministers, Brown surfaced from his early years most fully formed, with his qualities and deep flaws. His father was a minister in the Church of Scotland, a figure that Brown cited as often as Thatcher referred to Alderman Roberts. Brown suggested that his father gave him his moral compass. His father sought to do good in the Church. Brown saw politics as the vocation in which he could make a difference to people's lives. At the same time, he became a youthful star in the Scottish Labour Party, once described by another sparkling figure from Scotland, Robin Cook, as a 'nest of vipers'. Cook, who became Foreign Secretary in the New Labour era, was one of several figures Brown fell out with. Brown learned that politics could be brutal, and sometimes should be brutal. For Brown, the ends justified the means, whether the end was his own ascent to the top of the Labour Party or prevailing with colleagues in order to pursue causes related to his interpretation of social justice.

He was a student at Edinburgh University by the age of sixteen, a youthful rector of the university, a writer of books and pamphlets, a reader of many books, a campaigner for Labour and, by 1983, an MP. He had been briefly a BBC producer, giving him some sense of how the media worked, in a parliamentary party incapable of conveying any message effectively to a wider audience. Brown was also intensely competitive. Some of the hunger to win was purged by taking part in various sports. Most modern prime ministers felt the need to affect an interest in football. Brown was genuinely passionate. While a student, he lost the sight in one eye playing rugby. He continued to play tennis and some other sports, but after that terrible injury much of Brown's competitive energy was focused on politics. He ached to win, for his party to win, for himself to win – and for his policies to be the ones that triumphed in internal battles.

In opposition and in government, Brown was responsible for Labour's economic policy for fifteen years. Few of his colleagues, including Tony Blair, gave much detailed thought to economic policy. This is partly because Brown would fume ferociously if anyone ventured onto his terrain. He was the most controlling of control freaks. At the top of the Labour Party, it was only Brown and his closest advisers who thought deeply about economic policy for more than a decade. From the left, John McDonnell reflected from the safety of the backbenches on economic policy, and these reflections gave him authentic authority when he became Jeremy Corbyn's shadow chancellor in 2015. None of Blair's frontbenchers dared to show any interest, in the face of the intimidating Brown. This was in marked contrast to the 1970s, when most Labour Cabinet ministers thought of little else other than economic policy, whatever their theoretical department briefs.

The background to Brown's thorny ascent merits a quick view. The circumstances at the start of his phase as a pivotal Labour figure partly explain the dramas that followed, and are as important in terms of making sense of his tempestuous career as his complex personality.

After the party's fourth defeat in 1992, the new Labour leader, John Smith, made Brown shadow chancellor. This is one of the toughest jobs in British politics at the best of times. But for a Labour politician of insatiable ambition, this was the very worst of times. The outcome of the 1992 election had been the most painful of the party's four successive losses. The party leadership had hopes they might win, even if Blair and Brown never thought they would, and most commentators predicted a Labour victory with Neil Kinnock as prime minister. The distinguished political columnist Peter Jenkins headed for Lancashire during the campaign, an area with several marginal seats, and concluded in his *Independent* column that Labour would win.[1] Most polls pointed to a Labour victory or a hung parliament. Yet Labour lost again, triggering much speculation – not least in Labour's ranks – that the party might never win. The conditions had seemed favourable: since the previous election in 1987, Kinnock had seen off the threat from the SDP, the Conservative government had introduced the deeply unpopular poll tax, the economy was in serious trouble and John Major was, in some ways, an awkward public performer. But Labour lost, a defeat that suggested seemingly never-ending opposition.

At Labour's National Executive post-election meeting the party's polling and focus-group guru, Philip Gould, was blunt. He told the shell-shocked and funereal gathering that Labour had lost again because it was not trusted with the voters' money. Specifically, voters did not trust Labour to 'tax and spend' – the narrow and distorting prism through which UK elections are largely fought. Labour's outgoing leader, Neil Kinnock, had tried hard to appear more like a technocratic bank manager, in an attempt to reassure voters. Kinnock tried so hard to become what he was not that he lost the exuberant qualities that had propelled him to the leadership in the first place. Yet he had reformed his party and modified its policies over nine draining years. His shadow chancellor, John Smith, had introduced carefully costed proposals, every halfpenny accounted for, even if he had mistakenly unveiled a 'shadow budget', which the Conservatives leapt upon gratefully.

Smith looked, and sounded, even more like a reassuring bank manager. Kinnock had wanted to propose an earmarked tax to pay for much-needed NHS improvements as part of the party's manifesto in 1992. With good cause, he wanted to add some verve to the party's pitch. Smith vetoed the idea. In spite of the carefully calibrated and fearful caution, the party was still regarded as a reckless spender by a significant section of the electorate and a hostile media. The projection of a leader and shadow chancellor as two bank managers, when the banks were still trusted, did not remotely purge the party's reputation for profligacy.[2]

So this was Brown's joyless inheritance as shadow chancellor. Labour was not trusted to run the economy, and the mistrust was shaped by a distorted but potent 'tax and spend' debate that his party always seemed to lose.

For Brown, the challenge was even more daunting. Labour was not trusted to raise money, but money was obviously needed. By 1992 public services in the UK were in deep decline. NHS waiting times were dangerously long, and the quality of health provision lagged behind equivalent countries, as did investment levels. Public transport creaked along unreliably and would get even worse with the ill-thought-through privatization of the railways. In schools there was much talk of teacher shortages, rundown buildings and the use of battered old textbooks. Everywhere there were vivid images that suggested public spending needed to rise. So how would Brown, as shadow chancellor, square the circle? Labour was not trusted to tax and spend, and yet money was urgently required for public services.

In a way that was too easily overlooked when Brown went out of fashion, he managed it. By Labour's second term, the government was investing in services, sometimes by huge amounts, without becoming unpopular or losing credibility with the markets. Even much of the media remained onside – a miraculous development, as most newspapers had worked on the assumption that services could be improved without spending any additional money.

At the beginning, as the new shadow chancellor, Brown condemned every tax rise introduced by the Conservative government, describing them repeatedly as 'Tory Tax Rises'. In his ubiquitous condemnations he sought to change the perception that Labour put up taxes while Conservatives cut them. There were obvious risks in his relentless attacks. Brown allowed little space for a left-of-centre narrative in which tax ceased to be a 'burden'. But after the election defeat in 1992 there was no such space for Labour. The party could not risk fighting another orthodox 'tax and spend' election, when it had so much evidence this led to electoral slaughter. Instead on Brown went, like a 'Speak your weight' machine: 'Tory tax rises…! Tory tax rises…' The New Labour era can only be understood in the context of the 1992 election and the gloomy lessons to which it pointed.

Brown was equally rigid in relation to Labour's spending plans. To their frustration, and sometimes fury, he would not allow shadow Cabinet colleagues to utter a word that implied an increase in expenditure. Brown eventually recognized that he must address the decay in public services and welfare provision, but at first he saw the necessity of winning over the trust of the media – however right-wing – business leaders and the wider electorate. In contrast to the profligate Conservatives, he would be Mr Prudence, and his frontbenchers would not be allowed to announce policies that implied any additional spending. The discipline and focus that Brown showed are qualifications of leadership. The message was painful for many in his party, but he needed to find a way of moving on from four election defeats. He imposed the pain like a brilliant surgeon who lacked a patient-friendly manner.

Brown's wooden and over-rehearsed declarations were formed partly because he was carrying the heavy weight of economic policy-making. He knew that one word out of place could bring the whole edifice down. Previous shadow chancellors had got into difficulties by going beyond a contrived phrase. He would not do so. As a former TV producer, he also assumed – wrongly – that the soundbite on a TV news bulletin was virtually all that mattered as a form of communication. He would reach that audience whenever he could, happily missing the second half of a live or televised rugby match on a Saturday afternoon to deliver twenty seconds on a TV news bulletin. This was a major sacrifice, as he was one of the few aspiring leaders, or actual leaders, who genuinely adored sport.

The repetitive messaging was only Act One of what Brown assumed would be a long drama, during which he would move on to expand on the purpose behind the prudence. He did not plan to spend the rest of his career railing against tax rises and banning hints of more investment. But as Act One was reaching a prudent climax, there was a dramatic twist in the plot when John Smith died suddenly in the summer of 1994.

Brown had ached to be leader of his party, so much so that he almost assumed he would be. He never recovered from the shock that Tony Blair had not only decided to stand in the 1994 leadership contest but, from the evidence, would probably beat him. There was a part of Brown that sensed, with little evidence to back him up, that he could have fought Blair from the left and won. But Brown did not contemplate doing so for long. Such positioning would have undone all his work as shadow chancellor, in which he had sought to reassure the mighty right-wing newspapers, even though beneath the deceptive surface he was, indeed, to the left of Blair. Instead, a traumatized Brown announced that he would not be standing for the leadership and, although in torment, wrote some of Blair's campaign speeches, and even parts of his victory speech. This is one of many ambiguously vivid images of the New Labour era: the anguished figure who thought he deserved the crown writing key speeches for the close ally who had become leader in his place.[3]

Brown's agonies over the leadership are a running theme for the rest of his political career. The path by which he became leader has its origins in the torment from 1994. He was a figure of unyielding ambition in every field. Like Edward Heath, he needed to prevail in all circumstances. He wanted to be leader more than Blair did. Indeed, when Roy Hattersley urged Blair to stand in 1994, Blair replied, 'But Gordon wants it more than me.'[4]

In many respects, by 1994 Brown deserved it more. He had been the senior partner in his relationship with Blair, teaching Blair the art of speech-writing to the point where Blair became much the better speech-maker. In relation to policy, Brown had been deeply involved in the pivotal area of economics, much the most demanding and complex of policy remits. As for the media, Brown began as the more obsessed and fascinated, although Blair caught up fast. It was Brown who composed Blair's most famous soundbite, when he was shadow Home Secretary. Blair declared that 'Labour would be tough on crime and tough on the causes of crime' – an early example of a clever soundbite that invited a big, bulging tent of support, but the line was Brown's.

In their cramped Westminster office, they watched TV reports of Neil Kinnock's initiatives, and Brown would instinctively offer a running commentary of what worked and what did not, in terms of presentation. He was, for a time, closer than Blair to Peter Mandelson, the party's presentational guru. Brown also arrived at Westminster with a deep sense of Labour's history, having written several books and pamphlets before becoming an MP, and being an avid bibliophile. With all these qualifications, Brown almost assumed that Blair would be his brilliant deputy, the modernizing English counter to his Scottish voice.

There was much talk in the early 1990s, and afterwards, about how close they were as friends. Younger allies of both were later bewildered by this, given the extent of the falling-out and their differing personalities. The explanation is partly that Brown did not, or could not, view politics in terms of friendships. He regarded the vocation as much bigger than that. Colleagues were friends if they served a purpose in the great political venture; they were often enemies if they did not. From 1983, when they both became MPs, Brown recognized Blair's great strengths. To some extent they viewed the political challenges in precisely the same way. They agreed on the need for Labour to change beyond recognition or face eternal opposition; on the centrality of reaching out beyond core support, in terms of messaging and the policies that made sense of the messages; on the sense that England in particular was a conservative country and would not turn to Labour until the leadership could reassure as well as inspire. These common assumptions bound them together as they worked relentlessly in their shared office. They also shared a sense of the ridiculous and laughed together quite a lot before the summer of 1994, as they were struck by the many absurdities in politics. There was little laughter after that summer.

Brown viewed the friendship in political terms. Here was an ally who could help in a joint project to revive Labour, and then become an even more important colleague when Brown went for the leadership. When this did not happen, the limited basis of the friendship more or less collapsed. In the summer of 1994 Brown could not see, or chose not to see, that all the momentum was with Blair. MPs across the party were urging Blair to stand. Influential columnists and newspaper editorials went for Blair. Polls suggested that Labour would soar if Blair became leader. Normally Brown was the most astute reader of the wider context, but this particular background was too bleak for him to contemplate.

His response to the loss of leadership was multi-layered. Above all, it made Brown even more determined to be the next Labour leader. He succeeded against the odds, a rare case of a leader-in-waiting becoming leader. Partly his response was to display aggressive rudeness to allies of Blair, and quite often to Blair himself. He rarely spoke to Mandelson or Blair's chief of staff, Jonathan Powell. Others in Blair's Number Ten, with political views closer in some respect to Brown's, were alienated by what they regarded as a thuggish approach that shocked and alarmed them. Brown's transparent anger was largely counter-productive. His fuming disappointment was too transparent. But it was partly the anger that drove him on. Most of Blair's close ministerial allies from the New Labour era were nowhere near as driven. As a result, they did not last very long, their shaky grasp of policies and the values that underpinned them combining with a lack of determined resolve to stay the course. Alan Milburn left the furnace twice, to spend more time with his family. Steve Byers was forced to resign and did not return. Patricia Hewitt left the fray soon after Blair stood down. John Reid moved from Cabinet post to post with such speed that he was never fully tested and headed off to be chair of Celtic Football Club soon after Blair stood down. They all had their qualities, but staying power was not one of them. Like the equally stubborn Edward Heath, Brown had no intention of moving to one side. He had a pretty clear idea of the course he wanted to take.

Those who seek to be a leader must make many calculations and face a multitude of dilemmas. The TV series *House of Cards* would not have been a hit if leadership and ambition were straightforward. Of all the modern prime ministers, Brown faced the most complex and multifaceted of dilemmas. The problems started to take shape when he knew that he could only challenge Blair from the left in the summer of 1994. After that, they grew into a conundrum that could only be addressed by increasingly painful contortions.

Brown calculated that he would be destroyed if either the media or the wider electorate learned that he was to the left of Blair, even if he was more relaxed about his party recognizing the difference between the two of them. There were genuine ideological and strategic differences over the role of the state and markets in the provision of public services, tax and spend, welfare reform, the euro and how best to present the way the Labour Party had changed.[5] These ideological tensions became more marked over time, but they placed Brown in a straitjacket. He concluded – probably correctly, given the way New Labour had chosen to project itself – that if he were seen as being a millimetre to the left of Blair, he was doomed. As Blair moved further to the right, Brown's anguish intensified. He opposed quite a lot of what Blair was doing and saying, but could not articulate in full the nature of his opposition without alienating what he regarded as the mighty newspapers. He was especially preoccupied by the *Sun* and *The Times*. Like Blair, he developed politically in the 1980s, a time when the newspapers contributed to the destruction of Labour leaders. He worked on the assumption that if the *Sun* turned against him, he would not have the space to succeed in British politics. Ironically, the *Sun* still turned, although by then Brown was prime minister and was probably going to lose anyway. This dilemma lingered, even when he became prime minister, as he ached for the endorsement of the newspapers in an election, while seeking to mark the distance from Blair.

The dance between the two New Labour figures was more or less the sole focus of the media for thirteen years.[6] The soap opera of conflicting ambitions was usually the focus. But the New Labour era was always more subtle and interesting than it seemed. From the summer of 1994, Brown was by no means only in torment about the leadership. For big political figures, many emotions can run in parallel. Brown was also partly excited by his new freedom under Blair's leadership. He had been close to Blair's predecessor, John Smith, but their views on economic policy, and the strategy that arose from it, did not always coincide.

Under Blair's leadership, Brown had much more space, at least in the early years. He famously insisted on a huge degree of control when he agreed not to contest the 1994 leadership contest. Whatever else happened when Blair and Brown met at Granita, the restaurant in Islington where they made their pact in the summer of 1994, both agreed that Brown had demanded control over key policy areas. Such was the unprecedented degree of autonomy he had secured that when the *Guardian*'s political columnist, Hugo Young, went to see Brown for a cup of tea, after it was clear Blair would be the new leader, he discovered Brown on something of a high. 'I'll be able to do a lot more now,' he said. Young saw Brown at his Westminster office on 24 May 1994 and noted: 'GB seemed oddly liberated. No sign of the uptight neurotic fellow I've seen before. Perhaps not a man desperately worried about the leadership?'

Brown was unquestionably worried about the leadership, but as ever in the New Labour era, there was another dimension. Young went on to observe: 'As with Margaret Beckett [Labour's then acting leader] death seems to have released confidence. Not that they are not more reckless with their words: they just seem less defensive.'[7]

Brown made the most of the space, once Blair was leader, and worked intensively with his young special adviser, Ed Balls. Theirs is an under-explored relationship, partly because the two of them are wary of exploration. Indeed, one of the challenges to understanding the New Labour era is the one-sided nature of the memoirs published so far. Blair and his allies have published detailed onslaughts against Brown, as part of their vivid and surprisingly well-written reflections on their time at the top. There are fewer books from the alternative perspective, partly because the key figures are unsure how to make sense of what happened, and why.

The Brown/Balls partnership was as important as any other relationship in the New Labour era, and more significant in policy terms than the relationship between Blair and Alastair Campbell. Working intensively in opposition, as well as in government, the duo sought a new economic framework that would help to resolve the impossible conundrum of how Labour was not trusted to spend money and yet public services needed investment. Balls was the economist and Brown the obsessive strategist. Their objective was to establish a reputation for prudence that ultimately gave the government space to increase public spending. Brown espoused 'prudence for a purpose', another soundbite aimed at the big tent of support. The right-wing newspapers hailed the prudence, but the purpose was focused on higher pay for low earners and more cash for public services, previously dismissed by the media as reckless profligacy. Brown and Balls planned for Bank of England independence, a policy implemented immediately after the 1997 election. Shortly before the general election in 1997, Brown announced that there would be no increases in income tax for an entire parliament. He would stick to government spending plans, which the outgoing chancellor, Ken Clarke, had regarded as 'eye-wateringly tight'. In government, Brown kept to those targets, which Clarke had every intention of breaking if he had been returned to the Treasury.

———

Brown was too prudent after Labour won a landslide in 1997. The need to secure 'trust' trumped the demands of public services. Hospitals, schools and public transport continued to totter in the early years of the Labour government. But over time, Brown secured the space to increase spending in ways that made Labour electorally popular, rather than fatally mistrusted. Crucially, he kept the markets from panicking. He found other ways of raising money without putting up totemic taxes in ways that drove the newspapers into a frenzy. Some of the revenue-raising policies got him into deep trouble retrospectively. He sold gold when prices were low. He launched costly and convoluted Private Finance Initiatives in order to raise cash for hospitals. These short-term emergency measures were a consequence of a political and media culture that assumed public services could be improved without raising taxes. That had been Blair and Brown's experience of fighting elections in the 1980s and in 1992. Until Labour's second term, Brown worked on the assumption that no Labour chancellor could overtly raise taxes on income.

His alternative searches for much-needed revenue were unavoidable. He needed the money. But over time they had an impact on his reputation. Brown became famous for raising taxes stealthily – a comical contradiction in terms. His reputation as the stealth chancellor suggested he was not being anywhere near stealthy enough, or else he would not have been well known for raising hidden taxes. The same contradiction applied to Harold Wilson, who became famous for being devious. If Wilson had been devious, he would not have been known for this characteristic. The successfully devious prime ministers act in ways that make the trickery almost impossible to recognize. Wilson did not acquire this reputation until he had been prime minister for several years. Brown became well known for his stealthiness long before he was prime minister. He arrived in Number Ten with a well-developed reputation. Here is another lesson: leadership is more straightforward in its early phase if leaders have more of a blurred image. The fuzziness gives them space to develop their public persona.

In his early years as chancellor, Brown managed to combine prudence with purpose. He was one of the few chancellors to direct the Treasury rather than be directed by it. The already mighty department became mightier still, with an expanded remit to consider the needs of public services and to narrow inequality. Brown began to invest in tax credits for the lower-paid and raised a one-off tax on privatized utilities. This was cleverly chosen as a popular tax, another contradiction in terms. The money funded a largely effective welfare-to-work programme, branded as a 'new deal'. In his first term, when Brown did find extra money for public services, he diverted the cash to poorer areas. The prudence – or the appearance of prudence – kept the Tory newspapers and their readers on board. After the 1999 budget the *Daily Telegraph*'s front page declared: 'Brown's Budget for Middle England'. In reality, quite a lot of Middle England was being asked to pay more in order to finance projects for those on low incomes and benefits. Over time, there was a downside for Labour, and for Brown, in the messaging. Those on lower incomes did not always make the connection between their higher pay and the government policies that brought about the increases.

To the surprise of Blair and the relief of Brown, the big tent of support survived an overt tax rise to pay for a substantial increase in NHS spending in 2003. Brown's route towards the announcement of a big tax rise for most earners proves that he could be an epic strategist, and also shows how quickly political orthodoxies can change. The saga is worth a book in itself, and is like going back to ancient history.

Brown sought respectability by being associated with revered senior bankers. This was another strategic move. How could he be perceived as to the left of Blair when being seen with Alan Greenspan, the chair of the Federal Reserve in the US; or when playing a prominent role in the opening of the Lehman Brothers' bank in London? Brown assumed in that distant era that being seen with bankers helped his political project, rather than the opposite. He was right to do so. The bankers were the trusty wealth-creators, the innovators making the global economy spin. In order to acquire a protective shield for the planned tax rise to pay for NHS funding, he asked Derek Wanless, the former chairman of NatWest Bank, to conduct a review of how the increase could be paid for.

Wanless soon concluded what Brown had indicated he wanted as a conclusion: a substantial increase in National Insurance payments was needed. When Brown made the announcement in his 2002 budget, he made sure that Wanless was cited repeatedly: 'Wanless says the only feasible way is through an increase in National Insurance contributions...' Wanless got the citations, Brown got the credit. Voters gave his 2002 budget the thumbs up, with polls indicating that a large majority of voters supported the tax rise enthusiastically. One of Brown's other senior advisers, Ed Miliband, noted in the immediate aftermath that Brown showed his authentic voice in the 2002 budget. Yet his voice was smothered again, as internal battles erupted over what reforms should accompany the additional cash.[8]

Eventually Brown became the longest-serving Labour chancellor. This was too long, as far as he was concerned. Still, to be a Labour chancellor for ten years is a momentous achievement, not least because the media and markets are more wary of Labour chancellors. The scrutiny is much greater. Denis Healey, a robust political figure, was chancellor for five years and was physically ill by the end. Healey was responsible for the economy in tumultuous times, but Brown's task was mountainous, too. He became chancellor following four election defeats and lasted a decade at the Treasury, having already been responsible for economic policy in opposition from 1992. Although the economy he inherited was far more stable than the one Healey took over in 1974, public services were in decay. He also faced epic decisions over whether the UK should join the single currency, an issue that Blair, as prime minister, saw as his historic role. If nothing else, Brown's tenure was a feat of endurance and ruthlessness.

In standing his ground with admirable powers of endurance, he also went way over the top, alienating some potential allies. In the Blair court that Brown loathed, there were advisers who were in some respects closer to Brown's politics than they were to Blair's. Peter Hyman, in his book *1 Out of 10*, about his time as an aide to Blair, noted that the prime minister did not see the need for higher public spending beyond existing commitments, after the 2001 election. Hyman could see that more increases were evidently required. In some ways, Hyman was closer to Brown politically, but he was utterly loyal to Blair and disdainful of Brown, partly because of the chancellor's behaviour. Alastair Campbell's *Diaries* are punctuated with tense exchanges with Brown, even as Brown points out that Campbell is politically closer to him than he is to Blair. Part of the fascination with Campbell as a chronicler is that he does not disclose whether or not he agrees with Brown. In the later volumes, as important and revelatory as the earlier ones, he reports on a whole range of people who were critical of Blair's reforms, from his GP and psychiatrist, to his partner, Fiona Millar, but does not expand on where he stands in terms of policy. His loyalty to Blair is unyielding and his despair of Brown is intense. If Brown had managed some of Blair's allies less brutally, they would have become stauncher allies. His angry frustration drove him on to the top, but it was also a cause of his downfall. When he finally got to the top, there were a lot of influential Labour figures who wanted him to fall.

Brown's anger was not only about unfulfilled ambition. The division became more starkly ideological and strategic over time. Along with Alastair Campbell's GP, Brown had genuine concerns about Blair's public-service reforms. One instance of this emerged in 2003, when Brown laid out in a speech why the markets do not always work when services are financed centrally and delivered free at the point of use. He focused mainly on the NHS.[9]

In his relentless critical scrutiny of Blair's reforms, Brown saw that 'patient choice' would only become a reality if hospitals were half-empty. If they were full, the choice became non-existent. Yet if hospitals were half-empty, there would be fury about the waste and inefficiency. Similarly, if there was a particularly good local school, not all nearby children would be able to attend or it would become packed and would then cease to be as appealing. The good schools tended to find ways of picking the pupils, and not the other way round. Brown delivered the speech to the Social Market Foundation in February 2003 and tried to outline where the markets worked and did not work – a key area for any government, but a theme rarely explored. What is striking retrospectively is how characteristically cautious Brown was in exposing the limits of the markets. At the time the Blairite wing regarded the speech as an act of provocative treachery.

Brown hailed the markets in most areas and was careful to distance himself from some on the left. Once again, he wanted to make a case from the left, but did not want to be seen as to the left of Blair. He put the case for a different kind of 'third way':

> The argument that is often put as public versus private, or markets versus state, does not reflect the complexity of the challenges we face: that markets are part of advancing the public interest and the left are wrong to say they are not; but also that markets are not always in the public interest and the right is wrong to automatically equate the imposition of markets with the public interest. The challenge for New Labour is, while remaining true to our values and goals, to have the courage to affirm that markets are a means of advancing the public interest; to strengthen markets where they work and to tackle market failures to enable markets to work better. And instead of the left's old, often knee-jerk, anti-market sentiment, to assert with confidence that promoting the market economy helps us achieve our goals of a stronger economy and a fairer society.

Having cautiously set out the general terrain, Brown focused on the NHS:

> In healthcare we know that the consumer is not sovereign: use of healthcare is unpredictable and can never be planned by the

consumer in the way that, for example, weekly food consumption can. So we know that: the ordinary market simply cannot function…[10]

The speech was a subtle way of engaging with the internal battle over NHS reform but, weeks away as it was from the Iraq War, it got little attention. As far as the commentariat noticed, Brown's carefully chosen words were regarded as a leadership bid, an attempt to please 'old Labour'. While the leadership was always on Brown's mind, his motives were more multi-layered, as was the speech. Brown knew why he opposed some of Blair's reforms, and it was not just about winning support for a leadership bid.

Brown was the only figure in the New Labour era capable of stepping back and reflecting more deeply. The other modern prime minister who had a similar capacity was Edward Heath. As both Brown and Heath endured traumatic times in Number Ten, perhaps one lesson of leadership is that a capacity to delve beyond the surface is no requirement for lengthy leadership.

Still, leadership was always on his mind. If Brown had been told, when he delivered the speech on the markets and public services, that he would have to wait more than four years before he became prime minister, he would have been horrified. The haul was a long one. By the time Brown acquired the crown he was exhausted. He had been at the centre of the political stage, as shadow chancellor or chancellor, for thirteen years. He had calculated that a modern prominent politician had a shelf life of seven or eight years, given the level of round-the-clock scrutiny. On that basis, Brown had gone well beyond his shelf life even before he became prime minister.

The seemingly calm and yet deranged circumstances in which he finally acquired the crown were part of a pattern of ambiguously Shakespearean sequences. Blair was typical of prime ministers. From the outside, the stresses of leadership in his final phase seemed nightmarish, with Iraq, a police investigation into allegations of 'cash for honours' and the polls suggesting that, for the first time since he became leader, the Conservatives were well ahead. But Blair was reluctant to let go. From within Number Ten, cosily cocooned at times, power retains its attractions. Later the same applied to Theresa May. Governing was a form of hell, but she wanted more of it. Being prime minister can be like the Woody Allen joke: 'The food in this restaurant is awful… and the portions are so small.'

Blair rationalized that he was staying on to ensure Brown had no choice but to follow his version of New Labour. The trap for Brown was that Blair's version of New Labour was different from his in some respects, and yet he did not want to define himself too clearly, fearing he would be seen as moving to the 'vote-losing left'. The dynamic produced one of the whackier dances between the duo, in a highly competitive field of awkward choreography. Eventually, under pressure from Brown and his supporters, Blair announced in 2006 that he would serve for one more year. True to form, Blair had hit upon a third way in resignations, and his announcement triggered a mountain of tributes. After he made the farewell announcement he returned to work as prime minister. For the next year – more so than ever before – Brown was on formal trial as the prime minister-in-waiting. Every word he uttered, and every policy announced, was made with this in mind. Unsurprisingly, the pressure was too much, even for a figure who had been a leader-in-waiting since 1994. Brown began to make big mistakes. In his final budget, assuming that he was sowing the seeds of a prime ministerial triumph, he contributed to his traumatic downfall. This took the form of an income-tax cut to come into effect later in the parliament, by which time he would be in Number Ten. The cut would be paid for by cuts in tax credits, a policy to which he had been passionately committed. As a result, there was another political crisis when Brown became Prime Minister as low earners faced a drop in their income.

Brown was neurotically determined that he should face no other candidate when Blair stood down. This desire has generated several myths. Above all, his many internal critics complained of the thuggishness of his operation. They complained that if an embryonic leadership candidate seemed to be emerging, he or she would be pushed aside by Brown's entourage in vicious briefings to the media. In fact they were being far too precious, and were treated too generously by those parts of the media that loathed Brown. If any of Brown's internal opponents had been fully formed politically, they would have stood their ground. Instead they ran away and told political journalists what a bully Brown was, not exactly a substantial manifesto for leadership from his critics. The political temperature was much lower than in the 1970s, when major figures, from Tony Benn to Roy Jenkins, were fighting for causes and their own ambitions. They kept going in spite of the intense heat of the political battle. Brown's opponents did not. The New Labour era was so dominated by two individuals, and their advisers, that no one else grew into a big political figure. The reason Brown faced no formidable rival was that there were no formidable rivals.[11]

Curiously, the other myth from this time contradicts the first one – namely, that Brown was so fearful of confrontation that he could not contemplate a challenge. This was not the case. In 2007 Brown would have beaten David Miliband, David Blunkett, Alan Johnson or any other candidate who might have stood. The reason he wanted to avoid a contest was that persistent fear of having to define his position. He would have to publicly compete against a so-called Blairite opponent from the left, when he wanted to be seen as the prime ministerial 'father of the nation'. Brown and his advisers described the contest without an opponent as a 'smooth transition'. In retrospect, this is a laughable description, but at the time it was partially accurate. When Brown became prime minister, support for Labour soared in the opinion polls.

Ironically, Brown's honeymoon was another cause of his fall. He had not expected to be popular quickly. Blair had set him several tests of leadership, as had the newspapers, and Brown assumed he would have to prove himself as prime minister before voters would give him their backing. He ached to win an election on his own terms, but had calculated that he would need a year in Number Ten before he would be in a position to do so. The reality was that voters immediately approved of Brown's 'father of the nation' act. He worked around the clock to show he was up to the job, breaking off his holiday in the late summer of 2007 to respond to a foot-and-mouth outbreak, visiting President Bush and subtly conveying a degree of distance and yet continued support, announcing cautiously constitutional reforms that sought to symbolize a rebuilding of trust between government and voters. In September 2007 the Northern Rock bank nearly went bankrupt, a preview of the drama that was to erupt the following year. As account holders queued outside branches to withdraw their cash, Brown feared his honeymoon was ending. Instead, his support went up. It was at this point that he contemplated for the first time calling an early election. If the near-collapse of a bank made him more popular, perhaps he could realize his dream of winning an election in order to get his own mandate.

As he wondered, he made a spectacular – and in many respects fatal – miscalculation. Without deciding whether to call an election, he assumed the speculation about one would destabilize the Conservatives under their newish leader, David Cameron. Brown encouraged his allies to fuel the speculation in interviews. Predictably, Cameron stayed calm, while the feverish media focus on the possibility of an early election intensified to the point where momentum alone almost demanded that one was held. Labour's conference in September 2007 was dominated by this one issue. Cabinet ministers close to Brown asked journalists a single question: should we call the election? As they were asking the question, Brown was receiving private opinion polls suggesting that marginal seats were swinging towards the Conservatives, even though they also indicated that Labour would win by a smaller majority. The polls triggered a second question that Cabinet ministers close to Brown began to agonize over: if they won with a smaller majority than the one secured in 2005, would this be regarded as a form of defeat rather than an authority-enhancing victory? Brown was used to being in various forms of torment, but this decision became a unique form of agony. After thirteen years he had finally become prime minister, yet he was faced with the possibility of throwing it away after a few months by losing an election. But what would happen if he did not call an election, having stirred up speculation? Over this hung the possibility that if he called the election, and won, Brown would escape the ghost of Blairite New Labour.

Here is another lesson of leadership. Early elections are dangerous, whether or not they are held. Edward Heath lost when he called one in February 1974, and Theresa May lost her majority in 2017. By not holding an early election, having so publicly contemplated going ahead, Brown lost his political voice, his credibility and his momentum. He never recovered.

An over-rehearsed and inauthentic public voice will be exposed if a leader stays on the political stage for a long time. Brown was not in reality a 'father of the nation' apolitical figure – the image that he sought to project in his early months as prime minister. On the contrary, he hoped to slaughter the Conservatives in an election and press ahead, after an authority-enhancing victory, with an agenda that was to the left of Blair's, but nowhere near as left-wing as the programme Labour was to adopt a decade later.

In the first few months Brown moved incrementally, but each tiny move symbolized greater ambition. This had been New Labour's tactical approach in the early years: the party's pledge card in the 1997 election included relatively puny offers, but offered hopes of a leap towards new priorities for government. Initially Brown hinted at a new constitutional settlement, a different debate about how most effectively to reform hospitals and schools, and a less hawkish approach to the UK's continuing role in Iraq and Afghanistan. But after deciding against the early election in October 2007, Brown was doomed to carry on until close to the end of the parliament in 2010. He could hardly generate speculation about another early election, having failed to call one. Suddenly his small incremental changes made no sense any more. They were not designed for a parliament that would last until 2010, and yet he had no authority to develop his personal agenda without winning an election.

As he struggled to work out what he stood for, and what he could do without holding an election until 2010, Brown foolishly denied that the opinion polls were a factor in his decision not to call one in the autumn of 2007. At the Prime Minister's Questions held a few days after Brown had announced there would be no early election, David Cameron wittily declared that his suddenly bewildered opponent 'was the only Prime Minister in history not to call an election because the polls suggested he was going to win'.

Brown arrived at that parliamentary session looking as pale as a ghost, and left looking even ghostlier. For an obsessively calculating leader, he was oddly readable, unable to disguise gloom or haunted ambition when Blair was prime minister and long afterwards. He had realized he could no longer pretend to be the impartial 'father of the nation' when he had been caught plotting an early election. Subsequently he needed to find another public voice, and yet he never managed to do so. Brown failed to do what Blair did almost effortlessly – Blair's public voice was close to his private one. Privately, Brown was capable of being funny. He had a sense of humour and could laugh with a guttural spontaneity. Humour and his love of football could have been points of connection with some voters. But he could not make them so. Instead there were darkly comical attempts to connect, from contorted claims about listening to the Arctic Monkeys at breakfast, to awkward appearances on YouTube in which he sought to speak unmediated to the electorate.

There was a third consequence to the non-early election, to do with Brown's allies. At the best of times, prime ministers need a team of trusted advisers; they become insecure and exposed without them. Theresa May's senior advisers, Nick Timothy and Fiona Hill, might have been the cause of some of her problems, but she was dependent on them. Timothy, in particular, gave her ideas and a sense of purpose. Without them May became less sure of who she was, when demands on her became immense. In the fallout of the non-election fiasco, Brown's close allies for many years viewed each other with fuming suspicion, and relations between them never recovered.

The disagreements were based on traumatic misunderstandings, but that only goes to show how fragile relations were in the first place. Some allies blamed Ed Balls for briefing against them in the immediate aftermath of the election saga. Balls emphatically denied doing so, but they did not believe him. Probably what happened was that Balls told journalists, truthfully, that he favoured the early election while others advising Brown did not. The differing newspaper accounts of what had happened triggered deep divisions within the Brown camp. The close-knit inner sanctum that had gathered many times over the previous years rarely did so again. When it did, it was in an atmosphere of mistrust. As a result, Brown was isolated when he needed reliable advice.[12]

Yet he still sought the advice. Even though Balls was now a Cabinet minister with his own distinct responsibilities, Brown would phone him at all times, seeking his views on issues well beyond his departmental brief. At one point Brown asked Balls to move back into Number Ten, to work more closely with him. Brown told Alistair Darling, the newly appointed chancellor, that at some point he wanted Balls to replace him at the Treasury, though it never happened. This is one example of many showing that Brown got his way less often after he became prime minister. He was not strong enough to move Alistair Darling; their old friendship never recovered. Brown is the only modern prime minister to have pulled more levers *before* he moved into Number Ten.

An example of his relative powerlessness arose before the early election-that-never-was. Trying to be too clever by half, Brown revived Blair's attempt to increase the time that suspects could be detained without charge. Playing a similar political game, Blair had sought a ninety-day period, but lost the vote in the Commons. Brown opted for a forty-five-day period, a move that reflected his weakness and made him weaker still. He had intended to show that he could be 'trusted' on security and achieve an extension at least to forty-five days, thereby guaranteeing glowing editorials in the *Sun* and the *Daily Mail* while exposing David Cameron, who was affecting to espouse civil liberties as part of his 'modernization' agenda. But Brown should have relaxed a little and not tried to reassure the doubters that he was 'strong' in ways that made him appear weak. Quickly it became clear that Brown's proposal would not secure support in Parliament, either. At one internal meeting, Labour's chief whip in the Lords warned Brown that he would lose the vote in the second chamber by more than 200. Brown's response was characteristic. He asked the chief whip, 'Who should I phone?', as if hundreds of prime ministerial calls could sway the dissenters. In the Commons, the situation was just as bad. Brown's loyal ally, Ed Miliband, now a minister, was asked to appear on BBC1's *Question Time*. He was keen for exposure on the programme, but turned down the invitation because he could not defend the forty-five-day extension. Here is yet another lesson of leadership. When prime ministers try too hard to please, and are so transparent in their desire to do so, they will end up pleasing no one. The proposal was eventually dropped when few people would notice, as the banks headed towards bankruptcy.

———

Bizarrely, the global financial crash of 2008 initially saved Brown, and then became the main cause of his fall. The crash was arguably the biggest test of leadership for a British prime minister since 1945, at least until Theresa May faced delivering Brexit. In the wake of the global economic downturn, several British banks hurtled towards the verge of bankruptcy. Brown and his chancellor, Alistair Darling, had to respond speedily to an emergency of seismic proportions.

Quickly and weightily, Brown delved below the surface panic, recognizing that governments around the world were facing what he called the first crisis of the globalized economy. A tremor in the US lending markets triggered mayhem across the world. Having lost a public voice and all sense of direction, Brown now had purpose thrust upon him.

The UK government spent an estimated £500 billion keeping the banks afloat, acting sometimes with hours to spare before they would have gone out of business. Alistair Darling noted with retrospective levity that before the crash he and Brown used to agonize over whether to allocate an additional few million here and there. Suddenly they were spending hundreds of billions. For Brown, the scale of intervention represented on one level a revolutionary leap, which he struggled with initially. The struggle was not because of his convictions, but out of fear over how he would be perceived – the stifling theme of his career.

When Northern Rock had collapsed the previous year, publications ranging from *The Economist* and the *Financial Times*, to respected political figures such as the Liberal Democrats' Vince Cable, were advocating nationalization. Brown resisted at first, fearing headlines about a return to the 1970s. When he eventually made the inevitable move, he could only describe the new policy as 'temporary ownership', such was his reluctance to use the word 'nationalization'. Sensing an opportunity, David Cameron and his shadow chancellor, George Osborne, held a rare joint press conference, making the precise claim that Brown feared. This was old Labour, a return to the failed past.

Fortunately for Brown, their claims had no impact and the nationalization proved to be popular in the polls. For different reasons, Brown, Cameron and Osborne could not make sense of the implosion of the lightly regulated order that had begun in the 1980s with the Reagan/Thatcher partnership. Brown could not see it at first because he was brought up politically in the 1970s and 1980s, when Labour lost the battle of ideas to Thatcher. Cameron and Osborne were blind partly for the same reason in reverse. The Conservatives won elections in the 1980s when Thatcher was privatizing rather than nationalizing.

Leaders look back to the past for warnings or guidance because they rarely have any idea what might happen next. At least the past has happened, though it is a treacherous guide.

Still, Brown was well suited to respond, once he fully understood that Northern Rock was a tiny hors d'oeuvre compared with what followed. He was the only elected world leader who had been responsible for economic policy for a decade. His contacts book was unrivalled, and he was on the phone relentlessly to key figures around the world, all of whom he had worked with. Brown was at his most authentic when he was gripped by the need to act. In emergencies he had no time to brood and scheme, instead channelling all his furious energy into achieving outcomes.

In response to the crash, Brown led a coordinated response from G20 world leaders, persuading even the most fiscally conservative to inject cash into the global economy. The recently elected President Obama, still mesmeric and glittering, also played a key role. But with London chairing a G20 conference in the aftermath of the crash, Brown became leaderly without, for once, worrying about how he might appear to sceptical voters and the media. At one point the Nobel Prize-winning *New York Times* columnist Paul Krugman wrote that Brown had saved the world. Brown accidentally quoted the words during Prime Minister's Questions, inadvertently revealing that he had not only read the complimentary column, but had clung on to it as rare praise. He was much mocked for this, but leaders are human beings. Each morning during the earlier days of his premiership he woke early and read the UK newspapers, encountering story after story that said he was both mad and useless. Suddenly a weighty columnist from the US credited him with saving the planet. Which leader would not retain such praise in the forefront of his or her troubled mind?

As far as Brown's leadership was concerned, the crisis gave him momentum, although his formidable response did not provide him with vote-winning arguments. Instead, David Cameron and George Osborne reframed the entire debate in the UK, with the willing or gullible support of most newspapers and parts of the BBC. This is how it happened. The government's pre-crash growth projections for the UK economy were way off the mark. Spending plans had been determined on what proved to be wildly optimistic assumptions about economic growth. After the crash, the economy went into recession. Meanwhile the government was spending huge sums to prop up the banks, while injecting cash into the economy, in place of consumers and the private sector. As a result, the UK accumulated a gaping deficit.

The financial crash was the cause of the deficit, but the Conservative leadership argued that Labour's profligate spending had caused the crash. A banking crisis became one about public spending. In the build-up to the 2010 election, Osborne devised clever soundbites warning that voters should never give the keys back to those who crashed the car. Instead of receiving sustained credit for his response to the crash, Brown was blamed for its origins. The build-up to the next general election – the only one contested by Brown as leader of his party – was framed in precisely the way he had spent his career seeking to avoid: Labour's reckless spending of the past versus Conservatives' sensible cuts in the future.

The situation was made worse by deep internal divisions within Brown's government. Darling, once a good friend of Brown, took a different strategic view. He argued, publicly and privately, that the deficit was so large that deep spending cuts were required, though not on the scale advocated by Osborne and Cameron. Brown saw the terrible danger of such a 'dividing line', a device he had used to considerable effect, especially in the 1997 and 2001 elections, and which was now being used against him. He told Balls that Labour was doomed if the dividing line at the election was between Labour's 'good cuts' versus the Conservatives' 'bad cuts'. Rightly, he could see the strategic dangers of moving onto the Conservatives' terrain by accepting their framing of the financial crash.

But he was trapped. Inadvertently, the supposedly impartial BBC came to regard the Osborne framing as a form of impartiality. In interviews, every senior Cabinet minister was asked relentlessly what they were going to do about the deficit, and to specify the cuts they would make. Long before the election, Osborne had won the argument, even though the evidence suggested that the Keynesian approach – the fiscal stimulus that required governments to spend more – worked in the immediate aftermath of the crash. Brown could not find the equivalent to Osborne's car-crash metaphors, which made sense of what seemed nonsensical: in order to address a deficit, governments sometimes needed to spend more.

There was little in the 2010 election about the role of bankers in recklessly triggering the crisis to the point, in some cases, of criminality. The central question was what to cut, by how much and why did Labour spend so recklessly in the first place? The orthodoxies of the time extended well beyond the Conservatives.

From outside Parliament, Blair confided to Alastair Campbell, 'We were against borrowing... now we're in favour... voters won't understand this Keynesianism', an observation that showed Blair tended to follow the surface game more than the substance of policy. He did not say whether he agreed with the Keynesian policy – only how it would be perceived.[13]

The more fundamental problem for Brown was that he had been chancellor for ten years. His adviser, Ed Miliband, was excited by the political implications of the crash and had good cause for his excitement. Miliband liked to give the example of hearing a guest pleading for the government to intervene in the financial markets, on the BBC's *Today* programme. He assumed the voice was from a left-wing think tank, only to discover at the end that the interviewee was a senior figure from Lehman Brothers in the UK. Here was a banker panicked into making the case for the kind of government intervention that Blair and Brown had been too scared to make. In the fallout from the crash, Miliband saw the opportunity at last for Brown to show he was a left-of-centre figure who believed in the benevolent power of the state. But Miliband overlooked one key point. Brown would get a lot of the blame for the crash. Voters and newspapers were asking: Why had he not regulated the financial sector more effectively? Why did he allegedly let spending get too high? The crash was thought to have happened 'on his watch'.

Here was the tragic New Labour irony. Brown had sought to be trusted in relation to the economy, as Blair had done in foreign policy. In trying so hard to please, they both ended up deeply mistrusted. In Brown's case, having connections with bankers was suddenly the least politically helpful association in the world. From the autumn of 2008 onwards, no politician wanted to be seen near a senior banker.

Although Brown's history as a long-serving chancellor became a problem for him in terms of perceived culpability, he was evidently well qualified to respond to the crash. Such was Labour's internal angst at the time that few of his critics noticed that Brown was responding effectively to an epic challenge. Alastair Campbell's brilliantly illuminating diaries from this period make virtually no reference to the financial crash, whereas criticisms of Brown dominate. There were more plots aimed at removing Brown than any previous prime minister had faced. All of them were absurd – another symptom of the Labour Party becoming almost as whackily dysfunctional as the Conservatives were to become.

The fact is there was no alternative figure capable of becoming prime minister in the aftermath of the crash. None of the potential candidates would have known what to do, or how to do it. No other Cabinet ministers, with the exception of Ed Balls, Ed Miliband and Alistair Darling, had given any deep thinking to economic policy, let alone how to navigate away from the cliff-edge a fragile economy dependent on a vibrant financial sector. But still dissenting MPs planned various coups, to no avail. This was an early sign that many Labour MPs brought up under the Blair/Brown duopoly were half-formed politicians lacking basic political skills. The attempted coups were laughably amateurish. One began just before a Prime Minister's Questions session in the Commons and had petered out late the same afternoon.[14] But the attempted coups reflected badly on Brown and his casual mishandling of egos. The former Cabinet minister Charles Clarke was one of the most active in seeking the removal of Brown, and Brown's handling of Clarke is telling. When he became prime minister, Brown tried to appease Clarke by suggesting that he become a special envoy in Iraq. Clarke noted that the life-threatening post was one way of dealing with an internal critic. Clarke stayed in the UK and became a deeper critic. Brown did not understand how best to deal with colleagues, especially dissenting ones – an essential qualification of leadership.

The wider issue of 'trust' tormented Brown, as it had Blair and Major. In opposition, Blair had played on the mistrust of John Major, only to leave office with questions raging about his own integrity. Before he became prime minister, Brown was fairly discreet when reflecting on Blair to journalists, although his sense of fuming frustration was conveyed more candidly by senior allies. But after the 2005 election Brown said to some journalists, 'Tony isn't trusted. We have this huge "trust" problem that can only be addressed when Tony goes.'[15] Instead of addressing the issue, Brown himself was brought down at a point where mistrust between voters and elected politicians ran deep.

On this, too, he was unlucky. The saga over MPs' expenses could have erupted at any time, but it did so while he was prime minister. For quite some time certain MPs had been maximizing their allowances, on the assumption that no one would know what they were claiming. This was widely seen as an alternative to higher salaries, which it was politically impossible to implement. When exposed under the Freedom of Information Act in 2009, the expense claims looked absurd or grotesque, and sometimes both. The sequence fuelled the already intense mistrust that voters felt towards those they elected. Historically the mistrust was often irrational, voters' anger and disdain being a substitute for engagement with politics and current affairs. But here was a scandal that looked terrible, and a few MPs went to prison. It was not lost on Brown that he had become prime minister hoping to restore trust, but by the time he left some MPs were facing criminal trials, while bankers were being exposed as reckless, self-seeking and greedy. In some cases, they too faced the possibility of criminal charges.

For leaders, 'trust' is too vaguely defined. They are unwise to proclaim a restoration of 'trust' as an objective – it rebounds on them every time. Politics is too stormy a vocation, defined by subjective judgements. Blair regretted slaughtering John Major with allegations of 'sleaze' in the build-up to the 1997 election, not least because he became mistrusted, too. Brown soon discovered that attempts to restore trust were overwhelmed by events, and by behaviour that fuelled further mistrust.

Perhaps if Brown had been a more effective political teacher, he could have made greater sense of what he was trying to do, both in his first phase as prime minister and then in his response to the crash. In his memoirs, Brown argued that he was not as interested in modern ways of communicating as he should have been. That is not the case. He was obsessed with the media in all its manifestations – a big difference from Edward Heath, who was another prime minister of depth, but one who was genuinely not that concerned about how to communicate in the media. Brown became friends with Paul Dacre, the editor of the *Daily Mail*, predominantly because he hoped that the newspaper might endorse him at the 2010 election. Similarly, Rebekah Brooks was wooed as she acquired ever greater influence over the Murdoch empire, especially the *Sun* newspaper. Both the *Mail* and the *Sun* endorsed the Conservatives in 2010. Elsewhere, Brown was interested in the potency of social media, but never mastered it. He assumed he understood how to project in the media because he recognized Labour's presentational failings in the 1980s and he had briefly been a BBC producer. But he never did fully understand.

However, at times his carefully calibrated messages resonated. Brown's genius as Labour's main economic policy-maker for so long was to convey messages that reassured, while giving him space to be radical. Sometimes the messaging worked and at other times it did not. Never has a modern leader enjoyed such an oscillating relationship with voters and the media – take a deep breath and come for the ride. In the late 1980s Brown was so popular that he was spoken of as a future Labour leader and made shadow chancellor after the party's 1992 election defeat. By 1994 he was so unpopular that the party turned to Blair after John Smith died. After the 1997 election Brown became a commanding chancellor, widely perceived as being the chief executive of the government. Following the 2001 election there was much talk of Brown being peripheral, as Blair commanded the world stage after the terrorist attacks on 11 September. After the Iraq War, Blair sensed that Brown was unpopular enough to marginalize his role in planning for the next election, yet Brown proved to be so popular that Blair then had to plead with him to play a central part in the election. By 2006 Brown was so unpopular there was talk of David Miliband standing in a leadership contest against him. After he became prime minister in 2007, he was so popular he was tempted to hold an early election. When he did not, he became the least-popular prime minister since polling began.

Partly Brown's wild ride reflects febrile times. Leaders can be hailed and despised in the space of the same week, let alone during many years at the top. The varying reactions also reflect the ambiguity of Brown as a political figure. Some of those who worked with him were devoted, in spite of the tantrums and the ongoing volatility. When he moved from the Treasury to Number Ten, a lot of those who had worked in his private office wanted to move with him. Balls and Miliband were devoted in their different ways, recognizing Brown's strengths and only later appreciating the flaws. Yet the devotees were joined by those within the government who loathed Brown. Some of the loathing was calculating and self-interested. After all, being friendly to Blair was much more useful to ambitious ministers with limited political talent. As chancellor, Brown had little patronage, whereas Blair had many posts to offer. Still, Brown's mishandling of people certainly played its part in his limited range of political allies.

Aspirant leaders must be ruthless but polite in their calculated brutality; the brittle egos of colleagues often cannot cope with rudeness. Brown could be rude, without thinking about what he was doing. For him, brought up in the bear pit of Scottish Labour Party politics, the means justified the ends. His close allies noted the noble worthiness of the ends and were sometimes impressed with his command of the means to bring them about. But his enemies noted only the apparent thuggishness. Sometimes voters thought he was on their side, sometimes they did not. The ambiguities were deep, complex and revealing of the oscillations in his reputation.

Latterly the 2010 election campaign proved to be appropriately ambiguous, too, a defeat that was not as bad as expected. On the whole, the campaign had been traumatic for Brown. The defining moment came during his nightmarish confrontation with a voter in Rochdale called Gillian Duffy. Brown had been on a walkabout, a form of contact with voters that he had never mastered. Indeed, he failed to fully master any forms of contact with voters. On this occasion, after they were introduced, Duffy started berating him about immigrants. Brown eventually escaped reasonably unscathed, but in the car afterwards, unaware that he still had a microphone on, he described Duffy as a 'bigoted woman'. Within minutes the words were broadcast across the news channels and Brown was devastated. Voters are allowed to attack leaders, but leaders are never allowed to criticize voters. Brown had been caught doing this at precisely the point when he most needed the support of voters. It was the voters who held the upper hand, as they often do. Brown assumed the sequence would destroy him and propel the Conservatives to power.

But this isn't quite what happened. In the end there was a hung parliament, a rare outcome in the UK. The last one had been in February 1974. Brown, the great survivor, wondered whether he could hang on. This time, however, he could not. The leader of the Liberal Democrats, Nick Clegg, chose to form a coalition with the Conservatives, after days of frantic negotiations.

Like Heath and Callaghan, Brown left office as a short-serving prime minister. He had dreaded being what Roy Jenkins described as a 'tail-end Charlie' and yet that became his fate. But like Heath, his prime ministerial role became renowned. In Brown's case, the financial crash – a tumultuous event that he never foresaw in all his neurotic planning – and his response were as historic as the acts of much longer-serving prime ministers. Taken with his reforms as chancellor, implemented when bankers were still revered and government activity of any kind was viewed with wariness by a still-mighty right-wing media, Brown goes down as one of the most significant figures in the history of the Labour Party.

He left Number Ten on the Tuesday after the 2010 election with his wife and two children. This was a rare sighting of his family together, and an image that humanized Brown when it was far too late. A short time later, David Cameron stood outside Number Ten as prime minister of a peacetime coalition in the midst of an ongoing economic crisis. Cameron could not have been more different from Brown in terms of personality, ideology and political experience, as an incoming prime minister. He not only had to face the consequences of the financial crash, but also had to manage the Conservative Party and a unique relationship with the Liberal Democrats.

While the Labour Party had been showing signs of an existential crisis, with its coup attempts against Brown, Blair's ambiguous legacy and Brown's awkward and complex efforts to move on from his predecessor, Cameron was to discover that the Conservatives had become at least as problematic to lead as Labour, and in some ways much more so.

8

DAVID CAMERON

David Cameron will be recalled as the prime minister that took the UK out of the EU, against his own wishes. Cameron possessed a sunnier personality than most leaders and yet his ending was uniquely dark. All the modern prime ministers left office with much to be gloomy about, and in some cases they despaired for the remainder of their lives. But the chaos unleashed on so many fronts by Cameron's decision to hold a referendum, and then lose it, was a uniquely bleak legacy. The nightmare of Iraq would still have happened if Blair had boldly opposed the war, because the US administration was determined to invade. Thatcher's poll tax was addressed by abolition. But Brexit became never-ending, sucking up all political energy for years to come. As with all modern prime ministers, the seeds were sown at the beginning. Cameron's referendum was not an aberration, but part of a pattern. Even as he fought what seemed like a distinctively refreshing leadership campaign in 2005, he was moving towards his fall.

David Cameron was only thirty-nine when he became leader of the Conservative Party in December 2005, younger even than the youthful Tony Blair had been when he became Labour leader. Significantly, Cameron had far less experience of formative political battles within his party and beyond. As a result, he became a leader without quite knowing who he was as a public figure, or what he was for. His polished poise, demeanour and apparent sense of political purpose obscured his deep inexperience for a time. He rose too speedily and was neither ready nor ideologically suited to lead the UK after the many traumas of the 2008 financial crash.

Early internal and external battles matter for aspirant leaders. They test recently elected politicians in many different ways. Are they resilient? Do they possess guile? What are their convictions and values? Can they express them effectively? Blair was Cameron's model as a leader, but the Labour leader had been an MP for eleven years by the time he acquired the crown, and had been heavily involved in several intense internal debates over the future of Labour's policy and strategy. Being a prominent participant in the battles over a party's future is one way that aspirant leaders acquire some shape and definition.

While neither Blair nor Cameron had been a minister before becoming leader, Cameron had been engaged in far fewer internal struggles about the future of his party. He had only been an MP for four and a half years when he became leader. His most senior post had been as a short-serving shadow Education Secretary, the same remit held by Neil Kinnock before he became Labour leader. The difference was that Kinnock had been prominent for many years in Labour's intense civil wars in the late 1970s and early 1980s. By the time he became leader in 1983, he was battle-scarred, with plenty more scars to come. Like Blair, Kinnock had been an MP for more than a decade when he became Labour leader. We will never know, but perhaps if Cameron had been similarly engaged, battling it out with sweaty intensity on one side or another in the Conservative Party, he would have been big and strong enough to have addressed the issue of Europe when he became leader. All we do know is that he made no such attempt.

Cameron had played a few roles with elegant agility, but they were ones that had kept him a safe distance from the political furnace. He had been Norman Lamont's adviser at the Treasury during the Exchange Rate Mechanism crisis in September 1992 – a good seat from which to witness ministers responding to a national emergency, but Cameron was an observer and not a central participant. He also had the task of advising John Major on how to handle Prime Minister's Questions, and subsequently gave similar advice to Michael Howard when the Conservatives were in opposition. Major rated Cameron highly. Howard's admiration was such that he wanted Cameron to be his successor and discreetly played a part in helping to bring about his meteoric rise. Such demands test the wit and intelligence of an aspirant leader – anyone who gave poor advice about how to handle Prime Minister's Questions would be dumped very quickly. Still, advising a prime minister is a minor qualification for becoming a prime minister.

Cameron's political activities were early signs that he was a talented politician – and that talent was acknowledged widely. One of Cameron's PPE tutors at Oxford, Vernon Bogdanor, described him as 'one of my ablest students', although he added the qualification, 'I am not responsible for his views.'[1] Such endorsements and experience suggested that Cameron had considerable potential. Again, though, these were puny qualifications for immediately assuming responsibility for the titanic demands of leadership in December 2005.

Before entering politics, Cameron had been Director of Communications at Carlton TV, a decent enough job, but not one that is normally regarded as adequate preparation for becoming prime minister. His media background triggered one early slight misperception: that he was obsessed, as a politician, with 'spin' – the message and not the substance.

While it is the case that Cameron was not always gripped by policy detail, it is wrong to assume that a spell at Carlton TV made him especially preoccupied with the media. It was his fascination with Tony Blair and New Labour that led him to woo the media, but in ways that were slightly less sophisticated and clunkier than the methods applied in the not-always-subtle Blair/Brown era. Largely for images in the media as a new leader of the Opposition, Cameron visited council estates in the hope of conveying a new, compassionate Conservatism, and dashed to the Arctic Circle to 'hug a husky', in order to develop his green credentials. The detailed policies were not in place to make sense of the images, but Cameron assumed that the images themselves would be potent.

To some extent, he was right. Non-Conservative newspapers, including the *Guardian* and the *Independent*, gave him an easy time. *The Times* was a cheerleader. Greatly influenced by *The Times*, parts of the BBC portrayed him as a 'modernizing centrist'. But without policies that reinforced the images, and with some policies that contradicted the 'spin', Cameron's media strategy lacked the force of Blair's at his peak. As a symbolic contrast, Blair hired as his media adviser Alastair Campbell, a tabloid Labour supporter, who read the rhythms of the news in a way that a masterful conductor reads music. Campbell was intensely tribal and passionately loyal. Ultimately, after a long period in which Cameron ran an endearingly tiny media operation, he hired Andy Coulson, hoping to have acquired a Campbell equivalent. Coulson made a positive difference to the media coverage, but he was not in Campbell's league and, as a former editor of *News of the World*, he ended up in jail as part of the phone-hacking scandal.

The Conservative leadership contest that Cameron won in 2005 was held after the party's third successive election defeat. There had already been several odd contests since the Conservatives had been slaughtered in 1997, including the eccentric 'dream ticket' of Ken Clarke and John Redwood the same year – the party's most passionate pro-European making an absurdly desperate pitch with its most ardent Eurosceptic, a *Monty Python* double act that did not last very long. Then there was Michael Portillo's strange candidacy in 2001; the once transparently ambitious politician had become a reluctant leadership contender. Bizarrely, the candidates who fared poorly in opinion polls of the wider electorate won with ease in the leadership contests. They did so because they took a tough line on Europe. The contests, their frequency and nature, were symptoms and causes of a party in crisis.

The 2005 campaign was particularly odd because it was defined by a *Britain's Got Talent*-style session during the Conservative party conference in Blackpool. Each candidate was given a short slot to make their case in front of the audience. The favourite, David Davis, blew it with a leaden and reactionary speech, although the address was not as bad as it was immediately perceived to be. Conversely, Cameron's speech was not as good as it was immediately judged to be, but the format lent itself to instant verdicts, first by journalists and then by those attending the conference.

Cameron delivered his speech well. There were good jokes. The theme was 'change' – not a bad one, after three election defeats. He said: 'We can change this party and we can change this country... a modern, compassionate conservative is right for our times.' But the performance and message were almost consciously Blair-like.

Formidable leaders tend to be authentically distinct and original in their pitch, rather than actively imitate a recent leader. There had been no leaders like Wilson, Thatcher and Blair, in style and demeanour, before they arrived on the political stage. Cameron was like Blair. Even so, he won the contest by a big margin. This was a significant achievement for a figure who was not widely known before he became a candidate, and who could not fully know who he was as a public figure.

One of his strengths was that he was wholly at ease with himself as a human being, but that is different from being fully developed as a potential prime minister. Still, the ease was impressive. To take a minor example: Cameron and his entourage would often take a political columnist with them for day-trips out of London. On one occasion, a columnist travelled with them to Norwich. On the train back, Cameron fell asleep opposite the columnist and at one point fleetingly and inadvertently put his legs on the columnist's lap. This shows how laid-back and comfortable he was. Most leaders never switch off when there are journalists accompanying them.[2]

Although the responsibilities were huge for such an inexperienced leader, the context when Cameron became leader was fairly benevolent. The Labour government was in the final throes of the Blair/Brown duel, still bewildered and demoralized by the war in Iraq and what the ongoing bloody conflict implied for an administration that had taken the decision to go to war. Yet the Conservatives had lost three successive elections. Their purpose was unclear and they were still split over Europe. In this respect, the Conservative Party was closer to Labour in 1983, with all its internal tensions and lack of clarity about what it stood for. Cameron mistakenly worked on the assumption that his party was more or less in the same position as Labour in 1994, when Blair became leader. This was his early and most fundamental misjudgement. Blair took over a party that had already been reformed beyond recognition, since its slaughter in 1983. Cameron acquired a party that was still largely the same as it had been after its slaughter in 1997, with Europe still the overwhelmingly debilitating fault line.

As leader, Cameron continued to be the 'modernizing' candidate. At times his projection became even more of a conscious act of imitation of Blair than it was during the leadership contest. Still prime minister during Cameron's early phase as leader, Blair noted privately, 'He's being me… it's an impersonation of me.'[3] Cameron adopted the same conversational approach in interviews and wore Blair-like casual clothes at weekends and on holidays. He was reported to have told newspaper executives at a dinner during the leadership contest in 2005 that he was the 'heir to Blair'.[4] His closest allies described a book written by Blair's close adviser, Philip Gould, as their 'bible'.[5]

Cameron and his allies set out to be New Labour from the other side of the political spectrum, at least during the early phase of his leadership. In policy terms, this meant they sought to address what were seen as fatal Conservative positions in the same way Blair and Brown had done with Labour's. They noted admiringly that in the 1980s and early 1990s Labour was not trusted to tax and spend, so Blair and Brown pledged to be overtly tough on both. Although the admiration was sincere, the emulation was limited.

As they lost elections from 1997 onwards, the Conservatives were seen as 'the nasty party'.[6] This was shorthand for saying they were more bothered about tax cuts for the wealthy than about public services, illiberal in social outlook and represented largely by elderly men. Under Cameron, the Conservatives would stick to Labour's spending plans, become 'green', commit to spending on Third World countries and encourage more gays, women and ethnic minorities to stand as candidates. They would be nice rather than nasty, and modern rather than backward-looking.

To some extent, Cameron's early project was indeed New Labour in reverse, but there were several big differences. Above all, his modernizing message did not address the fundamental problem of his party: division over Europe. Cameron's only early message on Europe was that his party should stop 'banging on' about it quite so much.[7] This would be the equivalent of Blair and Brown telling their party to stop banging on about tax rises, and then retaining the same tax-and-spend policies that had contributed to their defeat in 1992. Instead Blair and Brown delivered some tough messages to their party in areas where Labour had adopted vote-losing policies. Cameron avoided the issue of Europe when he was strongest to address it, at the beginning of his leadership. Leaders always have space to act at the beginning. Some of them do not have the confidence, or the inclination, to do so.

Cameron's reticence was also because he did not know decisively what he himself thought about Europe. His first move as a leadership candidate during the 2005 contest was to support the policy of Conservative MEPs (Members of the European Parliament) withdrawing from the formal centre-right grouping in the European Parliament. Cameron's press spokesman at the time, George Eustice, who became a Brexit-supporting minister, is convinced that Cameron believed in the policy as a matter of conviction. Cameron told Eustice that he was wary of the European People's Party (EPP) centre-right grouping and thought it best that Conservative MEPs broke away. Conversely Ken Clarke, who went on to serve in Cameron's Cabinet, is equally certain that Cameron acted solely to woo Eurosceptic MPs during the leadership contest.[8]

Perhaps both interpretations are true. Cameron convinced himself that the move was the 'right thing to do' – one of his favourite phrases lifted from Blair – while assuming the policy would help him win the leadership. He almost certainly would have won without the commitment.

Ironically his main opponent in the contest, David Davis, was opposed to leaving the EPP, bravely arguing that such a move would be counter-productive. Davis went on to support Brexit, becoming the first Brexit Secretary, his only Cabinet post. But in the context of 2005, when UK withdrawal was not on the agenda, he was opposed to Conservatives leaving the EPP and said so during the contest. Cameron did not take his party on over Europe – the most calamitous example of his weak-kneed inexperience and hazy ideological grip.

In failing to do so, he became the latest leader to sow the seeds of his downfall, in a bid to seize the crown. The German chancellor, Angela Merkel, never fully forgave Cameron for the EPP breakaway, one that weakened the centre right in the European Parliament and gave a degree of comfort to the far right. Cameron naively assumed that his Blair-like charm would be enough to woo Merkel when he needed her. He liked the idea of being a prime minister being shown on TV screens in convivial conversations with other powerful leaders in Europe, mistaking his ease in dealing with individuals as a deeper rapport. But Merkel focused more on policy positions when judging other leaders, and Cameron's first policy with EPP got him off to a bad start. In some respects, Merkel preferred dealing with Theresa May – a public figure, like her, who was less interested in politics as theatre – even though the context of their meetings was always ridiculously fraught because of Brexit.

Cameron's assumption that he could be the heir to Blair is also revealing. He might have had a similar approach to the election-winning Labour leader, but he was not leading in the same context. By the time Blair became leader, his two predecessors had done a significant amount of heavy lifting. Between them, Neil Kinnock and John Smith had transformed Labour, in terms of its policy and internal organization. This touched everything, from the methods by which the party chose its leader, to a detailed policy programme that was unrecognizable from the one the party proposed in 1983 when Margaret Thatcher won her first landslide.

In contrast, Cameron's predecessors had done little to address the reasons why the Conservatives had lost three times in a row. That is why Cameron's inheritance was closer to Neil Kinnock's in 1983. Both Kinnock and Cameron led parties that needed to be challenged in policy terms. Crucially, Kinnock had to challenge himself as well as his party. He was a unilateralist who turned his party towards multilateralism – a momentous shift for him, as well as Labour, in the 1980s. Cameron was fascinated by how a vote-losing party could win again, but he never challenged his own assumptions in quite the same way, except in the area of social liberalism. This was never quite as painful as it seemed, though, even when he became an advocate of gay marriage, a policy that triggered a substantial revolt in Parliament and amongst party members. The anger was fleeting. In the broad sweep, gay marriage was something of a red herring for both party and leader, creating the impression amongst some commentators and broadcasters that Cameron was a 'centrist' – that ill-defined term that distorts many perceptions in politics. He had become a social liberal, but on economic policy and public-service reform he struggled to move on from his Thatcherite upbringing. He became politically engaged when Thatcher was at her peak.

Indeed, his wider upbringing was not one made for a natural 'modernizer' or, to be more precise, a leader who would move his party away from the Thatcherite right. It is not Cameron's fault that he had a privileged start; that his father was an affluent stockbroker; that he himself went to Eton, Oxford and enjoyed the champagne-swilling Bullingdon Club while a student. Cameron did not disown his gilded past, but sought to play down elements of it. A photograph of Cameron and other Bullingdon Club members, including Boris Johnson, disappeared from public circulation. Cameron rarely referred to his time at Eton, whereas Johnson looked back at his school days with uninhibited affection.[9] But Cameron's upbringing was not one that led him to challenge many Thatcherite assumptions. Only the relentless election defeats of his party during the New Labour era belatedly led him to question previous orthodoxies, and in a fairly limited way.

———

Cameron's victory speech in December 2005, when he was elected leader of his party, highlighted an ambiguity that extended well beyond his partly contradictory views about Europe. He had won the leadership election with a simple message, essentially about being nicer, showing that the party cared about poor people, the NHS and the environment. After winning, he declared in his victory speech: 'There is such a thing as society… it's not the same as the state.' These are the most illuminating words Cameron uttered, although not for the reasons he intended. They tell us just as much about him as the phrase 'What works is what matters' gives insights into Blair, and 'prudence for a purpose' reveals much about Brown.

Cameron's construction was as clever as those phrases from the New Labour era. The words seem to reject Margaret Thatcher's view that there was no such thing as society, while – on closer inspection – echoing Thatcher's famous assertion. He appeared to be moving on from Thatcherism while marching at one with her own simplistic assumptions. Cameron was unsure how to handle Thatcher's legacy. A friend of his recalls that in his early phase as leader, Cameron feared that his party could not move on until the death of Thatcher, such was her potency in the party. He was not being morbid, but making a political point about her spellbinding capacities, now that she had become a living legend. Yet Cameron was one of those in Thatcher's thrall, in policy terms, and most significantly on how he saw the role of the state.[10]

Thatcher argued in an interview in the autumn of 1987 that the state could not be, or should not be, a binding agency – one that people always turned to for their problems to be addressed.[11] She had been making the same argument since the mid-1970s. There were other institutions that could perform the tasks of the state, such as charities, churches and businesses. As Cameron was arguing that the state was not the binding agency, he was essentially agreeing with Thatcher. The difference was tonal. She was happy to declare, unsubtly, that there was no such thing as society. He was happy to assert, by implication, that society could and should thrive with a smaller state – a more diplomatic argument for advancing her convictions.

Here was a fundamental difference with the leader he imitated. Tony Blair came to believe passionately in the version of New Labour he advocated, and in his rejection of old Labour, a force from the past that he understood with only limited knowledge. For good and bad, at different points in his leadership, Blair sought constant definition against his party's past. Cameron did not do so in relation to his own party. He knew his party had to change, or be seen to be changing. He planted trees, toured council estates, turned up at hospital wards and appeared to distance himself from his party's support for the war in Iraq. But in policy terms, he could not bring himself to make the leaps that Kinnock and Smith had made with their party, let alone Blair. This is not necessarily a flaw. Cameron was a figure of the right, leading a party on the right. It became a flaw because Cameron claimed that his party was moving to the centre and breaking away from its past, the definition of a 'modernizer' – that overused term in British politics.

Cameron's galvanizing idea was the 'Big Society', an objective that reinforced and deepened the ambiguity of his leadership. In opposition, the 'Big Society' was explored as an idea in seminars organized mainly by Cameron's friend and senior adviser, Steve Hilton. The MP Oliver Letwin, a former shadow chancellor, was the other key organizer. Hilton appeared to personify Cameron's modernizing project. Usually he wore a T-shirt and jeans or shorts. Quite often he was barefoot at these seminars, and later in Downing Street. He was engaging and unstuffy, without any pomposity. He was also right-wing, a reminder that fun-loving libertarians are usually closer to the right than the left. In Hilton's case, he was wary of the state as a provider of services. He had some interesting ideas about the state as a regulator, intervening to challenge the excesses of big corporate companies, which he viewed with an illuminating disdain. Mostly he disapproved of the state. In his early years as leader, Cameron regarded Hilton as a close friend and the originator of big new ideas. Hilton did not last very long in Number Ten, and the two of them fell out permanently when Hilton campaigned for Brexit from the safe distance of Silicon Valley in California where, amongst other ventures, he hosted a series for Fox News, President Trump's favourite channel. This shocked some UK commentators, not least because Hilton showed support for some of Trump's more outrageous comments. But really he had not changed at all.

Letwin was charming, thoughtful and a committed Thatcherite, who had to be hidden away in an earlier election campaign for speaking too candidly about the Conservatives' planned spending cuts. He had not changed his views significantly on any element of policy, but as he was genuinely decent, thoughtful and close to Cameron, the media changed its view of him, hailing Letwin as a key modernizer in Cameron's team. Letwin worked closely with Cameron for the rest of his leadership, a behind-the-scenes fixer and generator of ideas. Quite often his ideological instincts clashed with his role as the fixer. It was Letwin who gave the go-ahead for the coalition's early calamitous health reforms, not because he was careless, but because he agreed with them. Cameron had asked his friend to check out the planned changes. Letwin gave them the thumbs up, at least initially.

The early Big Society seminars were private events, but some commentators were invited to attend. On one level the seminars were hugely impressive: here was an opposition party with energy and ideological verve. They were also a warning of what was to follow. At these events senior shadow Cabinet members expressed their determination to devolve power away from Whitehall departments. By way of example, the shadow Health Secretary, Andrew Lansley, argued that when there were crises in parts of the Health Service, he should not be on the *Today* programme to take responsibility. In 'empowering patients', NHS providers lower down the system would be in control and accountable. Other shadow Cabinet members argued along similar lines in relation to their policy briefs.

As a new model of public-service delivery, Hilton spoke enthusiastically of a large vegetable cooperative he had seen in Brooklyn; it was innovative, dynamic and owned and run by its workers. He argued that this was a model for public services, especially housing estates, where tenants could – and should – take responsibility.

At one point the Big Society had a clumsy subtitle, the 'Post-Bureaucratic Age'. This is how Cameron explained his vision while leader of the Opposition:

> This is what we mean by the Post-Bureaucratic Age. The information revolution meets the progressive Conservative philosophy: sceptical about big state power; committed to social responsibility and non-state collective action. The effects of this redistribution of power will be felt throughout our politics, with people in control of the things that matter to them, a country where the political system is open and trustworthy, and power redistributed from the political elite to the man and woman in the street.[12]

But the seminars that explored the Big Society and the Post-Bureaucratic Age inadvertently exposed some of the problems. Who decides how much government money is devolved to various local initiatives? How is the money accounted for? Which agency is responsible for ensuring that high standards are maintained? Who or which agency represents taxpayers contributing the money to cooperatives and other self-run bodies, in order to ensure that the money is spent efficiently? By the end of the session, thousands of additional bureaucrats had been deemed necessary to administer the Post-Bureaucratic Age.

The same problems applied to ministerial responsibility. Was a Health Secretary not going to be held to account for the NHS, when the taxpayer was funding the service so that patients could be treated free at the point of use? How were patients being empowered, as more agencies became involved in the provision of services? At one point Letwin declared that he had an answer to issues relating to 'accountability'. He suggested that accountability was a lesser issue compared with the principle of giving away power.[13] This was only a limited answer.

Cameron played a curious role at the seminars. He was an assiduous attender, sitting in one of the rows, taking notes modestly. At the end he would often close the sessions of meandering and inconclusive discussions with a declaration that a 'redistribution of power' was the Conservatives' big idea. Again, the meaning was partly vague. Where was the power going to lie, and in what form? In a speech given to the World Economic Forum in Davos in 2006 he suggested that 'exhortation' from government was the way in which the state should play its role. He cited the TV chef Jamie Oliver as having more impact than regulation or changes to the law. But Oliver's campaigns were always aimed at changing laws and regulations; they were never limited to exhortation. Cameron did not seem especially interested in detailed answers. He was animated by the way these sessions were changing how the party was perceived, and seemed less bothered by the complexities. But one complexity soon surfaced. At first, charities applauded the Big Society and charity leaders flocked to the seminars, conferences and talks held by Cameron. That was until they learned that the Conservative leadership proposed significant cuts to grants for charities.

To his credit, at least Cameron surrounded himself with lively and radical thinkers. The only other leader of the Opposition to have done so was Margaret Thatcher in the late 1970s. But Thatcher tended to lead the ideological debates. Cameron was more passive, giving space to the likes of Hilton and Letwin. Hilton played a major part in composing Cameron's early speeches. Cameron appeared much more conventional than Hilton, but the new Conservative leader liked the company of right-wing radicals, partly because he was more radical than he appeared to be. His radicalism was largely rooted on the right. His genuinely charming demeanour fooled some in the media that he was more expedient than he was.

Before securing power in 2010, Cameron succeeded in his goal of changing perceptions of his party. Non-Conservative newspapers were beguiled for a time. In the build-up to the 2010 election there were rumours that the left-leaning *Guardian* might endorse the Conservatives under Cameron, a move that would have been as dramatic as the *Sun* backing Labour in 1997. It did not happen, but its deputy editor at the time, Ian Katz, became a fan of Cameron's when the Conservative leader was the new fashion. Katz would note approvingly, 'Cameron's the future… he's the real deal.'[14] The *Independent* also presented approvingly the new leader as green, progressive, sceptical of the war in Iraq and a true modernizer. Labour went into the 2010 election with only the clear support of the *Daily Mirror*.

If the Big Society was the galvanizing idea, then the political framework of Cameron's pitch was lifted transparently from the New Labour rulebook on how to win elections. Before the 1997 election, Blair and Brown announced they would stick with the Conservative government's spending levels for two years and would not raise income-tax levels for an entire parliament. Cameron and George Osborne announced, at the beginning of what was almost a joint leadership team, that they would stick to Labour's spending levels and that tax cuts were not a priority for them.

Later the message became that the 'proceeds of growth' would focus on public services and some tax cuts. Cameron's plan was spelt out vaguely in an 'Aims and Values' document sent to party members for ratification, in another imitation of Blair. As with all Cameron's policy gestures, the superficial appearance implied a change of approach, but the substance much less so. The document put the case for tax cuts along with some spending rises – the familiar message from Conservative leaders in their vote-losing era from 1997, and indeed from long before that:

> We will put economic stability and fiscal responsibility first. They must come before tax cuts. Over time, we will share the proceeds of growth between public services and lower taxes – instead of letting government spend an ever-increasing share of national income.[15]

At the 2006 party conference, Osborne warned that tax cuts could not be a priority. Facing the possibility of an early election a year later, he made a tax cut the centrepiece of his speech, with Cameron's enthusiastic support, pledging the near-abolition of inheritance tax. The move was politically smart and unnerved an increasingly nervy Gordon Brown, but the new policy contradicted the central theme when Cameron/Osborne were playing at being New Labour in reverse. Tax cuts were not supposed to be a priority. Cameron and Osborne were agile tacticians, but wobbly modernizers.

During the 2005 party conference, when he was still a leadership candidate but clear favourite to win, Cameron had told journalists that recent party leaders had pledged to take a different approach to 'tax and spend', then quickly reverted to the familiar Tory approach. He insisted that he would never change direction and was strong enough to resist pressure from within his party and the powerful Conservative-supporting newspapers.

But unlike Kinnock, who had to change his own views as well as his party's, Cameron's heart was never fully in it. He knew that he had to reposition his party, so at the 2006 conference the Conservative Party had posters attacking Brown for not spending enough on the NHS, with the implication that Cameron planned to spend much more. Similarly the slogan 'Vote blue, go green' was devised when the party's pollsters pointed out that a Conservative majority could be secured partly by wooing Liberal Democrat voters. Cameron had no previous record of passionate environmental activity. At a special green fringe meeting during the 2006 conference he told the *Independent*'s deputy editor, Ian Birrell, that Margaret Thatcher had inspired his green convictions – a revealing insight in so far as Thatcher only discovered a passing interest in environmental matters after the 1988 European elections in the UK, when the Green Party performed unexpectedly well. Her interest did not last. For a time, Cameron appeared to be passionate and was hailed as a radical environmentalist by some extremely generous newspapers.

But the financial crash of 2008 revealed Cameron's truer political self. Here was an epoch-changing event that raised deep questions about the UK's light regulatory rules and its dependence on the financial sector. If Cameron had been serious about changing his party's approach to the economy, he would have cited historic chaos and suddenly dwindling living standards as vivid examples of the failings of the Thatcher/Reagan era. If he had been following the admittedly crude New Labour model for winning elections with conviction, he would have argued that 'old' Conservatism had been right for the 1980s, but that it had gone too far and the appropriate response was a leap towards modern 'one nation' Conservatism.

Instead, Cameron's response to the crash out-Thatchered Thatcherism. Cameron and Osborne were the only mainstream leaders in the Western world to argue for real-term spending cuts. Even President Bush in the US supported an emergency fiscal stimulus. The supposedly modernizing Conservative duo chose to blame government profligacy for the crash. None of Cameron's ideological advisers were thrown by the shift after the crash. They were enthused by the leap rightwards. Steve Hilton noted in the autumn of 2008 that Cameron's calls for spending cuts would boost the Big Society rather than hinder it. The smaller state was the essential backdrop to Hilton's vision.[16]

Cameron carried on wooing non-Conservative commentators who, in most cases, continued to fall for the charm and genuine decency of the political personality. When Cameron insisted that his main priority could be summed up in three letters – 'NHS' – he was widely praised as a new type of Conservative leader, even though his then shadow Health Secretary, Andrew Lansley, was devising a reform to the NHS that would challenge the basic premises of the institution. Although he later denied it, Cameron knew what Lansley was up to. Indeed, Lansley was being guided partly by the principle that Cameron's historic objective was the 'redistribution of power'. In the case of the NHS, this meant the government accepting no further formal responsibility for the delivery of healthcare. Cameron presented the vaguely explored proposition as giving greater power to patients, and his plans received little scrutiny up to and during the 2010 election.

Occasionally, though, his mask slipped. In his 2009 party conference speech Cameron attacked the state, in the manner of a right-wing tabloid columnist, less subtle than Thatcher at her most strident:

Why is our society broken? Because government got too big, did too much and undermined responsibility. Why are our politics broken? Because government got too big, promised too much and pretended it had all the answers... This idea that for every problem there's a government solution, for every issue an initiative, for every situation a czar... It ends with them making you register with the government to help out your child's football team. With police officers punished for babysitting each other's children. With laws so bureaucratic and complicated even their own Attorney General can't obey them. Do you know the worst thing about their big government? It's not the cost, though that's bad enough. It is the steady erosion of responsibility. Our task is to lead Britain in a completely different direction. So no, we are not going to solve our problems with bigger government. We are going to solve our problems with a stronger society. Stronger families. Stronger communities. A stronger country. All by rebuilding responsibility.

'For every situation a czar?' Only the *Daily Mail*'s most polemical columnists would try that one out. This was meant to be a modernizing, centrist leader in his final conference before the next election. But Cameron's theme was clear: the state was the problem. He was equally blunt a few weeks later, in front of most of the *Guardian*'s staff, when he delivered the annual Hugo Young Lecture at Kings Place, the paper's HQ: 'The recent growth of the state has promoted not social solidarity, but selfishness and individualism.'[17]

Cameron's pitch as a centrist leader was partly because he focused on what are often seen as left-wing themes. His Hugo Young Lecture was partly about tackling poverty. His arguments might have been made from the right, but he appeared to be a compassionate Conservative, in that he gave the impression that he sought progressive objectives. Indeed, he deployed the term 'progressive' often.

Cameron was also close to some who were more 'centrist' in outlook. *The Times'* columnist Daniel Finkelstein and his own internal pollster, Andrew Cooper, both of whom originated from the SDP, were allies and friends. His head of office, Ed Llewellyn, had worked for the former Liberal Democrats' leader, Paddy Ashdown, in Bosnia. They were nuanced and thoughtful. But rather than achieving a unique synthesis of radical right and SDP-style moderation, the combination made Cameron a confused leader.

The synthesis was problematic, but the strategic objective was clear. Cameron ached to be seen as being on the 'centre ground'. During the 2006 party conference, Osborne reflected with journalists on a chart that traced where voters saw politicians across the political spectrum. Osborne pointed to the middle point of the chart: 'That's where voters see Tony Blair… bang in the centre. That's where we need to be.' Within two years Osborne was to announce economic policies that were to the right of Margaret Thatcher's, in response to the 2008 crash, proposing those real-term spending cuts. Cameron and Osborne mistook a desire to be on the centre ground with being *on* the centre ground.

Yet away from economic policy and public-service reform, they made some headway. They genuinely changed the look of their party. Within a few years those attending Conservative conferences were much younger and more diverse. There were many more women. Debates were livelier and sharper than at Labour conferences, where deadening control freakery reduced fringe meetings to exchanges of cautious banalities – a stifling political atmosphere that partly enabled the rise of Jeremy Corbyn, a figure not known for his expedient caution. By copying Blair in terms of leadership style, Cameron personified the change in the Conservative Party. He was energetic and witty, and he conveyed a sense of dynamic purpose, even if that purpose was more muddled than it seemed, in terms of policy and party.

————

The muddle played a part in the 2010 election result. Cameron failed to win an overall majority, in fairly propitious circumstances: it was the aftermath of the crash, living standards were falling, the long-serving Labour government had lost most of the media, and the prime minister was unpopular. Even though the Conservatives won more seats than Labour by a considerable margin, they did not secure an overall majority. Steve Hilton's 'Big Society' theme took centre-stage at the Conservatives' epic manifesto launch, held at Battersea Power Station. In effect, the voters were asked to do more for their country as the state got smaller. This request was billed as 'an invitation to join the government of Great Britain'. Not enough voters accepted the invitation for Cameron to win outright.

The outcome was a hung parliament – the first since February 1974. This was both a symptom and a warning. Voters were breaking away from familiar patterns. In this case, they were unable to elect a government with a decisive majority. Cameron had campaigned as a dynamic and youthful leader who was accessible, charming and articulate. Yet he was privileged – the Old Etonian and a child of Thatcherism. He did not quite come together as a convincing political figure, as his role model Blair had done in 1997. Some voters detected, perhaps, the internal confusion behind the confident exterior. Cameron arrived in Number Ten unsure, deep down, about what he wanted to do. The confusion was never fully resolved.

But in order to get to Number Ten he acted with leader-like brilliance in the immediate aftermath of the election. The outcome, while disappointing for him, played to his strengths. He was fascinated by the choreography of politics – how to win, how to secure power, how to outmanoeuvre opponents. In the days after the vote, he made a dramatic and 'comprehensive' offer to the Liberal Democrats to form a coalition, offering Nick Clegg the post of deputy prime minister. A key figure in this course of action was Oliver Letwin, who had done something highly unusual in British politics. He had read the speeches of his opponents and had noted that Clegg's various addresses had chimed with the ideas of the Conservative leadership. Letwin had observed what voters had failed to do. Most voters backed the Liberal Democrats in 2010 on the assumption they were to the left of New Labour. After all, the Liberal Democrats were opponents of the Iraq War, pledged to abolish tuition fees and advocated a fiscal stimulus, rather than Osborne economics. But Clegg's speeches in the years leading up to the 2010 election had been scathing of Labour's record, and not necessarily from a left-wing perspective. He argued that social democracy had failed and that the state was too often seen as part of the solution, when it should not be. He was an economic liberal of a purer form than his recent predecessors. Ming Campbell, Charles Kennedy and David Steel were all social democrats, openly on the left of centre. By closely reading Clegg's speeches, Letwin identified his ideological essence and its uses to the Conservative Party. Still, the parliamentary arithmetic was key: a Con/Lib coalition had a safe majority. A partnership with Labour would not have been secure, in terms of numbers in the Commons. Within days, Clegg had accepted Cameron's offer. Cameron had achieved his ambition. With Liberal Democrat support, he was prime minister.

Cameron's response to the 2010 election showed great agility – an important qualification for leadership. He had little space on the political stage, as a leader who had not won in the way many of his admirers assumed he would. But within hours of the result he had created acres of political space, a route to Number Ten and an arrangement that allowed him and Osborne to pursue most of their radical objectives in policy terms. No other potential Conservative leader from that era could have pulled off such a feat in such difficult circumstances. Cameron accomplished it with energetic aplomb. The energy he displayed during the tortuous coalition negotiations was miraculous, particularly given how tiring the election campaign was. But the prospect of power can light up ambitious politicians as if it were the equivalent of a high-voltage charge from the National Grid. Cameron was lit up, even agreeing to Clegg's demand for a referendum on electoral reform. In his creation of the coalition and its subsequent management, Cameron passed a key test of leadership. He was an astute manager of people and could lead effectively in a hung parliament. He would have been much more effective at working with other parties over Brexit than Theresa May, who was incapable of reaching out in any meaningful way.

What followed the formation of the coalition was extraordinary. The Con/Lib government implemented radical policies at the political equivalent of the speed of light. In pursuit of its ideological goals, Cameron's government was far bolder than New Labour in 1997, yet New Labour had won a landslide majority, while Cameron had not even secured a majority of one. The dazzling speed of implementation suited Cameron's lack of interest in complex policy detail. This is not to suggest that he was lazy or too relaxed, another inaccurate caricature of modern prime ministers.

He worked long hours, as any prime minister must. But he was not excited by policy detail. Strategy and projection animated him more.

Within a year his government had pledged to wipe out the UK's huge deficit by the end of the parliament through the introduction of real-term spending cuts; announced sweeping reforms of the NHS; pledged referendums on all future EU treaties; implemented a Fixed-term Parliaments Act; imposed new rules on schools, while further fragmenting the structures governing education; and, in effect, almost privatized universities by announcing a trebling of tuition fees, while beginning a massive overhaul of welfare provision and holding a referendum on electoral reform.

Each radical reform had historic or chaotic consequences – and quite often both. Policy implementation is the best guide to a prime minister's character, and whether he or she is up to the job. On this basis, Cameron was not a laid-back Etonian, but a restless reformer. This is also the context for his decision to hold the Brexit referendum. He sought to clear the ground in order to embark on more reforms in his second term. But there was no ground-clearing with Brexit.

The economic policy of unyielding ambition failed, on its own terms. The deficit had not by any means been wiped out by the end of the parliament. With the self-confident chutzpah that defined the coalition, both governing parties went into the next election pledging to wipe out the deficit in the following parliament, and mocking Labour for failing to make the same pledge. Eventually the pledge was dropped in 2016. Apart from other considerations, the policy was threatening to wreck the Conservatives' electoral chances. The framing of the policy had been obviously fruitful for a time, but it sowed the seeds for later political trouble, not least the Brexit referendum and the 2017 election in which Conservative MPs warned that the cuts were biting too hard, even in affluent constituencies. When senior Conservative ministers declared that wiping out the deficit was no longer an immediate objective, the media no longer focused on the issue, having previously been obsessed by it.

Austerity's role in the Brexit referendum was significant. 'Leave' voters were rebelling partly against the impact of the cuts. They felt 'left behind' and sought 'control', because outside London and a few of the more affluent cities, the state had left them to cope with the consequences of globalization. In her party conference speech in October 2018 Theresa May announced the 'end of austerity' with the deficit still far from wiped out, but with some public services, welfare reform and local government in a state of crisis. Significantly, quite a few Conservative MPs were highlighting the crises.

The coalition's new NHS reforms were as chaotic as they were ambitious. Cameron's Health Secretary, Andrew Lansley, unveiled a White Paper almost as large as the one that introduced the NHS in the first place. Although Clegg was enthusiastic at first, naively seeing the plan as a celebratory conflation of the Liberal Democrats' support for localism and the Conservatives' attachment to markets, his party was alarmed.[18]

Cameron had been supportive of Lansley, partly because he was excited by the political implications of Lansley's proposal. He assumed the changes would have the support of Tony Blair and the vocal Blairites in the parliamentary Labour Party, thereby fuelling tensions in the post-Blair Labour Party. Cameron was alarmed when Blairites, including the former Health Secretary Alan Milburn, expressed their opposition. Lansley's reforms, as originally envisaged and as largely implemented, formed the most extensive reorganization of the NHS in its history. Wholly in line with the 'Post-Bureaucratic Age' seminars that Cameron held while in opposition, Lansley proposed removing formal responsibility for health provision from the Secretary of State for Health. The aim was to make local providers more accountable and, by increasing competition, to deliver better outcomes for patients. As ever with the 'Post-Bureaucratic Age', the outcome was many additional mediating agencies often competing with each other, and none of them taking responsibility as the lines of accountability became blurred.

Cameron dodged responsibility for the proposed reforms by coming up with a curious excuse. He claimed that he had not known what Lansley was up to, and announced 'a pause' – a rare example of the coalition catching a breath rather than accelerating further. The breath was limited. Under the changes after the 'pause', the NHS was further fragmented and more agencies were involved in the delivery of healthcare, in what had already become a complicated flowchart of lines of responsibility and accountability. The fragmentation began at the top, where it was never clear whether a supposedly mighty quango, NHS England, pulled the strings or whether this was still the responsibility and prerogative of the Health Secretary. Cameron was one of those who became confused.

Fearing a winter flu crisis before the looming 2015 general election, Cameron asked his Health Secretary, Jeremy Hunt, to phone the managers of hospitals individually and demand that preparatory actions be taken. Hunt pointed out to Cameron that the government had given away the powers to act in such a way. In fairness to Cameron, he smiled at the ironic impotence.[19] The effects were already being felt and, when a series of scandals surfaced in relation to Mid Staffs hospital in 2013, the government decided to make a parliamentary statement. Cameron made the statement himself, pledging to take personal responsibility to ensure the hospital improved and the lessons were learned. But the spirit of the NHS reforms contradicted this act of prime ministerial muscularity. Again Cameron had not determined clearly in his own mind what he believed, or what the implications of whatever beliefs he possessed would be, when they were put into action.

His former head of policy, Camilla Cavendish, concluded in a perceptive article from 2018 that fragmentation had failed:

> I have observed the NHS for more than 10 years: as a journalist, as a non-executive director of the NHS regulator Care Quality Commission, as a patient and relative, and as head of David Cameron's policy unit in No. 10. Unlike many patients, I have a map. Yet like many patients, I can still feel lost. There are more job titles in the NHS than in many multinational corporations – some of them jobs that exist simply to tie together the disparate pieces.

What if we really had one truly unified national medical system?[20]

The same question could have been asked in terms of the costs of paying all the mediating agencies required to regulate and supervise them.

Moving so fast in eye-catching policy areas, such as the economy and the NHS, Cameron's constitutional reforms did not receive the scrutiny they required. After losing the referendum on Brexit in 2016, Cameron was widely accused of being too casual and complacent in his approach. The signs were there much earlier, when he had legislated to hold referendums on all future EU treaties. This meant that if Cameron had not held his later

In/Out plebiscite, the UK would probably have left the EU anyway. A referendum on an EU treaty would almost certainly not have been winnable – harder to win, in some ways, than a binary choice of such vastness as the one he posed to voters in 2016. If the UK could not have signed a treaty, it would have been on its way out of the EU.

The Fixed-term Parliaments Act had more precise consequences, which have been felt ever since it was passed. The reform was rushed through in 2011 largely for short-term considerations. In a hung parliament, Cameron wanted to be prime minister for a full term, and Osborne was similarly enthused about being chancellor for a long time. The Act essentially facilitated this, making an early election much less possible. But the policy had a perverse consequence.

If a prime minister is popular there is usually no need for an election. Popularity suggests a degree of stability. Yet it is only when a prime minister is well ahead in the polls that an early election becomes possible, under the Act. The MPs from the governing party will only vote for an election if they are confident they will win. In effect, under the Act, MPs from the governing party must support an early election. Conversely, when a government is in trouble and Parliament is close to paralysis, an election is almost impossible. MPs from a governing party are unlikely to back a dissolution that will lead to their political demise. These consequences were tested in dramatic circumstances when Theresa May called an early election in 2017, at a time when she was twenty points ahead in the polls. As her subsequent minority government struggled to stay afloat in a near-paralysed hung parliament, she and her senior colleagues showed no similar hunger for an election. This was the consequence of the Fixed-term Parliaments Act. Yes, the coalition served a full term, but the UK was left with a situation in which when there might be a need for an election, there would never be one. When there was no need for an election, a popular prime minister might be tempted to hold one. The 2017 Conservative manifesto pledged to scrap the Fixed-term Parliaments Act, one of several sensible proposals that were not implemented when Theresa May lost her party's majority.

Elsewhere in Cameron's raft of rushed-through policies, the decision in the summer of 2010 to triple university tuition fees had echoes of the NHS reforms that were unveiled that autumn. He assumed that Blairite Labour MPs would be sympathetic to the rise in fees for students. Blair and his adviser in Number Ten, Andrew Adonis, had introduced tuition fees during Labour's second term. But so-called Blairites were alarmed at the leap, regarding the increases as far too steep. Adonis was a passionate opponent. There were many consequences. Disillusioned students faced significant debts. Universities started to pretend they were in a marketplace when they were not, paying out vast incomes to vice-chancellors and other senior staff for doing very little – the corruption of a pretend market. The Open University was a sad victim, unable to attract as many students, with the higher fees.

The rapid decline of the Liberal Democrats from strong third force to a puny parliamentary party of near-irrelevance can be traced to this single policy. Clegg's party had pledged to scrap tuition fees, but within months of the election it supported the increase. Indeed, as is often the case with newly elected British governments, the seeds of the coalition's fall were being sown during its honeymoon. As political commentators praised the coalition for showing how two parties could work together to 'save' the UK – wondering all the while whether a new permanent realignment of British politics was taking place – policies were being implemented that made the chance of a second coalition impossible. The Liberal Democrats were heading for an electoral meltdown in 2015, to the benefit of Cameron, who went on to win a small overall majority.

In the summer of 2010 Cameron wondered too about whether he had been an agent of a permanent realignment on the centre right between his party and the Liberal Democrats.[21] By 2018 the agents of the realignment, Cameron and Clegg, were out of Parliament; and Cameron's successor, Theresa May, had announced a review of tuition fees, with some of her senior advisers convinced they had to reduce the costs to students if they were ever to win another election. Under Jeremy Corbyn, Labour had pledged in the 2017 election to abolish tuition fees. The coalition's 300 per cent increase in student fees was radical and yet fragile.

Cameron's economic policies and public-service reforms were often an outdated cheer for Thatcherism. Because they came so late in the long era in which Thatcher cast her spell, they showed few signs of enduring. The Fixed-term Parliaments Act would have been scrapped, had May won a majority. Subsequent Health Secretaries concluded, like Camilla Cavendish, that the NHS needed greater centralization rather than fragmentation. Elsewhere, May announced the 'end of austerity' in her 2018 party conference speech, and the UK had voted to leave the EU before a new treaty could be tested in a referendum. Never had a newly elected government moved so quickly and with such ambitious range, yet most of the reforms did not last long.

The one that will endure is the legalization of gay marriage, a socially liberal reform that enhanced the lives of many, but served to confuse the way Cameron was perceived. Cameron had moved on from possessing a Bullingdon Club lofty machismo to being a sincere social liberal. At his final Prime Minister's Questions in the summer of 2016, he cited gay marriage as the change that had given him most satisfaction. He and Osborne clung to the reform as proof that they were 'centrists', and quite a few commentators bought into the idea. But the conflation of social and economic liberalism is deceptive. Thatcher was an economic liberal and was defiantly assertive about not being on the centre ground, warning that people get run over if they walk in the middle of the road. Cameron and Osborne were also economic liberals, like her. They were, on economic matters at least, to the right of Theresa May. On social matters they were more 'liberal' and metropolitan than her, but that did not alter their position on economic policy and the role of the state. Yet several commentators reported, as objective fact, that the Conservatives had moved to the right under May. This was misleading.

Perhaps because Cameron won the referendum on electoral reform with ease, he became complacent about the anomalies and risks of direct democracy. His leadership is defined by referendums, which is odd for a British prime minister. There was a time when the UK hardly ever held referendums – for instance, under Margaret Thatcher and John Major. In the 1997 election, Tony Blair offered many, but didn't hold them all, once in power. Like the fragile Labour government in the 1970s, Cameron offered one to Scotland, this time on independence rather than devolution; and then the referendum on Europe that brought him down. In the 1970s Callaghan's referendum on devolution led to his fall, but earlier in that decade Wilson had won the plebiscite on Europe. In Cameron's case, the reverse happened. He moved on from the Scottish referendum and then lost the Brexit referendum.

The campaign on electoral reform was not exactly preparation for the referendum storms that were to follow. In the run-up to the vote, Cameron constantly outmanoeuvred Clegg, with charm and a far greater fascination with the game of politics than the politically naive Lib Dem leader. Cameron's offer of a referendum had clinched the deal during the coalition negotiations, but there was one crucial condition that Clegg meekly accepted. The referendum would be on the Alternative Vote (AV) – a different option from First Past the Post – which was not proportional and had not been previously advocated by the Liberal Democrats. In an act of comically brutal ruthlessness, the campaign against AV, authorized by Cameron, argued that voters could not trust Clegg on the basis of the way he had betrayed them in the coalition. Cameron won the referendum with ease. The Labour leadership was theoretically supportive of AV but, in reality, was indifferent at best. It would not campaign with Clegg, partly because he had opted for a coalition of the radical right, but also because the Labour leadership had its private doubts about electoral reform. Few voters showed much interest, either. The turnout was low.

As such, the referendum campaign on electoral reform was highly deceptive, dull and soporific, resulting in the status quo. But on other fronts, voters were starting to stir. The 2010 election result was a better guide to what was to come: the unusual irresolution of a hung parliament. Cameron became casual with referendums, after winning his first one with such ease. He called two when he did not necessarily have to hold either. The first destabilized British politics and yet inadvertently helped Cameron win a tiny overall majority in 2015. The second led to his dramatic fall.

After the leader of the SNP, Alex Salmond, won a majority in the Scottish Parliament in 2011, the issue of independence for Scotland soared up the agenda. At least it did for Cameron. Salmond, a leader of agile cunning, spoke often about a referendum, but had no intention of calling for one with a precise date until the polls suggested he would win. In spite of his historic triumph in elections for the Scottish Parliament, there was still no definitive evidence in the polling that he would win a referendum. He twisted and turned, when asked about when he would expect the vote to be held.

In contrast, Cameron went for it, displaying the usual impatient flair that defined his speedy, risky radicalism. He did so on the assumption that he would win. No prime minister calls a referendum on the assumption he or she will lose. A prime ministerial passion for direct democracy is kindled only when victory is on the cards. Cameron named the date for the referendum on independence and rolled up his sleeves. It was only towards the very end of the campaign that he feared he might lose. He was brilliant at staying calm – perhaps too brilliant – but when a poll suggested that a majority of voters would back independence, even he was alarmed. The poll was either wrong or the mood changed in the final days. In light of the result of the Brexit referendum, the modest victory for the union of 55–45 per cent was a triumph, but the campaign in Scotland unleashed passions that fed on themselves. Although the status quo prevailed, the referendum transformed British politics and did not resolve the issue of independence.

Early the next morning Cameron stood outside Number Ten and declared that he would introduce 'English votes for English laws' in the Westminster Parliament, to appease some of his MPs who feared that too much had been given away to the Scottish executive in order to win the referendum. Cameron was the latest of a long line of Conservative leaders who felt obliged to appease his right-wing MPs, only to land in more trouble as a result of the appeasement.

In Scotland, Cameron's early-morning announcement was widely seen as further evidence of betrayal from London, a prime minister acting differently once the votes had been cast. Support for the SNP soared the weekend after the referendum, partly as a consequence of Cameron's conduct. Salmond departed, to be replaced by the equally smart Nicola Sturgeon, who instantly became commanding. The observant Labour politician Barbara Castle once said of Margaret Thatcher that 'power made her beautiful'. Castle meant that leadership suited Thatcher and gave her space to fulfil her potential. The same applied to Sturgeon. She had been nervous and gauche in her early days as Salmond's deputy. But when she took over, she was ready: a clear-sighted and articulate social democrat. Labour had ruled Scotland like a fiefdom. Under Sturgeon, the SNP became an even more dominant force.

Cameron had not planned the rise of the SNP and its destabilizing impact on the UK, but the subsequent near wipe-out of Labour in Scotland in the 2015 general election enabled him to win his overall majority. Labour's leader, Ed Miliband, had been nervily fearful of much that could go wrong under his fragile regime, but never anticipated Labour being destroyed in Scotland. Miliband was reduced to tears in the immediate aftermath of the 2015 general election, when reflecting on what happened in Scotland. After all, he would have been prime minister if Labour had performed even reasonably well there. But for Cameron, the wipe-out of Labour was an accidental consequence of his referendum. His objective had been to resolve the independence question for a generation, but his referendum failed to do so. Indeed, it heightened the intensity of the question.

There was, however, a case for Cameron's decision to hold the Scottish referendum when he did. In leadership, decisions are nearly always nightmarish, and more nuanced than the media allow. Blair once characterized most decisions that he had to take as 'Do you want to cut your wrist or slit your throat?'[22] There were no easy routes. If Cameron had not offered the referendum in Scotland, Salmond would have played games, teasing the British government and making the Westminster politicians seem defensive and uncooperative. There was a case for Cameron taking the initiative, especially when there had not been a single opinion poll suggesting that he would lose. But equally, Cameron could have called Salmond's bluff, put forward the case for the union and got on with the rest of his crammed agenda. This is what Theresa May did, when Sturgeon called vaguely for a second referendum in Scotland after the Brexit referendum. May said 'No' and Sturgeon's calls became vaguer. In a few respects May was more leaderly than Cameron, arriving in Number Ten more fully formed. But she faced Cameron's thorny legacy, and her fatal flaws soon doomed her, too.

———

His legacy took the form of Brexit. All the themes of Cameron's leadership came together in the Brexit saga. Far from being the laid-back Etonian prime minister, he was taking yet another big risk. Of all the modern prime ministers, Cameron was the greatest risk taker. He was over-confident in his ability to win the referendum, and yet lacking in confidence in his sense that he needed to make such an offer in order to survive in office. His renegotiation with the rest of the EU was rushed and ill-thought-through, and yet it might have been the basis for a long-term settlement if Cameron had not proved yet again that he was an unreliable vote-winner, this time in the referendum.

When Cameron offered the In/Out referendum during a speech in 2013, the EU was low down the list of voters' concerns, according to opinion polls. He made the offer against the advice of Osborne and his then close friend Michael Gove, because he feared more defections from his parliamentary party and voters turning to the UK Independence Party (UKIP), a party campaigning for a referendum on whether to leave the EU. Cameron calculated that a referendum would blunt the appeal of UKIP and be a winning card in a general election. Again, his calculations were understandable. UKIP's leader, Nigel Farage, claimed that he was speaking to several Conservative MPs who planned to defect. Cameron's press secretary, Sir Craig Oliver, revealed subsequently that Number Ten worried that up to twenty Conservative MPs could defect.[23]

There is nothing more terrifying for party leaders than defections to another party, and nothing more gratifying than travel in the opposite direction. Defections are evidence of momentum to one side rather than another, and of fatal disunity. They are a more reliable guide to the wider mood than opinion polls. The defections from the Conservative Party to Labour in the New Labour era were regarded as hugely significant at the time, confirming and reinforcing Labour's soaring rise and the Conservatives' fall. When the likes of Alan Howarth, Sean Woodward and Quentin Davies changed sides, they were not household names, but made huge waves because of the symbolism.

In the early 1980s the defections from Labour to the SDP were also a sign that Labour was heading for electoral catastrophe. Cameron and Osborne ached for defectors to join them in their early phase, wooing in particular the Liberal Democrat MP David Laws, who supported much of their economic policy. Their failure to attract defections reflected the fragility of their project. Defectors are attracted to a project that appears to have depth and durability. They are making a big leap. Cameron was acutely aware that if several Tory MPs switched to UKIP, the latter would be greatly strengthened and he would be conversely weakened. The right would be split at a general election, in the way the left had been in the 1980s. The Independent Group, formed in 2019 from defecting Labour and Conservative MPs, outlined the vaguest of programmes on the basis of a banal set of values, but the leaderships of the other parties feared more defections and to some extent changed their tunes accordingly. Leaders loathe defections or the prospect of them.

But while anxiety was a natural response to the stirrings of UKIP, Cameron moved too speedily towards the seemingly magical solution of the referendum. He made the pledge to hold an In/Out plebiscite before the trauma of the Scottish referendum, but after the easy ride of the vote on electoral reform. Again he acted because he assumed he would win. Partly he was paying the price of failing to challenge his party over the issue of Europe when he was strong in the early days of his leadership, preferring to take the easier path of visiting council estates as a symbol of a new compassionate conservatism or visiting Greenland to highlight concern for global warming. On Europe he had chosen appeasement when he was strong, the same mistake that May made when she was on an authority-enhancing honeymoon. Having supported his party leaving the European People's Party during his leadership contest, Cameron sought to act tough with Europe as prime minister, wielding his veto ostentatiously at key moments, while seeking and failing to block the appointment of a new EU president. By 2013 he was relatively weak. He was behind in the polls, the leader of a coalition rather than a Conservative government, and the self-confident swagger was replaced with some degree of panic.

Cameron found the art of politics compelling and yet he was not always an astute reader of its complex rhythms. His tendency to copy Blair meant that he read the rhythms as if they arose from the mid- to late 1990s, an altogether different era. Cameron was navigating his way through the aftermath of the 2008 financial crash while leading a party as riven over Europe as it was when his role model, Blair, slaughtered it in 1997.

UKIP was never as strong as it seemed, or at least as it seemed to Cameron. The party attracted two defectors during the coalition era, the ineffectual Mark Reckless and the ideologically eccentric Douglas Carswell. Both had left UKIP by 2018 and were out of the UK Parliament. Other Tory hard-liners showed little inclination to join them in defecting. They were as tribal as any other part of the Conservative Party.[24]

Support for UKIP peaked in the European elections in 2014 after Cameron had made the referendum pledge, suggesting that the offer was not a decisive factor for voters. UKIP topped the poll in terms of votes cast – a staggering achievement and a warning about what might happen in a referendum on EU membership. The result was simultaneously a warning and a red herring. Voters were stirring in unprecedented numbers, making any referendums extremely dangerous. Yet their chosen vehicle, UKIP, was weak and fragile. Its leader, Nigel Farage, was a laddishly appealing performer, who managed to keep the show on the road. Below him were a bunch of weird amateurs espousing incoherent views. When Farage resigned after the 2016 referendum, UKIP had a series of bizarre leaders who were elected during even odder leadership contests. UKIP was not the formidable force it appeared to be. By 2019 Farage had formed The Brexit Party – even he had had enough of UKIP.

After his unexpected victory in 2015, Cameron announced, with characteristically impatient speed, that the Brexit referendum would be held in the summer of the following year. There is a common myth that he offered the referendum on the assumption that he would never have to hold it – calculating that there would be a second coalition and the Liberal Democrats would veto the referendum. This is not the case. Cameron knew when he made the offer of a referendum, largely to his party, that he would have to deliver, whether leading a coalition or a single-party government. He had been unequivocal. He made the offer of the referendum because he thought he would win, not because he hoped he would never have to hold the vote.[25]

Cameron might well have won the referendum if it had not been for a series of miscalculations. The first was to overestimate his own persuasive powers, both in his negotiations with the EU and in his pitch to UK voters. He made the mistake of assuming that a few charming bilateral meetings with individual EU leaders would deliver a substantial renegotiation of the UK's already generous membership arrangements.

As usual, the EU acted as a coherent whole, and Cameron's sleepless visits to Berlin and other capitals produced only limited results. Meanwhile, in parts of the UK where his turbo-charged Thatcherite economic policies had hit hard, voters were not inclined to give him their backing in a referendum. Cameron should have taken more notice of Harold Wilson's approach to the 1975 referendum on UK membership. More than aware of his unpopularity, Wilson kept a low profile, timed the referendum when polls pointed to a huge victory, and used his 'renegotiation' to achieve some easy accessible gains, mostly relating to the price of New Zealand butter.

The context of Cameron's renegotiation was determined by his other major miscalculation. Wilson knew that his Cabinet and party were split and that his 'renegotiation' had no hope of uniting the two sides of the divide. His cosmetic deal was merely a peg to justify Wilson supporting membership, having opposed it when the UK joined under Edward Heath.

In contrast, Cameron hoped to keep his Cabinet on board and united behind his 'renegotiation'. He was also fairly optimistic of wooing the then highly popular Conservative MP Boris Johnson. The stakes in relation to his renegotiation were impossibly high, and only late in the day did he accept with great reluctance that collective responsibility had to be dropped. This was when his deal with the EU failed to satisfy several Eurosceptics in his Cabinet, including his friend Michael Gove. According to Sir Craig Oliver, Cameron knew Johnson was unreliable, but was devastated by what he saw as Gove's betrayal.[26] Cameron was fairly unflappable, but Oliver recalls how Cameron had his head in his hands in fuming despair as he heard that Gove, campaigning for 'Leave', had co-written an article with Johnson suggesting that his old prime ministerial friend could not be trusted with some of his claims in relation to Europe. Cameron was naive to expect friendship to trump conviction on an issue as emotive as Europe. In some respects, he was a leader with strong views weakly held, as the historian A. J. P. Taylor once described himself. Gove had strong views, held with a determination that would end a friendship.[27]

Probably the 'Remain' campaign was doomed from the beginning. Across the democratic world voters were giving perceived 'elites' a kicking. Looking back to 1975, although the elite (in the form of current and former prime ministers, most MPs and business leaders) campaigned for the UK to remain in Europe, their advocacy was not seen as counter-productive. In 2016 the support of a charismatic US president, as well as all current and former living prime ministers, turned out to be deeply unhelpful.

But Cameron did not perform with the agility required to give him any chance of avoiding the torrents that were sweeping perceived elites from power. Indeed, the fragile career of the onetime self-confident Etonian highlights the wild politics that carried him away. He became the prime minister of a rare peacetime coalition and never served with a hefty Commons majority. In a country that rarely held referendums, Cameron implemented three of historic significance. If prime ministers hold referendums, they must win them. Cameron lost one and, barely a year after winning an overall majority in the 2015 general election, he was gone. It was an unprecedented fall, from major triumph to fatal humiliation in just twelve months.

For a youthful prime minister, Cameron proved masterly in creating and managing a coalition. Both were epic achievements – managing people and parties is a major part of leadership. Cameron had to manage his party and its relationship with another in government. Against the expectations of many, the coalition lasted the full five years and this was largely down to his skilful dealings with colleagues. He also led the Cabinet with aplomb, avoiding too many reshuffles and keeping on board throughout the coalition years social democrats such as Vince Cable and Tory radicals like Iain Duncan Smith. IDS resigned in the build-up to the referendum, when the Conservatives had an overall majority. He stayed put during the coalition, working well with the Liberal Democrats' Steve Webb. Cameron had created the space for unlikely partnerships to form and flourish.

Fatally, though, Cameron did not know who he was as a political figure, arriving as prime minister more underdeveloped than any post-war leader. His early passion for the 'Big Society' was dropped soon after he became prime minister. He was reported as describing the Liberal Democrats' concerns for the environment as 'green crap' towards the end of his leadership, having affected a commitment to green issues early in his leadership.

Ultimately Cameron had wanted to be a different type of Conservative leader, and yet he shared many of the views espoused by recent Tory predecessors. Tony Blair was his model, but while Blair believed – rightly or wrongly – that his party should change beyond recognition, Cameron was less sure whether he could, or should, challenge the Conservatives to the same extent. He was reluctant on some policy areas to challenge himself in the way that a figure like Neil Kinnock had done. But unlike Kinnock, he won an election and was prime minister for six years. He could have ruled considerably longer, if his inexperienced ambiguity and shallow tactical instincts had not led him to fight and lose a referendum on the UK's membership of the EU. He had been too quick to assume he could convince the electorate that the EU was close to a form of paradise, despite having been largely Eurosceptic for most of his leadership. The other related trauma for Cameron was how the referendum outcome suggested that he had not understood the country he had led for six years, assuming it was close to the one that elected New Labour in 1997. But the country had changed in ways that he and his media supporters had not seen.

While Cameron had insisted in public that he would remain prime minister if he lost the referendum, privately he had told his closest advisers he would go.[28] One of those who believed his public statement was his then Home Secretary, Theresa May. She had kept a low profile during the referendum, on the assumption that a vacancy would arise at some point during the parliament. After all, Cameron had pledged, unwisely, not to seek a third term; May thought he would probably win the referendum or stay on in defeat. Wholly unexpectedly for her, he lost the vote and then stepped down. Within days she was prime minister, thrown to the top of the pile in a context, and at a time, that she had not anticipated. Cameron's sudden departure was as premature as his speedy rise. Theresa May arrived in Number Ten less prepared for the burdens of leadership than any other prime minister in modern times.

9

THERESA MAY

Theresa May's nerve-shredding, energy-sapping and joyless prime ministerial career serves as a warning to current and aspiring leaders: expect a hellish time, unless you have certain essential qualifications. May had a story to tell about Brexit and the rest of her agenda, but she was not a political teacher. She not only failed to tell her story, but did not even make an attempt. This was her fatal flaw – not only a failure to communicate, but an indifference to the art.

She also lacked a second qualification of leadership. She was not an astute reader of the political rhythms. She did at times have space on the political stage, but failed to see when she had the room to be bold and when she did not. In relation to Brexit she acted weakly when she was politically strong, and finally told her party of the need for compromise when she was hopelessly weak. Fatally she got the sequence the wrong way round.

She became weak after calling the early election in 2017, just a year into her premiership, and losing her party's overall majority. Many lessons of leadership arise from the collapse of her authority. Most fundamentally that early elections can be dangerous – either contemplating them or holding them.

As May made her moves, she worked assiduously, and at times wilfully, to deliver her view of the form that Brexit should take. Soon the volcanic explosions began. Ministers resigned. Her Brexit deal was defeated in the Commons three times. There was a vote of confidence amongst Conservative MPs, in an attempt to remove her. The Brexit deadline was extended from March 2019, in spite of endless prime ministerial proclamations that the UK would be out of the EU by then. May was at the centre of it all and yet determinedly separate from the drama – a form of political isolation that was both a protective shield and a further source of her fragility.

Most incoming prime ministers have had some time to prepare for the tasks ahead. May had none. With dizzying speed, the UK had a new leader in the aftermath of the 2016 referendum, one who had never had cause to think deeply about Brexit. Her direct ministerial experience of the European Union was acquired in the Home Office. She had not been a leader of the Opposition, where it is necessary to frame arguments and reflect more widely on the UK's relationship with Europe. She had no ministerial perspective from the Treasury or the Foreign Office. Her experience of the EU as a minister had been in the more straightforward, though highly charged and important area of security. On the whole, members of the EU agree that security concerns require coordination and the sharing of information. The UK was respected for its willingness to share and coordinate. As Home Secretary, if May wanted to opt out of some EU agreements and opt into others, she prevailed with ease. The Home Office tests many qualities in a politician, but it is not the best preparation for becoming an authoritative expert on all aspects of the European Union.

Theresa May also had no idea in advance that the Conservatives' whacky leadership battle of July 2016 was going to end almost before it had begun. She assumed that she would face a second round of party members and would have until September to finalize her thoughts around Brexit, before entering Number Ten – if, indeed, she won. The immediate context of her rise is pivotal. As the contest got under way she was not to know that there would be no second round. Her thoughts about Brexit were on a single question: how to win a Conservative leadership contest when a majority of members were strongly pro-Brexit?

Her early post-referendum discussions, which were confined to her two special advisers of the time, Nick Timothy and Fiona Hill, focused largely on this narrow question: 'How can we convince the party that we are deadly serious about Brexit?' In reflecting on that question, May began to frame answers that led towards her fall. As is often the case with prime ministers, the seeds of her fragility were sown in the period in which she rose triumphantly to the top. She had no time to think for very long about what Brexit meant. She had no time to learn how the EU operates at the highest level.

Other prime ministers sought to find words to make sense of a chaotic situation, or tried to change the situation. May did neither. She was widely seen as dutiful, as she twisted and turned to stay on her chosen path – a triumph of deviousness. But her indifference to words and persuasion, essential arts of leadership, became the main cause of her undoing. Long-serving prime ministers are the ones who seek constantly to engage with MPs, voters and the media, telling stories that appear to make sense of what is happening. Margaret Thatcher was an instinctive teacher, reducing the complexities of monetarism to homilies about how her father never spent more than he earned. As she made her moves, Thatcher proclaimed that her aim was to set people free. And who is opposed to freedom? Wilson and Blair deployed the evasive term 'modernization' to explain their early initiatives. Some of the shorter-serving prime ministers were more effective than May. Edward Heath was an adequate communicator in the 1975 Common Market referendum after he had ceased to be prime minister, explaining better than most why pooled sovereignty was not a threat to democracy. Gordon Brown sparkled as a speaker before he became shadow chancellor and even, at times, after he acquired the stifling, dehumanizing economic brief. He framed some of the enduring soundbites of the New Labour era, from 'Tough on crime, tough on the causes of crime' to 'prudence for a purpose'. Nick Timothy devised May's best lines and, after he left, there were no memorable lines at all. May was not a 'teacher' prime minister, with the language and performance skills to make sense of what – in the case of Brexit – could often be nonsensical.

There were times when May needed to be opaque in order to keep her government together, but a political teacher can be evasive while appearing to be clear. When Thatcher declared famously in October 1980 that the 'lady's not for turning', she was, in reality, overseeing a U-turn in her economic policy. The lady *was* for turning from pure monetarism, but her skill as a teacher disguised the haphazard route she was taking. When Blair tormented John Major by asserting, 'I lead my party, you follow yours', he was referring to Major's equivocations over the single currency. Blair was equivocating in precisely the same way, but he was a communicator who could deploy words to convey resolute leadership, when he was keeping options open. Words are a political weapon. May did not have the necessary ammunition.

At the beginning of her premiership in the summer of 2016, with Brexit looming large, she said there would be no 'running commentary' on the process. In the many months that followed, both within government and outside it, May was the only person who followed this laughably unrealistic instruction. Standing apart from the political noise, there was no focus from May on strategy as the storms erupted. Instead, an unruly pattern emerged: as the latest crisis erupted, May kept going till the following day, when she inevitably became politically trapped again, wriggled awkwardly, spoke evasively and created a little more space until the next incarceration. She proved to be a durable political contortionist, but did not seek to explain what her latest painful position might be.

This determinedly insular pattern formed during the gradual phase of May's ascent. As with other modern prime ministers, the pattern of the early years recurred after May acquired the crown, and therefore merit further scrutiny. When an ambitious politician becomes prime minister, he or she often assumes that past patterns are a guide to future successful rule. But quite often they are a warning of how *not* to rule, when leading in the very different context of Number Ten. Most fundamentally, May assumed that the way she had operated as Home Secretary, and as a senior Opposition frontbencher, could be applied in Number Ten. In those previous roles she had kept public and media appearances to a minimum, decided on policies with a few trusted advisers and then made sure she prevailed, if colleagues sought to prevent her policies from being implemented.

May was not interested in engaging with journalists, either as an ambitious potential leader or as prime minister. She met them because her advisers told her to do so. No journalist can recall a noteworthy exchange. She was bewildered and disapproving of her colleagues who spoke endlessly to those in the media, assuming – often correctly – that they saw politics merely as a game. When she was Home Secretary in the coalition, and as prime minister, some of her colleagues did become far too intoxicated with the fleeting thrill of engaging with political journalists, both in private and in the broadcasting studio. The exchanges were an affirmation of their significance and, they often assumed, a further boost to their ambitions to become more significant still. Quite often the sole consequences were to provide lines for journalists – lines that came and went in the daily hurly-burly of politics.

Even so, an indifference to the art of being a political teacher is a form of neglect, and it is the media that mediates between leader and the electorate. May did not try to be a guide through the storms. If she had been an effective teacher, she would have had more followers, because there would have been a more clearly defined path for them to follow.

Instead, she saw her political past as a form of vindication. She had got to the top by focusing on policy implementation, while largely hiding away from the media and the public. This was how she had succeeded where others had failed. In her previous job she was used to making policy without great public scrutiny. She had often turned down interviews on the *Today* programme and BBC1's *Andrew Marr Show* as she navigated her course. On being made prime minister, May assumed that she could still get away with this evasiveness, even in relation to the most significant change in UK policy since 1945.

There is an important qualification to May's determination to lie low. Every now and again throughout her career she would surface dramatically, before hiding away again. For much of the time May made little public impact during her years on her party's frontbench, toiling away behind the scenes without feeling the need to explain very often what she was doing, or why. But, every now and again, she uttered words that would make waves. She was the equivalent of the plodding tennis player who occasionally had a tantrum and played spectacularly.

May had wanted to be prime minister for much of her adult life, being ambitious for the top job for longer than Thatcher or Blair. She was brought up as an only child in Oxfordshire. Her father was a vicar and her mother was an active Conservative Party member. Like Thatcher, May was hooked on politics from her teenage years, becoming a member of the Conservative Party and active at Oxford. She met her future husband, Philip, at a Conservative social evening at the university. Even as prime minister, she liked nothing more than canvassing in Maidenhead, her constituency, and taking part in local political meetings. She seemed most at ease politically when canvassing at home. Coincidentally, the UK had both a prime minister and a leader of the Opposition, Jeremy Corbyn, who flourished in their constituencies, while being much less at ease responding to national and international historic events. As Brexit raged on, both liked nothing more than to return to their home patch. May became an MP in 1997 – Tony Blair's first landslide victory – and slowly rose through the ranks as a solid, determined MP who had more time on her hands than most of her colleagues. Like Edward Heath, she had no children and few other interests to distract her from politics. Unlike Heath, she had a partner, in Philip, who shared her passion for Conservative politics. They were in it together. Heath was alone.

At the Conservative conference in 2002 May made her mark as the newish party chairwoman. Here was an early example of her making waves, before returning to semi-darkness away from the intense media glare. For a politician who rarely delivered memorable speeches, her words at that conference were never forgotten and were often quoted in the years to follow. In some respects, they defined her in the most flattering light possible – as a figure brave enough to tell her party hard truths. She was speaking early on in Labour's second term, after the Conservatives had been slaughtered in both the 1997 and 2001 elections:

Yes, we've made progress, but let's not kid ourselves. There's a way to go before we can return to government. There's a lot we need to do in this party of ours. Our base is too narrow and so, occasionally, are our sympathies. You know what some people call us: the nasty party.

She was not posturing. She meant it. May was a politician who tended to say what she believed. Quite often her beliefs were pragmatic and uninteresting, but her speech stood out at the time, along with her daring leopard-skin shoes – exuberantly ostentatious footwear at odds with her reticent personality, as if she assumed that the wearing of attention-grabbing shoes would help her to acquire a public personality. In a way they did. The shoes were almost an act of disguise.

On the whole, May plodded on without becoming a big crusader for internal reform, after her 'nasty party' speech. As would later prove to be the case with the Brexit saga, she had uttered some words of apparent significance and then carried on, almost as if the words had not been said. Her chance for greater prominence came when she moved to the Home Office as part of the coalition in 2010. She remained Home Secretary until she became prime minister in 2016. To have survived as Home Secretary for six years was in itself a qualification for leadership. The Home Office is a tough testing ground, to the extent that few Home Secretaries become leaders. Only James Callaghan, among modern prime ministers, had served at the Home Office. In the final phase of the New Labour era Home Secretaries came and went on a regular basis. May lasted the course – a genuine triumph.

Perhaps there is a reason why this senior post is not a natural part of the path towards Number Ten. The Home Office is, in some respects, atypical. The demands are nightmarishly intense and unpredictable. A terrorist threat can disturb a Home Secretary at any time. A prison escape can trigger demands for the resignation of a Home Secretary. Immigration is an emotive issue, as well as one that is politically and practically complex. But the Home Secretary is to some extent cocooned from the rest of the government, working tirelessly, with little time to reflect on economic policy and foreign affairs or wider public-service reforms. May worked with the smallest possible team, relying mainly on her two advisers, Nick Timothy and Fiona Hill. They were utterly loyal to her and she was dependent on them, regarding them almost as oracles who were guiding her to the top. But May also worked well with senior Home Office officials, which is not always the case with Home Secretaries. Her civil servants respected her and broadly agreed with her own assessment, which was formed quietly, modestly and determinedly, that she was a potential prime minister.[1]

At the Home Office she kept a relatively low profile, compared with the more theatrical members of the coalition – the ones May regarded partly as players of politics as a game, rather than as a wholly serious vocation. Lunches with journalists or colleagues were awkward and unrewarding occasions. Shortly before the start of the 2016 referendum campaign David Cameron's director of communications, Sir Craig Oliver, took May out to lunch. He noted later, 'I tried every example of small talk I could think of in an attempt to get a conversation started. After around twenty minutes I started to feel physically sick.'[2]

Yet periodically, when she was largely hidden away as Home Secretary, May delivered a sensational speech, as she had done in opposition, lighting up the political stage in ways that made her more ostentatious colleagues seem shy and retiring. In May 2014 she addressed the Police Federation's annual conference and went for them. Referring to various topical and highly charged controversies involving police misconduct and racist attitudes, she declared:

> If there is anybody in this hall who doubts that our model of policing is at risk, if there is anybody who underestimates the damage recent events and revelations have done to the relationship between the public and the police, if anybody here questions the need for the police to change, I am here to tell you that it's time to face up to reality... It is an attitude that betrays contempt for the public these officers are supposed to serve – and every police officer in the land, every single police leader, and everybody in the Police Federation should confront it and expunge it from the ranks... It is not enough to mouth platitudes about a few bad apples. The problem might lie with a minority of officers, but it is still a significant problem, and a problem that needs to be addressed... Polls show two-thirds of the public trust the police... We should never accept a situation in which a third of people do not trust police officers to tell the truth.

The speech was one of the most powerful to be delivered by a Cabinet minister during the coalition era – courageous, principled and, to deploy Cameron's favourite political term, 'modern'. Leading members of the Police Federation were taken aback, but their response was a tribute to the force of the speech. Once she had delivered her brutal message, May disappeared again from public view.

So it was with Brexit. May made a set-piece speech every few months and acted as if no more needed to be said for some time. With Brexit, much needed to be said – nearly every hour of every day. Ironically, May did have a strategy of sorts for Brexit, and a premise to justify her plan. The strategy, premise and plan were contentious and inelegant, but they were not as calamitous as her growing number of detractors were to claim. There was a case, but she never found a way of putting it: memorable phrases, the framing of an argument, a compelling narrative. Here was May's thinking on Brexit and how it evolved.

At the beginning she decided that she had a democratic duty to deliver the referendum. As far as she was concerned, the referendum was her mandate. Parliament had played its role by voting for the referendum to be held after the 2015 election. Now it was her duty to deliver and, in her view, Parliament's role would be peripheral. She did not want Parliament to have a vote on the triggering of Article 50, the move that formally began the Brexit process. MPs demanded a 'meaningful vote' on her deal. She did not want to grant them such a potent weapon. After she had negotiated her Brexit deal, she sought to bludgeon Parliament into submission with threats of far worse alternatives. As far as she was concerned, she was responding to the referendum result and, in doing so, saving the UK from a crisis of trust, if a 'Remain'-dominated Parliament took control.

In terms of the deal she sought, May had a point in claiming that Brexiteers won the referendum because of voters' opposition to free movement. Her final deal ended free movement and potentially allowed the UK to trade with other countries. As her negotiations intensified, May became more aware that the soft border in Ireland was threatened by the UK's departure from the customs union.

Acutely aware that the soft border was central to the peace process in Northern Ireland, she agreed a backstop compromise, whereby the UK remained in the customs union until alternative arrangements were agreed. Her position was not too distant from that of the Labour leadership, which sought membership of a customs union.

The flaws in May's strategy and assumptions were deep, and should have been more obvious to her. Parliament would not allow her to treat it with disdain. Her Brexit deal was a convoluted set of compromises. But given that there had been a majority in the referendum for 'Leave', and she had a plan for leaving, she did not necessarily have to endure the various forms of Brexit hell that followed. Her failure to make accessible sense of what she was doing was the main reason she struggled to prevail and her government fell apart. There were more ministerial resignations and sackings under May than any other modern prime minister, by a huge margin.

Unlike Margaret Thatcher, May was also a poor reader of the political stage. Thatcher perceived clearly when she had space to be bold and when she had no room for manoeuvre. Instead, as the Brexit prime minister, May made the right moves at the wrong times. Had she been assertive when she was politically strong, she might have suffered a slightly less draining nightmare in Number Ten. Instead, she endured a period of rule that made even James Callaghan's tempestuous leadership in the late 1970s, or Gordon Brown's after the 2008 crash, seem like a model of calm.

At the beginning of her leadership, in the summer of 2016, May was in a formidably strong and authoritative position. This was partly for the simple reason that there was not going to be another leadership contest in the months that followed her speedy victory. If she had announced that she was planning to fly to the moon, there would have been no challenge. The party had just held a traumatic contest and was hardly going to trigger another. May was walking on water, according to the opinion polls, with soaring personal ratings. Popularity is authority-enhancing for a prime minister – if polls suggest a prime minister could win an election, then he or she becomes almost as commanding as when they do hold and win a general election. As a result of winning a leadership contest with ease, May's popularity among voters rose; thanks to her steely and distant manner, Cabinet ministers were in submissive awe of her. Even in private, few said a word against her. Instead they cited May as if she was the oracle. Ministers repeated her words to journalists as if they came from a political titan. With some justification at the time, ministers – and much of the media – assumed that May would be prime minister for a long time, another assumption that often feeds on itself.

But in relation to Brexit, May did not recognize her strength when she became prime minister. As a Remainer, she felt the insecure need to reassure her party that she would deliver on the referendum. Her senior adviser, Nick Timothy, invented the phrase 'Brexit means Brexit' – words that she repeated like a machine for the first six months of her leadership. She made the phrase seem like a defiant act, but Timothy meant the words to be soothingly reassuring for Brexiteers, a promise that she would deliver on the referendum.

May was too aware of her awkward position, as the Remainer who had leapt into Number Ten on the back of a Brexit victory in the referendum. Her acute awareness became a trap. Subsequently she felt a need to please hard-line Brexiteers far more than she did the smaller number on the other side of her party who had backed Remain. In doing so, she chose to be incarcerated, in relation to Brexit, at an early phase in her leadership when she had no need to be. With reckless defiance she proclaimed her Brexit 'red lines': no customs union, no single market, no jurisdiction from the European Court of Justice (ECJ), no freedom of movement. In response, hard-liners in her party purred during those early months. Like John Major and David Cameron, Theresa May tried hard from the beginning to please her potential tormentors but, in doing so (as with Major and Cameron), she was sealing her fate.

By the beginning of October 2016 she had declared that the UK would leave the single market and the customs union and would no longer be under the jurisdiction of the ECJ. She had promised to trigger Article 50 by March of the following year. At the same time she envisaged retaining the benefits that were conferred on the UK on the basis of its membership of the EU. At no point in this early phase – her period of greatest untouchable authority – did May explain to her party that Brexit would involve some very tough choices. She could have done so in the opening months of her leadership. Some in her party would not have liked being told candid truths, but would have had no choice but to listen. She could have cleared some of the ground that became impossibly cluttered when she started to make the awkward choices that she had pretended were not there.

Instead, in the early months, May was having her cake and eating it. Later, when ministers were being publicly critical of her (in some cases defying the whip in Brexit votes) and MPs were calling on her to go, she had no choice but to be assertive, lecturing her stroppy party about the importance of maintaining the soft border in Ireland, and on the need for the UK to consider being part of a customs union until the issue of the Irish border and the backstop was answered. But at that point she was telling hard truths when few would listen.

Leaders often get the sequence wrong. Tony Blair and Gordon Brown were politically untouchable in 1997 and yet acted cautiously. When voters turned hard against Blair, he had no choice but to be strong in defending the calamity of Iraq. He became a crusading evangelical as voters were becoming restive. When he had much less to say, voters paid homage to him. Harold Wilson had more space than he dared to realize after winning a landslide in 1966. The example of May is more vivid. As prime ministers often do at the beginning of a reign, she made a series of rushed decisions when she was mighty. These decisions were the product of insecurity, but were hailed in the Eurosceptic newspapers as acts of Thatcher-like strength.

Yet prime ministers are complex human beings. May was both insecure about her relationship with the party in relation to Brexit, and over-confident on other matters. These are the kinds of contradictory forces that shape many early prime ministerial careers. Early over-confidence arises from the fact that prime ministers have reached the pinnacle that so many dream of attaining. They dare to wonder whether they are special. At the summit, the few who make it inhale a whiff of intoxicating power. During the coalition years, May must have heard much speculation that George Osborne might well be Cameron's successor, or maybe Michael Gove; or, days before she acquired the crown, she would have noted that Boris Johnson was the favourite to lead. Yet she was the one who got there. The victory gave her a partial sense of imperious triumph – as misjudged as her early insecurity about being a prime minister who voted 'Remain'.

With a ruthless swagger, she triggered a purge of Cameron's allies across Number Ten, the Treasury and the wider government. George Osborne was one of those who was brutally sacked – told to go off and learn more about the Conservative Party, an early sign that sensitivity with colleagues was not May's greatest asset. The purge had many consequences. From day one, she acquired enemies who would never forgive her brutality, when it should have been obvious to her that she would need all the goodwill she could get in order to deal with Brexit.

A more serious and overlooked consequence of the purge was a sudden loss of collective memory in relation to the European Union. The mistakes David Cameron made in his renegotiation with the EU, and the lessons learned from that flawed negotiation, would have been invaluable to a novice prime minister suddenly exposed to the task of Brexit. To have had some ministers involved in the torrid twists and turns of the late-Cameron era in the room with May and her advisers, when they were having dangerously naive conversations about Brexit, might have made her approach more agile. Instead, those who had learned lessons from Cameron's renegotiation were largely in exile. May had felt confident enough to sack them.

The early over-confidence took a deeper form, which impaired her political vision. She hoped to lead a government that instigated many historic domestic reforms. She did not realize, or accept, that Brexit would overwhelm all other ambition. This was part of her early misreading of the overcrowded political stage. Some of the early ideas were substantial and marked a genuine leap from the Conservatives' recent past, but they did not have a hope of taking shape, with the Brexit mountain to climb. The early hopes for radical domestic reform took an ideological form, influenced greatly by Nick Timothy. As an adviser, Timothy had ideas that were a distinctive and interesting blend, combining a hint of Enoch Powell's Midlands nationalism and Ed Miliband's faith in the state. He was a genuine radical and innovative thinker, who was also a committed Brexiteer. There is speculation as to whether May was a mere vessel for Timothy's bold ideas or whether she shared his distinct values. It does not matter greatly – she chose to share them, albeit erratically.

———

Like most prime ministers, May was not a good judge of colleagues or how best to deal with them. Leaders, often more insecure than they seem, self-absorbed and with no choice but to become wholly immersed in the frenzied rush of each day, have little time or inclination to reflect on the characters around them. Most value loyalty as a winning characteristic. They are often poor at evaluating who will be an effective administrator or reformer, and rarely value those who challenge and question what is happening.

Some said of Margaret Thatcher that she liked nothing more than to be challenged by other ministers. There is little evidence of this. Her test, when making appointments, was the question 'Is he one of us?' – a theme so defining that an early biography by the columnist Hugo Young took the question as its title.[3] Her chancellors shared Thatcher's economic approach and, when they ceased to do so, they were gone. Those she promoted tended to be doting admirers. Those who questioned her did not last very long. Tony Blair sought to promote 'Blairites', colleagues who had decided to agree with him in the internal battles with Gordon Brown. Cameron assumed that he had loyal colleagues until he called the referendum and discovered, in some cases – namely, Boris Johnson and Michael Gove – that their convictions or ambition trumped their loyalty to him. Wilson and Callaghan had to balance their Cabinets politically. The art of managing fascinated both of them in different ways, but like other prime ministers they were not especially curious about what made their colleagues tick. Blair was a poor judge of who would flourish in government. At the beginning he was very keen on appointing as ministers those with experience of business. Few survived in the more brutal world of politics for very long.

Immediately after becoming prime minister, May appointed three controversial Brexit supporters to key Cabinet posts. Two of them were gone within days of May finally putting a Brexit deal to the Cabinet in the summer of 2018. At the beginning, Boris Johnson was made Foreign Secretary, David Davis was Brexit Secretary in a new department, and Liam Fox was given responsibility to pursue embryonic trade deals that would be ready when the UK left the EU. Nick Timothy outlined the thinking behind the appointments:

> I can remember when we were planning the reshuffle and we went through all the different options and the way she described what she wanted to do, I remember sort of summarising it as Brexit abroad, social reform at home. And that was actually really the intent of that reshuffle. So there were leading Brexit supporters who were given the foreign-facing department, so Boris went to the Foreign Office, David Davis was in the Brexit department, Liam went to trade, Priti Patel went to International Development and then people like Amber Rudd went to the Home Office and Damian Green to DWP [Department for Work and Pensions]. And that was the logic and it was partly because I think Theresa felt that it was important that the people responsible for developing the Brexit policy should be people who really get it and really mean it. And to be honest, there probably was a calculation too that compromise would need to happen at some point and that it would be important that the leading Brexiteers were party to those compromises and that they'd helped to make the decisions.[4]

Timothy's assessment is illuminating. Here is further confirmation of May's early underestimation of the Brexit task. She assumed that Cabinet ministers in non-Brexit departments would have the space to embark on historic reforms. They never got the chance. Brexit swallowed up all political energy.

Davis had qualities as a campaigning and rebellious backbencher, but had shown limited interest in governing. Yet May gave him the brief of setting up a new government department, while negotiating Brexit with the rest of the EU and being the main navigator in a tricky UK Parliament. This was a gargantuan set of tasks. Davis was ill-equipped to accomplish them. They demanded patience, a mastery of detail, a form of administrative genius to make the new department work, a deep understanding of how the EU functioned and a capacity to work with a wilfully insular prime minister. Davis did not possess the range, experience or interests to meet any of these tasks, and his appointment reflected May's poor judgement of people.

Crucially, May did not go out of her way to engage with the new Brexit department. She reconfigured Whitehall and then proceeded to take decisions with her small group in Number Ten, as she had done at the Home Office. One of the few friends of David Cameron to be offered a post in May's first government, George Bridges, was the Brexit Minister in the House of Lords:

I found at times I was learning more from the *Financial Times*, in terms of its reporting of what was going on in Brexit, than I was from internal papers I was being shown. And I found at times I was being asked questions in the House of Lords, very searching questions, which, given a Member of the House of Lords could think that this is an important issue, we as government should have been able to answer. And the fact that I didn't – I was often skating on very thin ice, or even trying to walk on water – I felt deeply troubled. Number Ten felt very, very closed. Should I have banged on the door more often? Every so often I did raise a flag saying: what is going on? But it felt very closed and I have to say that was one of the major frustrations that led me to resign.[5]

Bridges resigned after the 2017 election, one of many Brexit ministers who walked away during the years of May's rule.

May was taking the decisions in Number Ten, becoming trapped in stages. Having declared that the end of free movement was a 'red line', and having appointed senior Cabinet ministers with the obvious potential to make her life hellish, the next key step towards her incarceration was a special speech that she delivered on Brexit at the start of the Conservative party conference in October 2016. It was during the address that she pledged to trigger Article 50 by the end of the following March. She made the pledge not because she had a clear idea of the route ahead, once the Article had been triggered – she was in the dark about that. Like so many previous prime ministers in relation to Europe, May acted for reasons of party management. Unlike previous prime ministers, she was triggering a timetable from which there was no escape. Once Article 50 was triggered, the UK was scheduled to leave two years later.

Throughout the summer before the conference, Conservative MPs had been popping up, asking why she had not already triggered Article 50. They did so politely but firmly. In response to their demands, May thought she had hit upon a balanced approach – a third way. She rationalized to herself that she had not triggered Article 50 immediately when she became prime minister, as some of her MPs had wanted, but at the same time she was assuring impatient backbenchers and the newspapers that they did not have to wait beyond 31 March 2017 for Article 50 to be triggered.

Her third way was widely hailed again as a Thatcher-like act of assertion, by the Eurosceptic newspapers, but the opposite was closer to the truth. She could have waited longer and a delay would have been a display of courageous strength – a leader defying the foolish impatience of hard-liners in her party. Well ahead in the polls, May was in a strong enough position to resolve at least some of the internal differences within her Cabinet before starting the clock. An attempt at resolution would have been tough for her, but she could have prevailed at this early stage, the phase when she assumed she would be prime minister for a decade at least. Instead, the Article 50 clock was ticking, without May having any clear sense of how she would bring about her objectives of leaving the EU while retaining the benefits of the EU and keeping her Cabinet united.

As a nervy communicator, May's preferred form of address was the occasional set-piece speech on Brexit. There is much to be said for the long prime ministerial address, forcing a leader and advisers to put a case at length for what they are seeking to do. But speeches twice a year were not enough to persuade voters and MPs of May's chosen course. A Brexit prime minister needed to be communicating constantly and accessibly.

When she made her first big speech on Britain exiting the EU, at Lancaster House in January 2017, May was not clear what precise course she would take. Once again she outlined her 'red lines', to the delight of Brexiteers – no single market or customs union, and no ECJ rule – but even at her most defiant, there was ambiguity running through her careful words, in a speech that was still being written and rewritten the day before it was delivered. May spoke about the possibility of 'associate membership' of the customs union. The imprecise term papered over the cracks. She was clever enough to realize the potentially dark consequences of a complete break with the customs union and yet she needed to declare, and genuinely wanted to assert, that the UK would negotiate its own deals. Liam Fox and others had convinced her that countries were queuing up to sign new deals. Although May spoke vaguely about future customs relations, Nick Timothy insists that if there was ambiguity, it was tactical. As far as he was concerned, there would be no customs union of any form under May's leadership – and he helped to write the speech. His exchange, in a BBC interview, highlights the multi-layered calculations:

> It definitely wasn't the case that she was wrestling with the possibility of staying in the customs union. Theresa has an instinctive dislike of policy options being reduced to binary outcomes and so that was her way, I think, of trying to leave open the possibility of reducing the friction in trade between the UK and EU whilst still retaining the ability to pursue an independent trade policy.
>
> **When you say she has a reluctance of binary choice, is that another way of saying perhaps she has to be, or chooses to be, quite opaque at times in this Brexit journey?**
>
> Yeah, I think a bit of both. I mean I think it's partly she has had to deal in ambiguity because that's the reality of negotiating sometimes. It's also the reality of trying to hold together complicated coalitions of factions. So I think it's probably partly that, but it does genuinely also reflect a way of thinking, which is to not leap to a particular position because it appears like you have a choice between a and b policy options.[6]

Around the time May delivered her Lancaster House speech, many within her party, including David Davis, were advising her to call an early election. The reasons for this were twofold. Most obviously, the bigger majority that Davis and others assumed the Conservatives would secure would make the Brexit legislative path much more straightforward. Of equal importance, as far as Davis was concerned, was that an election in 2017 meant there would be no need for another one in the immediate aftermath of Brexit. Instead, the government could breathe freely until 2022.

May listened to Davis and gave no indication of what she herself was thinking. She was an enigma to her Cabinet ministers, but also quite possibly to herself. She had publicly declared there would be no early election and, if she had kept to that position, she would have been much stronger. Before the 2017 election, May was one of the more commanding prime ministers of recent times.

At least she was in every respect apart from one. She had secured no mandate of her own, and yet she was openly pursuing an agenda that was different from David Cameron's. She wanted to leave the Cameron era behind. She faced the same problem Gordon Brown had faced in 2007, but with one key difference: Brown wanted to move on from Blairism without losing the support of the pro-Blair newspapers; May felt no need to worship at the altar of Cameron's leadership or to be seen doing so.

The early election of 2017 had a Shakespearean quality. For several reasons, it was the most significant since 1979, and arguably had more historic consequences than Margaret Thatcher's first victory. Unusually, the two main parties campaigned on manifestos that celebrated the potential of the state, which had the possibility of making the management of Brexit even more of a nightmare.

May is not to be compared with King Lear or Macbeth in terms of character, but there are parallels with Shakespeare's tragic heroes. Shakespeare had a theory, widely held at the time he was writing, that if leaders break with the natural order, they unleash forces that turn on them. Macbeth killed Duncan to seize the crown and began a sequence that destroyed him. Lear broke up his estate and became homeless. May called an early election in order to win big, and almost lost everything. She had declared several times that she would not call an early election, and she meant it. A cautious leader in some respects, she was partly at ease with the natural order: she was a commanding figure, with several years before the next election was due. But in the end she succumbed and called an election. Expecting a sizeable majority to reinforce her dominance, she unleashed forces that turned upon her. The early election transformed the politics of Brexit under May, as she failed to secure the mandate she needed in order to deliver her version of Britain's withdrawal.

Voters in the UK tend to elect prime ministers who are partly actors, and although they (and much of the media) claim not to like the artifice of politics, they need the artistry. Margaret Thatcher was an actress. She was nowhere near as self-confident as her public stridency suggested. Tony Blair could have acted Macbeth and Hamlet simultaneously. David Cameron was an imitator of Blair – almost consciously an imitator, in the style of Rory Bremner. These prime ministers were all fascinated by their place on the political stage and how they appeared at any given time. May was not interested in politics as a performance. Her shyness and awkwardness were, in some respects, endearing qualities. Although self-absorbed, she was not mesmerized by the glamour and glitter of politics. But in spite of her reticence, her hired strategists made the election about her. When she was the star guest on BBC1's *The One Show*, in arguably the softest interview ever given, the toughest question to be asked of her and her husband was 'Who puts out the bins at night?' May looked fleetingly horrified at this question, as if she had been asked to reveal her whole hand in the Brexit negotiation. She was shy and uneasy throughout the contest and, in a twist of historic significance, lost her majority.

Her manifesto was crammed with radical ideas, including a strong defence of the state, and it dared to put forward a policy to raise much-needed money for elderly care. Yet at no point in the campaign did May expand on the radical spirit in her programme. Instead she repeated, in a machine-like manner, that her new government would be 'strong and stable', as if the daring manifesto had no connection with her robotic pitch. The specific policy for elderly care was misjudged and mistimed. Those who needed care would have to pay substantially more from the value of their property. The policy became known as the 'dementia tax' because, unlike patients in the tax-funded NHS, the sufferer would meet the costs. The details were flawed, but it was the manner of the announcement that was so bizarre. In the New Labour era – albeit in ways that were too cautious – Blair and Brown spent months, and sometimes years, clearing the ground before announcing a specific fund-raising policy. May introduced hers in the middle of an election campaign, without the capacity to explain. Instead, the Conservatives were forced to revise the policy in a panic, only for May to declare that 'nothing had changed'. This was an early example of her tendency to make statements at odds with what was happening around her. She lacked the language to manage and explain the eruption of wild events about her. There was no greater misreading than the introduction of a deeply contentious measure during a campaign.

After the election, May faced Brexit with no overall majority. Her fragility was unique. Normally when prime ministers lose their majorities, they cease to be prime minister. Ted Heath is one of the other prime ministers who called an early election, only to find forces turning on him. In February 1974 he lost his overall majority, tried to stay on, but was gone by the Monday. Although Harold Wilson then took over as a minority prime minister, he was seen to have won. In this case, May, despite having won almost as many votes as Margaret Thatcher at her peak, was seen to have lost. It was in this context that she navigated Brexit. Yet her Cabinet stuck by her. In the months that followed, she endured more resignations than any modern prime minister, although none immediately after the election. She was no longer strong enough to act with ruthlessness, in terms of purging another batch of perceived enemies. In a Shakespearean contrast, having sacked Osborne and Gove as she acquired the crown, May was now forced to remove her two close advisers, Nick Timothy and Fiona Hill. She was almost alone, comforted only by the presence of Damian Green as her unofficial deputy prime minister. Then she had to sack him, when he faced allegations of sexual harassment.

May was often described as 'weak'. The term is close to useless in casting light on a leader, but as far as it means anything, it points us in the wrong direction here. Politically she was in a much weaker position, but as a personality she remained the most stubborn prime minister to occupy Number Ten for many decades – arguably more so than Margaret Thatcher. Often Thatcher was more expedient than she seemed. May was a wilful leader in a weak position: an explosive combination.

She mistook being stubborn for integrity. If she committed publicly to an absurd immigration target, she felt she had to stick to it. If she said that the UK must leave the single market and, ultimately, the customs union, then the UK would have to depart at the assigned date. She was not a leader of guile. May's aims in relation to Brexit were more or less constant and publicly expressed.

Yet she could not escape her early 'red lines'. The hard-liners clung to them with exuberant hope, even when May came to realize that she could not wholly deliver the contradictory objectives. The post-election sequence – 'red lines' becoming blurred, a divided party and a hung parliament – was something of a roller-coaster ride. May was one of the least ostentatious prime ministers in modern history and yet, without a great ego or a hint of narcissism, her ride was spectacular.

Leadership is partly a conjuring trick. Leaders can get away with a huge amount, if they are popular and able to win elections. For most of the time they are in power, colleagues judge them largely on this limited basis. Jack Straw once sought to explain the lack of intense Cabinet scrutiny of Blair's conduct in the build-up to Iraq by pointing out that he had made a lot of correct calls. He had won a landslide for a second time. Thatcher won elections, so the Cabinet went along with her, even when some ministers had doubts about what she was doing.

While personally stubborn after the early election, May was in a weak position because she could perform no tricks. She had been seen to be useless during an election. She would not be allowed to contest another, and therefore the art of appearing to rule into the long-distant future had gone. Instead of being the new political fashion, May became immediately the frail leader. When she proclaimed her thoughts on Brexit, the ministerial and media instinct was to question what she was saying, rather than to pay homage. If she had returned from Brussels with her Brexit deal after a landslide election win, much of her party and the media would have hailed a negotiating triumph. We choose to see what we want to see. After the 2017 election, it was the default position of Conservative MPs and May's opponents to declare her efforts to have been a disaster.

May's moves towards her Brexit deal were made even more complex by her own growing insights into what Brexit meant for Ireland and the peace process. Soon after the election, she came to realize that her early Brexit assumptions had been too simplistic. In January 2017 the UK's EU ambassador, Sir Ivan Rogers, resigned, complaining in his resignation letter of 'muddled thinking' and 'ill-founded arguments'. He went on to give a series of illuminating talks on the muddle, touching on the fundamental misunderstanding of how the EU worked, the false hope of playing some members off against others, and the unjustified swagger. He left while May still assumed that the UK could have its cake and eat it. Rogers' concerns were unwelcome to her. At that point she did not want to hear that Brexit would be more complicated than she wanted it to be. By the early autumn of the same year May came to realize that some of what Rogers had been warning her about was urgently pertinent, and that the simplistic assertions of her Brexit Secretary, David Davis, were unreliable at best. In September 2017 the senior official at the Brexit Department, Olly Robbins, moved into Number Ten. This was a symbolic and practical move of great importance. Number Ten was taking control because Davis had failed to do so at his new department. After his resignation in the summer of 2018, Davis told journalists that a key moment for him was when May changed her approach to Brexit from his fantasy version. As ever with May, she said nothing to indicate any fresh thinking. That is partly because she was incapable of articulating what she was doing.

Even if May had won a landslide, she would still have faced mountainous problems in delivering an impossible 'have your cake and eat it' strategy. She would still have found the negotiations almost impossible, and she would still have had to make her speech in Florence at the end of September 2017 on the eve of the party-conference season. Her Florence speech was intended to secure a breakthrough with the EU, as she started to appreciate that the early flourishes of UK machismo were wholly unrealizable. Tonally, the speech was conciliatory and internationalist. May agreed that the UK would pay a Brexit bill – the sum conveniently unspecified. In interviews surrounding the speech she made clear what was implicit in it: she ached for a deal. The UK machismo around 'no deal' had gone. There was no reference to 'no deal' in the speech, only a warning about what such an outcome would mean.

The Florence speech was elegantly constructed. Reading it retrospectively makes sense of all that followed: May's determination to avoid no deal, a recognition that the Irish Question must be answered, and her intention to regain a degree of democratic control, as she saw it. For her, above all that meant ending free movement, the element of Brexit that she believed in with unyielding conviction.

It was only in December 2017, when she signed up to phase one of the Brexit deal, that her willingness to compromise became more tangible. Both the UK and the EU agreed that there must be no hard border separating Northern Ireland from the rest of Ireland. Barring a technological breakthrough that no one could confidently envisage in the short term at least, that meant the UK remaining in a customs union or Northern Ireland being treated differently from the rest of the UK. When this issue surfaced the following year, it seemed to come as a surprise to some hard-line Brexiteers, but although May remained evasive and vague, the words were there for them to read in the December document. Her hard-liners were not careful at reading them, or chose not to reflect on what the words implied. May did not encourage any such reflections. Instead she did what she always did and kept going, hoping the dissenters would be won round at the final moment.

May might have told Osborne to get to know the Conservative Party better, but she displayed a lack of understanding herself –

namely, the degree to which the parliamentary party had changed from being largely pragmatic and expedient to becoming an ideological crusade, one in which a purist view of accountability and sovereignty meant far more to them than loyalty to a national leadership.

———

In the summer of 2018 May outlined her proposed Brexit deal. Although based on the Florence speech and the December agreement, the proposals came as a shock to her Cabinet and a lot of her MPs. But the alarm that greeted what became known as her 'Chequers plan' was also a reflection of her closed, insular style of leadership. May did not explain her thinking in the months leading up to Chequers. There was no attempt to prepare the ground. With good cause, she knew she had to sideline David Davis, but she lacked the skills to make her hard-liners feel fragile and insecure. On the contrary, she returned them to their comfort zone. They flourished as evangelical dissenters and martyrs to their imprecise cause.

The contrast between May's approach and Tony Blair's, in relation to Iraq, is striking. Blair gave a constant running commentary as he sought to persuade his party, the media and the wider electorate to support his timid decision to back the Bush administration. He spoke at regular press conferences, gave many interviews and delivered a vast number of speeches. His call to back Bush was weak and misjudged, but he showed how a leader can persuade by the power of argument. He framed arguments about the weapons of mass destruction, and about his conviction that Iraqis would hail the imposition of democracy. In some respects May had a better case than Blair's shaky one, as she sought to deliver Brexit while protecting the Irish soft border and the supply chains for the manufacturing sector. Her Chequers plan, though deeply flawed, had points in its favour. But she never made the case for it, neither before nor after it was published. By the time MPs came to vote on whether or not to support Blair in relation to Iraq, he had succeeded in the art of persuasion, admittedly helped by the willingness of most Conservative MPs to back him before he had uttered a word. He knew little about Iraq or the wider region, but could deploy words to make a case. On Brexit, May could not – and did not – deploy words artfully.

She put her Brexit deal to the Cabinet at Chequers in July 2018. Ministers were told that if any of them resigned, they would lose their cars and would have to book a taxi home. Their mobile phones were confiscated. At the end of a long, hot summer's day, May issued a statement asserting that her proposals had the backing of her Cabinet. This was the beginning of another pattern. The vicar's daughter with a sense of moral duty uttered words that were true at the time, but were to prove to be untrue very quickly. The Chequers gathering was on the Friday. Davis and Johnson resigned the following Monday, and May responded as she always did: she replaced the two outgoing ministers and carried on as if nothing had happened.

En route to the torrid summer of 2018, May had largely stopped reading the newspapers, relying on a daily digest from media advisers. She was cocooned in Number Ten, dealing only with colleagues who served her. Prime ministers tend to enjoy elements of the role, even when they appear to be under impossible pressure. With the exception of Wilson, none have left voluntarily. May flourished when faced with long hours of work. She had got to the top, when so many others had not. She looked better than when she was twenty years younger – slimmer and more coiffured. This is all part of a pattern of leadership: prime ministers tend to look good until they leave, and then they very quickly show signs of decline. In power, the adrenaline fires them up. A diabetic who had to inject insulin, May was not short of energy-enhancing adrenaline, but she was attempting the impossible.

On one level, her Chequers plan was a work of art in its attempt to bind together conflicting and contradictory forces. But May had done nowhere near enough between September 2017 and July 2018 to clear the ground. Perhaps there could be no clearing of the ground, given the circumstances, and her dogged, insular focus was the only option available. We will never know. What we do know is that May began to lose control – or even more control – after her day-long Cabinet meeting at Chequers in July 2018.

The final deal that May and her senior negotiators secured with the EU was partly based on Chequers, but inevitably some of her more contorted proposals were dropped. Instead of guaranteeing a soft border in Ireland, through impossibly complex trading arrangements, there would be a so-called 'backstop', to come into effect if no other solution was found during the transition. The UK would remain in a customs union until such a solution was found. There could be no unilateral withdrawal from this arrangement, or else it would not be a backstop. Again the proposition arose directly from the phase-one agreement the previous December, when both sides were committed to the soft border. As long as May secured an end to free movement, she was ready to accept other compromises. Again the compromises came as an apparent shock to her Cabinet and MPs, when she unveiled the deal in November 2018.

The dramas that erupted after May had published her deal highlighted once again her inability to persuade, her failure to read the political stage and her unique detached wilfulness. Through the months that followed she was both the most fragile of modern prime ministers and yet the most pivotal. She continued to make the key decisions, often without much consultation, that would shape her country's history. Yet she could have fallen at any point, and at one stage in the spring of 2019 offered to resign under certain circumstances. In true May tradition, she made the offer and then carried on as if nothing had happened.

The immediate aftermath of the Cabinet meeting that discussed her Brexit deal for the first time in November 2018 was typical. May gave a statement declaring that the Cabinet had supported the deal. The words were true at the time, but as she must have known as she delivered them, they would not be true for more than a few hours. The following morning the Brexit Minister, Dominic Raab, resigned, along with several other ministers. May had become even more of an unreliable narrator. Shortly after Raab's resignation, she gave a statement to the Commons on her deal. For an hour not a single MP had a good word to say about it. May might have thought, at the end of such a draining session, one that followed ministerial resignations, that her deal was doomed. Wilson, Blair, Brown and Cameron would have been in a state of neurotic hyperactivity after such a sequence, working out what the hell to do next, contemplating a thousand different ploys that might change the situation.

May was quite different. Instead, she acted as she always did – as if the volcanic eruptions were separate from her, and from what she was doing. She appointed a new Brexit Secretary and made other replacements. Then she conducted a bizarre nationwide tour to put the case for her deal, as if she were fighting a general election. Those warning May that her deal would be defeated in the Commons included the chair of the 1922 Committee, Sir Graham Brady. He was one of the few politicians May listened to and liked. It was his job to convey the views of backbenchers. On the several occasions when Brady warned her about a terrible defeat over her deal, May gave nothing away. She looked at him and then moved on to other issues.[7]

May was a sheltered prime minister, hearing only what she wanted to hear. In discussions with a small number of advisers, she calculated that her threat of no Brexit, or no deal, would bludgeon MPs into backing her deal. She devised no memorable phrases to make her deal accessibly appealing. Indeed, her deal was spoken of as if it were an abstract art form, rather than a dense, detailed document. Yet in spite of the density of the Withdrawal Agreement itself, it proved to be another evasive exercise in kicking the can down the road. The Irish Question was still to be resolved. The much thornier issue of the UK's future relationship with the EU was not addressed. May was asking MPs to take the historic decision to leave the EU without having a clue as to what would happen next.

Inevitably, she pulled the vote the day before it was due to be held in December. When the vote eventually did take place the following month, her deal was defeated by a historic majority of 230 votes. Her senior advisers looked on in alarm when the vote was declared in the Commons. The margin of defeat was higher than any of them had anticipated. May returned to Number Ten and carried on as if nothing much had happened, once again behaving as though she was separate from such seismic events.

After the vote, May said she would reach out in order to get parliamentary approval. She did not mean it. Her sole focus was to persuade her Brexit hard-liners and the Democratic Unionist Party (DUP) to back her. She hoped also to secure the support of some Labour MPs, but she was not going to pivot significantly. She had never done so in her career, and she did not consider doing so now. During the leadership contest back in 2016 the former chancellor, Ken Clarke, had been recorded, when he was off air, describing May as a 'bloody difficult woman'. He meant that she was obstinate to the point of destructiveness at times. She clung to her deal, whatever the external circumstances.

In two more votes she failed to win the support of the DUP or a sufficient number of her hard-liners. Only a few Labour MPs were gullible enough to back her, not least after a televised statement in which May placed herself on the side of 'the people' against Parliament. The misjudged TV statement, delivered in March 2019 on the eve of another vote on her deal, was the most vivid example of her inability to read the rhythms of politics. She needed to woo MPs and she attacked them live on TV.

To be defeated three times, on the most significant proposition since the Second World War, normally would – and should – trigger a prime ministerial resignation. But May led in a weak parliament of largely half-formed politicians. Her internal opponents enjoyed the limelight, appearing on the media so often they appeared to be numerically stronger than they were. But they were hopeless strategists, not having had to think strategically very often in the past, and unable to do so when their moment came. Crucially, her critics mistimed their vote of confidence on May, holding it in December when her deal had not been put to the vote, and when she was evidently regarded as the least-bad option to most Conservative MPs. May won the vote of confidence – another event that would have traumatized most prime ministers, but one she characteristically treated as if it was just another drama that had little to do with her. In theory, Conservative MPs had no formal means of removing her for another twelve months – she was, briefly, the least secure and most secure prime minister of modern times.

Like all prime ministers, May clung to power for much longer than the surrounding political and media frenzy suggested was possible, but her approach to survival was unique. Most prime ministers who know they are in deep trouble become obsessed by the political noise erupting around them. They scheme and then watch obsessively the consequences of their manoeuvrings. In contrast, May stood apart from the noise as if she was separate from it. The detachment was breathtaking, because her fate was to become the Brexit prime minister, the most darkly demanding destiny of any post-war prime minister.

To take one emblematic example, during Prime Minister's Questions on the day her MPs held a confidence vote on her leadership in December 2018, the Liberal Democrat leader, Vince Cable, asked her a mischievous question. Cable wondered whether she preferred her own MPs condemning her or the entire House of Commons doing so, in a vote of confidence in her government. Characteristically, May did not recognize mischief, and neither could she respond to provocative questions with wit. She responded to Cable by pointing out, in a matter-of-fact way, that there was a vote of confidence in her leadership taking place amongst Conservative MPs that day. It was as if she was talking about items on a shopping list – somebody else's shopping list. She then sat down and awaited the next question on another issue. For May, detachment of this kind was constant, to such an extent that the disconnect between her public words and what was happening around her became stark.

———

Context partly determines the fate of leaders, and May faced the toughest set of tasks of any modern prime minister. Yet her approach to leadership made the demands more mountainous. Tellingly, she became the third modern prime minister, following Blair and Cameron, to announce her departure from Number Ten in advance – the most humiliating of pledges. The announcement is a symptom of disorder and fuels the sense of crisis, rather than alleviating it. Immediately after May told MPs she would resign if they backed her Withdrawal Agreement in March 2019, potential successors of unproven mettle made their moves. None of them were remotely qualified. Sajid Javid had been Home Secretary for a few months. Jeremy Hunt was a similarly short-serving Foreign Secretary. Boris Johnson had his chance at the Foreign Office and blew it. Others were measured by their views on Brexit, as if the fact that Penny Mordaunt had been equivocal about May's Brexit deal meant she was ready for the epic demands of leadership. Thatcher had big figures breathing down her neck, ready to lead. Blair had one big figure breathing down his. May had none.

Looking back, as a Labour politician responsible for his party's economic policy from 1992, Gordon Brown faced the most persistent set of external challenges. The markets and the media in the UK set a much higher bar for Labour, in relation to the economy. Edward Heath had to deal with the consequences of the quadrupling of oil prices, a seismic event over which he had no control. In 1974 Harold Wilson inherited raging inflation and industrial chaos. James Callaghan took over in 1976 with none of those challenges remotely resolved. Yet, by some distance, May faced the biggest mountain of the lot. Brexit would have challenged a leader of titanic qualities. When she first became prime minister she inherited a tiny majority of fifteen, nowhere near big enough to avoid parliamentary trouble. After her 2017 election she had no majority at all, although that was her fault for the way she had conducted the campaign.

There are some myths about May's misjudgements. From her exhausted chief whip, Julian Smith, to many Labour MPs, she was unfairly accused of failing to reach out to other parties after the general election. Smith told the BBC that a softer Brexit was inevitable after the election.[8] Many others have observed it was obvious, after the election, that May's approach to Brexit was doomed in a hung parliament, and as a result she should have engaged formally with Labour in the summer of 2017, as she finally did in April 2019 when, in theory, the UK was about to leave the EU.

The accusation of self-interested tribalism fits the stereotype that May could only think of her party and never beyond its fractious boundaries. In truth, she was trapped after the election. If she had opened talks with Jeremy Corbyn in the aftermath of what, for her, had been a terrible campaign – one in which Corbyn had fared better than most assumed – and she had performed much worse, she would have been removed.

Her internal Cabinet critics were strategically inept and, for all their macho posturing, dreaded taking responsibility for Brexit. Even so, they would not have allowed May to give Corbyn even more credibility than he had already acquired after the election, by being consulted over Brexit. That option was not available to her. The likes of Johnson, Davis and others, who had contemplated telling May that she had to resign on the night of the election, would have acted to remove her.

Instead of leading with Labour in the new hung parliament, she behaved with a degree of political courage by sidelining Davis in his Brexit department, fantasizing about a deal that the EU would never have agreed to. In private meetings she also dared to challenge the likes of Jacob Rees-Mogg on the seriousness of the Irish Question. Indeed, it is hard to sustain the common thesis that May put her party before the national interest, when much of her party was incandescent with rage over her Withdrawal Agreement. If May had the wit of Wilson or Blair, she would have made a virtue of the internal defiance by joking that if she had put her party first, it did not seem to be working. But May never joked, at least not spontaneously. Wit is an important weapon for leaders. May did not, or could not, deploy humour.

Looking back, that first Cabinet points to the tragedy of May's premiership. Nick Timothy's explanation of the appointments highlights an early reforming zeal that was never to be realized. May hoped that the likes of Amber Rudd, Damian Green and Greg Clark might assist her and her senior advisers to move the party on from Thatcherism. Indeed, nothing irritates Timothy more than reading commentators or hearing broadcasters observe, as if a matter of fact, that May's leadership marked a move to the right after Cameron and Osborne. Timothy had planned for a domestic agenda that was to the left of what had preceded it. Without Brexit, May might have been a genuine modernizer, the first 'one nation' Tory leader since Heath. Instead, she was doomed to become the Brexit prime minister. By the time the UK was supposed to have left the EU in March 2019, voters were more divided than when the referendum was held, and her party was in turmoil. Brexit in a hung parliament demanded a leader of imagination, empathy, tenacity, guile and mesmeric persuasive gifts. Instead it was Theresa May, emerging from the relative shelter of the Home Office: shy, stubborn, detached and inflexibly wilful.

In some respects, May was the dullest of modern prime ministers, and yet her premiership was by some margin the closest to an impossibly gripping thriller. During her misjudged early election, May told an interviewer that her most daring venture had been to run through a wheat field. Yet as prime minister, she played the starring role in the political equivalent to a James Bond film, confronting many villains (mainly in her own Cabinet and parliamentary party), racing around European capitals, sometimes flying out suddenly in the middle of the night. All the while, no one knew how the drama would end – May became utterly compelling, in spite of herself.

Finally, May ran out of road. She tried to revive her deal a fourth time, presenting a Withdrawal Bill aimed at wooing Labour MPs with various imprecise concessions that may or may not have taken effect if her bill was passed. Her MPs were alarmed at the concessions, while Labour MPs were unimpressed by the tentative nature of her offer to them. The bill was doomed and so was she. May announced her resignation tearfully on Friday 24 May 2019, stressing the need for compromise and a parliamentary solution to Brexit. If those themes had been her focus when she was politically strong, she might have been Prime Minister for longer. Instead, at the beginning, she had sought to please her hardliners. Three years later she was making her resignation statement from more or less the same spot outside Number Ten where Cameron had announced his departure. Within a day or so, more than ten Conservatives had expressed a passionate interest in replacing her. So many ached still to wear the thorny crown. But only one – Boris Johnson – was perceived by most Conservative MPs and party members as a vote-winner who could deliver Brexit. May was no fan of Johnson's and yet her leadership and the manner of her departure cleared the way for his breathtaking ascent to the top.

10

BORIS JOHNSON

Boris Johnson's first year in Number Ten was as crammed with epoch-changing events and personal dramas as Winston Churchill's opening months as prime minister in 1940. Johnson wilfully determined the course of history in relation to Brexit. He took the UK out of the EU with his own distinctly provocative strategy. Then the coronavirus (Covid-19) pandemic hit, and he had to respond to a global emergency rather than act as a leader shaping events. Other modern prime ministers had much cause to feel stressed, but the most casually ebullient of them all endured a uniquely draining sequence of events.

Johnson presided over a wholly unplanned revolution – one triggered not by Brexit or the ideas of his restless insurrectionary adviser Dominic Cummings, but by the spread of a pandemic. Like other world leaders, Johnson used the term 'war', but not as some pathetically contrived metaphor to place him in the same league as his hero, Churchill; he was a prime minister at war with the coronavirus, the gravest threat to the UK for many decades – a threat so grave that it almost killed him when he was hospitalized in April 2020. Quite unexpectedly he became a leader facing a challenge on a Churchillian scale.

When Johnson had viewed leadership from the safe distance of an aspiring prime minister, he encouraged comparisons with Churchill, writing a biography of the wartime leader that read at times as if it were autobiographical. Soon after becoming the actual prime minister, Johnson was tasked with making the UK as safe as was feasible while a virus wreaked deadly havoc. Coronavirus triggered a deep economic crisis as well as threatening lives. The emergency would have challenged a leader of great depth, range and experience. And Johnson had been prime minister for only a short time when the virus started to take hold. His senior ministers and advisers were not especially experienced, either, having been chosen more for their commitment to Brexit than for any great weightiness or sense of how government worked. Although the Conservatives were ruling for a fourth successive term, and Johnson had been a prominent public figure for years, he and his team were not used to pulling levers in power and turning announcements or slogans into the hard grind of policy implementation.

This bizarre and contradictory juxtaposition of an inexperienced team in its fourth term of government arose partly because in the autumn of 2019 Johnson had purged his parliamentary party of some senior figures. Former chancellors and other well-known Cabinet ministers had lost the whip in the Brexit battle – a conflict that was also epic in its historic significance. Additionally, after Johnson's triumphant election victory in December of that year, he turned with even greater relish to his fellow Brexiteers to take up key posts in his government. Behind-the-scenes advisers of equally limited experience danced fearfully to Cummings' tunes.

Johnson led a government of largely unproven lightweights, almost out of choice. There were few brilliant economists as powerful advisers, or weighty policy specialists. Instead there were those who met with Cummings' approval – the main qualification for survival. They were mostly timid figures willing to echo Cummings' sometimes insightful, but often eccentric, thoughts; he was fuelled by restless and impatient anger.

Such a team of shallow radicals flourished when the mood amongst a significant part of the electorate was one of anger. Suddenly that mood changed. From March 2020 the prevailing emotion amongst voters switched from Brexit-related fury to fear about the impact of coronavirus. Johnson and Cummings were equipped to make the most of anger, fuelling it at times with provocative statements about 'Parliament versus the people'. They were at their most determined when acting like manipulative conductors leading an orchestra. Fear was an altogether different emotion. Voters became frightened as they contemplated the impending health and economic crises. Their loathing of most elected politicians could be manipulated by the swagger of jingoistic radicalism from a new prime minister pledging, 'Let's get Brexit done.' Fear required a reassuring solidity rather than revolutionary fervour.

For Johnson personally, there was a formidable challenge of leadership. He had to change as a public figure while already at the centre of the stage, with the spotlight glaring on him. He could no longer play the clown, as he did sometimes as Mayor of London, and even as a marginalized Foreign Secretary when he occasionally still went for laughter rather than gravity. He found that he could not deliver evasively provocative slogans, as he had in relation to Brexit, when it came to the virus.

For some leaders, a near-metamorphosis on the public stage would be impossibly awkward. Johnson more or less managed such a transition because he possessed a textured authenticity. He could play the joker, but he was also capable of genuine seriousness. Like

Wilson, Thatcher and Blair, he was a wholly unique and distinct public figure. Some of the other modern prime ministers were more transparently self-conscious about how they sought to project their public images. Johnson was who he was. If it was an act, he had been acting for decades. Unlike May who was shy, Cameron who imitated Blair, or Brown who affected to be the 'father of the nation' when he was in reality passionately partisan, Johnson was at ease cracking jokes and, in terms of his demeanour, at responding to a dark and tragic crisis. His video recorded on the day he left hospital to recuperate at Chequers was hailed across the political spectrum for its authenticity. For five fluent minutes he thanked those who had saved his life, naming two nurses in particular, one from New Zealand and the other from Portugal. He was unavoidably serious about the nature of the virus, yet managed to joke that most of those who had treated him were called Nick. There could be no easier context for a prime minister to flourish fleetingly, but some of his predecessors would not have pulled it off.

Johnson's public ease was not the same as being in command of policy. At first, during February and early March 2020, he underestimated the threat posed by the virus, boasting that he had visited a hospital treating patients who were suffering from coronavirus and shook hands with all those he met. This was at a point where the limit of government advice was to avoid shaking hands and to wash one's hands regularly. Then, in vivid, frightening contrast, Johnson personified the danger of the virus when he fell ill in April 2020 – a turn of events that was hardly surprising, given that he ignored his own warnings about social distancing.

During the seven days that the prime minister was seriously ill there was an extraordinary development, one that adds a new layer to the perceptions of a leader. As he lay in intensive care, breathing with the assistance of an oxygen mask, Johnson became more prime ministerial than he had been when he was healthy. Obviously this was not because he was displaying a new mastery of detail and titanic leadership. He was struggling to breathe. It was the new misleading narrative in response to his vulnerability that turned him briefly into an imperious figure.

This was partly because doting newspapers projected Johnson as a martyr for the nation. Their message was that he had risked his life in order to save ours. Such reporting placed his deeply flawed responses to the virus earlier on in a heroic new context. There was a precedent for this: newspapers deified their favoured leaders at key points in their careers, most notably Margaret Thatcher during and after the Falklands War.

But more distinctly illuminating was the way in which the virus narrative developed as Johnson lay in intensive care. The media always needs new lines in a crisis. It was only getting two updates a day on the health of the prime minister, so it had no choice but to pose other questions in order to keep the news rolling forward. Who was in charge? How would the government – and, indeed, the entire country – cope in the absence of the prime minister? These were legitimate questions in the sense that the prime minister is the key decision-maker during a national emergency. There were also doubts within the government about the qualities of his chosen stand-in, Foreign Secretary Dominic Raab. But the frenzied way in which these questions intensified conveyed the false impression that Johnson, when healthy, had been a mighty leader, galvanizing his colleagues at the click of his fingers, capable of protecting the country from the killer virus on his own. In reality, Johnson's early responses had been confused, contradictory and less effective than those of some other leaders facing the same dilemma across the globe.

Because he fell ill, perceptions of him had changed. As questions raged about how the country would cope in his absence, Johnson became a titan. Normally when prime ministers fall ill, they are perceived as puny and fragile, which is why their medical conditions are often downplayed. Johnson nearly died, and he became wrongly but widely seen as herculean. It was one example among many in which he overturned the orthodoxies of modern leadership.

Yet perceptions of a leader can change many times. Even as Johnson was being hailed as a heroic prime minister who had risked his life to save his country, questions were being posed in parts of the less supportive media, and by Opposition MPs, about the government's response to the pandemic. The multi-layered emergency demanded deep thinking, a capacity to make connections and to recognize that each complex decision would have profound consequences that would also need to be addressed. Also required were skills to read the rhythms of a crisis and to stay ahead of the curve, a deep sense of how government works and, most specifically, how the NHS was structured, after a series of haphazard reforms.

Gordon Brown was an unlucky prime minister in some respects, but he had one stroke of luck. He was supremely well qualified to respond to the apocalyptic financial crisis in 2008, having been chancellor for ten years.[1] He could quickly read the scale of the crisis, and he had contacts around the world that enabled him to be a global leader, coordinating international action. Johnson was ill-suited to lead in a similar way. Being a former polemical columnist, Mayor of London and a poor Foreign Secretary was not the equivalent preparation for leadership amidst seismic events. This was not entirely Johnson's fault. By definition, a leader cannot automatically acquire the qualifications for the unexpected, or determine the timing of huge events. Johnson had been famous for many years, but prime minister for just six months, when coronavirus spread through Europe. It was a momentous test of leadership.

———

Johnson's first six months before the global pandemic had been historic, too. He became prime minister in July 2019. That quickly felt like ancient history when the virus transformed the way we lived and were governed, but what happened before this was hugely significant. By February 2020 Johnson had removed the whip from some of the best-known Conservative MPs in the land, had unlawfully prorogued Parliament, negotiated a Brexit deal with the European Union – albeit one that was more economically and constitutionally risky than the one he had deemed to be unacceptable – lost key votes in the Commons, won a general election with a landslide, formally taken the UK out of the EU and lost a chancellor before the government's first budget. It took a virus to make such a sequence seem like small beer.

After the December 2019 election Johnson was the most powerful prime minister of modern times. Awestruck political commentators compared his mighty omnipotence with Tony Blair's after Labour's 1997 landslide win.[2] The comparison was imprecise. Johnson wielded much greater power than Blair, who had to negotiate with the formidable Gordon Brown at the Treasury.

Brown had his own distinct agenda. In contrast, Johnson's first chancellor was Sajid Javid, a figure grateful to be in the post and dependent solely on the prime minister's patronage. When Javid dared to raise the occasional question about Number Ten's plans for the economy, he was in trouble. He was given no choice but to resign in February 2020 even before he had delivered his first budget, his fate being sealed when Johnson told him that, at Cummings' insistence, Javid must sack his special advisers. Normally the resignation of a chancellor is a volcanic event in British politics. Such was Johnson's early might, however, that Javid's departure caused little more than a day's excitement. He was replaced by Rishi Sunak, his slick and capable deputy at the Treasury, and Number Ten's omnipotence was unshaken.

Until the spread of coronavirus, Johnson and his chosen senior adviser, Dominic Cummings, made all the calls, without having to worry about the reaction of ministerial colleagues, MPs or the media. Johnson had been a journalist and yet he shunned the media. There was no need for regular appearances. For a time he could do as he wanted.

The closest to this, in terms of unconstrained power, was Margaret Thatcher after her landslide victories in 1983 and 1987, but she was surrounded by senior ministers who were capable of thinking for themselves and even daring occasionally to challenge her. The likes of Michael Heseltine, Nigel Lawson, Ken Clarke and Geoffrey Howe were substantial figures in their own right. Thatcher had to bear some of them in mind as she made her moves. At the end of 2019 Johnson didn't need to listen to anyone. He faced no equivalent independently minded figures. If ministers or advisers had sought to be challenging, they would almost certainly have been removed.

The twist is that Johnson did not know exactly what to do with his theoretically unlimited power. Although he had some clear objectives, they were contradictory ones. He was a crusader for free trade, and yet sought a Brexit that threatened the end of frictionless trade with the UK's biggest overseas market. He was genuinely passionate about the need for new infrastructure projects, being the first modern prime minister who dared to declare railways and buses to be a priority. As he did so, he also pledged to invest heavily in other public services. At the same time he remained a fan of relatively low taxation, while his Brexit plans threatened to hinder economic growth. Without the prospect of a booming economy or significantly higher taxes, it wasn't clear where the money would come from to fund Johnson's ambitious spending plans.

Still, he was well to the left of David Cameron and, to some extent, Theresa May in his willingness to use the levers of power, at least until the virus revolutionized economic policy. Indeed, Johnson was more overtly 'statist' than either Blair or Brown in the early New Labour years. Yet as part of the contradictory pattern, his first Cabinet was well to the right of either Cameron's or May's. His first chancellor, Javid, worshipped at the altar of the small-state libertarian economist Ayn Rand. Javid's successor, Rishi Sunak, had no record of being a fan of an active state. The Foreign Secretary, Dominic Raab, was a protégé of the former Brexit Secretary, David Davis, who regarded tax rises as a form of political sin. Johnson's choice of Home Secretary was Priti Patel, a hard-liner on immigration, when the prime minister had affected to be 'liberal' on the issue in the past. Even before coronavirus transformed the role and size of the state, Johnson led a government that sought to be hyperactive while being composed largely of small-state Thatcherites.

Johnson's political personality was equally contradictory. On any stage he was ebullient, often posing questions to an audience like a pantomime star encouraging participation. 'We're going to get Brexit done, aren't we?' he would ask, in the build-up to the

December election. His fans replied ecstatically in the affirmative. Away from the stage, he was more of a loner, without many close political friends. He could be shy in some situations and exuberant in others. At times Johnson was unusually confrontational, both in the Commons and when dealing with ministers. His reshuffles were brutal. Yet he wanted also to be liked, and he turned away from confrontation if he could find a Blair-like 'third way' in terms of policy.

Famously, Johnson could show an indifference to detail and hard work, while being capable of working tirelessly and productively when he chose to do so. When he wanted to be, he was the master of detail; when he lost interest, as he frequently did, he failed to grasp the most basic information. He was the easiest of prime ministers to caricature and yet he was hard to pin down. He relished being evasive as a public figure, and this evasiveness extended to his own self-perception: he was not sure who he was, as a public figure or as prime minister.

————

During his early months as prime minister, Johnson sought to rule strongly when he was weak – the opposite of May, who began in a strong position but chose to tamely appease hard-line Brexiteers.

On 24 July 2019 he delivered his opening words outside Number Ten with a self-confidence that defied the fragile political context in which he spoke. He was a new prime minister in a hung parliament, but he made his statement as if he were a leader with a huge majority. He repeated the theme of his triumphant leadership campaign (which had also been conducted as if he were about to inherit a big majority, rather than a minority government). For the first time as prime minister, Johnson insisted that he would bring about Brexit by 31 October: 'The doubters, the doomsters, the gloomsters – they are going to get it wrong again. The people who bet against Britain are going to lose their shirts because we are going to restore trust in our democracy and we are going to fulfil the repeated promises of parliament to the people and come out of the EU on October 31st ... no ifs or buts.'

He was already behaving as no prime minister had previously. All his predecessors left themselves wriggle-room over Europe. In a hung parliament, they left themselves wriggle-room over virtually everything. Johnson did not do so. Within seconds of getting the top job he was a breaker of prime ministerial orthodoxies. He went on to repeat his other consistent theme: his determination to 'level up' the poorer parts of the UK. This part of his message could almost have been delivered by a Labour prime minister. He pledged to answer 'at last the plea of the forgotten people and the left-behind towns by physically and literally renewing the ties that bind us together, so that with safer streets and better education and fantastic new road and rail infrastructure and full fibre broadband we level up across Britain with higher wages, and a higher living wage, and higher productivity. We close the opportunity gap.'

Johnson was the second successive Tory prime minister to make the case for government intervention during an opening proclamation. Theresa May had done the same in her first speech outside Number Ten three years earlier. In their attitude towards the role of the state, Conservative leaders were, in theory at least, finally escaping the spell cast by Margaret Thatcher. David Cameron was the last to be held in her thrall. His successors were moving leftwards in their public statements.

In normal circumstances the implicit shift to the left, the recognition of the good that government could do, would have commanded much attention. As was true for much of 2019, everything was overshadowed by Brexit. Johnson's plans were impossibly ambitious. He was leading in the same House of Commons that had tormented May. MPs had opposed May's deal by huge margins in three separate votes. Yet Johnson was pledging to leave the EU by 31 October – with a new deal or no deal.

At the same time, although government forecasts suggested the UK economy would suffer from the consequences of Brexit, Johnson was implying that he would find vast additional resources to boost poorer areas. The phrase 'levelling up' was a revealing one. Johnson was suggesting a boost for poorer regions and lower earners, without in any way hitting the incomes of the better-off. He did not say he would level downwards, only upwards. The term 'redistribution' was never uttered. The means that Johnson envisaged for 'levelling up' only became clearer in his government's first budget in March 2020. It would borrow on the Keynesian basis that extra spending would boost growth and productivity. Since 2010 Tory prime ministers and their chancellors had argued that stringent limits on spending and borrowing would boost the economy. Johnson's government was arguing the precise opposite.

What followed his opening words in July 2019 was even more unprecedented. Traditionally prime ministers schemed tirelessly in a hung parliament, wooing internal critics and reaching out to other parties. They assumed it was their only route to survival. Harold Wilson manoeuvred to the point of disillusioned exhaustion in order to keep his governing party together after the February 1974 election. He appointed a Cabinet that represented the 'broad church' of the Labour Party. The leading left-winger Tony Benn held a prominent post, and so did Roy Jenkins from the right of the party. Radical policies that had featured prominently in Labour's manifesto were moderated and, in the more contentious cases, dropped. And when he became prime minister in 1976, the tribal James Callaghan reached out to another tribe, the Liberal Party, in order to keep going.

When John Major lost his majority heading towards the 1997 election he told his party there was a need to twist and turn at times. In one of his contortions, Major appointed a potential rival, the pro-European Michael Heseltine, as his deputy, but he also wooed Eurosceptics by starting a 'beef war' with the European Union, a conflict that he knew to be an absurd contrivance. When David Cameron had no overall majority in 2010 he reached out to the Liberal Democrats. And after losing her party's small majority in 2017 Theresa May wooed the DUP, while working sleeplessly to keep her party together over Brexit and, more particularly, her Brexit deal.

Johnson did not twist and turn. He did not woo internal critics or reach out to other parties. He broke all the informal rules established by his predecessors concerning how to behave in a hung parliament. His chosen route was fraught, but ultimately triumphant – at least, he was triumphant in terms of his short-term objectives: winning an election and leaving the EU. For Johnson, securing these objectives was a stunning achievement, assisted by some of the most gullible political opponents that a prime minister could dream of facing.

Johnson's first act of machismo was a ruthless reshuffle. Every new member of the government had to agree in advance to back his overriding pledge to leave the EU by 31 October, with or without a deal. As a symbolic statement of intent, committed Brexiteers were appointed to senior positions. Dominic Raab became Foreign Secretary. Michael Gove was placed in the Cabinet Office in charge of stepping up the planning for 'no deal'. Priti Patel moved to the Home Office as Home Secretary. All had campaigned for Brexit in the 2016 referendum. Most sensationally, Johnson appointed Dominic Cummings as his chief adviser.

As far as Johnson was concerned, Cummings was his most important appointment. Prime ministers' chosen advisers reveal far more about them as political figures, and as human beings, than the appointments they make to senior Cabinet posts. Cabinet selections are determined by the limited cast of suitable MPs. There are also stars who expect senior posts in a government and would not accept middle-ranking departments, even if the prime minister at the time would prefer them to be more peripheral. Prime ministers have immense powers of patronage in terms of ministerial appointments, but they are constrained by the broader political context, even when they are at their most powerful.

When choosing their most senior advisers in Number Ten, leaders are free to do as they wish. Harold Wilson kept the temperamental but devotedly loyal and shrewd Marcia Williams close to his side throughout his leadership. Tony Blair spent more time with Alastair Campbell than he did with any Cabinet ministers, with the possible exception of Gordon Brown. David Cameron opted for Steve Hilton, the eccentric bare-footed libertarian. Theresa May was reliant on Nick Timothy and Fiona Hill for ideas and drive; she had little time for her chancellor, Philip Hammond, or her Foreign Secretary, Boris Johnson.

Johnson chose Cummings, who was more of an outsider than Hilton, in that he was not a Conservative Party member. Although famously ambitious, Johnson did not spend huge amounts of time cultivating backbenchers, understandably opting to edit *The Spectator* and then to become Tory candidate for Mayor of London – one of several risky moves that he navigated successfully, at least in terms of his career. He was not a brilliant speaker in the Commons, and his addiction to politics did not extend to spending vast amounts of time in Parliament. He did not socialize much with David Cameron's so-called 'Notting Hill set'. Some of Cameron's ministerial colleagues were also his friends; Johnson had few such friends.

The senior MPs that Johnson knew best were fellow Brexit campaigners. A lot of them were rewarded with Cabinet posts, but without huge doses of excitement on Johnson's part. In contrast, he passionately wanted to secure the appointment of Cummings and was thrilled when he persuaded the legendary Brexit campaigner to join him. An indication of his excitement was reflected in his self-discipline – the appointment did not leak in advance.

Johnson could see virtues in some of his ministerial colleagues, but rarely went as far as intense admiration of them. He admired Cummings, however, and became convinced that it was Cummings above all who had turned the Brexit referendum in Leave's favour. Probably, if there had been no Brexit campaign, Brexit would still have won, but in the heat of battle Johnson saw Cummings – the author of the slogan 'take back control' – as the key. He wanted Cummings at the heart of his government, a sign that he saw the first phase of his leadership as a campaign.

Although Cummings had been Michael Gove's adviser at the Department of Education during the first phase of the coalition, he flourished as a campaigner and viewed politics as an eternal battle. In Number Ten he envisaged conflicts that challenged the conservative complacency of the institutions. He would take on the Civil Service, the bureaucracy of Brussels, the judiciary or the extravagantly over-managed and biased BBC.

Cummings' appointment meant that Johnson was never going to woo a hung parliament; he was going to take it on aggressively. But while Cummings generated a vast amount of media attention, it was Johnson who made the appointment. If he had not wanted a battle with Parliament he would not have given Cummings a central role. Some ministers and Tory MPs were quick to curse Cummings, but the elected prime minister is the one with the patronage; in the end he or she decides on the style of leadership and the policies. If ministers were cursing Cummings, they were also condemning Johnson.

Those Cabinet ministers who had supported May's Brexit deal resigned before they were sacked in July 2019. The chancellor for three years, Philip Hammond – hardly a revolutionary figure – moved to the backbenches, and was viewed by the new regime with some justification as an enemy. He was joined by Rory Stewart, a charismatic contender in that summer's Tory leadership campaign; and David Gauke, a witty, mild-mannered figure who had served in several departments.

They had left government even before they knew Cummings was joining, already aware, from Johnson's leadership campaign, that he had left no space for nuance – and apparently no flexibility as to the date of the UK's departure from the European Union. Johnson had therefore left no space for them. Even before he had moved into Number Ten, there were more formidable critics on the backbenches.

He made more internal enemies in the following months, as if wilfully making his position in the hung parliament even more precarious. Johnson acted with apparent recklessness because he was astutely aware of the one ace card in his otherwise poor hand. He gambled that his disparate enemies in the Commons would never unite to inflict a fatal blow. In ultimately being vindicated, he showed it was possible to prevail in a hung parliament by being assertive rather than accommodating. No other prime minister had dared to be so determinedly unyielding in such circumstances.

The summer and autumn of 2019 were bizarre, erupting with possibilities for Johnson's opponents that were never realized. The summer recess began almost immediately after Johnson had become prime minister. Throughout August a strange dance played out. There was a majority in the Commons against the UK leaving the EU without a deal by 31 October. Johnson's disparate parliamentary critics were at least united in their opposition to 'no deal'. Yet they were not sitting. Throughout the summer recess Johnson acted imperiously without parliamentary constraint. Wherever he went he continued to insist that the UK would be out on 31 October, 'come what may'.

There was much feverish speculation at that time about how the government could leave on a 'no deal' basis, given that in the early autumn a majority of MPs planned to take legislative control with a single objective in mind. They intended to make it unlawful for Johnson to step away from the EU without a deal. But Johnson was having none of it and continued to act as if he could do what he wanted, pretending that Parliament was an irrelevance. He could act this way when Parliament was not sitting in August, but what about when MPs returned to Westminster?

In early September the answer was both alarming and reassuring, as far as Johnson was concerned. Some MPs, especially on the Labour side, threatened to call a vote of confidence in Johnson and his new government. They did so knowing there was no point in making such a move, if they were defeated. Led by Nicola Sturgeon, SNP MPs indicated they would support the attempt to bring Johnson down. If the government was defeated in such a vote, the SNP would support a brief interregnum under Labour's Jeremy Corbyn. Johnson and Cummings might have been out of Number Ten within weeks of making it to the heart of power, if the rest of their parliamentary critics had been ready to act.

But Johnson's swagger throughout the summer was partly justified. Some Labour MPs were wary of a vote of confidence, dreading Corbyn becoming prime minister, even for a few weeks. The loudest dissenter was the new leader of the Liberal Democrats, Jo Swinson. Her party had enjoyed a strong performance in the European elections the previous June and had attracted some defectors from Labour. Swinson was also from the wing of the Liberal Democrats that was more hostile to Labour than the Conservatives, even if she did not recognize – let alone acknowledge – the inclination. She was not willing to cooperate with the Labour leadership. And Swinson was not alone. The internal Tory dissenters were equally alarmed at being in any way instrumental in making Corbyn prime minister. Some of the anti-Johnson Tories were also opposed to a second referendum. In contrast, Swinson backed a second referendum, as did the SNP. Johnson's opponents were all over the place.

He was lucky in facing opponents who were so divided, but he was also politically courageous by daring to assume they would give him all the space he needed. Johnson was the biggest risk-taker of all modern prime ministers, by a considerable margin. Only Thatcher came close.

From Johnson's perspective, he had no choice but to be bold. The Brexit Party, led by Nigel Farage, had topped the European elections in terms of the popular vote the previous June. The Conservatives had languished in fifth place, in terms of votes cast. Johnson concluded that the Conservative Party faced an existential threat. If the party did not deliver on Brexit, it was finished. For him, the conclusion was conveniently self-serving: only he could save the party.

The merits of Brexit, as he'd once seen them, rarely entered Johnson's calculations after he became prime minister; they were hardly ever mentioned during the autumnal parliamentary battles of 2019 or the December election. The issue had moved on from the claimed benefits of Brexit to a battle over 'trust' – the most emotive and misleading theme in British politics. While other candidates had wavered in terms of the timing for Brexit during the leadership contest, Johnson was unequivocal about delivering it by 31 October. That was the only message that mattered. Nigel Farage and his new party were breathing down the Conservatives' neck. They had to be dealt with.

When MPs returned from the summer recess, Johnson's enemies briefly held the upper hand. At the end of August, Johnson announced the prorogation – or suspension – of Parliament, to take effect from sometime between 9 and 12 September until the state opening of Parliament on 14 October. The announcement triggered uproar. From day one, Johnson had behaved as if he was all-powerful. Now he sought to make Parliament irrelevant by closing it for a crucial period in the lead-up to his deadline for leaving the EU.

The move was astonishing on many levels. At its most funda-mental, the prorogation was the most vivid illustration of the impossible divide. 'The people' had voted for Brexit in the 2016 referendum. Parliament at least wanted to mitigate the huge risks of leaving, and some MPs sought ways in which the UK could remain in the EU. Johnson was acting to implement the referendum and had no time for a parliament that challenged him, even though the Commons had been elected at a point when he was a senior member of Theresa May's Cabinet.

With a chutzpah never seen in a modern prime minister, Johnson insisted that the move to prorogue Parliament had been made to facilitate a Queen's Speech. Few believed him. His entourage reinforced the scepticism by briefing journalists that MPs wouldn't have time to introduce legislation making it unlawful for the UK to leave the EU without a deal. The government with no majority wanted a free hand, as if it had a landslide. Without the landslide, it sought to remove Parliament.

What followed showed that Johnson and Cummings were haphazard in their strategic cunning. They did not navigate a smooth path, and their actions often made their chosen route far more difficult. The proposed prorogation united their disparate opponents within seconds of its announcement. The different groupings that could not agree on very much came together with uncharacteristic speed and resolution. Before Parliament was prorogued, MPs passed an emergency motion to take control of the Order Paper (the order of parliamentary business) the following day. The bill that made leaving the EU without a deal unlawful was rushed through all its Commons stages in a day, contrary to those initial briefings from Number Ten. Suddenly Johnson was in the worst of both worlds. He was facing a furore for proroguing Parliament and he had not stopped MPs from blocking 'no deal'.

Yet amidst the raging storms, he added to the turbulence. There was no attempt to appease Parliament; instead all previous orthodoxies were challenged once more. Johnson removed the whip from all those Tory MPs who backed the legislation blocking a no-deal Brexit, expelling some of the best-known names in the parliamentary party. Those who lost the whip as well as Hammond, Gauke and Stewart included Ken Clarke and Oliver Letwin, a government loyalist who had been a key figure in the Cameron era. Whenever these prominent figures appeared on TV they were given the label 'Independent'. Johnson had turned the orthodox Conservatives into near-revolutionary figures. None of them could quite believe what had happened. When Churchill's grandson, the normally exuberant and loyal Nicholas Soames, reflected on his fate in the Commons he was close to tears.

Johnson's treatment of prominent Tory MPs seemed masochistic, as if he was formalizing a schism when most leaders would instead paper over the cracks, in the hope of presenting a facade of unity. But this was an act of ruthlessness that worked brilliantly. Johnson knew that, one way or another, an election was not far away. The contest would be a Brexit election. When the campaign got under way, he could not have prominent Tory candidates taking a different view from him. By removing the whip from those who were doubtful about his Brexit stance, he ensured that when the election was called the party would field candidates delivering the same message.

In the short term Johnson faced accusations from the likes of Ken Clarke that the Conservative Party was becoming the Brexit Party. He did not mind such jibes. Indeed he welcomed them, in the same way Blair was relatively relaxed about being described as 'Bush's poodle' in the build-up to the war in Iraq. Blair wanted to be seen as pro-American, and such onslaughts helped him bind stronger ties with Atlanticists like Rupert Murdoch. Johnson knew that in order to destroy the Brexit Party, the Conservatives would have to take an unyielding line on Brexit.

With the party-conference season under way, the prorogued Parliament was not due to return until shortly before the UK would leave the EU. But, in another dramatic twist, the Supreme Court found the prorogation to be unlawful in late September 2019. As Lady Hale, president of the Supreme Court, calmly read the judgment without qualification, it felt as if another political earthquake was erupting around Johnson. Political journalists at the Labour conference in Brighton rushed back to London. Johnson, who was in New York, held an urgent phone conference with his Cabinet before dashing back earlier than planned. The Commons' Speaker, John Bercow, declared there would be plenty of time for MPs to question ministers, and indeed the prime minister when he had returned from the US. All were reflecting on Lady Hale's words when delivering the unanimous judgment: 'The decision to advise Her Majesty to prorogue Parliament was unlawful because it had the effect of frustrating or preventing the ability of Parliament to carry out its constitutional functions without reasonable justification.'

The Supreme Court ruling and the act that made a 'no deal' departure from the EU illegal were the high points for Johnson's opponents. But they were also red herrings. The drama felt far more significant than it actually was. MPs had already passed the key legislation that would bind Johnson's hands in terms of a no-deal Brexit. That legislation, although an important insurance policy, was also less significant than it appeared to be.

There was another twist. Johnson was almost as determined as his opponents to avoid a no-deal Brexit. He partially agreed with them about the risks. He also thought, wrongly, that the threat of no deal was of use to him in his negotiations with the EU, but he had no intention of walking out without a deal if he could possibly avoid it. Johnson was reckless, but he was not daft. He had been briefed on the consequences and knew the risks involved. Meanwhile the court's verdict that the government had acted unlawfully made no practical difference to Parliament's power over the government, and even made Johnson more popular with target voters. Once more he could affect to be the victim of an 'elite' that was apparently indifferent to the 2016 referendum result. The Old Etonian prime minister was on the side of 'the people'.

Nonetheless, Johnson and Cummings had not anticipated the consequences of their high-wire sequence. Cummings calculated that the prorogation would prevent Parliament from passing legislation that made 'no deal' illegal. They also believed they had legal cover by pretending that their sole objective was to prorogue so that a Queen's Speech could be delivered. They were wrong on both counts. Quite often they played their hand as badly as their inept opponents did.

———

After the drama of the early autumn, Johnson faced a different dynamic. He had arrived in Number Ten convinced that he needed to deliver Brexit before calling a general election. But as he was repeatedly defeated in votes in the Commons he began to change his mind. As ever with Johnson, his declarations were at odds with reality – in this case claiming that he could deliver Brexit in a hung parliament. When reality caught up with him, he found another way through: he became an advocate for an election in advance of Brexit.

By October, Johnson could not be clearer about his hunger for a dissolution: 'We will campaign day after day for the people of this country to be released from subjection to a parliament that has outlived its usefulness.'[3] In a way, this was his dream scenario: another campaign against Parliament. Johnson and Cummings were most at ease when they had a campaign to fight, a cause or a crusade. The hard grind of policy implementation was of less interest to them.

Johnson made one key move that made an election more attractive: he secured a Brexit deal, as he had always hoped to. In meeting after meeting with doubting Tories he insisted he wanted a deal. He told David Lidington, a key figure in the May era, that he knew 'no deal' carried big risks.[4] Lidington was not the only former Remainer to hear this message. Johnson sought to reassure his Welfare Secretary, Amber Rudd, that he was working for a deal. With good cause, Rudd did not believe him; there was little evidence of the government seeking such an outcome. Rudd was one of several ministerial resignations. Another was Jo Johnson, the prime minister's brother. Neither believed Johnson would secure a deal. In this respect, he pulled off a conjuring trick. Fortunately the deal didn't require huge amounts of government activity – for the most part, Johnson reverted to the deal the EU had originally proposed to Theresa May.

Towards the end of 2017 the EU had suggested that a border should be placed in the Irish Sea as a way of resolving the UK's desire to leave the customs union. This would avoid the need for a border being re-established between Northern Ireland and Ireland. May rejected the proposition, not least because it was strongly opposed by the DUP. Johnson adopted a version of the original EU plan, because it allowed him to avoid 'no deal' and claim to have delivered on his pledge to dump the 'backstop', the thorniest part of May's deal. Under May's proposals, the UK would have remained in the customs union until both sides could agree on vaguely defined technological ways of avoiding a hard border between the Republic of Ireland and Northern Ireland.[5]

Although Johnson had denounced May's deal during the Tory leadership contest, he now accepted large elements of what she had negotiated, while reneging on a pledge to the DUP that he would never support arrangements that placed Northern Ireland in a different position from the rest of the UK.[6] Here was a characteristic of Johnson that would cause him considerable difficulty in the coronavirus crisis: a tendency to make claims or pledges that could not be delivered.

Even so, his deal was politically astute. He was in a trap and he escaped. From his perspective, he wanted to take the UK out of the EU, and he wanted a deal that would not include Theresa May's backstop. The EU had insisted it would not reopen negotiations, but by reverting to its earlier offer, Johnson could claim a negotiating triumph to a broadly supportive media. The EU had reopened negotiations in the sense that it scrapped the backstop and happily reverted to its earlier proposal – one that was a better deal for it and much worse for the UK than May's agreement.

Johnson's admirers in his party and the media came to believe sincerely that he had pulled off a great coup. Crucially, Johnson, Cummings and other hard-line Brexiteers in the new government also came to believe their own propaganda. They convinced themselves that, by being assertive, they had got what they wanted. This view made no sense. Why did the EU, and the Irish government in particular, agree to the new arrangements so swiftly? They no longer feared a no-deal outcome because that had been made unlawful by the UK Parliament. They could have played for time. They responded with such speed because Johnson was broadly adopting the proposals they had made in the first place. Yet his escape from the trap was mesmerizing for the previously incarcerated Johnson. On one level, he had pulled it off. The UK was leaving with a deal that was not precisely May's deal. Like Cameron, Johnson was fascinated by leadership as a performance art. And the performer fell for the performance.

Parliament intervened one more time. On a rare Saturday sitting a majority of MPs backed Johnson's deal, but they also supported an amendment demanding more time to scrutinize the details. This was perfectly reasonable, as the deal marked the biggest change to the UK's place in the world since 1945. Johnson refused to grant the additional time. Instead he withdrew the legislation and began to demand a general election with even greater intensity than before. Parliament had supported his deal, and yet Johnson still argued that this was part of a sequence in which the Commons defied 'the people'. Again, this was nonsense.

There were few consistent patterns in Johnson's leadership, but fear of scrutiny was another constant factor. From proroguing Parliament, to refusing MPs any significant time to study his withdrawal agreement, and on to being elusive with the media, Johnson preferred to make a broad case and leave it at that. In relation to his Brexit deal he knew there were details that contradicted previous pledges. These would surface if former Conservative MPs with a forensic grip were given the time to question him at length in Parliament. There were also some Labour and SNP figures who would expose flaws in his apparent diplomatic triumph. Then there were the Lords, who were ready to unpick the sweeping claims from the government that this deal was great news for the UK. Johnson could do without such lengthy examination.

He had another motive, too. Being seen to be 'against' Parliament was helping him considerably in the wider electoral battle. Johnson led at a time when a significant number of voters loathed elected politicians. Here again was a chance to ally himself with the people against Parliament. On the Saturday night after Parliament had voted to demand extra time for scrutiny, Johnson had no choice but to sign a letter to the EU asking for an extension to the UK's membership until 31 January 2020. In the letter he made clear this was not his wish. Johnson had not met his 'do or die' pledge. He was untroubled by his failure to do so, and moved on as he always did when his previous words clashed with reality.

The failure to deliver by 31 October did him no harm whatsoever. 'The people' – or enough of them – blamed Parliament for blocking the wishes of their hero, even though Johnson had made the pledge in the full knowledge that MPs were not inclined to bring about such an objective. He got away with his deceit. Here is another pattern in Johnson's rise: he made claims that were often at odds with reality, and some pledges that he knew could not be met. When the claims were exposed and the pledges were unrealized, he moved on, often to the cheers of those lauding him as he made his original contentious assertions.

Having escaped the bind of not wanting a 'no deal' while opposing May's deal, Johnson became fleetingly trapped again. He had no majority, and after expelling several of his MPs the parliamentary arithmetic made the situation even more hopeless for him. He kept on losing votes in the Commons. The Fixed-term Parliaments Act meant that Johnson was trapped, even though he ached for an election. He was on his political honeymoon. He had a Brexit deal. He wanted a majority. He faced an Opposition leader, Jeremy Corbyn, who was trailing badly in the polls. Although any early election held risks for him, a pre-Christmas Brexit election was his dream scenario.

With no need to do so, and with hubristic naivety, the opposition parties delivered for him. There they were, pulling the strings in a hung parliament, making Johnson look weak, with more than two years to run in the fixed term. The opposing parties had every right to keep Parliament going and it was obviously in their interest to do so. Why give the prime minister a general election on the date he sought, at the height of his honeymoon period as a newish leader, and on the theme that he wanted to put centre-stage?

For the SNP leader and First Minister, Nicola Sturgeon, the answer to this question was obvious. Her party was riding high in the polls in Scotland. She had every reason to give Johnson his election. But in her support she was now joined by the Liberal Democrats' leader, Jo Swinson. Once again a Liberal Democrat leader was behaving in precisely the way a Conservative prime minister hoped. By the end of October, Swinson declared with a flourish that she would join the SNP in backing a December election. She conveyed a message that was both confused and gullibly simplistic: 'A general election on our proposed timetable would take no-deal off the table, and give the public the chance to elect a Liberal Democrat government who will revoke Article 50 or increase the number of MPs who support a People's Vote.'[7]

There were a number of miscalculations in a single sentence, not least the assumption that the Liberal Democrats were on the eve of securing power and that their proposal to revoke Article 50 was a vote-winner. Confusingly, Swinson continued to advocate a referendum on Brexit while arguing that the Liberal Democrats backed revocation without further consultation. While seemingly on a high, and ignoring the advice of former leaders Vince Cable and Ming Campbell, Swinson was striding towards her doom.

If Jeremy Corbyn had been a more leaderly figure, perhaps he could have worked with Sturgeon and Swinson more constructively. Instead he had little choice but to back an election, when the other two main opposition parties were doing so. Even at this point Labour had the numbers to prevent an election from going ahead, and could have done so. But Corbyn and his insular team were viewing the fast-moving events through the prism of the 2017 campaign, when they had successfully reversed appalling poll ratings. His advisers were enthusiastic, believing that when broadcasters were bound by the rigid rules of impartiality, Corbyn would shine. This was as naive as Swinson's calculations.

Quite a lot of the shadow Cabinet were opposed to giving Johnson his election, including senior figures such as John McDonnell and Emily Thornberry, much sharper readers of the political rhythms than their leader. But for Corbyn, campaigning was one of the few pleasures of leadership. He could not wait to get going again and to feel liberated from all the other burdens of his role. He meant it when he declared, soon after Sturgeon and Swinson: 'We will now launch the most ambitious and radical campaign for real change our country has ever seen.' Michael Foot felt the same in 1983. Once an election gets under way, many of the burdens of leading an unleadable party are lifted.

Johnson was a lucky leader – the luckiest since Margaret Thatcher, who had the great fortune to face an Opposition that had formally split between Labour and the SDP. In Johnson's case, with the exception of Sturgeon, the leaders who opposed him were weak. They had him under their thumbs and they let him go. But they did more than that. In the subsequent election they fought poor campaigns – as great a favour to Johnson as granting him the election on the date he wanted. Corbyn had failed to frame and win an argument in advance of the election. Since his genuinely significant semi-triumph in the 2017 election he had been largely invisible, fearing partly – for good reason – the bias of the mainstream outlets. A more agile leader would have accepted the bias and sought to overcome it rather than opt for invisibility. There had been no sustained and accessible argument from him, or anyone else, about why the state could be a benevolent force. Then suddenly at the start of the 2019 election Corbyn unveiled a manifesto with hundreds of policies, as if they were in themselves an explanation of the state's potential. The few election-winning Opposition leaders have addressed the 'why' question before outlining detailed policies. Corbyn was not a teacher; he asserted but did not explain.

Beyond the issue of Europe, the Liberal Democrats had little idea of who they were or what they stood for. There had been no detailed post-mortem of their role in the Cameron-led coalition, even though it was the cause of their slaughter in the 2015 election. In the months leading up to December 2019 they had been joined by the likes of Labour's Chuka Umunna, who continued to describe himself as a social democrat; and by Conservative MPs who regarded themselves as economic liberals, who had enthusiastically supported the austerity policies of the coalition. Swinson had been a minister in that government and remained in close contact with Nick Clegg, Cameron's gullible partner.

Swinson assumed she would sweep up the 'Remain' vote, not least because her promise to revoke Article 50 was more hard-line than Labour's offer of a referendum. Instead she was still being criticized by voters on some TV programmes for her role in the coalition, and there was considerable opposition even from Remainers to her 'revoke' policy. She had also claimed that she could be the next prime minister, when she did not have a chance of seizing the crown. If the Liberal Democrats had soared, they would have made gains at least in the south-west of England at the expense of the Conservatives. Instead, they fell back calamitously. From the summer onwards, when she publicly refused to contemplate working even briefly with Labour to dethrone Johnson, Swinson had made one inept move after another.

In contrast to such ineptitude from Labour and the Liberal Democrats, Johnson's campaign was ruthless. Because of the victory that followed his campaign, Johnson passed a key test of leadership. He was an election winner: victorious twice in London's mayoral elections, winning a leadership contest easily and, most triumphant of all, securing the Conservatives' biggest majority since the Thatcher landslide in 1987. His opponents helped him – and so did a supportive, or confused, media – but it was a massive personal victory as well.

He secured the victory by fighting as a one-man show. Most of his colleagues were nowhere to be seen. But Johnson's stardom took a strictly limited form. When the BBC announced a series of interviews with the party leaders, it assumed they would all agree to be made to look incompetent and crooked, as Andrew Neil demanded short answers to complex or unflattering questions, interrupting interviewees if he did not get a quick response. Johnson and his advisers took the simple step of refusing to go on the programmes. The BBC hit the roof and sanctioned Neil to deliver a monologue about what he would have asked Johnson. There would have been questions about why he was not trusted, and many other questions on equally unflattering themes. Few voters noticed. A general election is not a public education exercise, but a battle for power. Johnson was not obliged to appear for an interrogation and did not do so. The outcome of the election showed that he made the right decision. Voters are not bothered if leaders do not appear on interview programmes that most people do not watch.

Johnson's absence was part of a wider campaign strategy. He had one message: wherever he went he repeated the words 'Let's get Brexit done.' Although Brexit was far from done, there was a scintilla of truth in the campaign's only memorable slogan. In visual stunts, video monologues on social media and interviews with less aggressive interviewers, Johnson's sole purpose was to convey that message and not to make big mistakes on other fronts. In contrast to Labour's manifesto, the Tory programme was tiny. Johnson wanted to win by promising to get Brexit done. Corbyn campaigned as if Brexit was a peripheral issue. Swinson's Brexit message, as far as it was heard, seemed illiberal and confused. Johnson had the stage to himself and he chose carefully which parts of it he occupied.

The campaign was viewed through the prism of the recent past. Tory strategists were nervy because of what had happened in 2017, when most polls suggested Theresa May was heading for victory. Even when the polls consistently pointed to a decent majority for Johnson, Tory strategists did not dare to believe them. Conversely, some Labour strategists were more confident than they should have been, on the basis of their performance in 2017. Their manifesto made no impact on the polls. Corbyn's campaign did not come to life. Yet on the evening of 12 December 2019, as the UK awaited the outcome of the exit poll, there were still some senior Tories and senior Labour figures who at least contemplated the possibility of a hung parliament or a tiny Tory majority.

The outcome was obvious from the beginning, but many chose not to see it. Campaign strategists looked back to the 2017 election for clues as to what would happen next, only to discover that the past can be a dangerously unreliable guide. In a Brexit election, Johnson won a triumphant eighty-seat majority against weak and divided opponents. The 2017 election had provided no guidance whatsoever. On the night of his triumph, Johnson was restrained. As a former journalist, he understood how he would be reported and therefore how he would be perceived. His victory was the result of traditional Labour seats in the north of England and the Midlands switching to the Conservatives. The dramatic transformation of the political landscape was mainly a result of Brexit. Wisely, Johnson noted that some people had 'lent' their votes to the Conservatives, and said that the party would now work tirelessly to retain their new support. The 2014 Scottish independence referendum had killed off support for Labour in its once-mighty political stronghold; the Brexit referendum had destroyed support for Labour in its English and Welsh heartlands. Unintentionally, in holding two referendums, David Cameron had created the space for a huge Tory victory. Cameron had inadvertently created Prime Minister Johnson, just as Edward Heath had unintentionally propelled Margaret Thatcher to the top.[8]

But it also took the resolute swagger of Johnson and Cummings to make the most of the space. They risked being cast aside in a hung parliament, or formalizing a split in their party that would wreck their plans. Instead it was the Brexit Party that was destroyed, emerging with no seats and several of its senior figures declaring their support for Johnson's Tories.

———

The election was the biggest transformation of the political landscape since 1997. Like Tony Blair, Johnson was both triumphant and facing a daunting challenge. Blair saw himself as the custodian of Labour's new support amongst previously Conservative-supporting voters and the newspapers they read. This made him wary of tax rises while desperate to improve public services. Johnson needed to be an interventionist to boost his new base of electoral support, without alienating the Thatcherites in his party.

His early decisions and declarations reflected the tensions of leading a party that had been brought up on Thatcherite economics – an upbringing given a turbocharged boost under the confused leadership of David Cameron. Some of Johnson's early moves were to the left of what Blair and Brown would have done in 1997. In January 2020 the government intervened to save the ailing airline Flybe from closure, on the grounds that domestic flights connected the regions of the UK. New Labour would not have dared make such a move in the early years of its rule, fearing that Middle England and the mighty newspapers would detect a return to the 1970s. There were murmurs of criticism in parts of the right-wing media, but little else. Johnson was on his honeymoon, seen to be 'getting Brexit done'. That was enough for quite a lot of the media. A few weeks later Flybe did stop operating, an early casualty of coronavirus, as flying came to a halt. Nonetheless, Johnson had sought to save it. During the same month the government took Arriva Rail North into public ownership, another move that early New Labour would have been terrified to make. Overcrowding and unreliability had become the norm for those dependent on trains in the north of England. The government took responsibility.

The role and accountability of government in the delivery of public services had been more or less taboo for decades in the UK. The fashion for fragmentation and government keeping its distance reached a peak with the publication of the coalition's original NHS reforms, published in 2011 and taking modified legislative form a year later.

This was a useful break with prime ministerial orthodoxy. Unusually for a British prime minister, Johnson recognized that the key to decent public-service delivery comprised clear lines of accountability. Based on his experience as Mayor of London, he knew that when individuals or bodies were held directly responsible for public transport, the services improved and became more affordable. During the leadership contest in 2019 he noted at one of the many hustings, when contemplating the chaos of the UK's railways, that the key was always to know 'whose backside you can kick'. He was moving close to Tony Benn's test: 'who is accountable to whom?'

Fearing any echo of Bennite Labour, Blair and Brown rarely explored the theme of accountability in public services. Cameron echoed Blair's commitment to 'reform'. They sought the empowerment of public-service users, but the endless mediating agencies meant that users became disempowered. One of the more valid reasons for Johnson's initial disdain for the BBC was the number of managers only loosely connected to the output, without clear lines of accountability.

Soon Johnson and Cummings wondered why they had so little control over what happened in the NHS, when they would be held to account for its performance. A huge quango, NHS England, took many of the key strategic decisions. *The Times* newspaper published a leaked government paper in February 2020 in which it dared to challenge the assumptions of the non-elected quango: 'The proposals NHS England brought forward were designed in a different parliament than the one we have now, with an underlying principle to avoid an extensive reorganisation ... they do not deliver the fundamental reform of the 2012 Act that we and the system believe will be needed.'9

Johnson had entered Number Ten with a clearer sense of the need for investment in infrastructure – and for the government to take responsibility for public services – than any prime minister in decades, particularly Thatcher, Major, Cameron and May.

Yet Brexit was not done. For all the optimistic hyperactivity in Number Ten in relation to public services and much more, Brexit remained an unresolved challenge. In a speech in February 2020 Johnson laid out his terms for the forthcoming trade deal with the EU. The context was already fraught. The entire trade deal with the EU, as far as Johnson was concerned, was meant to be agreed by the end of 2020. He thought this to be possible on the bizarre basis that the EU and the UK began in the same place, and so a new agreement could be reached speedily. This would have had some logic to it if Johnson shared the EU's vision for a deal, but he did not. In his speech he declared: 'We have made our choice: we want a comprehensive free trade agreement, similar to Canada's. But in the very unlikely event that we do not succeed, then our trade will have to be based on our existing Withdrawal Agreement with the EU … The question is whether we agree a trading relationship with the EU comparable to Canada's – or more like Australia's.'[10]

Australia did not have a deal with the EU, so Johnson had opted for a euphemism. 'No deal' became an 'Australia'-style arrangement. The UK was back where it was before the signing of the Withdrawal Agreement in 2019, getting ready for the possibility of 'no deal'.

Johnson's leadership style after the election was not greatly different from his approach before he won a big majority. In relation to Europe he acted as if he believed his own earlier narrative: that by being assertive he had achieved what he called an 'oven-ready deal'. His assertiveness this time took many forms, above all as self-destructive impatience. As the negotiations opened, Johnson insisted that he would seek no extension.

He was in a rush, while Cummings was in an angry rush. Having taken on the European Union, Cummings now wanted to confront the BBC, the judiciary and the Civil Service. As Johnson had agreed to give Cummings full control over ministerial special advisers, he had no choice but to be as assertive with his own government as he had been during the early phase of the EU trade talks. Resignations followed.

Until the outbreak of coronavirus this was still the Brexit government, led with the bravado that characterized the Vote Leave campaign in the 2016 referendum. By early 2020 the Brexit Cabinet committee consisted only of those who had campaigned for Brexit. Johnson's main negotiator, David Frost, was a Brexit-supporting adviser, convinced that the UK would flourish alone in the world, seemingly unaware that the EU was much the bigger of the two parties and therefore the body holding the cards in the negotiations. Frost espoused a naive jingoism. On the whole, the key jobs in government went to the Brexiteers. Sajid Javid's successor as Chancellor, Rishi Sunak, had been a Brexiteer as well as an early backer of Johnson in the leadership contest. As far as Johnson was concerned, the Brexit government wanted only those committed to the cause.

Another pattern of his leadership was evident at this time: the overwhelming impression was one of fearful disorder. Before the election, senior Tory MPs lost the whip. After the election, special advisers lived in fear. The former Permanent Secretary at the Home Office was by no means the only senior civil servant alarmed at the revolutionary fervour in Number Ten. Yet Johnson was not a visible figure as the early revolution took shape. Even when forces beyond his control added to the apocalyptic mood, he was nowhere to be seen. In February 2020, when coronavirus spread around the globe and floods of biblical proportions were wrecking homes, Johnson was not seen for more than a week. The political showman chose not to perform.

By lying low, Johnson broke another unwritten law of leadership. Other prime ministers felt the need to be seen at times of crisis, whatever the context. Blair decided he was obliged to comment when a popular character in *Coronation Street* was jailed. Cameron was similarly ubiquitous. Earlier prime ministers were highly visible, as if they were presidents. Thatcher could not bear holidays and would be back in the fray as soon as possible, sometimes cutting short her unwanted vacations. Brown ended his short break when there was a minor outbreak of foot-and-mouth disease infecting cattle in 2007. But in the first few weeks after his December election victory, Johnson was nowhere to be seen.

Part of this was a mature calculation. The government had a big majority. There was no need to feed the Westminster media machine around the clock. Ministers would not play the game. They would get on with the hard work rather than explaining what they were supposed to be doing. This was sensible, given the vast number of media outlets. A minister committed to giving interviews on breakfast programmes alone would be inundated with requests. Understandably, the Johnson regime decided to boycott some of these programmes.

There was another reasonable explanation: Johnson's only leadership experience was as Mayor of London. He won a second term and ruled the city with his limited powers by delegating widely. To deploy one of Harold Wilson's favourite metaphors, Johnson did not feel the need to be goalkeeper, defender, midfielder and striker.

He had a team that he more or less trusted; others were dealing with the floods, the spread of the virus and the start of trade talks with the EU. But Wilson was at the exhausted end of his leadership when he insisted that his colleagues could score some of the goals. At the beginning he played in virtually every position. More significantly, being Mayor of London is like running a lower-league football team compared with the demands of being prime minister.

A discordant theme took shape. Johnson's Number Ten sought to be omnipotent, challenging even the might of the Treasury, while the prime minister insisted that he could delegate to his ministerial team. There was a contradiction in Johnson's desire to be laid-back and yet overwhelmingly dominant at the same time. His ministers were inevitably confused, seeking to please a uniquely powerful Number Ten and then finding that they were being asked to take command in relation to specific issues, or to be the public face of the government.

Another reason for Johnson's erratic and contradictory approach to leadership follows the pattern of previous modern prime ministers. He had not been leader of the Opposition – a role that is in many ways the best preparation for being prime minister. Theresa May had not been tested in that role, either, and it showed. Johnson had been a poor Foreign Secretary and that was his sole experience of national government. A leader of the Opposition has to respond nimbly to a range of events while managing a frontbench team, the parliamentary party, the wider party and seeking to satisfy an increasingly noisy and fragmented media. These demands are closer to those facing a prime minister, though nowhere near as testing. Still, the rhythms are similar.

May struggled with the wild oscillations. Being a long-serving Home Secretary was no preparation. Johnson struggled too, misjudging when to play a leading role and the form it should take. He was also poor at managing a team, as May had been. Ironically, May was the prime minister he resembled most in some respects. Both were political loners. Both turned to their chosen special advisers to give them ideological purpose they themselves did not possess, and the language to articulate their crusades. Nick Timothy devised the phrase 'the good that government can do' for May, as well as 'Brexit means Brexit', a phrase that she repeated like a machine. Cummings gave Johnson the election-winning slogan 'Let's get Brexit done' and arrived in Number Ten with a thousand radical ideas every day. The media became obsessed with Cummings, just as it had been with Alastair Campbell in the Blair era. But in the end Johnson decided how much space Cummings could have, just as May did with Timothy. Johnson controlled Cummings and not the other way round. Johnson had to answer for whatever happened in his government. Cummings ruled only if Johnson was content to be held to account for what followed.

Cummings had some input over policy, although he did not always prevail. He was an opponent of HS2, the costly high-speed rail project, but Johnson gave it the go-ahead. Cummings was more interested in shaking up process – the means rather than the ends. He had loathed the education establishment when he worked for Michael Gove at the Department of Education. One of his many angry conclusions was that the department would have been far more effective if the numbers working there had been cut by two-thirds.[11] Cummings may well have been right. Government departments were never knowingly understaffed. But he got too worked up, dismissing the wider establishment as the 'blob' when specialists dared to question his or Gove's crusading zeal. Cummings was less precise about the ends.

This incoherence also applied to his approach to the creation of 'free schools'. At the Department of Education, Cummings liked the idea of schools being liberated from the loathed bureaucrats, and yet prescribed what should be taught for virtually every minute of the school day, leaving teachers less 'free' than before. He was the same under Johnson. He had control over special advisers and, as a result, sought to centralize power in Number Ten. Advisers were sacked or moved to other ministers if they were not behaving as Cummings required. He sought 'weirdos' to join him in Number Ten, to think the unthinkable. He viewed the Civil Service, the EU, Parliament and parts of the Conservative Party with impatient disdain. Once again, shaking up the means to the ends sucked up Cummings' energy. The 'ends' were unclear: a hard Brexit that would have a severe impact on the economy of the north of England, combined with economic policies aimed at reviving the north of England, being one vivid example. Johnson looked on admiringly, in the same way May listened to Timothy as if his ideas would take her to the Promised Land. She did so until she sacked him after the 2017 election. Advisers are both mighty and precarious.

Nick Timothy was an incomparably more substantial and original thinker than Cummings, but Johnson felt he could not do without his wayward guru. Even when Cummings had appeared to break the government's own coronavirus lockdown rules, Johnson's instinct was to stand by him. It emerged in May 2020 that Cummings had driven to his parents' home in Durham and also taken an excursion several miles from there, at a point in the lockdown when most voters were fastidiously obeying government instructions to 'stay at home'. A significant number of Tory MPs called on Cummings to go. Opinion polls suggested a slump in support for the Conservatives. Yet Johnson and senior ministers immediately defended Cummings, retrospectively rewriting lockdown rules in order to justify the adviser's trip to the North East. Increasingly out of his depth, Johnson concluded he could not do without his advisor.

The decision to keep Cummings lay firmly with Johnson. He was willing to risk all in order to retain the services of an intimidating maverick whom he wrongly regarded as a genius. Tame ministers tweeted contorted messages of support because of the hold that Johnson had over them. Cummings was powerful but only because Johnson let him be. Johnson's early defiance and the ministers speaking up for Cummings were vivid examples of what a Prime Minister could attempt to get away with when he or she had recently won an election with a big majority. Although the furore was triggered by the conduct of Cummings, this was a saga about Johnson, his chaotic style of leadership and his lack of what Gordon Brown used to call a 'moral compass'. When Johnson arrived in Number Ten he did not know what to do or say. He chose to let Cummings give him the words and some of the deeds. He also allowed Cummings to rule special advisers across government with a regime of fear. Johnson chose to make Cummings powerful. Cummings' power did not determine how Johnson responded to his apparent misdeeds.

———

With the eruption of coronavirus, the challenges of leadership changed beyond recognition. Even huge events, such as a big election win and Brexit, became ancient history. The priorities and dynamics of Johnson's leadership were turned on their head just as speedily as the virus spread. All the assumptions that had excited his entourage before the crisis no longer applied. The prime minister who had broken most prime ministerial norms in his bid to 'get Brexit done' had no choice but to be more orthodox as he sought to guide the UK through a real-life horror film, in which no one could see what form the end would take.

Ministers now appeared on the BBC's *Today* programme, having boycotted it since the election on the instructions of Johnson's advisers. When the virus struck, Johnson accepted scrutiny of his government in daily press conferences, having been more or less invisible between the election and the spread of the pandemic. There were attempts to explain what was happening and to seek some form of consensus rather than crush opponents and then lie low, again the opposite to Johnson's post-general-election leadership.

Suddenly the government needed, and valued at times, the relatively sober reporting and analysis of the BBC. Before the crisis one of Johnson's advisers had briefed *The Sunday Times* that the government would 'whack' the BBC – an aggressive metaphor indicative of the hunger for confrontation in parts of Johnson's team.[12]

The attacks on the Civil Service from Number Ten's advisers also largely stopped, as ministers relied on Whitehall to rise to the challenge of the pandemic. More widely, instead of framing politics as an eternal battle with enemies on every front, Johnson and his senior ministers liaised with Opposition frontbenchers, business leaders and trade-union leaders. Again this was in marked contrast to their approach to Brexit and to virtually all other policy areas.

Yet it took some time for the newish prime minister – fairly laid-back about the demands of leadership, not feeling the need to prove himself after winning an election, and with a largely supportive media – to recognize the urgency of the situation. He and his government were behind the curve in the crucial early weeks. Considerable time that could have been spent preparing for the crisis was squandered. The World Health Organization first warned of the risk of a deadly global pandemic in mid-January, by which point coronavirus was spreading rapidly in China and parts of Asia. Yet Johnson's advisers spent much of February distracted by their familiar fights with the Civil Service, the judiciary and the BBC. They were still enjoying themselves far too much. When Parliament took a half-term recess, Johnson disappeared from view for a week in the middle of the month. He opted to stay put in Chevening, a grace-and-favour home in Kent, unseen and unheard in public. He did not preside over his first emergency Cobra meeting to discuss the crisis until 3 March.

Even as the scale of the emergency became apparent in the UK, Johnson's response was erratic. For most of the first half of March the official advice was simply to wash your hands for twenty seconds: the time it takes to sing 'Happy Birthday' twice. On 12 March, as countries across Europe and the world closed schools, restaurants, bars and shops and introduced lockdowns and travel bans, the government merely advised that those who were ill with coronavirus symptoms should self-isolate for seven days. At the same time it announced that it would stop testing all except those with the most severe symptoms, in defiance of international medical opinion. Indeed, the testing programme was incoherent at this crucial phase. Journalists were briefed that the government's strategy was no longer to stop the spread of the virus, but merely to 'delay' its spread in pursuit of a goal of 'herd immunity', which it said might be achieved once 60 per cent of the population had been infected.

That strategy imploded four days later when the government did a U-turn, requiring all households to quarantine for fourteen days if any one member exhibited symptoms, and advising the public to stay away from pubs and restaurants. Johnson insisted that he had been guided by science all along and that the advice had changed. But he did not explain *how* it had changed, or why Britain's science differed so much from that of the rest of the world. Instead, he insisted the government was following its planned timetable. He was not being a political teacher making sense of what appeared to be haphazard. Even after this U-turn, the strategy was opaque.

Schools remained open for far longer than in other countries. They finally shut on the same day that pubs, restaurants, cafés and leisure centres were ordered to close. Before then, despite calls for social distancing, large crowds visited parks and public spaces across the country. Only on 23 March did Johnson finally announce a partial lockdown, instructing most people to stay at home for much of each day. The virus took hold in the UK later than other European countries, but a libertarian instinct in Johnson and some of his colleagues, combined with early indecisiveness over the most effective response to the threat, meant that the UK did not benefit from having the extra time to prepare.

He was imprecise throughout. Only 'essential workers' should be going to work, he declared in a televised broadcast watched by millions when the partial lockdown was announced. People should not pay visits to other homes, except to call on 'vulnerable' people. But who was 'vulnerable'? What was deemed 'essential'?

Huge financial packages were drawn up to help those in staff posts, but the self-employed were left waiting for days before hearing of equivalent assistance. Too often Johnson preferred to deploy repeated phrases, as if the government was simply fighting another campaign. He would do 'whatever it takes'; the UK would 'be turning the tide' soon. What did that metaphor mean, when no one could tell how long it would be before life would return to what it had vaguely resembled before? Once again he was blustering in order to get by.

The challenges of the virus would have been an almost unbearable strain for any of the modern prime ministers: a health crisis and an economic emergency raging simultaneously. But most prime ministers, with their capacity for hard work and their eye for future dangers, would have been alert to the virus earlier than Johnson was. They would have bombproofed their responses before unveiling them, in a way that Johnson did not. Indeed, when Gordon Brown and Tony Blair appeared separately on the BBC's *Today* programme in mid-March to reflect on the scale of the crisis, many commentators hailed their mastery of the detail. How perspectives change! Some of the same commentators had vilified Brown and Blair when they had been in power. Leaders move in and out of fashion long after their period of leadership comes to an end.

The arc of Johnson's leadership changed dramatically. From being a prime minister who could do more or less what he wanted, he faced a virus that took no notice of slogans or campaigning. The virus would respond only to the hard grind of around-the-clock government activity. This was an emergency for the long haul.

In his first post-election phase as prime minister, Johnson had become the showman who chose not to perform, rarely seen in public, not giving many interviews. Suddenly he had to perform in public every day, not as a showman, but as a leader responding to a seismic event. At the end of March he managed to combine the two approaches by catching the virus. The story dominated media coverage and yet Johnson partially disappeared once again, seen only for a time on video – unsurprisingly, not looking especially well. When he was moved briefly to intensive care at St Thomas' Hospital, his absence was a unique form of prime ministerial projection, highlighting the terrible dangers posed by the virus. Already under immense pressure, Johnson had the added burden of falling ill at a time when decisions were required speedily, based on a total mastery of the complex implications. The pressures were heightened when other senior ministers, advisers and top scientists also caught the virus. Coronavirus was not only the biggest challenge of leadership since 1945, but one being faced by leaders who were falling ill.

As a relatively inexperienced prime minister, Johnson led with some significant advantages. Although the NHS had been underfunded for ten years compared with health services in equivalent EU countries, it was still a national service. There had been chaotic attempts at reforming the NHS under David Cameron, resulting in confused lines of command, but it had not been dismantled entirely. A prime minister or a Health Secretary could pull levers and the system would respond. In March, when the scale of the emergency became apparent, ministers galvanized a nationwide response from the NHS. Grateful voters applauded hospital workers at prescribed times as they came to the rescue. The contrast with the US was especially marked, where a system reliant on private insurance struggled to deliver a service for all those who became dependent on it.

But the government's confused attitude to the importance of testing meant that the UK lagged far behind several other countries in its knowledge of who had the virus. In early April, Germany had tested more than 500,000 people. The UK had tested fewer than 10,000. Although polls suggested high levels of support for Johnson's leadership at a time of national emergency, this was becoming a huge trial for him. Why had he not taken action earlier, and what was he going to do about it? Did he know which levers to pull? Once again Johnson was being asked, as a matter of urgency, to use the full power of the state to get more testing done. On this issue he pledged to utilize the state to expand testing rapidly. Across the board Johnson's government was all about proving that the state could save lives – and the economy.

Here was the ultimate twist in Johnson's career of jagged patterns. Brexit had been the passionate cause of small-state Thatcherites seeking to complete Margaret Thatcher's revolution by shrinking the role of government even further. Johnson rose to the top because of his support for Brexit. Yet in the spring of 2020, in response to the virus, he became the most statist prime minister since the Second World War, borrowing hundreds of billions of pounds to keep the economy afloat and taking powers to force people to suspend the order of their lives. He was acting well to the left of any proposal espoused by Jeremy Corbyn when he was Labour leader.

Economic rescue packages of impressive range were unveiled by Rishi Sunak. He got deserved praise for the substance and the presentation. Johnson deserves praise, too, for the degree to which he was willing to let the state come to the rescue. Given the dominance of Johnson's Number Ten over the entire government, Sunak could not have acted without its permission and encouragement. Johnson's misguided wariness of the so-called 'nanny state', as expressed in many of his newspaper columns, led him to be slow at imposing restrictions on people's behaviour. His inattentiveness arguably delayed the UK's response to the emergency, so that the country lacked the equipment to test for the virus, and the ventilators to keep patients alive. In contrast, his economic interventionism was at least on the same scale as that in other countries. His more ardent Brexit supporters would have to wait for their dream of a much smaller state – a dream that Johnson showed little sign of sharing.

———

Most aspiring prime ministers have some time to plan how they would rule, in advance of entering Number Ten. Even Johnson, not one of life's most ardent planners, had a concept of how he would lead (based around his experience as Mayor of London) and how he would deliver Brexit. But leaders cannot plan for the unexpected. Often they are defined by their response to crises that they cannot anticipate.

With an energetic flourish, Johnson had achieved his long-held ambition to acquire the crown. With a calculated ruthlessness, he had made the crown secure by winning an election. He had seen off Theresa May, the incumbent who had to be removed; Nigel Farage, the leader of the Brexit Party, who had fleetingly threatened the existence of the Conservatives; Jeremy Corbyn, the leader of the Opposition; and even those who doubted Brexit within his own party. Then the unforeseen struck and he was overwhelmed by a single challenge. Coronavirus was the one force that did not recognize a big majority or the aura of unconstrained power. Almost out of the blue, Johnson faced a more formidable and deadly foe. In a dark and gruesome twist, he became the first prime minister in modern times who would be judged partly by the number of deaths in the UK on his watch.

CONCLUSION

There is a leadership crisis in the UK. Leaders, or potential leaders, seek to rule in an era when right-wing populists are flourishing, globalization generates deep insecurities and Brexit presents a seemingly never-ending set of explosive demands. Yet none appear to possess the communication skills, the depth, guile, ability to manage parties and the capacity to espouse credible policies that chime with values or deeply held convictions. Most of those contemplating putting themselves forward show a shortage of qualifications, though no lack of self-confidence. A successful TV interview, well received on Twitter, is enough to get some politicians wondering whether they can be the next prime minister. The demands of leadership are high. The bar is set low.

The decline in the quality of potential leaders can be traced in the leadership contests of the modern era. In 1975 the former Cabinet minister Margaret Thatcher took on the former prime minister, Edward Heath. Willie Whitelaw, another weighty former Cabinet minister, was seen as a possible leader at the time and entered the contest in a later round. The following year, when Harold Wilson resigned, the candidates in the leadership contest included James Callaghan, Michael Foot, Roy Jenkins, Anthony Crosland, Denis Healey and Tony Benn, all mighty figures in their different ways. Fast-forward to the summer of 2019 and those contemplating becoming a candidate to be the next prime minister included Esther McVey, Andrea Leadsom, Sajid Javid, Jeremy Hunt, Boris Johnson and Dominic Raab. Whatever the qualities of these individuals, even their most ardent admirers would not claim that they possessed the depth, conviction and experience of those engaged in Tory and Labour battles during 1975 and 1976.

Recent Labour contests also descended to levels of banality that would have horrified the Labour candidates in 1976. In 2015, after Labour's defeat at the general election, vacuous phrases such as 'We turned the page back... now it's time to turn the page forward' were prominent – an attempt to disguise ideological confusion and insecurity. As candidates agonized over whether to accept media claims that over-spending by the last Labour government had been a cause of the financial crash of 2008, Jeremy Corbyn entered the fray and declared, without qualification, that the Labour government had not spent enough. He won a landslide.

Corbyn did more to change politics than any leader of the Opposition in modern times. He created a mass-membership party, at a time when membership of parties is in alarming decline. He moved his party to the left and, in doing so, widened the scope of the national political debate. Before Corbyn became Labour leader, *Newsnight* would often invite onto the programme a panel of commentators, all agreeing that Labour was doomed until it broadly endorsed George Osborne's economic policies. After the rise of Corbyn, a range of voices from the left became part of the national debate. In depriving Theresa May of her majority in the 2017 election, Corbyn also transformed the dynamics of Brexit and challenged assumptions, in parts of his party and the media, that if Labour moved to the left it would be slaughtered.

These were significant achievements. Even so, Corbyn never wanted to be leader during his decades as a backbench MP, and it showed when he soared to the top. Of all the eruptions in British politics – Brexit, the dominance of the SNP in Scotland, a rare peacetime coalition – Corbyn's rise from backbench MP to leader is the most remarkable. He had few qualifications for leadership. Although he could command huge, doting audiences, he was not a political teacher, rarely explaining why he espoused various policy positions. He was not greatly interested in policy detail, or in how to translate policies into accessible messages. He was more pragmatic than caricatures of him allowed, especially in relation to Brexit, and yet he contrived to make expediency seem like a weak and pathetic 'fudge'. He was not interested in managing colleagues, or in spending every waking hour facing the ceaseless demands of leadership. Often Corbyn opted for invisibility or silence as issues erupted around him. He was only regularly seen on national TV leaving his house, looking furious at the number of journalists and cameras gathered outside. The fury was understandable and was not typical of his emollient personality. But the art of leadership is to hide one's annoyance in such weird situations. The most effective leaders are partly artists. Corbyn was no artist and led his party to a calamitous fourth successive defeat in December 2019.

Oddly, as the quality of leaders and potential leaders declined, the focus on them intensified. The door-stepping of Corbyn on a regular basis was one example of the new intensity. British politics has a presidential culture, without a president. The disjunction adds to the pressures on party leaders. Unlike presidents, or potential presidents, they have to lead and manage their parties. Their power is dependent on their parties and, if they become prime minister, they are accountable to Parliament, too. Since Thatcher – the era of the Iron Lady who was not for turning – there is a huge pressure on prime ministers to appear presidential, in command of all situations, when the constraints are such that they cannot be. Even Boris Johnson discovered during his honeymoon after his triumphant election victory in December 2019, that there were nightmarish dilemmas. With freakishly unconstrained power in early 2020, Johnson worried over what to do about HS2 (the high-speed rail project), the 5G contract with Huawei that President Trump angrily opposed and even the nature of the Brexit 'celebrations' that were to be officially sanctioned on 31 January when the UK left the EU.

Indeed, what is most striking about modern prime ministers is not how strong they are, but how weak. Or at least most of them felt weak and tormented a lot of the time. With the partial exception of Margaret Thatcher, they agonized over the limits of their power. 'What do we do now?', 'How do we get out of this?', 'How can the BBC be leading with that story?', 'We're screwed' – these are the panic-stricken questions and proclamations that punctuate prime ministerial lives.

There is a dangerous, darkly comical mismatch between widely held perceptions of mightily arrogant prime ministers, loftily indifferent to voters' lives, and the sense of toiling fragility at the summit of supposed power. The near-impotent toil is a gift for political outsiders. The likes of Nigel Farage can cry, 'Betrayal' from the safety of the campaign trail. Yet, to follow the Farage example, it was not that Theresa May sought to let down his ardent Brexit-supporting followers; indeed, she worked sleeplessly to deliver for them. There were many other reasons why Brexit did not take the shape that Farage claimed to seek.

This prevailing mood of fearful paralysis was unavoidable for the modern prime ministers who led in hung parliaments or with tiny majorities. From 1974 to 1979 Harold Wilson and Jim Callaghan manoeuvred endlessly to keep their fragile administrations in place, losing key votes, viewing colleagues with justified wariness. John Major lost his small majority by the end of his rule, twisting and turning to secure parliamentary support for the Maastricht Treaty and other policies – a prime ministerial trauma that was a mere walk in the park, compared with the Brexit saga that was to follow. When Theresa May called an early election and lost her majority, she faced a period of near-impotence. Johnson lost virtually every vote in the Commons when he first became Prime Minister.

Even those prime ministers with big majorities are alert to the precariousness of their position. Soon after winning a landslide in 1966, Harold Wilson saw enemies all around him. The seemingly self-confident Margaret Thatcher did not always feel secure. In his brilliant memoir *Cold Cream*, Thatcher's former adviser Ferdinand Mount chronicles her fears about calling an election in June 1983. Nervily she put the case for a postponement to her advisers. She did not want to face the risk of an election. She panicked again in 1987, falling out with the likes of her close ally Norman Tebbit in her alarm at the way the campaign was going. Tony Blair, with his landslide majorities, had been so used to losing elections in the 1980s that he had a similar fear of losing. 'The Tories are only sleeping... they'll be back,' he warned in his conference speech in 1998, when Labour was even further ahead in the polls than Thatcher was in 1983 and 1987. But Blair always worried that it would take very little for Middle England to return to the Conservatives. That fear weighed heavily on one of his prime ministerial shoulders; the intense pressure from Gordon Brown weighed on the other.

Thatcher's faith in the poll tax was partly driven by a fear of the impact of big rises in local rates, the system in place before the poll tax. Properties were being re-valued at the time and, in many Conservative-held seats, values had soared. Thatcher's solution was to scrap the property-based tax, assuming that the measure would be popular. Blair's support for the war in Iraq was based partly on a sense that his coalition of support would collapse if he did not support the United States. David Cameron's pledge to hold a referendum on the UK's membership of the EU stemmed from a fear of defections from his party to UKIP; the referendum was not a pledge made with an Etonian swagger. Fear, rather than arrogance, forms the backdrop to much policy-making. Prime ministers might affect crusading evangelism, but quite often this is an attempt to disguise timid insecurity.

In all cases, democracy constrains. Arguably it constrains too much, inadvertently giving vast amounts of space to the posturing 'strong leader' from the outside. The impact of local elections, by-elections, the prospect of a looming general election and the composition of the Commons all play their part in what a prime minister feels he or she can do. In some cases a single by-election can trigger a fall. The Conservatives' defeat in the Eastbourne by-election in October 1990 played a significant part in the quickly forming avalanche that propelled Thatcher from power a month later. Modern prime ministers also led in an era of never-ending opinion polls and the rise of the focus group. They might have been seen as out of touch but, if anything, they were too in touch with the public mood. They could be in touch to the point of paralysis.

Many in the media would argue that it is their job to hold power to account. They are less effective at highlighting the limits of power, and are also fickle in their levels of scrutiny. Read most columnists on Theresa May before the early election in 2017 and, when she was riding high in the polls, there was much talk of the 'May era' and even 'May-ism'. When she leapt out of fashion after the election, she became a disaster area. In the early years of the Lib-Con coalition much of the media hailed two parties working together to 'save the country'. In reality, decisions were being taken that were virtually to kill off the Liberal Democrats and make Cameron a fatal advocate when he called the 2016 Brexit referendum.

There are several reasons why the weightiness of actual or potential leaders has declined, at least in the UK Parliament. Scotland has produced some formidable leaders, including Nicola Sturgeon and, although untested by power, Ruth Davidson, the former leader of the Scottish Conservatives. The fashion when selecting candidates for the Westminster Parliament is on 'localism'. Candidates are more likely to be selected if they are from the constituency. For some trade unionists or councillors, becoming a Labour candidate is sometimes a reward for long service. There are equivalent rewards for local Conservatives. Any attempt to 'impose' a candidate is frowned upon, to the point where it is almost impossible for figures without credible local connections to become candidates in safe seats. The fashion might be admirable in some respects, but local parties are selecting candidates who might become ministers or even prime ministers. The ability to lead, or to represent their party at a national level, is rarely a criterion.

Probably some big figures are also deterred by the level of scrutiny in modern politics, preferring better-paid jobs in the City, the legal profession or the media. From Edward Heath to Roy Jenkins, Denis Healey and Tony Benn, the wartime generation ached to go into politics and to stay in politics, even when they were no longer in government.

Perhaps some are also deterred by the constraints of power. An owner of a big business will have more power than some ministers. Prime ministers can wield considerable power, but they must keep a party on board; win elections with majorities, or face a nightmare in a hung parliament; respond to a relentless around-the-clock media and social media; and, accept that some powers are now devolved to other elected bodies or quangos. They do not even have the power to set interest rates any more, although they are probably relieved that those decisions lie with the Bank of England. Everywhere there are obstacles – perhaps constraints that are necessary, but often frustrating for leaders wanting to lead.

No prime minister can ever relax on the domestic front, and most of the time prime ministers are miserable. Trips abroad are different. This is when power can become a pleasure – in locations where there is uncritical recognition of a prime minister's apparent greatness. The consequences of the red-carpet treatment can be dangerous. Only Heath and, to some extent, Wilson turned away from the intoxicating draw of a visit to a president in the US. Margaret Thatcher's genuinely warm and close relationship with President Reagan was a boost to her image in the UK and beyond. There she was a powerful world leader, with the US president hailing her with gushing sincerity. Her rapport with a US president had a big impact on the youthful Blair, observing vote-losing Labour leaders being given short shrift in the US. But even with Thatcher, the 'special relationship' was limited. At the start of the Falklands War, Reagan was ambiguous, not rushing to support his close ally, on whom he doted. Reagan was also friendly with the Argentinian junta that had become Thatcher's enemy. When the US attacked Grenada in October 1983 – more than a year after the two leaders' tensions over the Falklands – Reagan did not inform Thatcher in advance. She needed him much more than he needed her.

Blair's determination to show that he could work as closely with a Republican president as he had with President Clinton was the starting point for his moves towards the darkness of Iraq. Brown ached to be seen with Obama, whenever the opportunity arose, and yet there was little evidence that Obama yearned to spend too much time with Brown. Cameron was similarly smitten, regarding Obama's speech in London against Brexit, in the build-up to the 2016 referendum, as a great coup at the time. The evidence suggests that Obama's intervention boosted the Brexit campaign. Yet still the modern prime ministers could not resist the lure. May wooed President Trump, even though he was publicly dismissive of her Brexit negotiations and praised her more exuberant rival, Boris Johnson. Modern prime ministers liked to be seen as standing 'shoulder-to-shoulder' with US presidents. The glittering vindication of their place in the world compensated for the frenetic grind of making sense of their troubled leaderships in the UK. Their search for the glamour of power distorted UK foreign policy, often for the worse.

———

Vanity and ego play their part in the characters of modern prime ministers. This is unsurprising. Who could not be flattered by the attention and constant sense of historic significance that applies to their roles? In all cases there was also a sense of public duty and conviction. The essence of democracy is to fume about, or support, the consequences of prime ministerial conduct, but whatever our views on the individuals, modern prime ministers were motivated by a desire to make changes for the better.

In Wilson's much-derided final phase of leadership he won a referendum on Europe and introduced two substantial measures, the Sex Discrimination Act of 1975 and the Race Relations Act of 1976, enhancing work opportunities for women and ethnic minorities. Heath guided the UK into Europe in the first place, and displayed a dogged integrity in his tortuous negotiations with the trade unions. Callaghan left office with even greater levels of economic turmoil than Heath and Wilson, but he had to some extent controlled raging inflation. He had hopes of doing much more, but had no political space in which to act. Thatcher was the great game-changer, putting her radical instincts into effect, finding language to make them accessible and appealing. The UK in 1990 was unrecognizably different from the country in 1979 when she became prime minister – no wonder being forced out was such a blow for her, from which she did not recover. John Major was being sincere when he declared that he wanted to lead a country more at ease with itself. Subsequently he accepted that he failed in his mission, but the purpose was there. Blair and Brown introduced a mountain of life-enhancing changes, even if they sought to be far less radical from the left than Thatcher had been from the right. Cameron assumed, sincerely, that he was coming to the UK's rescue in forming a coalition in 2010. Although his government reformed speedily, May had more radical ambition than Cameron to make a leap away from Thatcherism, even if the precariously held convictions were acquired from her senior advisers. She was stifled by Brexit, but even she rationalized a historic purpose in her attempts to deliver the outcome of the 2016 referendum. I make this point not to imply preposterously that modern prime ministers were all saintly figures. The consequences of some of their policies and political outlooks were dire. There will always be intense disagreement about which were especially calamitous and which were beneficial, a timeless debate that is the essence of politics. I highlight the common desire to do good amongst this diverse group of flawed, often beleaguered prime ministers because the anti-politics mood is dangerously intense, fuelled by the lazy assumption that elected prime ministers were wilfully malevolent and indifferent to voters' concerns.

A colleague suggested that I compile a league table of modern prime ministers and put the unexpected at the top, in order to whip up a controversy or two. I could easily have done so, and with a hint of conviction. For their depth, range and seriousness of purpose, I could have put Edward Heath and Gordon Brown at the top. As reinforcement against the deliberately provoked mockery that would have followed, I would have cited Heath's epic moves to secure the UK's place in what was then the Common Market, and Brown's formidable response to the financial crash in 2008.

Such an act of provocation highlights the absurdity of the prime ministerial league table. There is a strong case for that unlikely duo, but they evidently lacked several of the qualifications for the impossible task of leadership and were prime ministers only fleetingly. The truth is that the modern prime ministers were all so different that it is, in some senses, remarkable they ended up in the same job.

They all passionately wanted to end up there. Modern prime ministers have one common quality: a ruthless hunger for the top job. They acquire the focused determination to become leader at different points in their careers, but at one stage or another they cast aside much else in life to win the leadership. For Wilson, Heath, Callaghan, Brown and May, ambition came early. Thatcher wanted to become leader only a few months before she actually did so, but once she had decided, she acted with hyper-energetic courage, challenging her old boss, Heath. John Major knew he was one of Thatcher's favourites and yet he was to the left of her. When she fell, he was ruthlessly ready to pitch for support across the broad church of his party. Blair knew that Brown wanted to be leader more than him and yet, when the opportunity arose, Blair took it with resolute focus. Brown also got there in the end because he wanted it far more than his weak-kneed colleagues of fleeting shallow ambition. Cameron was more or less ready when the time came, self-confident in his steely exuberance. May had done the hard grind of endless constituency visits while keeping a low profile on Brexit. When Cameron fell, she had done the work to win a leadership contest.

Perhaps the 2017 election will prove to be a turning point for future prime ministers. For the first time, once-powerful newspapers raged against a Labour leader and seemed to have no impact. After the election, Jeremy Corbyn was able to joke that he hoped the *Daily Mail* would attack him even more next time. Labour had performed far better than the commentariat had assumed or predicted. In that election, both Corbyn and May focused partly on the role of the state – the great taboo after Thatcher waved her wand and virtually silenced the pivotal debate. The Conservative manifesto was tonally contradictory, hailing backward-looking fox-hunting in one section and then, in a modernizing leap, articulating the 'good the state can do' in another. It advocated an industrial strategy and interventions in some markets. Labour's manifesto was closer to the programmes of social democrats in northern Europe, implying that the state could be a benevolent force, with its proposed national education service and incremental nationalizations.

In the outcome of the 2017 election it felt as if the rules that had governed British politics for decades were changing once again. Voters were stirring, and had been since the 2008 crash. And then in the elections for the European Parliament in May 2019 voters punished both the Conservative and Labour parties in relation to Brexit. The Brexit Party soared. The Liberal Democrats returned to the fray. The Green Party made waves. The SNP topped the poll in Scotland. The 2017 general election was an affirmation of the two-party system. By 2019, the two bigger UK parties were in Brexit-related crisis.

Only at the end of the year was there a resolution of sorts. Johnson secured a Brexit deal and managed to call an election with the theme 'Let's get Brexit done.' He won a big majority and yet, paradoxically, the pattern became more fractured. His majority was won on the back of gains in Labour strongholds. The Liberal Democrats were slaughtered and Corbyn more than undid the gains he had made in 2017.

There had been plenty of signs of the unruly times: the inconclusive 2010 election, the rare peacetime coalition, the stormy referendum in Scotland and, of course, the Brexit referendum. There were more signs to come, with new parties being formed and – in the case of the Brexit Party – becoming popular immediately in the summer of 2019 only to collapse in the general election at the end of the year. Leaders are slow to respond to changing times, instinctively using the past as their guide, even when all the evidence suggests that the assumptions of the past no longer apply. Most of them come up against mountainous obstacles. Rising to the very top, they feel special. They are part of a small group that has realized their ambition to lead. Then the Shakespearean themes take hold, and the prime ministers struggle with what they soon discover to be the wretched powerlessness of power.

NOTES

1 Harold Wilson

1 Ben Pimlott, *Harold Wilson*, HarperCollins, 1993

2 Labour won 301 seats, four more than the Conservatives. The Conservatives won 37.9 per cent of the vote compared to Labour's 37.2 per cent.

3 Tony Benn, *Against the Tide: Diaries, 1973–77*, Hutchinson, 1989, p.114

4 Roy Jenkins, *A Life at the Centre*, Macmillan, 1991, p.365

5 Bernard Donoughue, *The Heat of the Kitchen*, Politico's Publishing, 2003

6 See the following chapter on Edward Heath.

7 In October 1974 Labour won an overall majority of four.

8 See the David Cameron chapter. This was a highly significant difference with Wilson. Cameron hoped to avoid an internal split, but that put much greater weight on his 'renegotiation' with the EU.

9 Healey never did change his mind and remained a critic of Wilson for the rest of his life. He much preferred working with Jim Callaghan, Wilson's successor. Michael Foot was similar, being curiously scathing for a writer and politician capable of insightful and counter-intuitive empathy. Other Cabinet ministers came to realize Wilson's formidable achievements in what was often a dark context.

10 Barbara Castle, interview with the author, *New Statesman*, February 2000; available online. By then Castle was almost blind and yet was exuberant in her energetic and politically engaged mischievousness. Wilson liked and admired her. He also managed her smartly. I interviewed Castle during New Labour's first term, when Tony Blair was walking on water. She was also perceptive about the limitations of Blair's political project.

11 The story is related in Joe Haines' compelling memoir, *Glimmers of Twilight*, Politico's, 2003. The recollections of Haines and Donoughue in their various books and diaries are vivid, brilliantly written and almost Shakespearean in their tragicomic evocations.

12 Haines writes that Marcia Williams claimed to have had a brief affair with Wilson in the 1950s. She denied the affair and remained friends with Wilson's wife, Mary, after Wilson died.

13 Bernard Donoughue writes in *The Heat of the Kitchen* that Marcia Williams was another who told him on the eve of the February 1974 election that she did not expect, or want, Wilson to win. She wanted him away from the stressful exhaustion of the political stage. For her, Wilson was a human being as well as an aspirant prime minister. She had seen a human being at the end of his tether.

14 Harold Wilson, *Memoirs: The Making of a Prime Minister*, Michael Joseph, 1986, p.34

15 A fear of devaluation partly explained Gordon Brown's tentative support for the single currency when he was shadow chancellor up until the 1997 election. Independence of the Bank of England, implemented in the immediate aftermath of the 1997 election, addressed his fear and, under the influence of his senior adviser, Ed Balls, Brown became an opponent of the UK joining the euro.

16 The Conservative-supporting newspapers reverted to type, but arguably more shocking was the way in which the BBC joined in the bullying of Wilson – an early example of the BBC feeling compelled to join the political fashions of the time, as defined by the newspapers. This was not bias of a partisan nature, but bias in favour of what was fashionable. The documentary *Yesterday's Men*, broadcast soon after the 1970 election, is the most vivid example. It portrayed Wilson and much of his frontbench team as a bunch

of losers who were out of touch with the times. This was the team planning to fight the next election. Wilson was justifiably furious.

17 Speech at a May Day rally in London, 4 May 1969

18 He did so with the author in 2006 at a hotel in Nottingham during a prime ministerial trip to the city. I listed the large number of aspirant leaders in Wilson's Cabinets, compared to the one who had wanted Blair's job from the beginning. For understandable reasons, he agreed with me that there were advantages in having six or seven rivals, all formidable in their different ways and yet all of them cancelling each other out. Brown was more determinedly wilful than Wilson's ambitious Cabinet ministers.

19 Tony Benn, *Against the Tide: Diaries*, p.397

20 Giles Radice's book *Friends and Rivals* (Little, Brown, 2002) brilliantly shows how Roy Jenkins, Denis Healey and Tony Crosland, and their respective supporters, could not agree on which of the trio should become the candidate for Labour's social-democratic wing. In the 1976 leadership contest they all stood, and all almost certainly would have done if Wilson had left earlier.

21 Tony Benn, *Against the Tide*, p.394

22 Hansard, 24 May 1995

23 Roy Jenkins' *A Life at the Centre* has several unexpectedly flattering references to Wilson's leadership, as well as quite a few critical ones. Away from the intensity of the internal party battles, Jenkins saw how impossible it all must have been for a leader. Perhaps his own fraught leadership of the SDP lent additional personal perspective.

2 Edward Heath

1 Edward Heath, *The Course of My Life*, Hodder & Stoughton, 1998, p.31

2 Ibid., p.179

3 Ibid., p.194

4 In a powerful speech in November 2018 Gordon Brown compared Macmillan's extensive preparations for membership of the Common Market to the shallow approach of Cameron and May, the two prime ministers who moved the UK towards leaving, without much detailed thinking in advance.

5 Edward Heath, *The Course of My Life*, p.260

6 This applied to all aspects of Heath's life. When Heath invited Roy Jenkins to his house in Salisbury, his guest noted politely, 'This must have one of the best views in England.' Heath replied, 'What do you mean "one of the best views"?' Heath had to have the best views. Similarly, he had to be a leader and prime minister.

7 Obituary in the *Daily Telegraph*, 18 July 2005

8 William Waldegrave reviewing Philip Ziegler's biography of Heath, *Edward Heath*, in *The Spectator*, 16 June 2010.

9 *Daily Telegraph*, 7 June 2008

10 *A Question of Sovereignty* was broadcast on ITV on 13 May 1975 during the referendum campaign. The theme was also explored in depth when Roy Jenkins and Tony Benn debated UK membership on BBC1's *Panorama*, two Labour Cabinet ministers taking opposing views on peak-time television. Both programmes are available on YouTube and show that TV was capable of greater depth then, and that the potential loss of sovereignty was explored in more detail in 1975 than in 2016, when it was claimed by some Brexiteers that the UK had been duped into supporting membership. Michael Foot later became a strong supporter of the UK's membership. Benn remained an opponent.

11 I was that BBC political correspondent, dreading the task in case the moody Heath resented being interrupted while preparing for *Question Time*. He was on such a high that he would have given an interview to a chimpanzee.

12 In John Campbell's excellent unauthorized *Edward Heath: A Biography* (Jonathan Cape, 1993) he wonders about a possible gay affair in the army, but uncovered none of the scandalous allegations that were made after Heath's death. Campbell's insightful and fair account was published while Heath was still alive. The biography was too fair for Heath, who could cope with little less than unqualified praise.

13 Edward Heath, interview with Nanette Newman, 2000 (no date specified). The interview was carried out at his home in Salisbury and is available on YouTube. Heath is at his most relaxed, but even

in this exchange he does not look at the sympathetic interviewer. He was a shy performer.

3 James Callaghan

1   Denis Healey, *The Time of My Life*, Michael Joseph, 1989, p.427

2   Callaghan was a good actor, but there were limits. His chancellor being booed on live television as he spoke from the floor, within strict constraints, stretched those limits. Initially Callaghan advised Healey not to attend the conference, but then recognized that the situation was so grave he changed his mind.

3   Peter Jenkins, *Guardian*, 31 March 1976

4   Roy Jenkins was now Home Secretary for a second time, aching to escape from British politics for a bit, which he soon did. Jenkins became the UK's first president of the European Commission in Brussels, before returning to lead the SDP.

5   Edmund Dell was Trade Secretary during the IMF drama.

6   Denis Healey, *The Time of My Life*, p.431

7   GMTV's *Sunday Programme*, 4 March 2007. In the same programme Hattersley was joined by Tony Benn and David Owen for a discussion about the 1970s Labour governments and what followed. It was the first time the three of them had been in a studio together. I chaired the discussion, which was surprisingly convivial, given the epic scale of the falling-out. The programme is still available on YouTube.

8   This comes from the same ITV programme, available on YouTube. Benn deployed a genuine politeness and wit in order to defuse tense situations with his leaders. Callaghan was often furious with Benn for voting against government policy on the NEC, even though he was in the Cabinet. But in face-to-face meetings Benn was so friendly and engaged that Callaghan's fury melted fleetingly. Politeness is an underused political weapon. Others who have deployed it effectively include Michael Gove and Jacob Rees-Mogg. Coincidentally, both are partial Bennites in relation to the issue of parliamentary sovereignty and Europe.

9   In his autobiography and in subsequent interviews, Healey spoke of often being ill as a result of the pressures of being chancellor.

10 John Major's government was split over Europe, as was Theresa May's. Callaghan's government was divided several ways over economic policy, state ownership, relations with the trade unions and, of course, Europe, although this division had been fleetingly muted by the 1975 referendum.

11 The terms 'strong' and 'weak' in relation to leadership are two of the most misleading ones in British politics. Nearly always when the Greek chorus hails a prime minister for being strong, he or she is acting weakly. The same applies the other way round. There are countless examples of Margaret Thatcher being celebrated as the lady who was not for turning, at a point when she was revising her economic policies, to Tony Blair in the build-up to Iraq. See the chapters on Thatcher and Blair for more detail.

12 Jim Callaghan, interview with the author, *New Statesman*, December 1996

13 *Panorama*, BBC1, November 1977

14 I attended a dinner at Foot's house in 1998. Foot and his wife, Jill, sang Callaghan's praises as a leader, but were utterly and unfairly dismissive of Wilson. They both hailed Callaghan's trustworthiness and modesty while insisting that Wilson was mendacious and immodest.

15 Michael Foot won the next Labour leadership contest in 1980, the last in which Labour MPs alone elected the party's leader.

16 Giles Radice, *Friends and Rivals*, Little, Brown, 2002

17 Tony Benn, *Against the Tide*, p.653

18 Bernard Donoughue, *The Heat of the Kitchen*, p.234

19 The chapter on Margaret Thatcher shows that she was a good actress, not quite as polished as some of the actors, lacking tonal variety, but highly effective nonetheless.

20 *Guardian*, Monday 28 March 2005

21 *This Week*, ITV, 28 July 1978. The programme is available on YouTube and is an example of Callaghan as an authoritative and yet relaxed prime ministerial interviewee. He was a natural. No spin doctor advised him on the arts of broadcasting. He was wholly at ease with the medium. In contrast, Margaret Thatcher

was a shrill interviewee at times, although – as we shall see in the next chapter – a courageous one.

22 Prime ministerial broadcast, 7 September 1978

23 *Sun*, 10 January 1979

24 The others were Stanley Baldwin and Ramsay MacDonald.

25 *Guardian*, 22 February 2018

26 Bernard Donoughue, *The Heat of the Kitchen*, p.277

27 Jim Callaghan, interview with the author, *New Statesman*, 21 December 1996

28 Bernard Donoughue, *The Heat of the Kitchen*, p.268

29 Denis Healey, *The Time of My Life*, p.432

30 Benn, at least, was seen by Callaghan as a wrecker. He had more time for Crosland.

31 TUC History Online, March 1999: http://www.unionhistory. info/; Callaghan interview available as a PDF.

32 When I interviewed Callaghan for the *New Statesman* in December 1996, he could not hide his disappointment that Blair had not consulted him more, as Labour's last prime minister.

4 Margaret Thatcher

1 As discussed in a previous chapter, Wilson learned the importance of party management and the advantages of evasive political positioning as he rose to the leadership. By the time of his resignation in 1976 he was tormented by accusations that he regarded deviousness and party management as an end in itself. The reality is that the most devious leaders are too sharp to acquire a reputation for being so tricksy. The common factor in Tony Blair's rise and fall is explored in a later chapter.

2 Thatcher Foundation speech, 10 August 1974. The Thatcher Foundation is a wonderful online resource, crammed with original documents from the archives. Her rise and fall can be traced vividly by a tour of the Foundation: https://www.margaretthatcher. org/

3 Whitelaw did stand, once Heath withdrew, but by then it was too late. Thatcher beat him with ease, securing 146 votes to Whitelaw's

79. Several other candidates also threw their hats belatedly into the ring and did even worse than Whitelaw.

4 *Guardian*, 12 February 1975

5 William Waldegrave, *A Different Kind of Weather: A Memoir*, Constable, 2015, pp.141–3

6 *Observer*, 18 February 1979

7 *Firing Line* with William Buckley, 9 September 1975, available on YouTube. There are many Thatcher interviews on YouTube from her phase as leader of the Opposition. In most of them she is formidable. There is also an interview between Buckley and Tony Benn, recorded in the summer of 1981 at the height of Benn's powers as a communicator and framer of arguments. Benn also more than holds his own from the left. He was the left's counter to Thatcher, although he never became leader of his party, let alone prime minister.

8 Ibid. Thatcher had been leader for only a few months, since February 1975, yet in her ideological populism she was already firing on all cylinders.

9 *Panorama*, BBC1, 11 July 1977

10 Conservative Party manifesto for May 1979

11 Hansard, 3 April 1982

12 David Owen was a much-misunderstood politician. Later he was to become a donor to Ed Miliband's Labour Party and, more surprisingly, made a smaller donation to Jeremy Corbyn's Labour Party. Towards the end of the New Labour era he despaired that inequality was not higher up the agenda of his old party's leadership. But in the mid-1980s there was part of Owen that admired Thatcher and viewed Labour with almost as much disdain as he regarded the Liberals, his partners in a fragile alliance.

13 Gilmour's book, *Dancing with Dogma* (Simon & Schuster, 1992), published shortly after Thatcher left office, should be compulsory reading for all those who believe that she presided over something close to an economic miracle. Tony Blair was too generous in his assessment of the 1980s. David Cameron even more so. Gilmour used to dine regularly with Michael Foot, John Cole (the BBC's political editor for much of the 1980s) and the *Observer's*

wonderful columnist William Keegan, at the Gay Hussar in Soho. Keegan's own book, written several years earlier, *Mrs Thatcher's Economic Experiment* (Allen Lane, 1984), is equally illuminating and should also be compulsory reading if only because, in a variation of Churchill's phrase, history has been too kind to Thatcher, partly because many of her admirers have written it. Cole was on the left, but managed to be scrupulously impartial as BBC political editor. I am told that his impartiality slipped during these lunches with friends, who were all well to the left of the political consensus that Thatcher managed to shape long after she left power.

14 One of Thatcher's most famous speeches came at the October 1980 Conservative party conference, when she delivered the famous phrase 'You may turn if you want to. The lady's not for turning.' She performed the lines with gusto, but by the time of the autumn conference, Thatcher and Howe had softened their attachment to rigid monetarism. The lady had turned a little.

15 On 4 February 1975, the day of Thatcher's election as Conservative leader, Benn recorded in his diary: 'I think we will be foolish to suppose that Mrs Thatcher won't be a formidable leader... I think the quality of the debate will be raised because the Tory Party will be driven to the right and there will then be a real choice being offered to the electorate.' *Against the Tide*, p.311. Benn made constant references to Thatcher's powers of persuasion as some of his colleagues derided her, viewing her as their best chance of electoral victory.

16 Decades later Neil Kinnock would spit out the name 'Scargill', blaming him for letting down the miners and wrecking the early phase of his leadership. Kinnock once told me, with a degree of melancholy: 'I was one of the few leaders who never had a political honeymoon.' 'Why?' I asked. 'Scargill,' Kinnock replied. After the long haul of impossible leadership, Kinnock recovered his magnetic, witty exuberance, but still had the capacity for intense anger. The other figure from the 1980s who continued to provoke fury in him was Margaret Thatcher.

17 In Norman Tebbit's autobiography, *Upwardly Mobile* (Weidenfeld & Nicolson, 1988), he makes several criticisms of Thatcher, while less surprisingly hailing her as a great prime minister. The need for greater intervention, after the strike was defeated, was also acknowledged by Sir Geoffrey Howe and Michael Heseltine in their weighty and significant memoirs.

18 Michael Heseltine, interview with Matt Forde, *The Political Party* podcast, 27 September 2017

19 I was the BBC's local government correspondent at the time. Neither Hunt nor the Environment Secretary, Chris Patten, supported the policy they were compelled to implement. There were echoes of Brexit after 2016, as Theresa May made her moves towards leaving the EU even though she did not support what she was doing.

20 Chris Patten often referred to his leader in private as 'Margaret Hilda', implying that she was an eccentric aunt. He was in the odd position of knowing the poll tax was a calamity, but having the task of implementation, similar to some ministers after the 2016 Brexit referendum who believed that leaving the EU would have bleak consequences for the UK.

21 The editor of BBC's *Today* programme suggested that we did our own survey of projected bills. I appeared on the programme virtually every day for a few months with the latest projections. Patten or Hunt would often be in the studio to respond. They tried to put the case, but their heart was never in it. They knew the poll tax was going to be calamitous.

5 John Major

1 John Major, interview with Elinor Goodman at the London School of Economics, 24 April 2007

2 On the Social Chapter, Labour was unequivocally enthusiastic and adopted it after the 1997 election. On the single currency, Labour was much more equivocal, like John Major.

3 The most important of the speeches was delivered in Bonn on 29 March 1991. The build-up to the speech and its contents reflected Major's ambiguity in relation to the EU and also those

of his prime ministerial successors. A great deal of effort was made in preparing the speech, with the objective partly of wooing Chancellor Helmut Kohl in Germany, but also of reassuring his Eurosceptics that Major would not go too far. While expressing the desire to be 'at the very heart of Europe', he also stressed that the UK would be bringing its own proposals on the single currency and political union. He would 'relish the debate' with other EU leaders. The balance was not greatly different from Thatcher's Bruges Speech of September 1988 and yet, following the final phase of her leadership, it marked a genuine attempt to establish warmer relations. Patten played a part in preparing the ground for the speech. One of his advisers, Sarah Hogg, helped to write it. Hogg was a supporter of the single currency as a way of bringing down inflation. As ever with UK prime ministers and Europe, the calculations were multi-layered.

4   John Major, interview with Ian Birrell at the Politics Festival, Kings Place, London, 22 June 2018

5   There are several examples on YouTube.

6   During the 1992 election campaign there were often panic-stricken meetings about what was going wrong, as polls suggested the Conservatives might lose. After the victory the director of communications, Shaun Woodward, toured the US giving lectures about how to win a campaign.

7   Major made Patten the final UK governor of Hong Kong, a historic posting. The appointment meant Patten was out of the UK during the many traumas that erupted around Major. The Major/Patten friendship was in some respects an unlikely one. Patten was the Oxford graduate who relished being part of the establishment. He became chair of the BBC and chancellor of Oxford University. Major did not go to university and although he made a lot of money in his post-prime ministerial career, he never sought or acquired similar posts. On the whole they were bound by a similar political outlook. They were both 'one nation' Tories when their party was leaving behind such an approach to politics. Neither was moneyed. Both had their doubts about Thatcher and Thatcherism,

although Major was smart enough not to reveal his doubts until he had been elected party leader.

8   I was one of the correspondents. The other was John Pienaar.

9   Although Redwood was scathing of the Maastricht Treaty, he did not mention leaving the EU as an option. At this point the Eurosceptics were not Brexiteers, but the logic of their position led to where they ended up. If the UK had not signed the Maastricht Treaty, it was not clear what would have happened next, but withdrawal would have soared up the agenda. As it was, in the end the UK Parliament voted for the Maastricht legislation.

10 Mellor told the Leveson Inquiry in June 2012 that he thought Major was determined to keep him because the prime minister feared that his own affair with Edwina Currie would be reported. The affair was not in fact revealed until after Major left Number Ten.

11 Kelvin MacKenzie confirmed this much-reported threat during the Leveson Inquiry in 2012, although John Major told the same inquiry that he could not recall this part of their exchange.

12 I was one of the journalists at the dining table. Once again, John Pienaar was the other. Heseltine had a conscience and was partly seeking to convince himself that the government had acted fairly. He appeared to be as drained as Major was after the ERM crisis. This was a government losing its nerve within months of winning an election.

13 In the end, and with great reluctance, Clarke supported a referendum, a decision of historic significance. After Major announced that his government would hold a referendum before joining the euro, Tony Blair felt obliged to make the same pledge. In effect, the two declarations meant that the UK was not going to join the euro, as no prime minister would have been remotely sure of winning a referendum. Blair saw joining the euro as his historic mission, and yet knew deep down that he could not win a referendum on the subject.

14 Michael Heseltine interview, Politics Festival, Edinburgh, 11 October 2018

15 Major offered Lamont the post of Environment Secretary, a significant demotion. Wisely, Lamont did not accept and never served in government again.

16 Major had both an outright majority and the necessary 15 per cent margin, but had received only three more votes than his private minimum target of 215. His allies organized a 'spin' operation, rushing to the TV studios to declare the result a prime ministerial triumph. The media became obsessed with 'spin' under New Labour, but this was an example of presenting a result one way when in reality, if a few more votes had gone against him, Major would have resigned. His contortion had not really worked – his authority as leader was as fragile after the contest as it had been before. Yet it offered clarity in one respect. Major would have the misfortune to lead his party in the forthcoming election. There would be no further leadership contests after this one until after the election.

17 Politics moves so fast that what seems overwhelmingly significant is soon largely forgotten. The 'back to basics' saga terrified some Conservative MPs. I was a BBC political correspondent at the time and I recall interviewing a married MP about another matter. Before recording, I asked him what he did for his holidays, in order to test the level of his voice. The MP replied, 'I stayed at a lovely hotel in Greece…' He paused and looked horrified, before quickly adding, 'with my wife'. One Conservative MP had been discovered in bed with another man in a hotel, in bizarre circumstances. During 'back to basics' an assertion of heterosexuality in an orthodox marriage became necessary at all times.

18 Leaders tend to view elections as a form of relief. Michael Foot found the chaotic 1983 campaign more fun than the hell of leadership, as most of the time he was out addressing adoring crowds rather than seeking to bind a divided party, even if some of the strife continued until polling day, when Labour was slaughtered.

19 Tony Blair later admitted that he regretted deploying the term 'sleaze' as a powerful political weapon. The weapon was turned upon him, once his prime ministerial honeymoon was over.

From the safety of opposition, Blair claimed that his ministers would have to be 'purer than pure' and that even a perception of sleaze would force a minister to resign. If applied to him, Blair would have had to resign. Sensibly, a perception of wrongdoing was not quite enough in itself to wreck political careers in the New Labour era, although preposterously in some cases it almost was.

6 Tony Blair

1   Michael Meacher was the only member of Blair's shadow Cabinet not to be made a Cabinet minister. He was a decent radical, but with both a naive and a vain streak. Meacher would have been excited by the rise of Jeremy Corbyn.

2   *Independent*, 15 February 2010

3   Hattersley told the author about Blair's indifference to ideas and the past in 2001, after he had become deeply disillusioned. When John Smith died suddenly in 1994, Hattersley was one of several senior party figures who told Blair he must stand.

4   However, this sequence would almost certainly not have applied to Smith, who was also elected at the beginning of a parliament. In his nearly two years as leader he had established a strong lead in the polls, and the Conservative government was imploding over Europe. Smith had a natural self-confidence, fuelled by the fact that, unusually for Labour by the early 1990s, he had been a Cabinet minister. Government was not a daunting mystery for Smith as it was for Neil Kinnock and Tony Blair, when they were leaders of the Opposition. Smith had been there, albeit briefly, in the Callaghan government. Significantly, in terms of their mindsets, Blair and close allies like Peter Mandelson and Labour strategist Philip Gould disagreed with this analysis. They assumed that Smith would lose the election.

5   He also offered a referendum in Wales on the proposal to establish a Welsh Assembly.

6   In his witty memoir *Who Goes Home?* (Little, Brown, 1995), Roy Hattersley recalls a rally that he spoke at in Cambridge as the party's deputy leader. The rally during the 1987 election was regarded as highly significant, targeting disaffected SDP voters

under the banner 'Come Home to Labour'. At the end of the rally Hattersley appeared live on the peak-time Saturday-night BBC bulletin, eagerly anticipating the chance to convey a sense that Labour was back in the game. The presenter asked him whether it was Labour's policy to increase income tax for those earning more than £22,000 a year. Hattersley dismissed the proposition haughtily. He did so as the party's shadow chancellor. The presenter replied: 'But that was what your leader, Neil Kinnock, said this afternoon.' Hattersley writes that he could tell he was suddenly part of a calamity for Labour, live on air, and adopted the only option available to him: 'I attacked the interviewer.' His memoir is hilarious. Anyone who believes, wrongly, that politics is boring should read it.

7   In July 1996 Blair gave a long interview to the *New Statesman*. At one point he was asked whether he, personally, was in favour of electoral reform. Highly uncharacteristically, he was caught off-guard and replied, 'No.' It took many phone calls to Paddy Ashdown to repair the damage, but the answer was an early sign of what was to follow. Blair never called the referendum on electoral reform.

8   Labour won a staggering 419 seats and a majority of 179.

9   I was at the Royal Festival Hall event and at one point found myself dancing next to David Miliband. He said to me revealingly, 'I'm sure we'll wake up in a few hours' time and find the Tories have won again.' Miliband spoke for much of the new administration, working on the assumption that they were imposters disturbing the natural order in which the Conservatives ruled.

10 I was the commentator. The minister was David Blunkett, the newly installed Education Secretary. He meant it partly as a joke and semi-approvingly, but the joke captures brilliantly the mood of exuberant caution.

11 The reform created a new model of accountability. After Margaret Thatcher abolished the GLC, ineffective, unaccountable quangos were responsible for running large swathes of the capital. As a result, public transport in particular was a shambles, with long

delays and even longer queues to buy tickets. The high-profile mayor became accountable for transport and had no choice but to make improvements in order to get re-elected. Transport for London even includes some figures who know a lot about transport. Because the grim culture in England determines that subsidies are a waste and do not contribute to the overall public good, fares in London are some of the highest in the world, but the services have improved beyond recognition. The model works, even if it had a haphazard beginning: Blair refused to endorse the left-wing Ken Livingstone as Labour's candidate. Livingstone won easily as an independent, an early sign that figures to the left of New Labour could perform well at elections, contrary to mythology. Livingstone was an innovative mayor, introducing the Congestion Charge for cars, a source of income that led to a huge improvement in bus services. Later Blair admitted publicly that he had made a mistake in not endorsing Livingstone.

12 Robin Cook, interview with the author, fringe meeting at the Labour party conference, September 2000

13 Blair's senior adviser, Jonathan Powell, was also central from within the UK government, having a forensic understanding of what was required and an instinctive ability to recognize how to deal with those whom British governments had theoretically refused to negotiate with, even if informal talks were frequent throughout the decades of violence.

14 *New Statesman*, 11 January 2000

15 The *Alastair Campbell Diaries* (Biteback), especially Vols 6 (2017) and 7 (2018), include many references to his discussions with Blair about Brown being tactical compared with his more strategic approach.

16 Tony Blair, interview with Andrew Grice and Don Macintyre, *Independent*, 28 September 1998

17 Brown's anger about Blair's conflicting demands was relayed to me separately by both Balls and Miliband early in the second term. Their views are corroborated by memoirs from Blair's closest allies, who suggest that after 2001 Blair had concluded there was no need for further spending increases, and tax cuts must

be a priority. Peter Hyman's book, *1 out of 10* (Vintage, 2005) – largely supportive of Blair and despairing of Brown – is especially illuminating about Blair's views after the 2001 election and how, even in Number Ten, close advisers worried that he was moving too far to the right.

18 See the chapter on James Callaghan. In 1976 Callaghan and Denis Healey, prime minister and chancellor, were proposing substantial spending cuts, Anthony Crosland was calling for selective cuts and some increases to generate growth, and Tony Benn was developing his Alternative Economic Strategy, which included import controls and wider state ownership amongst its proposals. Such internal differences caused huge problems, not least for Callaghan keeping them all together, but at least they were all thinking about economic policy, the most challenging issue of them all. In the New Labour era there was no such thinking, apart from by Gordon Brown and his senior advisers in the Treasury.

19 From 1994, when Blair became leader, at least until the end of the first term he acknowledged his dependency on Brown in relation to economic policy, although he became intensely frustrated at Brown's preoccupation with spending money on tax credits rather than public services. The dependency continued, but the acknowledgement of it waned.

20 This would have been the equivalent of a sacking, as Brown would not have accepted the post.

21 There is more detail on this in the chapter on Gordon Brown.

22 Ed Balls, *Speaking Out*, Hutchinson, 2016, pp.107–8

23 Smith told me of the meeting days later. It is similar to a conversation I had with Blair shortly after the 2001 election. Blair did not meet his first objective and struggled with the second. He met the third and faced dark consequences well beyond his long leadership of the Labour Party. Around about the same time, Brown outlined to me privately his objectives in policy terms for the second term. They included ensuring that the UK would not join the euro over the next few years, and raising the money to meet the NHS spending pledge. I was struck that Brown, as chancellor, met his objectives while Blair struggled to meet his.

24 After the war, in the 2005 election Rupert Murdoch's *Sun* newspaper endorsed Labour, but did so on the basis of Blair's foreign policies alone. In particular the newspaper praised his 'courage' in supporting the US in Iraq.

25 In a conversation with the author in July 2003, Blair made precisely this point: 'At least I won't be accused of being anti-American in the euro referendum.'

26 One of the most forgotten phrases in modern British politics is the 'Baghdad Bounce'. This was the phrase used in Number Ten in the immediate aftermath of Saddam's fall, as it anticipated a rise in support in the polls, similar to the 'Falklands Factor'. Blair misunderstood much about Iraq and the wider region, but his electoral calculations proved to be largely correct. He went on to win the 2005 election, even if Baghdad provided no Bounce.

27 *The Sunday Times*, 18 February 2003

28 Alastair Campbell, *Alastair Campbell Diaries*, Vol. 7

29 Chilcot Inquiry, July 2015

30 Clare Short was International Development Secretary at the time and claims Blair had assured her that a post-war plan had been worked through in considerable detail. She resigned when she realized there had been no such detailed plan. For her resignation to be regarded as weighty and significant, Short should have resigned with Cook before the war, but she had made some substantial and daring interventions in advance of the conflict. In September 2002 Short returned from Afghanistan and warned publicly, in an interview broadcast on ITV, that al-Qaeda would regroup around Kabul if US and UK forces were diverted to prepare for war in Iraq. Her warnings provoked angry disdain amongst Blair's advisers in Number Ten, but proved to be accurate.

31 I do not believe that Blair was untroubled by Iraq on the basis that the war had been 'the right thing to do'. At the end of one long conversation I had with him about a range of issues, he sighed spontaneously and exclaimed 'Iraq'. It was a despairing exclamation, and not a resolute one. On another occasion he paused as another topic was being discussed and declared to me, 'I could not have stopped America from invading Iraq.' No doubt

he has partly convinced himself that he followed the only course available to him, but he has reflected more than that. He can never express any doubt in public, because British soldiers died in the war. He cannot ever imply that they died in a war that proved to be not the right thing to do.

32 During his first term Blair declared that it was his 'historic objective to end Britain's ambiguous relationship with Europe'. He meant he wanted the UK to sign up to the euro. After the war in Iraq he renewed his mission. During one meeting Gordon Brown's senior adviser, Ed Balls, told Blair that he was jeopardizing the economy and the future of the government in his pursuit. Blair and Balls never spoke again until after the government had fallen, when they formed a convivial relationship bound by their opposition to the leadership of Jeremy Corbyn.

33 During the 2005 election Blair and Brown were seen together eating ice cream and took part in an awkward party election broadcast in which neither could disguise his unease.

7 Gordon Brown

1 *Independent*, 2 April 1992

2 When John McDonnell became Labour's most left-wing shadow chancellor in 2015 he often cited the 1992 election to justify his caution in opposing tax cuts introduced by the Conservative government. McDonnell had fought and lost a marginal seat in 1992. Even the poorest voters in the seat expressed concerns about 'Labour's tax bombshells', he told *Newsnight* in an interview broadcast on 5 November 2018.

3 Philip Gould, *The Unfinished Revolution*, Little, Brown, 1998

4 Roy Hattersley was to regret his endorsement of Tony Blair in 1994 and became a supporter of Gordon Brown from New Labour's second term, stating openly and often that Brown should replace Blair.

5 Tony Blair explores the ideological differences in his memoir *A Journey* (Hutchinson, 2010). Gordon Brown and Ed Balls are less expansive in their memoirs, but there are hints for the assiduous reader.

6 Roy Jenkins observed to the author in the autumn of 2001, over a glass or two of red wine, 'Political columnists in the past had so many big figures to write about. You only have Blair and Brown.'

7 Hugo Young, *The Hugo Young Papers*, Allen Lane, 2008, p.417

8 Ed Miliband made the observation to the author the week after the budget. Miliband was on a high, regarding the budget as an important moment of vindication for his toil in Brown's team. He went on to say that he and Brown would spend hours late at night discussing how to address inequality, the shared political mission of Miliband and Brown. Miliband doubted whether Blair ever reflected on the challenge. Looking back at his political career, Ed Balls also told the author that the tax rise to pay for NHS investment was his proudest achievement. Balls had become a famous *Strictly Come Dancing* performer by then, but still became animated when the topic switched from celebrity fame to politics. See the previous chapter for more detail on the NHS battle between Blair and Brown. There is also a fuller account of a key episode in the New Labour era in the author's book: Steve Richards, *Whatever It Takes: The Real Story of Gordon Brown and New Labour*, Vintage, 2010.

9 Although this was regarded as Brown's most publicly left-wing intervention, Ed Miliband told the author subsequently that as far as he was concerned, the speech was nowhere near as critical of the markets as it should have been. As a leader, Miliband failed to frame arguments effectively or in a way that he was comfortable with, but in the New Labour court he was ahead of the times, or a sharper reader of where the times were heading. After the financial crash of 2008, thoughtful figures across the political spectrum were less in awe of the markets.

10 Speech by Gordon Brown to the Social Market Foundation at the Cass Business School, 3 February 2003

11 Brown was challenged in 2007 by the then left-wing backbencher, John McDonnell. Brown was more than happy with this contender, as he could challenge him from the right. They held one public debate, chaired by the author. At the time McDonnell seemed a convenient irrelevance as Brown marched towards

Number Ten. Yet McDonnell's arguments for a more radical approach to policy-making were central to the rise of Jeremy Corbyn in 2015. McDonnell did not secure enough support from MPs to enter the final round of the contest, which Brown fought alone. McDonnell became shadow chancellor in 2015 and proved to be much the most formidable figure in Corbyn's Labour Party.

12 On BBC Radio 4's *The Brown Years*, broadcast in October 2010, written and presented by the author, several of Brown's allies blamed Balls for the newspaper reports. When the allegation was put to Balls, he denied it emphatically.

13 Alastair Campbell, *Alastair Campbell Diaries*, Vol. 7

14 This was in January 2010, months before the general election. Far from undermining Brown, the failure of the coup guaranteed that he would lead Labour at the election. There was no space for another coup.

15 At least he did to me and my editor at the time, the *Independent*'s Simon Kelner.

8 David Cameron

1 *Guardian*, 17 February 2009

2 The author was that columnist. I seemed to be on a grid where I was invited to accompany Cameron when he went to Norwich. I went with him three times to Norwich and back. He only fell asleep once.

3 Tony Blair made this observation to the author in February 2006, very early in Cameron's leadership.

4 The remarks were supposedly made at a dinner during the Tory conference in October 2005. The words ring true.

5 Oliver Letwin was especially keen, carrying Gould's book *The Unfinished Revolution* with him when he met journalists for dinners during the early Cameron era.

6 Theresa May famously coined the term at the Conservative conference in 2002. See the next chapter.

7 Cameron used the words, uttered very speedily, in his party conference speech in October 2006.

8   Ken Clarke, interviews with the author for BBC Radio 4's *The Cameron Years*, first broadcast in January 2018

9   The author interviewed Johnson for a Channel 4 series, *School Days*. The interview is available on YouTube.

10 Cameron's friend told the author about their conversation on Thatcher's continuing influence.

11 Margaret Thatcher, interview with *Woman's Own*, October 1987

12 David Cameron, *Guardian*, 25 May 2009

13 Oliver Letwin, interview with the author, the *Independent* fringe meeting at the Conservative party conference, October 2007

14 That is what Katz noted to the author in November 2007 at a dinner gathering that would make an excellent play. Other guests included left-of-centre commentators, all hailing Cameron and Steve Hilton as the great progressive thinkers with innovative ideas for a fairer society. As David Miliband noted to the author at around this time, 'Cameron is playing the *Guardian* like a cello.'

15 The Conservative Party's 'Aims and Values' document, February 2006

16 Steve Hilton, conversation with the author, January 2009

17 Hugo Young Lecture, November 2009

18 The author met Clegg for a coffee on the day of the White Paper's publication. He enthused, without qualification.

19 The author had a conversation with Cameron about the NHS reforms and the unplanned consequences. Like Blair, Cameron could see the absurd side to governing.

20 *The Sunday Times*, 7 January 2018

21 In the heady summer of 2010, as the coalition was getting into its radical stride, Cameron joked with the author that there had been thousands of articles about a realignment on the centre left in the mid-1990s, and it had happened overnight on the centre right. Letwin, too, enthused about the ideological overlap between Clegg and the Conservative leadership.

22 Conversation between Blair and author in 1998, when New Labour was enjoying a sunny honeymoon, but decisions were still nightmarish on many fronts.

23 Craig Oliver, interview with the author, BBC Radio 4,
    The Cameron Years, January 2018

24 In *The Cameron Years* the Brexiteer Jacob Rees-Mogg said he
    genuinely knew of no other Tory MPs planning to defect. He
    confirmed that he would not have switched to UKIP if there had
    been no referendum, but stressed that he would have campaigned
    hard for one, from within the Conservative Party.

25 If there had been a second coalition, Nick Clegg would not have
    vetoed the referendum. He had espoused referendums related
    to EU membership on several occasions during his leadership.
    Cameron would have made support for a referendum a condition
    of the coalition, and Clegg would have agreed, again on the
    assumption that his case would win. If there had been a coalition
    after the 2015 election, with both the Tory PM and the Lib Dem
    deputy PM arguing for 'Remain' – and losing – the coalition
    would have collapsed.

26 Craig Oliver, interview with the author, BBC Radio 4, *The
    Cameron Years*, January 2018

27 Gove's wife, Sarah Vine, told the author that the referendum ended
    several of their friendships. Brexit had many consequences, and
    one of them was the ending of friendships.

28 His long-serving adviser Gabby Bertin confirmed this in an
    interview for BBC Radio 4, *The Cameron Years*, January 2018.

9 Theresa May

1 Senior Home Office officials are quite often pleased to see the back
   of Home Secretaries. I spoke to two who rated May very highly
   towards the end of her time there. Both thought she deserved to be
   the next prime minister.

2 Sir Craig Oliver, interview for BBC Radio 4, *Theresa May – The
   Brexit Prime Minister*, March 2019

3 Hugo Young, *One of Us*, Macmillan, 1989

4 Nick Timothy, interview with the author, BBC Radio 4, *Theresa
   May – The Brexit Prime Minister*, March 2019

5 George Bridges, interview with the author, BBC Radio 4, *Theresa
   May – The Brexit Prime Minister*, March 2019

6   Nick Timothy, interview with the author, BBC Radio 4, *Theresa May – The Brexit Prime Minister*, March 2019

7   Sir Graham Brady, interview with the author, BBC Radio 4, *Theresa May – The Brexit Prime Minister*, March 2019

8   Julian Smith, interview with Laura Kuenssberg, BBC1, March 2019

10 Boris Johnson

1   See the earlier chapter on Gordon Brown.

2   Denis Staunton, 'How Boris Johnson became Britain's most powerful prime minister since Tony Blair', *Irish Times*, 28 December 2019, was typical. The *Financial Times* made the same comparison on 14 December 2019, but argued that their routes to power were very different, with Blair taking a more 'centrist' path.

3   BBC News interview, 24 October 2020

4   David Lidington, interview with Professor Anand Menon, 30 January 2020

5   See the chapter on Theresa May.

6   Johnson spoke at the DUP conference in November 2018. He received an ecstatic reception as he referred to them as 'my fellow unionists'. The DUP MPs voted against Johnson's deal.

7   The *Observer*, 26 October 2019

8   See the chapter on Margaret Thatcher. Heath gave her shadow Cabinet roles that he assumed were of little significance. Instead her frontbench positions were the key in helping her to soar.

9   *The Times*, 8 February 2020

10 Johnson speech, Greenwich, London, 3 February 2020

11 Dominic Cummings, IPPR speech, 19 November 2014. The speech is available on YouTube.

12 *The Sunday Times*, 23 February 2020

ILLUSTRATION CREDITS

Portrait of Harold Wilson (Bob Haswell/Stringer/Hulton Archive)

Jeremy Thorpe, Harold Wilson and Edward Heath (Central Press/ Stringer/Hulton Archive)

Edward Heath becomes prime minister (Rolls Press/Popperfoto)

Margaret Thatcher speaks on Europe (Central Press/Stringer/ Hulton Archive)

Portrait of James Callaghan (Central Press/Stringer/Hulton Archive)

Tony Benn and James Callaghan (Gary Weaser/Stringer/Hulton Archive)

Newly elected Prime Minister Margaret Thatcher (Tim Graham/ Hulton Archive)

President Reagan with Prime Minister Thatcher (Diana Walker/ The LIFE Images Collection)

John Major succeeds Margaret Thatcher (Bryn Colton/Hulton Archive)

Portrait of John Major (Gemma Levine/Premium Archive)

The Queen and the prime ministers (Terry O'Neill/Iconic Images)

Portrait of Tony and Cherie Blair (Tom Stoddart Archive/Premium Archive)

Blair and Brown at Labour conference 1999 (Steve Eason/Stringer/ Hulton Archive)

Blair and Brown at Labour conference 2006 (Scott Barbour/Getty Images News)

Tony Blair on Middle East trip (Christopher Furlong/Getty Images News)

Margaret Thatcher and Gordon Brown (Bloomberg)

David Cameron wins Conservative Party leadership contest (Bruno Vincent/Getty Images News)

David Cameron and Barack Obama (Charlie Ommanney/Getty Images News)

David Cameron and Theresa May (WRA Pool/Getty Images News)

Prime Minister May greets European Commission President Jean-Claude Juncker (Carl Court/Getty Images News)

Prime Minister Boris Johnson (Wiktor Szymanowicz/NurPhoto via Getty Images)

—

ACKNOWLEDGEMENTS

Huge thanks to the brilliant team at Atlantic – James Pulford, Mike Harpley and Mandy Greenfield; to Peter Knowles and Daniel Brittain-Catlin for commissioning and producing the unscripted BBC TV talks on modern prime ministers and to Leala Padmanabhan the producer of *The Cameron Years* and *The Brexit Prime Minister* on BBC Radio 4. The various BBC programmes gave me the idea for the book, but the words and judgements here are mine alone… And an equally big thanks to my agent, Andrew Gordon, at David Higham Associates. Thanks also to Andrew Godsell who suggested some revisions for this edition, all of which were acted on.

INDEX